Integrated Science

Volume 33

Editor-in-Chief
Nima Rezaei ⓘ, Tehran University of Medical Sciences, Tehran, Iran

The **Integrated Science** Series aims to publish the most relevant and novel research in all areas of Formal Sciences, Physical and Chemical Sciences, Biological Sciences, Medical Sciences, and Social Sciences. We are especially focused on the research involving the integration of two of more academic fields offering an innovative view, which is one of the main focuses of Universal Scientific Education and Research Network (USERN), science without borders.

Integrated Science is committed to upholding the integrity of the scientific record and will follow the Committee on Publication Ethics (COPE) guidelines on how to deal with potential acts of misconduct and correcting the literature.

Cristina Costescu
Editor

Digital Technologies for Learning and Psychological Interventions

Editor
Cristina Costescu
Faculty of Psychology and Educational
Sciences
Babeș-Bolyai University
Cluj-Napoca, Romania

ISSN 2662-9461　　　　　　　　ISSN 2662-947X　(electronic)
Integrated Science
ISBN 978-3-031-76413-4　　　　ISBN 978-3-031-76414-1　(eBook)
https://doi.org/10.1007/978-3-031-76414-1

© The Editor(s) (if applicable) and The Author(s), under exclusive license to Springer
Nature Switzerland AG 2024

This work is subject to copyright. All rights are solely and exclusively licensed by the Publisher, whether the whole or part of the material is concerned, specifically the rights of translation, reprinting, reuse of illustrations, recitation, broadcasting, reproduction on microfilms or in any other physical way, and transmission or information storage and retrieval, electronic adaptation, computer software, or by similar or dissimilar methodology now known or hereafter developed.
The use of general descriptive names, registered names, trademarks, service marks, etc. in this publication does not imply, even in the absence of a specific statement, that such names are exempt from the relevant protective laws and regulations and therefore free for general use.
The publisher, the authors and the editors are safe to assume that the advice and information in this book are believed to be true and accurate at the date of publication. Neither the publisher nor the authors or the editors give a warranty, expressed or implied, with respect to the material contained herein or for any errors or omissions that may have been made. The publisher remains neutral with regard to jurisdictional claims in published maps and institutional affiliations.

This Springer imprint is published by the registered company Springer Nature Switzerland AG
The registered company address is: Gewerbestrasse 11, 6330 Cham, Switzerland

If disposing of this product, please recycle the paper.

Introduction

In an era defined by rapid technological advancements, the intersection of digital technologies and psychological interventions has opened new frontiers in the realm of education and mental health. Digital technologies offer promising opportunities for enhancing mental health interventions and improving access to psychological treatments. These include internet-based interventions, smartphone apps, virtual reality, and web-based platforms [1–3]. Such behavioral intervention technologies can target behaviors, cognitions, and emotions to support mental health or to improve the learning process [4]. Recent studies have shown positive results in feasibility, acceptability, and preliminary evidence of improved therapy outcomes. However, challenges remain, including dropout rates, engagement issues, and the need for personalization and cultural adaptations [1]. Future developments in digital mental health and educational interventions may include digital phenotyping, chatbots, and hybrid models of care [1]. To realize the full potential of behavioral intervention technologies, multidisciplinary collaboration between psychologists and technology experts is crucial [4].

Recent research indicates promising developments in digital technologies for assessing and treating symptoms associated with neurodevelopmental disorders (NDDs) in children. Various technologies, including machine learning, neuroimaging, and web-based interventions, have shown potential in improving outcomes for neurodiverse population, particularly autistic individuals and attention-deficit/hyperactivity disorder (ADHD) individuals [5–6]. Assistive technologies have demonstrated effectiveness in enhancing cognitive skills, behavior, social communication, and academic performance in intellectually disabled children and autistic children [7]. Web-based interventions have shown promise in reducing symptoms in neurodiverse children, although more research is needed due to methodological limitations and small sample sizes [6]. Technologies such as mobile apps, robots, gaming, and virtual reality are being utilized for assessment and treatment across multiple NDDs [8]. However, further high-quality research, including randomized controlled trials with longer follow-up periods and economic evaluations, is necessary to establish the clinical effectiveness and feasibility of these technologies [5, 8].

Moreover, there is a significant lack of conclusive evidence regarding the effectiveness of digital mental health solutions. Studies have shown mixed outcomes, indicating a need for more rigorous and comprehensive research to establish clear efficacy [9]. Another important gap is the access and disparities, since there are populations with limited access to technology (low-income or rural areas), the extensive development and use of digital interventions may worsen the existing disparities in access to mental health care [10]. When developing digital based tools there is a challenge in effectively translating digital assessment tools into actionable and effective treatments, this gap highlights the need for better integration between diagnostic tools and therapeutic interventions [10]. Even if this challenge can be overcome and more effective digital tools are being developed, the scalability remains a challenge. Effective models need to be developed and tested to ensure widespread adaption [11].

When it comes to use of digital technologies for neurodiverse children many studies lack methodological rigor, and more research is needed on long-term effectiveness, economic impact, and user acceptability [8] (Valentine et al., 2020). Additionally, further investigation is required in low- and middle-income countries to fully understand the benefits of telemedicine for autistic children [12]. As technology becomes increasingly pervasive, it is crucial to focus on how neurodiverse children can benefit from its use [13].

This book *Digital Technologies for Learning and Psychological Intervention* delves into the multifaced landscape of utilizing cutting-edge digital tools to support neurodiverse individuals and presents a comprehensive exploration of the transformative role digital technologies play in addressing the unique challenges faced by them. The insights drawn from each chapter contribute to a nuanced understanding of the potential and complexities of leveraging technology for educational and psychological interventions. Digital platforms are educational tools that enhance learning by offering a range of resources for both synchronous and asynchronous interaction and communication. These platforms facilitate engagement among students and between teachers and their students [14]. A boarder definition of digital technologies, that can be used for common understanding among the chapters of this book, is a range of tools, devices, applications and systems design to support the developmental, educational, social and therapeutic needs of neurodiverse children and typically developing children. These technologies aim to enhance learning, communication, social interaction and daily living skills through tailored interventions and interactive experiences. In the forthcoming sections, we will offer a summary of the predominant themes that have arisen. The book is divided into two parts, the first one describes from different perspectives the process and the aspects involved in the development and usage of the technological devices for learning purposes, meanwhile the second section has several chapters where different ways of using technology are described in the process of educational or psychological interventions.

Chapter 1 written by Herrera Gutierrez and Vera provides a very comprehensive view in regard to the use of technology for autistic individuals. The exploration of generalization of learning and personalization of technology-supported interventions, which is described in Chap. 4, adds a layer of complexity to the use of technology for neurodiverse children. The chapter dedicated to technologies for intervention in autism provides a panoramic view of current research efforts. It underscores the advantages of technology, particularly its visual nature and predictability, while cautioning against potential risks.

Chapter 2 written by Herrera Gutierrez, Perez-Fuster and Costescu sheds light on the critical importance of involving autistic individuals in research and technology design. By exploring participatory approaches, they aim to ensure that the tools created truly meet the needs and preferences of those they are intended to assist. A pivotal theme revolves around the active participation of autistic individuals in the research and design of digital tools. Ethical implications and experimental designs for inclusive representation are explored. The chapter emphasizes the need for methodologies that allow autistic voices to define their real needs during the initial stages of technology development, with examples like gamification and web accessibility illustrating how genuine participation can be achieved.

The discussion on biomarkers from Chap. 3 written by Guldner, Ernst, Nees and Holz explores the potential for diagnostic and therapeutic strategies. Despite advancements, the elusive search for a single biomarker meeting optimal standards remains unfulfilled. The chapter advocates for developmentally informed research strategies to address the dynamic nature of NDDs. The surge of interest in digital biomarkers for neurodevelopmental health is explored in two chapters, presenting an overview of recent advances, potential improvements, and associated ethical challenges. The chapters emphasize the need for novel technologies to address persistent challenges in the field, such as long waiting times for diagnoses.

Chapter 4 written by Owotoki, Enseroth, Nieri Mbugua and Owotoki starts with the definitions of biomarkers and digital biomarkers. After discussing the current status of use of digital biomarkers for neurodiverse population, the authors briefly describe the most use technology, such as wearable devices and eye trackers an their measurements: fixation duration, saccade profiles, eye movements. They also describe how vocal biomarkers can be used, as well as pupil diameter and multimodal biomarkers can be used for screening and diagnosis, health and treatment monitoring. The chapter ends with a most general approach discussing about accuracy and authenticity of the biomarkers, autonomy and agency, and access and availability.

Chapter 5 written by Thill explores the implications of the growing prevalence of resultant algorithms in technology designed to aid neurodiverse children across various contexts. The authors distinguish between different uses of algorithms, including the description of observable data and its interpretation. Additionally, they delve into fundamental challenges, such as assessing vaguely defined mental states. Overall, the objective of this chapter is to raise awareness about the potential and limitations of machine learning approaches in supporting neurodiverse children across diverse situations.

Chapter 6 written by Neerinex, Brito, Couto, Camposn, de Graaf, Masthoff and Paiva offers a review of recent studies in child-robot interventions, and it provides a framework for designing educational and psychological involving children and social robots. Various characteristics of social robots and their role within the intervention protocols are presented within the chapter. Considering the intervention context, three different kinds of purposes are presented in detail, the use of social robots for mental well-being, educational purposes and for robot mediated therapy for autism spectrum disorders. The chapter ends with presenting some case studies where the robot is used as a storyteller or a mediator for improving social and emotional competence in children.

Part II of the book has seven chapters, from Chap. 7 to Chap. 13 and it provides an overview of the way digital technologies are used for different types of populations and for different outcomes.

Chapter 7 of the book written by Costescu explores the transformative impact of technological tools on the lives of autistic children. From innovative interventions to tailored learning experiences, the authors examine the ways in which technology can bridge communication gaps and provide avenues for skill development, offering hope and possibilities for individuals on the spectrum. Virtual reality, robots, computer-based interventions, and wearables have shown promise in enhancing learning processes. However, the inconclusive and mixed results highlight the need for rigorous experimental studies. The importance of considering co-design, gamification, technology integration, and cognitive availability in technology design emerges as critical for optimizing effectiveness.

Among the addressed deficits in neurodiverse children are executive functions therefore the next chapter (Chap. 8) written by Costescu, David and Roșan emphasizes the role of digital technologies in training and enhancing these critical cognitive processes. While acknowledging the advancements, the discussion also points out limitations in computerized training, urging future research to navigate these challenges and provide effective solutions, also because executive functions play a pivotal role in shaping a child's cognitive development. From cognitive training apps to interactive platforms, the authors explore the promising landscape of digital interventions that contribute to the optimum executive functioning of neurodiverse people.

Chapter 9 written by Montero de Espinosa Espino and Perez de la Maza describes the best practices in using handheld devices for autistic individuals with a focus on independent living and social interaction. Handheld devices offer support to adjust the person's response in a specific setting almost in real-time helping them to navigate daily life more independently. Despite the limited existing solid scientific evidence, ensuring a positive correlation between the use of handheld devices and an enhancement in independence levels remains a challenge. The authors emphasize the opportunities and challenges for using the devices considering their specific needs and cognitive profiles, concluding that the adaption of technological devices by autistic individuals is not only an opportunity but a need.

Some of the chapters describe one technology-based intervention technique in more detail. For example, Chap. 10 written by Chezan, Horn, Liu and Idol focuses on eCoaching as an evidence-based training method emphasizing its role in improving the implementation fidelity of evidence-based practices for neurodiverse learners. The chapter provides a foundation for understanding and applying eCoaching with bug-in-ear technology in various educational settings. The authors provide details about how personalized digital coaching can provide tailored support to individuals, enhancing their abilities and fostering a sense of self-efficacy.

Chapter 11 summarizes the available digital interventions for ADHD individuals. The authors of this chapter are Marten, Kaiser and Häge and they describe within their chapter different ways of delivering the digital interventions, such as web and PC-based interventions, mobile applications, wearables/sensors, virtual or augmented reality. The chapter offer an overview of how the above-mentioned technologies can be used for ADHD individuals and which are the opportunities and risks in each of the cases.

The last two chapters draws attention about the comprehension on the moral development and engagement in moral (dis)engagement mechanisms among neurodiverse children when confronted with cyberbullying situations. Chapter 12 written by Costa Ferreira, Veiga Simao, Stilwell, Lopes, Trindade, Perreira and Francisco explores the risks associated with Internet use, particularly cyberbullying, and underscores the potential of serious games as a valuable resource for understanding these processes and behaviors in neurodiverse children. The authors pave the way for future studies that investigate individual, behavioral, and contextual factors shaping how neurodiverse children, respond to, and cope with diverse strategies.

The final Chap. 13 written by Costa Ferreira, Veiga Simao, Stilwell, Lopez, Domingues, Trindade and Perreira investigates the role of computer-supported collaborative learning in regulating learning experiences for neurodiverse children from virtual classrooms to collaborative platforms, the authors explore how technology can facilitate a supportive and inclusive learning environment. The emphasis on self-regulation, co-regulation, and shared regulation strategies provides recommendations for best practices.

In conclusion, the book underscores the transformative potential of digital technologies in educational and psychological interventions for typically developing and\neurodiverse children. While promising, the field requires further research, inclusive design approaches, and attention to ethical and accessibility issues to fully realize these technologies' benefits.

References

1. Baños RM, Herrero R, & Vara MD (2022) What is the current and future status of digital mental health interventions? Span J Psychol 25, e5
2. Fernandez-Álvarez J, Díaz-García A, Colombo D, Botella C, Cipresso P, & Riva G (2020) Digital technologies for the intervention of emotion regulation. Reference module in neuroscience and biobehavioral psychology. Edinburgh: Elsevier, 10

3. Rus-Calafell M, & Schneider S (2020) Are we there yet?!—a literature review of recent digital technology advances for the treatment of early psychosis. Mhealth, 6
4. Schueller SM, Muñoz RF, & Mohr DC (2013) Realizing the potential of behavioral intervention technologies. Curr Dir Psychol Sci 22(6):478–483
5. Ribas MO, Micai M, Caruso A, Fulceri F, Fazio M, & Scattoni ML (2023) Technologies to support the diagnosis and/or treatment of neurodevelopmental disorders: A systematic review. Neuroscience and Biobehavioral Reviews, 145, 105021
6. Khan K, Hall CL, Davies EB, Hollis C, & Glazebrook C (2019) The effectiveness of web-based interventions delivered to children and young people with neurodevelopmental disorders: systematic review and meta-analysis. J Med Internet Res 21(11), e13478
7. Pontikas CM, Tsoukalas E, & Serdari A (2022) A map of assistive technology educative instruments in neurodevelopmental disorders. Disabil Rehabil: Assistive Technol 17(7):738–746
8. Valentine AZ, Brown BJ, Groom MJ, Young E, Hollis C, & Hall CL (2020) A systematic review evaluating the implementation of technologies to assess, monitor and treat neurodevelopmental disorders: A map of the current evidence. Clinical psychology review, 80, 101870
9. Jardine J, Bowman R, & Doherty G (2022) Digital interventions to enhance readiness for psychological therapy: scoping review. J Med Internet Res 24(8), e37851
10. Skorburg JA, & Friesen P (2021) Mind the gaps: ethical and epistemic issues in the digital mental health response to COVID-19. Hastings Cent Rep 51(6):23–26
11. Mudiyanselage KWW, De Santis KK, Jörg F, Saleem M, Stewart R, Zeeb H, & Busse H (2024). The effectiveness of mental health interventions involving non-specialists and digital technology in low-and middle-income countries–a systematic review. BMC Pub Health, 24(1), 77
12. Stuckey R, & Domingues-Montanari S (2017) Telemedicine is helping the parents of neurodiverse children living in remote and deprived areas. Paediatrics and International Child Health, 37(3):155–157
13. Fletcher-Watson S, & Durkin K (2014) Uses of new technologies by young people with neurodevelopmental disorders: Motivations, processes and cognition. In neurodevelopmental disorders (pp 242–267). Psychology Press
14. Alshammary FM, & Alhalafawy WS (2023) Digital platforms and the improvement of learning outcomes: evidence extracted from meta-analysis. Sustainability, 15(2), 1305

Contents

Part I Development and Usage of Technology for Learning

1. **Technologies for Intervention in Autism: Current Knowledge and Research Framework** 3
   Gerardo Herrera Gutiérrez and Lucía Vera

2. **Participation of Autistic People in Research and Technology Design** 25
   Gerardo Herrera Gutiérrez, Patricia Pérez-Fuster, and Cristina Costescu

3. **The Utility of Biomarkers for Assessment and Intervention in Neurodevelopmental Disorders** 43
   Stella Guldner, Julia Ernst, Frauke Nees, and Nathalie Holz

4. **Digital Biomarkers in Neurodevelopmental Health: Current Status, Promises, and Perils** 83
   Wamuyu Owotoki, Anninka Enseroth, Ruth Njeri Mbugua, and Peter Owotoki

5. **Support, But Do Not Replace, Human Expertise: A Few Considerations for the Deployment of Machine Learning in Support of Neurodiverse Children and Adolescents** 109
   Serge Thill

6. **Social Robotics in Psychological Interventions for Children** 123
   Anouk Neerinex, Joana Brito, Marta Couto, Joana Campos, Maartje de Graaf, Judith Masthoff, and Ana Paiva

Part II Applications of Technology Use for Interventions

7. **The Use of Technological Tools for Autistic Children** 151
   Cristina Costescu

8	Shaping Executive Functions of Neurodiverse Children Through Digital Technologies	165
	Cristina Costescu, Carmen David, and Adrian Roșan	
9	Best Practices to Improve Autonomy of People on the Spectrum Using Handheld Devices	189
	Guadalupe Montero de Espinosa Espino and Luis Perez de la Maza	
10	Using *e*Coaching to Promote Independent and Effective Functioning of Neurodiverse Learners	211
	Laura C. Chezan, Annemarie L. Horn, Jin Liu, and Whitney Idol	
11	Digital Interventions for Attention Deficit/Hyperactivity Disorder	235
	Leonhard Marten, Anna Kaiser, and Alexander Häge	
12	Moral Disengagement in Cyberbullying Through Serious Games in Neurodiverse Children	255
	Paula Costa Ferreira, Ana Margarida Veiga Simão, Diana Stilwell, Sara L. Lopes, Fátima Trindade, Nádia Pereira, and Sofia Francisco	
13	Computer-Supported Collaborative Learning and the Regulation of Learning in Neurodiverse Children	273
	Paula Costa Ferreira, Ana Margarida Veiga Simão, Diana Stilwell, Sara L. Lopes, Diogo Domingues, Fátima Trindade, and Nádia Pereira	

Conclusion 289

Index 295

Contributors

Joana Brito INESC-ID, Instituto Superior Técnico, University of Lisbon, Lisbon, Portugal

Joana Campos INESC-ID, Instituto Superior Técnico, University of Lisbon, Lisbon, Portugal

Laura C. Chezan Department of Human Movement Studies and Special Education, Old Dominion University, Norfolk, USA

Paula Costa Ferreira CICPSI, Faculdade de Psicologia, Universidade de Lisboa, Lisbon, Portugal

Cristina Costescu Special Education Department, Faculty of Psychology and Educational Sciences, Babeș-Bolyai University, Cluj-Napoca, Romania

Marta Couto INESC-ID, Instituto Superior Técnico, University of Lisbon, Lisbon, Portugal

Carmen David Special Education Department, Faculty of Psychology and Educational Sciences, Babeș-Bolyai University, Cluj-Napoca, Romania

Maartje de Graaf Utrecht University, Utrecht, The Netherlands

Diogo Domingues Facukdade de Psicologia, Universidade de Lisboa, Lisbon, Portugal

Anninka Enseroth Vitafluence.ai, Kronberg im Taunus, Germany

Julia Ernst Department of Child and Adolescent Psychiatry and Psychotherapy, Central Institute of Mental Health, Medical Faculty Mannheim, University of Heidelberg, Mannheim, Germany

Sofia Francisco CICPSI, Faculdade de Psicologia, Universidade de Lisboa, Lisbon, Portugal

Stella Guldner Department of Child and Adolescent Psychiatry and Psychotherapy, Central Institute of Mental Health, Medical Faculty Mannheim, University of Heidelberg, Mannheim, Germany

Gerardo Herrera Gutiérrez IRTIC Institute, Universitat de València, Valencia, Spain

Alexander Häge Department of Child and Adolescent Psychiatry and Psychotherapy, Central Institute of Mental Health, Mannheim, Germany

Nathalie Holz Department of Child and Adolescent Psychiatry and Psychotherapy, Central Institute of Mental Health, Medical Faculty Mannheim, University of Heidelberg, Mannheim, Germany

Annemarie L. Horn School of Teacher Education and Leadership, Radford University, Radford, USA

Whitney Idol School of Teacher Education and Leadership, Radford University, Radford, USA

Anna Kaiser Department of Child and Adolescent Psychiatry and Psychotherapy, Central Institute of Mental Health, Mannheim, Germany

Jin Liu Department of Educational Leadership and Policy Studies, University of Texas at Arlington, Arlington, USA

Sara L. Lopes Business School, Iscte-IUL, Lisbon, Portugal

Leonhard Marten Department of Child and Adolescent Psychiatry and Psychotherapy, Central Institute of Mental Health, Mannheim, Germany

Judith Masthoff Utrecht University, Utrecht, The Netherlands

Ruth Njeri Mbugua Vitafluence.ai, Kronberg im Taunus, Germany

Guadalupe Montero de Espinosa Espino Inclusive Education Department, Smile and Learn, Madrid, Spain

Anouk Neerinex Utrecht University, Utrecht, The Netherlands

Frauke Nees Institute of Medical Psychology and Medical Sociology, University Medical Center Schleswig-Holstein, Kiel University, Kiel, Germany

Peter Owotoki Vitafluence.ai, Kronberg im Taunus, Germany

Wamuyu Owotoki Vitafluence.ai, Kronberg im Taunus, Germany

Ana Paiva INESC-ID, Instituto Superior Técnico, University of Lisbon, Lisbon, Portugal

Nádia Pereira CICPSI, Faculdade de Psicologia, Universidade de Lisboa, Lisbon, Portugal

Luis Perez de la Maza Board, Fundación AUCAVI, Madrid, Spain

Patricia Pérez-Fuster Department of Developmental and Educational Psychology, Universitat de València, Valencia, Spain

Adrian Roşan Special Education Department, Faculty of Psychology and Educational Sciences, Babeş-Bolyai University, Cluj-Napoca, Romania

Diana Stilwell CICPSI, Faculdade de Psicologia, Universidade de Lisboa, Lisbon, Portugal

Serge Thill Donders Institute for Brain, Cognition, and Behaviour, Radboud University Nijmegen, Nijmegen, The Netherlands

Fátima Trindade PADS, Portuguese Association of Down Syndrome, Lisbon, Portugal

Ana Margarida Veiga Simão CICPSI, Faculdade de Psicologia, Universidade de Lisboa, Lisbon, Portugal

Lucía Vera IRTIC Institute, Universitat de València, Valencia, Spain

Part I
Development and Usage of Technology for Learning

Technologies for Intervention in Autism: Current Knowledge and Research Framework

Gerardo Herrera Gutiérrez and Lucía Vera

Abstract

This chapter begins by compiling some figures related to the number of publications, which reflect the current dimension of research efforts around technologies and autism. The main lines of research related to the use of technology in the intervention are also summarised, and the main potential advantages of technologies for intervention in autism are explored, related to their visual nature and predictability, as well as their possible risks. Other potential benefits, such as the generalisation of learning and possibilities for the personalisation of technology-supported interventions, are also discussed.

Keywords

Autism spectrum disorder · Innovative technologies · Visual supports · Generalization · Computer assisted learning · Customization

1 Introduction

The first research on technologies applied to ASD dates back to the seventies. Colby et al. [1, 2] developed one of the pioneering studies on using computers to teach autistic students. Seventeen autistic people who had not developed verbal language participated in this work. Colby used several games with different levels of complexity. The children who participated in these games had to press a key on

G. H. Gutiérrez · L. Vera (✉)
IRTIC Institute, Universitat de València, Valencia, Spain
e-mail: lucia.vera@uv.es

G. H. Gutiérrez
e-mail: gerardo.herrera@uv.es

the keyboard to simultaneously listen to how the computer responded and express the name of the character corresponding to the key pressed through sound.

In other games, participants touched a specific key (for example, the one corresponding to the letter "H") and then saw a horse trotting on the screen and heard it neighing (continuing with the example). This pioneering study aimed to help children increase their understanding of how letters and sounds form words, as well as how words create expressions, and improvements were found to be significant in 13 of the 17 participants. In immersive virtual reality, the first documented research is the study of two cases carried out by Strickland et al. [3] in which two autistic children were trained in the activity of crossing the street. Despite the inconvenience and cumbersome nature of the technology used, positive results were obtained. In the field of augmented reality, one of the first works was carried out by Parés et al. [4], in which an interactive, multisensory environment was created and whose objective was to provide autistic people with a sense of agency through the movement of their body, within the framework of an interactive dialogue with images.

More than fifty years after the first study by Colby [1] in which technology was used for the first time for intervention, the number of published works has begun to grow exponentially, and the advantages of technology are increasingly considered a reality rather than a potentiality. However, a significant research effort is still necessary.

2 Current Dimension of Research Efforts Around Technologies and Autism

As with autism research in general, the current number of autism studies specifically related to technology has exploded in recent decades, even more so in recent years. In 2023, a simple search on the Web Of Science with the string "autism AND technology" in the *topic* field (which, in turn, includes Title, Summary and Keywords) returns 5531 results. This increase is reflected in the results of searches in databases that operate on socio-health research journals, such as PubMed, and those that run on technological journals, such as ACM Digital Library. Figure 1 shows the evolution of publications in both databases in recent decades. The left side includes the growth of publications in Pubmed for the search for "autism AND technology" in the title or abstract, which returns a total of 1033 results, with the maximum in 2021, when 160 publications were made. The right side shows the evolution of publications that include the term "autism" in the ACM Digital Library, with a total of 3,352 results, which reaches a maximum in 2020, with 296 results.

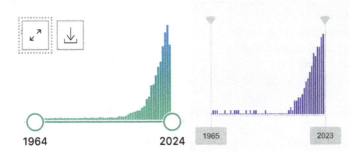

Fig. 1 Left: publications with "autism" and "technology" in PubMed between 1964 and 2023. Right: publications with the term "autism" in the ACM Digital Library between 1965 and 2023

3 Research Unrelated to Autism Intervention

More generally, considering the comprehensive set of results obtained in the searches, only part of the research focuses on using technology for intervention, as we will see later. In addition, there are other areas in which technology is used for purposes other than intervention:

- The use of technology for research into the nature of autism, for example, when using *eye trackers* to identify differences in the social attention patterns of autistic people compared to typically developing people [5].
- The use of technology for autism genetic research, in which chromosomal microarrays (CMA) are analysed to identify possible genes involved in the aetiology of ASD and other neurodevelopmental conditions [6, 7].
- The use of technology to improve the early detection of ASD, with classic screening tools that have been digitised [8–10] and the use of systems of *eye-tracker* to detect atypical attention patterns that may indicate the presence of ASD [11, 12] or a wide variety of technologies to detect autism both in the general population and in groups risk (see [13] for a systematic review on this topic).

4 Research Related to Intervention in Autism

In addition to the areas mentioned above, numerous investigations have been carried out in which technology is used either as a (focused) intervention tool or as support for intervention in any of the dimensions of development that are affected in autism.

In this area, we can find numerous systematic reviews around each dimension, having shown that specific technology-based supports are beneficial in the following areas:

- Alternative communication [14–16].
- Video modeling [17–19].
- Social communication [20–23].
- Emotion recognition [24–30].
- Physical activity [31].
- Access to employment [32–35].
- Access to medical services [36].
- Acquisition and improvement of academic skills [37–41].

We also find reviews and primary studies in which the role of a particular technology in autism intervention has been analysed:

- Studies with robots [42–44].
- Studies with mobile and/or touchscreen devices [45–48].
- *Wearables* [49, 50].
- Speech-generating devices which are used in the field of AAC [51].
- Virtual reality, augmented reality, and mixed reality [52–59].
- Tangible elements [60].
- Serious games, as described by Abt [61], in the studies of Hassan et al. [62] and Silva et al. [63].

Despite the enormous scope of research efforts, technology-based support with solid evidence of effectiveness is rarely commercially available [64]. And vice versa, of all the commercially available applications, only some have substantial evidence. For example, in digital applications for tablets and smartphones, a study analysed 695 commercially available applications for autism [65]. Of them, only 5 (less than 1%) had direct evidence of their effectiveness.

5 Use of Technologies by Autistic People

To understand the role that technologies play in autism, another source of information that should be observed is the use that autistic people make of technologies at home. An international survey of parental attitudes towards the use of technology by autistic children at home, involving 388 families in Spain, the United Kingdom and Belgium, found that tablets and smartphones are the most common devices used by autistic people, very significantly in children (higher than 70% in preschoolers and close to 80% in children), and closely followed using computers in adolescents and adults (between 70 and 80%) [66]. This same survey also analysed the purpose for which technologies were used in the homes of autistic people. According to the families themselves, the main uses of devices by their autistic children focus on uses related to leisure (Games, YouTube, Music and Photos), with uses related to some intervention (such as Alternative and Augmentative Communication or AAC) and with social media, email or videoconference having less weight.

As stated in the previous study, for autistic people who do not have intellectual disabilities, the use of technology does not usually pose any problem. In fact, in many cases, it will be a strength rather than a difficulty. But what happens to those autistic people with a significant intellectual disability? Will they also need support to handle the device?

There are still few studies on using tablets and smartphones by low-developmental autistic people. In a recent study [67], the abilities of a group of six autistic people without verbal language were analysed. It was found that the majority easily handled the touch functions (such as touching the screen and pressing large buttons). Still, everyone had difficulty turning on the tablet, rotating the image, navigating between applications (only one participant could do it), controlling the volume (also, only one participant could do it), and using the camera (again, only one of the six participants). This does not mean that these people cannot learn these functions. What is concluded in this study is that to do so, specific support and adult accompaniment are needed [67].

To these initial difficulties related to the devices, we must add those derived from the complexity of handling some digital applications, which may also require thorough training to learn how to use them.

6 Why Technologies?

Members of the autistic community find technology-based support particularly acceptable [68]. Research has also reported participants' enthusiasm for using technology [69, 70] and high motivation to complete tasks when performed with technology support [71, 72]. The reasons that may explain this tendency of autistic people to use technology will be analysed.

7 Visual Thinking in Autism

One of the factors that may explain the preference of autistic people for technology is the visual format of information presentation on these devices. Through their personal accounts, some autistic adults have explained that their way of processing information and their way of learning is primarily visual [73]. The nature of this visual thinking has been studied by different neuroscientists [74–76]. In Kana's pioneering study [74], a group of 12 autistic people and 13 others from a control group had to solve cognitively demanding tasks while brain activation was measured with magnetic resonance imaging (functional MRI). The tasks consisted of indicating whether the sentences proposed were true or false. These sentences were grouped into highly visual sentences (e.g., "If you take the number 8 and turn it 90°, then it becomes a pair of glasses") and others that are not very visual (e.g., "Both animals "As minerals are living beings, plants are not." The main finding of this study was that autistic people, unlike the control group, also used the areas of the brain dedicated to visual processing to solve tasks in which low-visual sentences were proposed.

A subsequent meta-analysis study by Samson et al. [75] concluded that—in autism—most cognitive tasks involving visual information (such as visual search, visual discrimination, and detection of embedded figures) lead to high activity in associative regions. That implies that sensory processing mechanisms play an atypically prominent role in supporting cognition in autistic people. However, in another study, Barbeau et al. [76] observed less task-related activity in visual areas in autistic participants compared to the control group, when they expected the opposite result based on Samson's meta-analysis. et al. [75]. These authors explain this lower activity in visual tasks due to the presence of highly efficient perceptual processing in ASD, citing the work of Soulieres et al. [77], which would require less activity to solve this type of task than that necessary in the participants with typical development in the control group.

This tendency to use areas intended for visual processing, even for tasks that we would a priori classify as non-visual, as well as the greater performance of visual processing areas, may also be an explanation for the visual approach and the effectiveness of some of the programs most used in autism, such as TEACCH [78] or PECS [79]. In TEACCH, visual supports are one of the bases to provide structure and aids at the receptive level of communication through daily agendas, individualised work systems or structured "step-by-step" tasks [78]. In PECS, visual supports are provided at the expressive level of communication, and autistic people use them both to communicate what they need—for example, when they hand over the water pictogram because they are thirsty—and to share ideas with others. others—for example, when they point to the sky to say that they have seen a plane passing by [79].

8 What Other Advantages Do Technologies Offer for Intervention in ASD?

Just over a decade after the first studies on technology and autism, in 1984 Panyan [80] analysed the potential benefits of technology for autistic people and anticipated many of the characteristics that were later elaborated upon in the following decades. Among the advantages that Panyan highlighted are the following:

(1) its potential to focus the attention of autistic people by capturing their interest.
(2) the possibility that they can contribute to reducing unwanted behaviours.
(3) the ability to provide continuous feedback to the autistic person.
(4) its different possibilities of helping language development and
(5) the possibility of allowing the autistic person to control the learning situation instead of passively participating.

Technology-based supports often result in benefits such as increased motivation, decreased outward signs of anxiety or distress, improved attention, and sometimes increased learning compared to traditional methods [81].

Below, other advantages that technologies represent in intervention in autism are analysed in greater detail, and the analysis of the transfer of learning and the possibility of personalisation is left for the following sections, which will be seen in greater detail.

8.1 Predictability

In its current definitions (DSM-5 [82] and ICD-11 [83]), autism involves difficulty thinking and behaving flexibly. This difficulty has many manifestations, including the difficulty in facing changes, which can occur at many levels. Small changes, such as an object not being in the same position in which it usually is inside the room or the light coming through the window at a different angle, are examples of changes that may be imperceptible to the eye for most people but in autism, they can be an important source of difficulties [84, 85]. Difficulties in attributing thoughts, beliefs, and intentions to other people are also a characteristic of autism [86]. These difficulties mean that it is difficult for autistic people to understand and predict the behaviour of others since these predictions must be made based on these mentalistic attributions and the events that happen. On the other hand, the information displayed on a digital device screen is generally always displayed in the same way, and the behaviour of these devices is generally much more predictable than that of people, which may also be behind the preferences of many autistic people for technology. With proper device configuration, interruptions, and appearances of unscheduled events in the digital context can also be reduced to a minimum.

8.2 Control of the Learning Situation

When the autistic child or adult does not use digital devices, whether at school, at home or on the street, life takes place in environments with a high load of stimuli in which these stimuli compete to capture the attention of the child or adult. It is known that, even in very controlled situations, the attention patterns of autistic people are different from those of typically developing people: autistic people show a pattern of interaction between perception and attention that results in excessive attention to parts over the whole, which contrasts with the tendency towards the whole over the parts typical of typical development [87, 88]. On the other hand, within a screen, and thanks to the good design and adequate usability of many digital applications, it is possible to have a format for presenting stimuli that is much more controlled and scheduled, in which there is planning for how they are presented. the stimuli and the quantity of these. There is also the possibility that the autistic person controls how these stimuli are presented, allowing them to assume—at least partially—control of the learning situation. That is, a situation of a priori use of technology can facilitate the conditions for learning to occur by having the user's attention and motivation and by reducing and controlling the stimulation load. This point will be returned to later in this chapter when learning transfer and generalisation are discussed.

8.3 Reduce the Speed at Which Information is Presented.

There are many stories from autistic people who express their difficulties processing information at the speed at which it is presented to them in everyday situations. For example, Donna Williams [89] expressed:

> When I was a little girl, my threshold for processing blah-blah-blah was only a few seconds. When I was about ten years old, this threshold had already passed from five to ten minutes. In adolescence and until reaching twenties, the threshold was already fifteen to thirty minutes. Currently, it is approximately twenty to forty-five minutes... If the environment had been more adapted... these thresholds could have been much better [89, p. 204].

These difficulties may, at least partially, explain autistic people's difficulties in facial, verbal, bodily, and socio-emotional interaction. When the information presented is generated in real-time by a computer or other device, it is possible to reduce the speed at which it is presented to adapt it to the preferences of the person receiving it.

Tardif et al. [90] evaluated the impact of slowed audio-visual information on verbal cognition and behaviour in 2 autistic children with delayed language acquisition. To do this, they used an application, **Logiral**, which allows them to record videos and display them at different speeds. During 15 sessions spread over four months, both children were presented with various stimuli (e.g., pictures, words, sentences, cartoons) and then asked questions or given instructions regarding the stimuli they finished. Both the audio-visual stimuli and the instructions/questions were presented on a screen and were viewed twice: once at the original speed and once slowed down. Both participants showed significant improvements in both their verbal performance and behaviour when the information was shown in a slowed manner and when it was shown in a slowed manner, followed by the original speed version.

8.4 Technology as Intrinsic Reinforcement

In the developmentally based naturalistic behavioural interventions (NDBI) [91], which represent the current reference model for early intervention in ASD, one of the requirements of the activities proposed to the child is that they have intrinsic reinforcement. They do not need an additional external reward when performing successfully. The high motivation for technologies shown by autistic people, at least partially explained by the previously stated reasons, already represents an intrinsic reinforcement when many educational or skill-oriented activities offered through technology are proposed. In addition, digital applications offer the possibility of programming and introducing reinforcements regularly within the intervention program, including videos, images, sounds or other elements that the autistic person prefers, to increase their motivation for the learning environment. In this sense, it is worth highlighting the possibility that reinforcements are provided immediately and contingently, which could improve the care of the autistic person in these situations. Again, implementing this type of support or reinforcement may be easier within a programmed environment than in a real context, such as a lesson with traditional classroom methods.

8.5 Risk Reduction

Reducing the risks associated with certain interventions is an advantage of some technologies. For example, when a person is taught to cross the street using an immersive virtual reality environment, the dangers will be lower than if done in a real environment [3]. Another study in which this advantage of virtual reality technologies, combined with *eye tracking* technologies, has already been positively exploited is that of Wade et al. [92], in which a simulator was successfully used. of driving whose behaviour was adapted to the direction of the user's gaze, with which the prominence of certain stimuli was increased (such as traffic lights or pedestrians crossing the street) until the autistic participants' attention was obtained towards the same.

9 Risks Associated with the Use of Technologies in ASD

Although this work aims to explore some advantages of technologies when used correctly, they can also entail some risks that need to be known.

Due to the characteristics of the technologies mentioned above, autistic people tend to feel very attracted to them [66]. This attraction or fascination with technology is precisely behind some of the main risks. In the last decade, different organisations such as the American Academy of Paediatrics (AAP) and the World Health Organization (WHO) have focused attention on the need to reduce the screen time to which children are exposed, recommending that do not have any exposure to screens until they are two years old (except video calls with loved ones), and that between the ages of two and five they use them for one hour a day, at most, and always in a supervised manner and with selected content [93]. These recommendations are based on some studies on the negative effects that we will see later in this section.

Very recently, the possible impact that such exposure at very early ages may have on the risk of ASD has been analysed. Slobodin et al. [94] conducted a systematic review of sixteen studies that supported the idea that autistic children are more exposed to screens than their typically developing peers and concluded that more research is needed to understand the long-term consequences. of exposure to screens in autistic children under three years of age. The most relevant study to date is the one developed in Japan by Kushima et al. [95]. In this work, 84,030 mother–child dyads were analysed using data derived from a large birth cohort study. Among boys, but not girls, having more screen exposure at one year of age was significantly associated with ASD diagnosis at three years of age. The strength of this association was generally greater as the number of hours of screen exposure increased, and the association was greatest in one-year-old children who spent between 2 and 4 h of screen time per day. The researchers themselves warn that there could be reverse causality, that is, that the presence of ASD at one year of age influenced the number of hours that children spent in front of the screen. To rule out this hypothesis, they carried out a second analysis, in which they excluded those children who—at one year of age—showed warning signs in any of the five ASQ items, and the results obtained support the argument that the time of screen at such a young age is a risk factor for ASD. Another systematic review of 11 studies [96] has recently found that the longer the period of screen exposure, the higher the risk that the child may develop ASD. Also, they have found that the earlier the child is exposed to screens, the higher the risk of developing ASD in children compared to children exposed later.

Some studies have examined the connection between characteristics of autism and compulsive Internet use in a non-clinical sample of 390 participants, finding consequences related to obsessive behaviours and social isolation [97]. Compared to people with fewer autistic characteristics, those with more autistic characteristics did not report a higher frequency of Internet use but were more likely to engage in compulsive Internet use.

Other effects that may occur immediately are related to the presence of epilepsy, which is estimated to be present in 12.1% of autistic people [98] or having a clinical history of migraine or vertigo. According to some organisations, the use of technologies that involve having screens very close to the eyes, such as virtual reality glasses, can induce seizures. The Epilepsy Foundation warns of this risk, although the mechanisms that cause these seizures remain unclear [99].

The potentially negative effects of technologies are not limited only to the moment in which autistic people are using them but can impact other aspects of their lives. Research on the use of technology, some carried out on the general population and others on autistic people, has identified other additional risks that must be considered when using technologies with autistic people.

One of the most obvious risks has to do with sleep. Especially when used before bed, technologies affect the quality and duration of sleep in the general population [100]. In autism, where sleep problems are more frequent than in the general population and where these problems also have important behavioural consequences

[101], even greater attention should be paid to this aspect when planning the use of devices.

Another risk is the reduced availability of time for other important activities, such as physical exercise or in-person social activities [102]. This is something that can occur from a very early age, also within the family. Furthermore, the possible negative effects are accentuated when children do not use screens in the company of other people [102]. At least one study has found that increased screen time correlates with decreased mother–child interaction time, both in typical development and autism [103]. Furthermore, in the long term, greater emotional and behavioural problems are found associated with the beginning of technology use before 18 months [104].

In general, the younger the developmental age of the autistic child, the more the risks will be related to excessive stimulation by technology and its difficult control, especially with those with greater communication difficulties. At more advanced levels of skill development, risks tend to be more related to a lack of understanding of social situations and the risks of deception and harassment on the Internet, with particular attention to social networks, online games, and other dangers. associated with this type of interaction [105].

The WHO recommendations were published before the COVID-19 pandemic, and precisely, this pandemic—especially in periods of confinement—posed a challenge to these recommendations in the entire child population, including the autistic population. Several surveys conducted after confinement revealed that children autistic had greater exposure to screens during the said period and that, in addition, they benefited less from that screen time to cope with the social isolation imposed by confinement [106, 107].

10 Generalisation of Learning Acquired with Technology

The generalisation in autism of skills acquired in learning situations to other situations has been analysed for several decades [108]. Generalisation *of a behaviour* is considered to have occurred when it appears under conditions different from those that occurred at the time in which said behaviour was trained [109]. Stories from autistic people have also addressed the issue of generalisation, describing some of the difficulties it presents [89]:

> I could learn to deal with a given situation in a given context. However, I felt lost when faced with that same situation in a different context. There was no connection between the two situations. If I learned something while standing in the kitchen with a woman in broad daylight on a summer day, what I had learned that day in that particular situation would not come to mind if I were, for example, in a bedroom. standing next to a man, it being night and winter. Things were stored, but the classification overhead was so subtle that the situations had to be practically identical to be considered comparable [89, p. 62].

Understanding this phenomenon from research needs to be completed. There are different processes and theories about these difficulties. On the one hand, the processes of formation of symbols and concepts have been analysed based on the experiences perceived in the different sensory modalities [84]:

> Before language, the process of symbol (concept) formation operates in sensory modalities. Aspects of the perceived experience are stored in long-term memory and form a kind of "perceptual symbol" file, which will later be used for reference. Visual images are acquired from vision. Auditory perceptual symbols are stored from hearing. "Olfactory images" are received from the sense of smell. "Flavour" files are added from the gustatory sense. Perceptual symbols for textures, pressure and temperatures are formed from the tactile sense. From proprioception, perceptual symbols for limb movements and body positions are organised [84].

Research in neuroscience indicates that each type of perceptual symbol is reached and stored in different brain areas and that if there is any alteration in the process, the conceptualisation of this modality can be interrupted [110, 111]. These neuroscience findings are compatible with one of the theories explaining the difficulties of autism that have had a long history: the theory of weak central coherence, which suggests that, in autism, there is greater attention to the parts than to the body. all, which can make it difficult to understand the global nature of the situations that the person faces and, consequently, the acquisition of significant learning that can be generalised to other situations that may be very similar but never identical [87, 88, 112, 113]. Other authors, such as Plaisted [114], suggest that difficulties in processing similarities at the perceptual and attentional levels translate into difficulties at the conceptual level that hinder generalisation.

In the initial intervention studies in this area, aimed at providing learning in educational centres and for these to be generalised to homes, it was identified that the generalisation results were better when children received training in several places instead of in one. alone and that, in this way, the school environment could be manipulated to simulate conditions more like those of home to facilitate the transfer of learning to the natural environment [115, 116].

In this sense, the role and advantages of technology can be twofold. On the one hand, in a computer-generated environment, it is possible to present a stimulus repeatedly so that, in each repetition, the stimulus is exactly the same (in its auditory and visual aspects) and use this strategy to provide learning that facilitates the acquisition of concepts (for example, those related to the functions of objects). On the other hand, the nature of some technologies in which reality is simulated would mean that a priori, better generalisation is expected, to the extent that there is less demand to process the similarities between both contexts. However, we know that, in the case of virtual reality, this approach only immediately provides ecological validity since many other factors influence the learning process, and excessive similarity can produce fewer effective results [117]. Other technologies, such as augmented and mixed reality, could be advantageous, as support is provided directly in the real environment.

Concern about the transfer of learning has been a constant in research carried out for decades. It has been observed that when children participate in naturalistic interventions, they receive instructions "in the place they want to be and doing what they want to do" and that these types of interventions are associated with a reduction in escape and avoidance behaviours [118, 119]. Currently, the application of naturalistic procedures to facilitate generalisation is one of the bases of the NDBI interventions [91]. However, it is considered necessary to adapt the different programs to the needs of each autistic person within a continuum that ranges from the highly structured to the naturalistic. When the intervention is to be provided in a non-naturalistic environment, the incorporation of naturalistic components will be essential to improve the generalisation of skills in natural environments [120].

Again, technologies can facilitate the fulfilment of the prerequisites for the learning situation to occur. In this sense, it is worth highlighting the intuitive and motivating nature of some technologies—which make the student quickly prepared to learn—compared to the difficulties of some natural contexts such as the classroom, in which, for some students, the difficulties to sit still or listen to the teacher can represent a huge learning barrier. Augmented and mixed reality technologies and other types of supports that can be provided ubiquitously through mobile devices can be an opportunity to adjust support to the level of structure that each person needs and to withdraw gradually said support as it acquires and generalises the learning.

11 Analysis of Customisation Options in Solutions Created for Autistic People

The needs of each autistic person and/or intellectual disabilities are different, and this means that the intervention responses proposed must be personalised. It is, therefore, a requirement of any intervention in autism, whether it involves using technologies. For example, in mobile applications, AAC applications that support communication must be personalised to the vocabulary and level of communication development of the autistic person. An activity agenda that needed to be adapted to the activity calendar of the user who benefits from this support would also be unthinkable. However, it is common to find applications of a different nature (such as educational ones) in which the customisation option is not always available despite its critical importance in autism.

12 The Current Reality of Personalisation in Technological Supports for ASD: A Systematic Mapping Study

In a systematic review and mapping work by Lopez-Herrejón et al. [121], the level and number of personalisation options in the technologies used in research on technology and autism were analysed in depth. In this work, the systematic mapping

(SMS) methodology was followed [122]. SMS are secondary studies intended to identify and classify the set of publications, the so-called *primary sources*, on a topic [122, 123]. To do this, guidelines are followed that describe a five-stage process: (1) Definition of research questions; (2) Conduct search; (3) Screening of papers; (4) Keywording using abstracts; and (5) Data extraction and Mapping process [122].

Nine research questions were posed in this study. The most relevant were those related to the *forms of personalisation*, the *sensory channels* through which this personalisation took place, and the level of help required by the participants in each study. In the searches carried out on the Web of Science and Scopus, 251 results were obtained, which, after eliminating duplicates (99) and detailed review, were reduced to 32 primary sources that were analysed in depth concerning each of the nine research questions. The most relevant results are collected below.

The different forms of personalisation that had been used, ordered from highest to lowest frequency, were:

- *Resources*: the possibility of adding content in image or sound format. It was the most frequent form of personalisation, present in 20 of the 32 studies analysed.
- *Functionality*: in some systems or applications, the contents and functions vary, depending on the beneficiary's profile. Half of the studies analysed dealt with systems or applications that presented this customisation form.
- *Interface*: customisation options related to the fonts used, their colours and sizes, background colours, etc. The third part of the studies analysed used systems that allowed the interface to be customised.
- *User-related data*: included different types of measurements, activity log, etc. Only 3 of the 32 studies presented this option.

The possibility of personalising technologies through external resources (not only images and sound but also video) has an added value in the intervention aimed at autism, which is the possibility of using these resources as reinforcements and thus increasing the motivation of the autistic person by the learning environment, thus contributing to the presence of the intrinsic reinforcements analysed above. When these reinforcements are provided immediately and contingently, an improvement in the attention levels of the autistic person towards the relevant elements can also be expected. Implementing this type of reinforcement can be relatively simple within a computer application, where everything is programmed. On the other hand, it is much more difficult to provide in real-time in the classroom context. The ease of automatic data collection and even the ease of automatic analysis and consultation of that data from any mobile device is another potential advantage of the technology and, at the same time, can facilitate personalisation.

Continuing with the review of López-Herrejón et al. [121], the technologies used to provide said personalisation were subsequently analysed (mainly computers and mobile devices such as tablets or smartphones). Next, the sensory dimensions around which the different systems allowed personalisation were analysed. The 32 studies analysed systems that allowed customisation of the visual channel. In 30 of them, sounds were allowed to be personalised. In 20 of them, the tactile function was allowed, with a much smaller number of studies allowing other sensory channels to be personalised (such as smell or taste), but the systems that considered the proprioceptive sense (11) and vestibular perception (9).

Another important aspect in terms of personalisation was whether the systems recorded the level of help of the users, establishing four levels or types of help, ordered from highest to lowest [121]:

- *High*: when it was explicitly stated that constant supervision was necessary in the use of technology or when its use involved a dyadic interaction (for example, between child and adult). A total of 9 studies analysed technologies that involved this level of help. They consisted mainly of working with robots that, by their nature, required the continuous presence of the support person.
- *Medium*: when it was indicated that a training period, help in installation or partial supervision was necessary when using the customisable system, which occurred in 10 of the studies, mainly related to digital or multimedia applications.
- *No help*: 7 of the papers explicitly mentioned that no help was needed to use the system.
- *Undetermined*: when this aspect was not mentioned in the sources analysed, something that occurred in 6 of the 32 studies analysed.

The other variables analysed in the primary sources of this systematic mapping review were the presence of intellectual disability in the study participants, the areas of development addressed (e.g., communication), the environment of use (laboratory, home, educational centre …) and the level of evidence obtained in each study. Overall, the analysis of the results around the nine research questions revealed a significant absence of robust customisation options and a notable need for greater evidence of effectiveness in using this type of system [121].

13   Conclusions

This chapter has described the current knowledge framework on technology use for autistic people. Starting with a review of the potentialities of IT to support autism intervention and the possible reasons behind the good fit of technologies and autistic people, different areas of intervention have been listed together with the most relevant works and studies. This framework would not be complete without considering the underlying risks of technology use in autism and the possible links between early exposure to digital screens and having an ASD diagnosis at an early age. Generalisation and customisation opportunities have also been explored.

Acknowledgements The research leading to these results is in the frame of the "EMPOWER. Design and evaluation of technological support tools to empower stakeholders in digital education" project, which has received funding from the European Union's Horizon Europe programme under grant agreement No 101060918. However, the views and opinions expressed are those of the authors(s) only and do not necessarily reflect those of the European Union. Neither the European Union nor the granting authority can be held responsible for them.

References

1. Colby KM, Smith DC (1971) Computers in the treatment of nonspeaking autistic children. In: Masserman JH (ed) Current psychiatric therapies. Grune & Stratton, New York
2. Colby KM (1973) The rationale for computer-based treatment of language difficulties in nonspeaking autistic children. J Autism Dev Disord 3:254–260
3. Strickland D, Marcus LM, Mesibov GB, Hogan K (1996) Brief report: two case studies using virtual reality as a learning tool for autistic children. J Autism Dev Disord 26(6):651–659. https://doi.org/10.1007/BF02172354
4. Parés N, Carreras A, Durany J, Ferrer J, Freixa P, Gomez D et al (2006) Starting research in interaction design with visuals for low-functioning children in the autistic spectrum: a protocol. Cyberpsychol Behav 9(2):218–223
5. Klin A, Jones W, Schultz R, Volkmar F (2003) The enactive mind, or from actions to cognition: lessons from autism. In: Frith H (ed) Autism: mind and Brain. Oxford University Press, Oxford
6. Heil KM, Schaaf CP (2013) The genetics of autism spectrum disorders—A guide for clinicians. Curr Psychiatry Rep 15(1):334. https://doi.org/10.1007/s11920-012-0334-3
7. Ho KS, Wassman ER, Baxter AL, Hensel CH, Martin MM, Prasad A, Twede H, Vanzo RJ, Butler MG (2016) Chromosomal microarray analysis of consecutive autistic individuals spectrum disorders using an ultra-high resolution chromosomal microarray optimized for neurodevelopmental disorders. Int J Mol Sci 17(12):2070. https://doi.org/10.3390/ijms17122070
8. Bauer NS, Sturm LA, Carroll AE, Downs SM (2013) Computer decision support to improve autism screening and care in community pediatric clinics. Infants Young Child 26:306–317. https://doi.org/10.1001/jamanetworkopen.2019.17676
9. Ben-Sasson A, Robins DL, Yom-Tov E (2018) Risk assessment for parents who suspect their child has autism spectrum disorder: machine learning approach. J Med Internet Res 20:e134. https://doi.org/10.2196/jmir.9496
10. Campbell K, Carpenter KL, Espinosa S, Hashemi J, Qiu Q, Tepper M, Dawson G (2017) Use of a digital modified checklist for autism in toddlers–revised with follow-up to improve quality of screening for autism. J Pediatr 183:133–139. https://doi.org/10.1016/j.jpeds.2017.01.021
11. Frazier TW, Klingemier EW, Parikh S, Speer L, Strauss MS, Eng C, Youngstrom EA (2018) Development and Validation of objective and quantitative eye tracking—Based measures of autism risk and symptom levels. J Am Acad Child Adolesc Psychiatr 57:858–866. https://doi.org/10.1016/j.jaac.2018.06.023
12. Moore A, Wozniak M, Yousef A, Barnes CC, Cha D, Courchesne E, Pierce K (2018) The geometric preference subtype in ASD: identifying a consistent, early-emerging phenomenon through eye tracking. Mol Autism 9:19. https://doi.org/10.1186/s13229-018-0202-z
13. Desideri L, Pérez-Fuster P, Herrera G (2021) Information and communication technologies to support early screening of autism spectrum disorder: a systematic review. Children 8:93. https://doi.org/10.3390/children8020093
14. Gilroy SP, Leader G, McCleery JP (2018) A pilot community-based randomized comparison of speech generating devices and the picture exchange communication system for children diagnosed with autism spectrum disorder. Autism Res 11(12):1701–1711
15. Lorah ER, Parnell A, Whitby PS, Hantula D (2014) A systematic review of tablet computers and portable media players as speech generating devices for autistic individuals spectrum disorder. J Autism Dev Disord 1–13

16. Brignell A, Chenausky KV, Song H, Zhu J, Suo C, Morgan AT (2018) Communication interventions for autism spectrum disorder in minimally verbal children. In: Cochrane database of systematic reviews. Wiley. https://doi.org/10.1002/14651858.CD012324.pub2
17. Stephenson J, Limbrick L (2013) A review of the use of touchscreen mobile devices by people with developmental disabilities. J Autism Dev Disorders 1–15
18. Den Brok WLJE, Sterkenburg PS (2014) Self-controlled technologies to support skill attainment in persons with an autism spectrum disorder and/or an intellectual disability: a systematic literature review. Disabil Rehabil Assist Technol 1–10
19. Huaqing C, Barton EE, Collier M, Lin Y (2018) A systematic review of single-case research studies on using video modeling interventions to improve social communication skills for autistic individuals spectrum disorder. Focus Autism Other Dev Disabil 33(4):249–257
20. Ramdoss S, Lang R, Fragale C, Britt C, O'Reilly M, Sigafoos J et al (2012) Use of computer-based interventions to promote daily living skills in individuals with intellectual disabilities: a systematic review. J Dev Phys Disabil 24(2):197–215. https://doi.org/10.1007/s10882-011-9259-8
21. Beaumont R, Sofronoff K (2008) A multi-component social skills intervention for children with Asperger syndrome: the junior detective training program. J Child Psychol Psychiatr 49:743–753
22. Hopkins IM, Gower MW, Perez TA, Smith DS, Amthor FR, Wimsatt FC, Biasini FJ (2011) Avatar assistant: improving social skills in students with an ASD through a computer-based intervention. J Autism Dev Disord 41(11):1543–1555
23. Thomeer ML, Smith RA, Lopata C, Volker MA, Lipinski AM, Rodgers JD, Lee GK (2015) Randomized controlled trial of mind reading and in vivo rehearsal for high-functioning children with ASD. J Autism Dev Disord 45(7):2115–2127
24. Berggren S, Fletcher-Watson S, Milenkovic N, Marschik PB, Bölte S, Jonsson U (2018) Emotion recognition training in autism spectrum disorder: a systematic review of challenges related to generalizability. Dev Neurorehabil 21:141–154
25. Bolte S, Hubl D, Feineis-Matthews S, Prvulovic D, Dierks T, Poustka F (2006) Facial affect recognition training in autism: can we animate the fusiform gyrus? Behav Neurosci 120:211–216. https://doi.org/10.1037/0735-7044.120.1.211
26. Rice LM, Wall CA, Fogel A, Shic F (2015) Computer-assisted face processing instruction improves emotion recognition, mentalizing, and social skills in students with ASD. J Autism Dev Disord 45(7):2176–2186
27. Russo-Ponsaran NM, Evans-Smith B, Johnson J, Russo J, McKown C (2015) Efficacy of a facial emotion training program for children and adolescents with autism spectrum disorders. J Nonverbal Behav 40(1):13–38. https://doi.org/10.1007/s10919-015-0217-5
28. Silver M, Oakes P (2001) Evaluation of a new computer intervention to teach people with autism or Asperger syndrome to recognize and predict emotions in others. Autism 5(3):299–316
29. Tanaka JW, Wolf JM, Klaiman C, Koenig K, Cockburn J, Herlihy L et al (2010) Using computerized games to teach face recognition skills to children with autism spectrum disorder: the let's face it! program. J Child Psychol Psychiatr Allied Discip 51(8):944–952
30. Voss C, Schwartz J, Daniels J, Kline A, Haber N, Washington P, Tariq Q, Robinson TN, Desai M, Phillips JM, Feinstein C, Winograd T, Wall DP (2019) Effect of wearable digital intervention for improving socialization in children with autism spectrum disorder: a randomized clinical trial. JAMA Pediatr 173:446–454. https://doi.org/10.1001/jamapediatrics.2019.0285
31. Dickinson K, Place M (2014) A randomised control trial of the impact of a computer-based activity programme upon the fitness of children with autism. Autism Res Treat
32. Gentry T, Kriner R, Sima A, McDonough J, Wehman P (2015) Reducing the need for personal supports among workers with autism using an iPod touch as an assistive technology: delayed randomized control trial. J Autism Dev Disord 45(3):669–684
33. Humm LB, Olsen D, Be M, Fleming M, Smith M (2014) Simulated job interview improves skills for adults with serious mental illnesses. Stud Health Technol Inform 199:50–54

34. Strickland DC, Coles CD, Southern LB (2013) JobTIPS: a transition to employment program for autistic individuals spectrum disorders. J Autism Dev Disord 43(10):2472–2483
35. Walsh E, Holloway J, McCoy A et al (2017) Technology-aided interventions for employment skills in adults with autism spectrum disorder: a systematic review. Rev J Autism Dev Disord 4:12–25. https://doi.org/10.1007/s40489-016-0093-x
36. Isong IA, Rao SR, Holifield C, Iannuzzi D, Hanson E, Ware J, Nelson LP (2014) Addressing dental fear in children with autism spectrum disorders: a randomized controlled pilot study using electronic screen media. Clin Pediatr 53(3):230
37. Massaro DW, Bosseler A (2006) Read my lips: the importance of the face in a computer-animated tutor for vocabulary learning by children with autism. Autism 10:495–510
38. Pennington RC (2010) Computer-assisted instruction for teaching academic skills to students with autism spectrum disorders: a review of literature. Focus Autism Other Dev Disabil 25:239–248
39. Knight V, McKissick BR, Saunders A (2013) A review of technology-based interventions to teach academic skills to students with autism spectrum disorder. J Autism Dev Disord 43(11):2628–2648
40. Ploog BO, Scharf A, Nelson D, Brooks PJ (2013) Use of computer assisted technologies (CAT) to enhance social communicative, and language development in children with autism spectrum disorders. J Autism Dev Disord 43(2):301–322
41. Root JR, Stevenson BS, Davis LL, Geddes-Hall J, Test DW (2017) Establishing computer-assisted instruction to teach academics to students with autism as an evidence-based practice. J Autism Dev Disord 47:275–284. https://doi.org/10.1007/s10803-016-2947-6
42. Billard A, Robins B, Nadel J, Dautenhahn K (2007) Building Robota, a mini-humanoid robot for the rehabilitation of children with autism. Assist Technol 19:37–49
43. van den Berk-Smeekens I, de Korte MWP, van Dongen-Boomsma M, Oosterling IJ, den Boer JC, Barakova EI, Lourens T, Glennon JC, Staal WG, Buitelaar JK (2021) Pivotal response treatment with and without robot-assistance for children with autism: a randomized controlled trial. Eur Child Adolesc Psychiatr. https://doi.org/10.1007/s00787-021-01804-8
44. Salimi Z, Jenabi E, Bashirian S (2021) Are social robots ready yet to be used in care and therapy of autism spectrum disorder: a systematic review of randomized controlled trials. Neurosci Biobehav Rev 129:1–16. https://doi.org/10.1016/j.neubiorev.2021.04.009
45. Campillo C, Herrera G, De Ganuza R et al (2014) Using Tic-Tac software to reduce anxiety-related behaviour in adults with autism and learning difficulties during waiting periods: a pilot study. Autism 18(3):264–271. https://doi.org/10.1177/1362361312472067
46. Cihak DF, Wright R, Ayres KM (2010) Use of self-modeling static-picture prompts via a handheld computer to facilitate self-monitoring in the general education classroom. Educ Train Autism Dev Disabil 136–149
47. Escobedo L, Nguyen DH, Boyd L, Hirano S, Rangel A, Garcia Rosas D, Tentori M, Hayes G (2012) MOSOCO: a mobile assistive tool to support children with autism practicing social skills in real-life situations. In: Proceedings of the SIGCHI conference on human factors in computing systems. ACM, pp 2589–2598
48. Al-Rashaida M, Amayra I, López-Paz JF, Martínez O, Lázaro E et al (2022) Studying the effects of mobile devices on young children with autism spectrum disorder: a systematic literature review. Rev J Autism Dev Disord 9:400–415. https://doi.org/10.1007/s40489-021-00264-9
49. Taj-Eldin M, Ryan C, O'Flynn B, Galvin P (2018) A review of wearable solutions for physiological and emotional monitoring for use by people with autism spectrum disorder and their caregivers. Sensors 18:4271. https://doi.org/10.3390/s18124271
50. Koumpouros Y, Kafazis T (2019) Wearables and mobile technologies in autism spectrum disorder interventions: a systematic literature review. Res Autism Spectrum Disord 66:101405. https://doi.org/10.1016/j.rasd.2019.05.005
51. Blischak DM, Schlosser RW (2003) Use of technology to support independent spelling by students with autism. Top Lang Disord 23(4):293–304. Consultado el 10 de abril de 2023 en https://www.learntechlib.org/p/97485/

52. Bradley R, Newbutt N (2018) Autism and virtual reality head-mounted displays: a state of the art systematic review. J Enabling Technol 12:101–113. https://doi.org/10.1108/JET-01-2018-0004
53. Mesa Gresa P, Gil Gómez H, Lozano Quilis JA, Gil Gómez JA (2018) Effectiveness of virtual reality for children and adolescents with autism spectrum disorder: an evidence-based systematic review. Sensors 18:2486. https://doi.org/10.3390/s18082486
54. Parsons S, Cobb S (2011) State-of-the-art of virtual reality technologies for children on the autism spectrum. Eur J Spec Needs Educ 26:355–366
55. Chen Y, Zhou Z, Cao M, Liu M, Lin Z, Yang W, Yang X, Dhaidhai D, Xiong P (2022) Extended Reality (XR) and telehealth interventions for children or adolescents with autism spectrum disorder: systematic review of qualitative and quantitative studies. Neurosci Biobehav Rev 138:104683. https://doi.org/10.1016/j.neubiorev.2022.104683
56. Dechsling A, Orm S, Kalandadze T, Sütterlin S, Øien RA, Shic F, Nordahl-Hansen A (2022) Virtual and augmented reality in social skills interventions for autistic individuals spectrum disorder: a scoping review. J Autism Dev Disord 52:4692–4707. https://doi.org/10.1007/s10803-021-05338-5
57. Khowaja K, Banire B, Al-Thani D, Sqalli MT, Aqle A, Shah A, Salim SS (2020) Augmented reality for learning of children and adolescents with autism spectrum disorder (ASD): a systematic review. IEEE Access. 8:78779–78807. https://doi.org/10.1109/ACCESS.2020.2986608
58. Parsons S (2016) Authenticity in virtual reality for assessment and intervention in autism: a conceptual review. Educ Res Rev 19:138–157. https://doi.org/10.1016/j.edurev.2016.08.001
59. Pérez-Fuster P, Herrera G, Kossyvaki L, Ferrer A (2022) Enhancing joint attention skills in children on the autism spectrum through an augmented reality technology-mediated intervention. Children 9:258. https://doi.org/10.3390/children9020258
60. Van Dijk J, Hummels C (2017) Designing for embodied being-in-the-world: two cases, seven principles and one framework. In: Proceedings of the 11th international conference on tangible, embedded, and embodied interaction (TEI), Yokohama (Japan), pp 47–56. https://doi.org/10.1145/3024969.3025007
61. Abt C (1987) Serious games. University Press of America, New York (New York: Viking Press, 1970)
62. Hassan A, Pinkwart N, Shafi M (2021) Serious games to improve social and emotional intelligence in children with autism. Entertain Comput 38:100417. https://doi.org/10.1016/j.entcom.2021.100417
63. Silva GM, Souto JJ, Fernandes TP, Bolis I, Santos NA (2021) Interventions with serious games and entertainment games in autism spectrum disorder: a systematic review. Dev Neuropsychol 46:463–485. https://doi.org/10.1080/87565641.2021.1981905
64. Kientz JA, Hayes GR, Goodwin MS, Gelsomini M, Abowd GD (2020) Interactive technologies and autism. In: Synthesis lectures on assistive, rehabilitative, and health-preserving technologies, 2nd edn, vol 9, pp i–229. https://doi.org/10.2200/S00988ED2V01Y202002ARH013
65. Kim JW, Nguyen TQ, Gipson SYMT, Shin AL, Torous J (2019) Smartphone apps for autism spectrum disorder—Understanding the evidence. J Technol Behav Sci 3:1–4. https://doi.org/10.1007/s41347-017-0040-4
66. Laurie MH, Warreyn P, Uriarte B, Boonen C, Fletcher-Watson S (2019) An international survey of parental attitudes to technology use by their autistic children at home. J Autism Dev Disord 49(4):1517–1530. https://doi.org/10.1007/s10803-018-3798-0
67. Scholle P, Herrera G, Sevilla J, Brosnan M (2020) A preliminary investigation assessing the basic digital capabilities of minimally verbal children on the autism spectrum with intellectual disability. J Enabling Technol 14(2):127–135. https://doi.org/10.1108/JET-06-2020-0025
68. Frauenberger C (2015) Disability and technology: a critical realist perspective. In: Proceedings of the 17th international ACM SIGACCESS conference on computers & accessibility. ACM, pp 89–96

69. Moore M, Calvert S (2000) Brief report: vocabulary acquisition for children with autism: teacher or computer instruction. J Autism Dev Disord 30:359–362
70. Williams C, Wright B, Callaghan G, Coughlan B (2002) Do children with autism learn to read more readily by computer assisted instruction or traditional book methods? A pilot study. Autism 6:71–91
71. Bernard-Opitz V, Sriram N, Nakhoda-Sapuan S (2001) Enhancing social problem solving in children with autism and normal children through computer-assisted instruction. J Autism Dev Disord 31:377–384
72. Heimann M, Nelson K, Tjus T, Gillberg C (1995) Increasing reading and communication-skills in children with autism through an interactive multimedia computer-program. J Autism Dev Disord 25:459–480
73. Grandin T (1996) Thinking in pictures: and other reports from my life with autism. Vintage Publishing, EE. UU. ISBN: 978-0679772897
74. Kana RK, Keller TA, Cherkassky VL, Minshew NJ, Just MA (2006) Sentence comprehension in autism: thinking in pictures with decreased functional connectivity. Brain 129:2484–2493
75. Samson F, Mottron L, Soulières I, Zeffiro TA (2012) Enhanced visual functioning in autism: an ALE meta-analysis. Hum Brain Mapp 33(7):1553–1581
76. Barbeau EB, Lewis JD, Doyon J, Benali H, Zeffiro TA, Mottron L (2015) A greater involvement of posterior brain areas in interhemispheric transfer in autism: fMRI, DWI and behavioral evidences. NeuroImage: Clin 8:267–280. ISSN 2213-1582. https://doi.org/10.1016/j.nicl.2015.04.019
77. Soulières I, Dawson M, Samson F, Barbeau EB, Sahyoun CP, Strangman GE et al (2009) Enhanced visual processing contributes to matrix reasoning in autism. Human Brain Map 30(12):4082–4107
78. Schopler E, Mesibov GB, Hearsey K (1995) Structured teaching in the TEACCH system. In: Schopler, Mesibov (eds) Learning and cognition in autism. Springer, pp 243–268
79. Frost L, Bondy A (2002) The picture exchange communication system (PECS) training manual, 2nd edn. Pyramid Products Inc., Newark, DE
80. Panyan MV (1984) Computer technology for autistic students. J Autism Dev Disord 14:375–382. https://doi.org/10.1007/BF02409828
81. Goldsmith TR, LeBlanc LA (2004) Use of technology in interventions for children with autism. J Early Intensive Behav Intervent 1:166
82. American Psychiatric Association (APA) (2013) Diagnostic and statistical manual of mental disorders, 5th edn. American Psychiatric Publishing, Arlington, VA
83. World Health Organisation (2019) International statistical classification of diseases and related health problems, 11th edn. https://icd.who.int/
84. Bogdashina O (2003) Sensory perceptual issues in autism and asperger syndrome: different sensory experiences—Different perceptual worlds. Jessica Kingsley Publishers. ISBN 978-1843101666
85. Peeters T (1997) Autism: from theoretical understanding to educational intervention. Wiley
86. Baron-Cohen S, Leslie AM, Frith U (1985) Does the autistic child have a "theory of mind"? Cognition 21(1):37–46. https://doi.org/10.1016/0010-0277(85)90022-8
87. Wang L, Mottron L, Peng D, Berthiaume C, Dawson M (2007) Local bias and local-to-global interference without global deficit: a robust finding in autism under various conditions of attention, exposure time and visual angle. Cogn Neuropsychol 24(5):550–574
88. Mottron L, Burack JA (2012) Sensory, motor and attention characteristics of autistic children. In: Tremblay RE, Boivin M, Peters RDV, Elsabbagh M, Clarke ME (eds) Encyclopedia on early childhood development. http://www.child-encyclopedia.com/autism/according-experts/sensory-motor-and-attention-characteristics-autistic-children
89. Williams D (1996) Autism. An inside-out approach. Jessica Kingsley Publishers, Londres
90. Tardif C, Latzko L, Arciszewski T, Gepner B (2017) Reducing information's speed improves verbal cognition and behavior in autism: a 2-cases report. Pediatrics 139(6):e20154207. https://doi.org/10.1542/peds.2015-4207

91. Schreibman L, Dawson G, Stahmer AC, Landa R, Rogers SJ, McGee GG, Kasari C, Ingersoll B, Kaiser AP, Bruinsma Y, McNerney E, Wetherby A, Halladay A (2015) Naturalistic developmental behavioral interventions: empirically validated treatments for autism spectrum disorder. J Autism Dev Disord 45(8):2411–2428. https://doi.org/10.1007/s10803-015-2407-8
92. Wade J, Zhang L, Bian D, Fan J, Swanson A, Weitlauf A et al (2016) A gaze-contingent adaptive virtual reality driving environment for intervention in autistic individuals spectrum disorders. ACM Trans Interact Intell Syst (TiiS) 6(1):1–23
93. World Health Oranisation (2019) Guidelines on physical activity, sedentary behaviour and sleep for children under 5 years of age. World Health Organization. https://apps.who.int/iris/handle/10665/311664
94. Slobodin O, Heffler KF, Davidovitch M (2019) Screen media and autism spectrum disorder: a systematic literature review. J Dev Behav Pediatr. Mayo de 40(4):303–311. https://doi.org/10.1097/DBP.0000000000000654. PMID: 30908423
95. Kushima M, Kojima R, Shinohara R et al (2022) Association between screen time exposure in children at 1 year of age and autism spectrum disorder at 3 years of age: the Japan environment and children's study. JAMA Pediatr 176(4):384–391. https://doi.org/10.1001/jamapediatrics.2021.5778
96. Sarfraz S, Shlaghya G, Narayana SH, Mushtaq U, Shaman Ameen B, Nie C, Nechi D, Mazhar IJ, Yasir M, Arcia Franchini AP (2023) Early screen-time exposure and its association with risk of developing autism spectrum disorder: a systematic review. Cureus 15(7):e42292. https://doi.org/10.7759/cureus.42292
97. Finkenauer C, Pollmann MM, Begeer S, Kerkhof P (2012) Brief report: examining the link between autistic traits and compulsive Internet use in a non-clinical sample. J Autism Dev Disord 42:2252–2256
98. Lukmanji S, Manji SA, Kadhim S, Sauro KM, Wirrell EC, Kwon CS, Jetté N (2019) The co-occurrence of epilepsy and autism: a systematic review. Epilepsy Behav E&B 98-A:238–248. https://doi.org/10.1016/j.yebeh.2019.07.037
99. Fisher RS, Acharya JN, Baumer FM, French JA, Parisi P, Solodar JH, Szaflarski JP, Thio LL, Tolchin B, Wilkins AJ, Kasteleijn-Nolst Trenité D (2022) Visually sensitive seizures: an updated review by the Epilepsy Foundation. Epilepsia 63(4):739–768. https://doi.org/10.1111/epi.17175
100. Chang AM, Aeschbach D, Duffy JF, Czeisler CA (2015) Evening use of light-emitting eReaders negatively affects sleep, circadian timing, and next-morning alertness PNAS 112(4):1232–1237. https://doi.org/10.1073/pnas.1418490112
101. Singh K, Zimmerman AW (2015) Sleep in autism spectrum disorder and attention deficit hyperactivity disorder. Semin Pediatr Neurol 22(2):113–125. https://doi.org/10.1016/j.spen.2015.03.006
102. Bernier RA, Dawson G, Nigg JT (2020) What science tells us about autism spectrum disorder: making the right choices for your child. Guilford Press, EE, UU
103. Krupa M, Boominathan P, Ramanan PV et al (2019) Relationship between screen time and mother-child reciprocal interaction in typically developing children and children with autism spectrum disorders. Indian J Pediatr 86:394. https://doi.org/10.1007
104. Lin J, Magiati I, Chiong SHR, Singhal S, Riard N, Ng IHX, Muller-Riemenschneider F, Wong CM (2019) The relationship among screen use, sleep, and emotional/behavioral difficulties in preschool children with neurodevelopmental disorders. J Dev Behav Pediatr 40(7):519–529. https://doi.org/10.1097/DBP.0000000000000683
105. Gwynette MF, Sidhu SS, Ceranoglu TA (2018) Electronic screen media use in youth with autism spectrum disorder. Child Adolesc Psychiatr Clin N Am 27(2):203–219. https://doi.org/10.1016/j.chc.2017.11.013
106. Cardy RE, Dupuis A, Anagnostou E, Ziolkowski J, Biddiss EA, Monga S, Brian J, Penner M, Kushki A (2021) Characterizing changes in screen time during the COVID-19 pandemic school closures in canada and its perceived impact on children with autism spectrum disorder. Front Psych 12:702774. https://doi.org/10.3389/fpsyt.2021.702774

107. Logrieco MG, Casula L, Ciuffreda GN et al. (2021) Autism spectrum disorder and screen time during lockdown: an italian study. [versión 1; revisada entre pares: 1 aprobado, 1 aprobado con reservas]. F1000Research 10:1263. https://doi.org/10.12688/f1000research.55299.1
108. Zifferblatt SM, Burton SD, Horner R, White T (1977) Establishing generalization effects among autistic children. J Autism Child Schizophr 7–4:337–347. https://doi.org/10.1007/BF01540392
109. Stokes TF, Baer DM (1977) An implicit technology of generalization. J Appl Behav Anal 10(2):349–367. https://doi.org/10.1901/jaba.1977.10-349
110. Damasio AR, Damasio H (1994) Cortical systems for retrieval of concrete knowledge: the convergence zone framework. In: Koch C, Davis JL (eds) Large-scale neuronal theories of the brain. MIT Press, Cambridge, MA
111. Gainotti G, Silveri MC, Daniele A, Giustolisi L (1995) Neuroanatomical correlates of category-specific semantic disorders: a critical survey. Memory 3:247–264
112. Brown SM, Bebko JM (2012) Generalization, overselectivity, and discrimination in the autism phenotype: a review. Res Autism Spectr Disord 6(2):733–740
113. Happé F, Frith U (2006) The weak coherence account: detail-focused cognitive style in autism spectrum disorders. J Autism Dev Disord 36(1):5–25
114. Plaisted KC (2001) Reduced generalization in autism: an alternative to weak central coherence. In: Burack JA, Charman T, Yirmiya N, Zelazo PR (eds) The development of autism: perspectives from theory and research. Lawrence Erlbaum Associates Publishers, pp 149–169
115. Handleman JS (1979) Generalization by autistic-type children of verbal responses across settings. J Appl Behav Anal 12(2):273–282. https://doi.org/10.1901/jaba.1979.12-273
116. Handleman JS, Harris SL (1980) Generalization from school to home with autistic children. J Autism Dev Disord 10:323–333. https://doi.org/10.1007/BF02408291
117. Schmidt M, Glaser N (2021) Investigating the usability and learner experience of a virtual reality adaptive skills intervention for adults with autism spectrum disorder. Educ Tech Res Dev 69(3):1665–1699
118. Koegel RL, Dyer K, Bell LK (1987) The influence of child-preferred activities on autistic children's social behavior. J Appl Behav Anal 20:243–252. https://doi.org/10.1901/jaba.1987.20-243
119. Koegel RL, O'Dell MC, Koegel LK (1987) A natural language teaching paradigm for non-verbal autistic children. J Autism Dev Disord 17:187–200. https://doi.org/10.1007/BF01495055
120. Gengoux GW, McNerney E, Minjarez MB (2020) Selecting meaningful skills for teaching in the natural environment. In: Bruinsma, Minjarez, Schreibman & Stahmer (eds) Naturalistic developmental behavioral interventions for autism spectrum disorder. Brookes Publishing
121. López-Herrejón RE, Poddar O, Herrera G, Sevilla J (2020) Customization support in computer-based technologies for autism: a systematic mapping study. Int J Hum Comput Interact. https://doi.org/10.1080/10447318.2020.1731673
122. Petersen K, Feldt R, Mujtaba S, Mattsson M (2008) Systematic mapping studies in software engineering. In: Ease 68–77 British computer society. http://dl.acm.org/citation.cfm?id=2227115.2227123
123. Kitchenham BA, Dyba T, Jorgensen M (2004) Evidence-based software engineering. In: Proceedings of the 26th international conference on software engineering. IEEE Computer Society, pp 273–281

Participation of Autistic People in Research and Technology Design

Gerardo Herrera Gutiérrez, Patricia Pérez-Fuster, and Cristina Costescu

Abstract

This chapter analyses the rights of autistic people to participate in the process of designing, developing and experimentally testing digital tools to address their needs. This active participation can be achieved and facilitated in at least two ways: in research studies and in the design processes of tools and intervention strategies. For the participation of autistic people in research, this chapter analyses ethical implications and relevant experimental designs that facilitate the representation of the autism spectrum. An evaluative method for assessing Evidence-Based Practices (EBP) in autism is also analysed. For the technology design, several methodologies facilitate this participation when expressing and defining their real needs in the initial stages of the technology development cycle. General methodologies for technology development are analysed with a focus on guaranteeing the best response to their needs. Finally, the case of gamification and web accessibility is analysed to illustrate how participation can be truly achieved.

Keywords

Participatory design · Autism spectrum disorders · Gamification · Web accessibility · Technology design

G. H. Gutiérrez
IRTIC Institute, Universitat de València, Valencia, Spain
e-mail: gerardo.herrera@uv.es

P. Pérez-Fuster
Department of Developmental and Educational Psychology, Universitat de València, Valencia, Spain
e-mail: Patricia.Perez-Fuster@uv.es

C. Costescu (✉)
Special Education Department, Babeș-Bolyai University, Cluj-Napoca, Romania
e-mail: cristina.costescu@ubbcluj.ro

1 Introduction

It is common for autistic people to participate in research aimed at testing the effectiveness of a specific intervention proposal. Those participants do not usually simultaneously present other neurodevelopmental conditions in addition to ASD. Homogeneous samples of participants are sought to identify and clearly delimit the target group to which a certain intervention is directed. However, in many cases, this means not including in the studies people who also have other conditions such as intellectual disability, attention deficit hyperactivity disorder or a language disorder. Consequently, the representation of the heterogeneity that characterises ASD may be limited within numerous investigations. Excluding certain groups from the research also has ethical consequences. This is an issue known as "the right to science" and is included in the Universal Declaration of Human Rights:

> Every person has the right [...] to participate in scientific progress and in the benefits that result from it [...] Every person has the right to protect the moral and material interests that correspond to him by reason of scientific productions...
>
> Universal Declaration of Human Rights. Article 27

This right may not be fulfilled for the reasons indicated above. Furthermore, it complements but does not replace the right to be protected in such research and to have the risks and benefits of such participation appropriately balanced, including making decisions about your participation in research whenever possible [1].

The active participation of autistic people can be proposed and facilitated in at least two ways: in research studies and the design processes of tools and intervention strategies. This chapter is aimed at exploring both pathways.

2 Language to Refer to Autism and Autistic People

In the last decade, various investigations have been carried out aimed at determining what is the most appropriate language to refer to autism and autistic people. Most studies have been conducted in English-speaking countries, and the results are not uniform. All of this research has been carried out in the current era, in which there is a strong social movement to defend neurodiversity, which not only demands the use of appropriate and respectful language for autistic people but also questions the need for certain research and studies, such as those dedicated to compensating for some of the difficulties that autistic people present, considering that they are not difficulties, but mere differences that, because they are part of human neurodiversity, should be celebrated and not attempted to be corrected [2–4]. Bottema-Beutel et al. [5] suggest that much of the language used to describe autistic people and their characteristics promotes this idea by conveying beliefs and practices that discriminate against people with disabilities.

These social movements have led to prominent researchers in the field of autism being recriminated by some autistic people for continuing to use medical terminology to refer to autism since they consider that words such as *disorder*, *deficit* or *alteration* are not appropriate to describe them.

One of the first surveys on preferences in language use was developed by Kenny et al. [6], who found a preference among autistic people themselves to be referred to in this way (*autistic*), while professionals preferred the term *person with autism* because they considered it more respectful. Keating et al. [7] developed a broader study, covering several English-speaking countries, on the preferences of autistic people for using various terms related to autism. The results obtained were similar, although not uniform, between these countries.

Another study, developed by Singer et al. [8] advocates the use of a broad spectrum of descriptive terms related to autism by doctors and researchers, without being the subject of recriminations. Words like *disorder*, they claim, are medically accurate when, for example, they describe people prone to "hitting the head so hard and frequently that it results in contusions". Discussing behaviour like this as mere "differences", they suggest, trivialises the severity of the condition and can translate into a reduction in the support these people need [8]. Certainly, it is not necessary to look for a situation as extreme as that described by Singer (*op. cit.*) since many of the early difficulties that characterise ASD—for example, the development of communicative intention—can have very important consequences in the child's development and trivialising them would divert attention from early intervention priorities.

The controversy arises from the heterogeneity of autism presentations, as indicated by Robison et al. [9], and from the fact that, within this variability, the symptoms of autism range from the extremes of typical human personality characteristics to the clear pathology. Singer et al. [8] point out that reducing disability and improving the quality of life of many autistic people will depend on the advances that arise from biomedical research, where the use of precise and objective language among scientists is necessary.

Dwyer et al. [10] also addressed the issue of language and provided suggestions for considering the use in scientific publications of terms that may be less harmful to autistic people. These researchers suggest how potentially harmful traditional terms can be easily and accurately replaced by alternatives. For example, in group studies, contrasting autistics with *normal controls or healthy* controls could easily be replaced with contrasting *autistics with non-autistics* or *neurotypicals*. Comorbidity could be replaced by *co-occurrence* when talking about commonly seen conditions, such as, for example, anxiety. The term *disorder* (which is embodied in the individual and linked to a medical model of conceptualisation of autism) can often be replaced by a reference to a *disability* that considers social and environmental factors (framing it in a more social model of conceptualisation of autism).

Considering all of the above and the fact that language use shapes one's conscious and unconscious perceptions and beliefs of autistic individuals, it is critical to identify the terminology that is preferred by people within the community [11].

However, the results obtained in studies conducted in English-speaking countries may not apply to other countries due to language and cultural differences. For instance, Buijsman et al. [12] recently explored language preferences in the Dutch autism community indicating that most autistic adults and parents preferred person-first language (i.e., person with autism) instead of identity-first language (i.e., autistic person). Another study conducted with the Dutch autism community highlighted the importance of the social psychological approach to study language preferences, as the autistic Dutch who had a stronger identification with the autism community and a later age of diagnosis predicted a stronger identity-first language preference [13]. This makes obvious the need for a better understanding of psychological and social factors that might underlie language use and preference within the autistic community. In this line, another recent study that examined quantitative predictors of language preferences through a social identity theoretical approach, found that a stronger autism identity was associated with a preference for identity-first terms while previous experiences of stigma were associated with finding identity-first language less favourable and more offensive [14].

Given the current situation and the need for more studies that can guide us better on the most appropriate language use, we advocate to use of a mix of person-first language and identity-first language in research and academic work to cover the full range of preferences identified so far.

3 Participation Within an Evidence-Based Practices Framework

Participating in research has ethical implications that need to be considered. Research efforts are focused on obtaining evidence-based practices for supporting autistic people to develop their potential fully and acquire a better quality of life. Therefore, this collective effort towards evidence-based practices frames their participation in research studies. Also, specific methodologies are more appropriate than others towards this end, and quality standards must be applied when evaluating studies to obtain evidence-based practices for autism intervention. This section explores all these ideas.

3.1 Participation in Research

To establish a methodological context for the participation of autistic people in experimental studies, it is necessary to know some ethical considerations, as well as identify methodologies that are compatible with them.

Addressing the needs of autistic participants involves implementing strategies that consider the common characteristics of autistic people, the broader socio-political context of autism research, and the unique needs of each autistic participant [15]. These unique needs, in turn, imply knowing the person's sensory and learning profile, how they interpret their identity, their life experiences and their family and social context. Therefore, addressing these individual needs is not only a methodological and design choice but also an ethical issue because it facilitates inclusion, reduces discomfort, and respects people [15].

Cascio and Racine [16] propose a *person-centred* research ethics framework that encourages researchers to consider these five indicators: respect for the holistic personality of each individual, personalisation and recognition of each participant's individual perspective, the relationships between researchers and participants, and empowerment in decision-making.

3.2 Experimental Designs that Facilitate the Representation of the Entire Autism Spectrum

As in any population within the autism spectrum, some minorities or subgroups have little or even no representation in studies, which has the double negative effect that their needs have not been considered and, therefore, the results from such studies may not apply to those subgroups. In this sense, *single-case designs* (also known as *single-subject designs*) have the advantage that they are applied to each autistic participant and that the result is interpreted individually. Traditionally, single-case designs have been considered a disadvantage, compared to *group designs*, as it has been assessed that the samples thus constituted (single cases or small series of cases) were not sufficiently representative. However, in autism and other neurodevelopmental disorders, many researchers opt for these types of designs due to the heterogeneity of the autism population and the sample constraints often faced, especially, when recruiting people to participate in intervention studies that may take several weeks or even months. Single-case designs are ideal for reporting improvements in individual learning and, when properly applied, their validity can be comparable to that of randomised controlled trials [17], which traditionally have been considered the *gold standard* in research. There is a wide variety of single-case designs [18], such as AB designs, reversible AB designs (ABAB) or multiple baseline designs, in which participants enter the intervention phase stepwise.

Many technology-mediated intervention studies in the autism field have used single-case designs and have demonstrated that, if well conducted and applying all possible controls to minimise the threats to the study validity, can offer a good level of methodological rigour and contribute to the establishment of Evidence-Based Practices (EBP) in the field [19, 20], as discussed in the next section.

What is the best design for each study? It mainly depends on the research question and the resources that one has access to, among others [21]. For instance, a research team wants to evaluate the effectiveness of a newly developed digital technology to improve social skills in autistic children. After contacting the organisations and schools participating in the research project, the researchers have identified around 30 autistic children who could potentially participate as they match the study inclusion criteria, and their parents are willing to sign the consent form. With this small sample, it would not be appropriate to do an RCT as 15 participants per group would not provide the results with sufficient statistical power to conclude the effectiveness of the tool adequately. Besides, the researchers do not want a traditional control group as they want all the autistic participants to benefit from the intervention. They could consider then a wait list control group. However, the timing of the project does not allow for it. As a result, they decide to apply a group design which is known as *stepped wedge randomised trial* (SWT) [22, 23], with two groups of 15 randomly assigned children each group. Both groups receive the treatment, but each group enters in the study phases at different moments and that time difference is what allows for the comparison of the scores between groups. This design also includes series of measurements both before and after intervention that can help to establish trends in outcome variables of interest prior to intervention (e.g., practice effects) and after intervention [24] and can help researchers to study non-linear trajectories in skill development [25]. This type of design can be of special interest for the autism community due to the amount of information that provides through the application of powerful statistical analysis and its potential to be applied in longitudinal studies which are so needed in the field.

3.3 Evaluating Evidence-Based Practices (EBP) in Autism

Researchers such as Horner et al. [26] and Romeiser et al. [27] propose a series of recommendations and quality indicators which can be applied to studies that have implemented single-case designs. Further are described the quality indicators for single-case designs:

A. Participants and framework illustration, which includes describing the participants with enough details so it can be used by other researchers for the selection of people with similar features (e.g., age, sex, disability, diagnosis), describing the selection of participants as accurately as possible so that it can be replicated, as well as the critical properties of the external surroundings and conditions.
B. Dependent variables which should be described with operational precision and should be measured with a method that results in a quantifiable index. The way in which the dependent variables are measured must be valid and thoroughly described so it is reproducible. Dependent variables must be measured again at different times. Data on reliability or interobserver agreement associated with each dependent variable are obtained, and IOA levels meet minimum standards (e.g., IOA = 80%; Kappa = 60%).
C. Independent variable must be described in such a way that it can be reproduced. It is systematically manipulated and under the control of the researcher conducting the experiment. The measurement of implementation fidelity for the independent variable should be clearly explained.
D. Base line. Most single-case studies include a baseline phase that makes possible a repeated measurement of a dependent variable and defines a response

pattern that can be used to predict the pattern of future performance if it has not already been defined. The conditions of baseline should be illustrated with accuracy so they can be reproduced.

E. Control/internal validity of the experiment. The study design must provide minimum three demonstrations of the effect of experiment at three different times. The internal validity is protected from common threats through design (e.g., allows for the elimination of rival hypotheses). The results must provide a model that proves control over the experiment.

F. External validity must be established by replicating the experiment with different participants, settings, or materials. G. Social validity. The dependent variable must be relevant from a social point of view as well as the size of the change in the dependent variable that results from the intervention. The implementation of the independent variable is both practical and efficient in terms of cost. Social validity should be broadened by applying the independent variable across longer time periods by using typical intervention agents and in typical physical and social contexts.

Reichow et al. [28] developed a method for evaluating the quality of research that can be applied to both group designs and single-case designs and that, in addition, allows several studies to be considered together, combining both group and case studies to determine the level of evidence available about a given intervention or practice. This method includes both primary quality indicators and secondary quality indicators for each of the design types (see Fig. 1).

A different classification system is proposed for each block of quality indicators, depending on whether they are primary or secondary. Primary indicators can be *high quality*, *acceptable quality*, and *unacceptable quality*. Secondary indicators can show *evidence* or *non-evidence* [28], developed in detail by Reichow in 2011 [29].

When a study is evaluated, whether with a group design or a single-case design, the strength of the evidence provided is assessed as follows:

- If it has all primary indicators of high quality and shows evidence on four or more (three or more for case designs) secondary indicators, it is considered *strong*.
- If it has four or more primary indicators of high quality and none of unacceptable quality and shows evidence of at least two secondary indicators, it is considered *adequate*.
- If it has fewer than four high-quality primary indicators or shows evidence of fewer than two secondary indicators, it is considered *weak*.

The application of these indicators and their accumulation throughout different studies is what can lead to the establishment of EBP. Research has shown that this evaluative method produced reliable and valid results [17, 30, 31], and in autism it

	Group research	**Single case research**
Primary quality indicators	Participant characteristics Independent variable Comparison condition Dependent variable Connection between hypothesis and analysis Adequate statistical analysis	Participant characteristics Independent variable Dependent variable Baseline condition Visual analysis Experimental control
Secondary quality indicators	Random assignment Interobserver agreement Blind raters Fidelity Attrition Generalization effect Effect size Social validity	Interobserver agreement Kappa Fidelity Blind raters Generalization effect Social validity

Fig. 1 Quality indicators to evaluate the rigour of the research report

has been used for the analysis of good practices related to video-supported mathematics training [32], with peer-mediated social interaction [33] and with social competence related to peers in the school environment [34].

3.4 Technology Design

The participation of autistic people in designing supports developed to address their needs is also vital. In this section, different approaches will be analysed to guarantee that their voice is heard when defining those supports' aims and functional requirements. Some methodologies are more appropriate than others for the full technology development cycle. Recent studies on gamification and web design for autistic people will also be analysed.

3.5 The Participatory Design of the Tools

When trying to build intervention strategies based on the needs of each individual, it is important to give autistic people an important role in defining said needs [35]. To this end, some researchers have developed strategies aimed at facilitating the participation of autistic people in the design processes of tools aimed at themselves, which is known as "participatory design" [36]. Participatory design is a form of "user-centred design" or UCD [37, 38].

A priori, communication and socialisation difficulties—as well as restricted interests—pose barriers to the participation of autistic people in co-design processes. However, suppose they are provided with the necessary support and structure. In that case, their participation in these processes offers an opportunity to practice communication, which, in turn, allows the tool created to be improved [36]. Brosnan et al. [39] points out numerous potential benefits of their participation in technology design teams, such as the creation of solutions well-adjusted to their specific needs, providing a structured context in which they can practice and improve their communication, and the satisfaction of having participated in the creation of a tool that they will find useful, which can also contribute to improving their self-esteem.

In recent decades, knowledge of the participatory design process has evolved rapidly. Among the most notable works are the following:

- Cooperative Inquiry Model [40]. It includes the roles of user, tester, informant, and member of the design team in the process of creating technological tools.
- Other authors, including Kientz et al. [41] have counted on parents and teachers of autistic people as informants and, sometimes, as designers. This is especially important when the aid is aimed at people who have not developed their communication skills enough to understand the process and contribute their own ideas.

- Benton et al. [36] have carried out numerous works to define and adjust the participation process of autistic people in developing technological tools intended for themselves. These authors have built a model called "participatory design." Benton et al. [36] report on some characteristics of autistic people that need to be addressed, such as difficulties with temporal organisation and sequencing, their preference for visual learning, their tendency to fixate on irrelevant details, managing distractors, as well as the supports they need to manage their impulses related to their topics of special interest and anxiety. Considering the perspective that autistic people have on how to address their own difficulties is a very enriching experience for everyone involved in the design team. It can also help the solutions created to be helpful, at the very least, for autistic people who participated in its design.

In the field of qualitative research studies, some strategies can be used to facilitate the participation of autistic people, both in research and in the design of tools. Focus groups are semi-structured interviews and dialogues that are designed to hear participants' perceptions about a particular area of interest [42]. Traditionally, these groups have been used to identify consensus among groups of experts in each discipline. Within this type of study, there are different methodologies, such as Delphi studies [43, 44] and other methodologies that are also considered appropriate for listening to the needs of people who have usually been excluded from research studies; They allow you to control the dynamics of each group efficiently to facilitate positive experiences for all participants [45].

3.6 App Design for Autistic People

In a previous work [46], different methodologies for the development of serious games and video games with virtual reality in the field of autism were analysed, as well as several specific projects for the development of virtual reality technologies. and increased for autism. In the field of video game development, Al-Azawi et al. [47] consider two archetypal development models, predictive and adaptive models. Predictive models create work planning as a separate pre-development task and are preferable when customer objectives and requirements are clear and fully defined. In the case of adaptive models, the requirements and objectives are not completely clear, and the client or user can add new objectives and requirements at each stage of the project. In these cases, the process is based on prototypes, tests and refinements. Each iteration includes analysis, design, implementation, testing and evaluation. Predictive models can be very useful for non-flexible application areas, but very inadequate for creating technology solutions for ASD [46]. Adaptive models are also most useful when the backgrounds of the participants vary greatly from one another, as occurs in a multidisciplinary design or a participatory design process. This is because not all people involved can predict the consequences of decisions made during design and development. Adaptive models also facilitate the refinement of tools to increase their usability [46].

Gamification is a very powerful resource to increase the engagement and to improve the learning process [48]. Camargo et al. developed a systematic review and analysed 30 studies to identify the status of gamification resources and user interface design for autistic people. Out of the 30 studies analyses, 46% of them aim to improve communication skills, and 13% of them aim to improve social interaction. The rest of the studies focused either on daily activities or facial recognition and basic education. The most used development approaches were Participatory Design and User-Centred Design, both considering specialists, such as psychologists and teachers, parents and end users in the design process.

Within the app development, several elements were investigated and are considered to create an attractive experience [49]: a. *narrative or storytelling*: the game must have a story behind the tasks, and in the case of autistic people, the stories should be simplified, and the languages used should be more concrete and avoiding metaphors; b. *progression*: the game should ensure the development and growth of some skills or abilities while playing the modules; c. *challenges*: the game should be intuitive. However, the tasks should require an effort to perform. When working with autistic people, their levels of understanding can be very different; therefore, several aspects should be considered. d. *competition*: the task should be described as something that involves winning or losing; e. rewards: the presentation of some benefits if they do certain actions, especially for autistic children, visual rewards should be provided; f. *feedback* is referring to some information that the user can receive regarding his performance, for autistic people the information needs to be transmitted immediate and in a way that can be easily understood; g. *avatars*: using a visual representation of the players helps better represent the actions within the game; h. *levels*: some well-defined steps that the player needs to follow to progress in the games; i. monitorisation: to represent visually where the player is situated with respect to others or how much from the activity they have left or to show their performance. Moreover, if the game is designed for multiple players, their achievements as a team or their points should be displayed during the game.

3.7 Gamification

According to the review from Camargo et al. [48], several studies considered and addressed gamification within their design out of the 30 analysed, which suggested increased awareness and willingness to move toward accessibility. For example, 50% of them used feedback, and 33% of them used a rewarding system. They used either virtual visual or auditory feedback or real-life tokens. 60% of the studies incorporated different levels of difficulty in their games, which includes the idea of mid- or long-term goals and is used to increase the motivation and interest in the game. Most of the studies allowed the teachers or users to customise the colours, the graphics, the photographs, text messages or other features, leading to a high degree of personalisation of the games. Moreover, 56% of the studies apply different types of control, either parental or teacher control, to customise learning and to monitor progress. Therefore, an integrated system is being used to select from different levels and custom learning objectives according to the level of each participant.

Regarding user interface design methods, studies reported visual presentations, such as using colours, illustrations, photographs, videos, sounds and voice. One of the major concerns in the development process is the use of colours; 76% of the studies considered either using more vibrant and vivid colours or calm and half-toned colours. However, the decision to change the colours was not based on the user's feedback since no re-evaluation of the used colours was reported. The same situation was in the case of the text used; 80% of the studies provided information regarding the text used but no further explanations concerning why they used one style or another. Only 30% of the studies included videos in their games, but 76% of them included illustrations, from simple, basic shapes to more complex ones (they also used real-life photographs—sometimes uploaded by the teachers). The sound is usually used to provide feedback, for example, associated with clicking a button, or to provide the narrative or as background music. It is reported in 56% of the studies.

There are still many challenges and obstacles in the path towards accessibility for autistic individuals. Even if there is a clear focus on applying methodologies that prioritise end users and involve them in the development process, most studies need to provide consistent data about the results achieved with the games. When it comes to designing games for autistic children, they are more prone to frustration when they must deal with interfaces that are not adapted to their cognitive and ability levels. Also, they are more focused on enjoying the activities and more impatient to receive feedback and immediate gratification after acting.

3.8 Web Accessibility in Autism and Intellectual Disabilities

The case of autistic people and people with intellectual disabilities in the definition of web accessibility guidelines is a recent and illustrative example of the issues raised in developing guidelines for technology design.

Web accessibility is a complex issue since it requires giving different answers to different individual profiles. For example, many of the accessibility options that we can find in browsers and devices are aimed at people with low vision and involve displaying information with high-contrast colours that, on the other hand, may not be suitable for autistic people who have visual hypersensitivity. The international body responsible for setting the technical standards on which the web operates, the World Wide Web Consortium, created the *Web Accessibility Initiative* (WAI), which developed and maintained the *Web Content Accessibility Guidelines* (WCAG). The WCAG provides a set of technical standards that were created largely by and for people with reduced mobility and people with sensory disabilities (primarily vision and hearing), and not by or for people with other conditions, such as NDDs. Traditionally, intellectual disability was excluded from the first sets of official recommendations in the field of web accessibility, which motivated some researchers to carry out experimental studies aimed at identifying web design guidelines that facilitate cognitive accessibility to the web, such as the one carried out by [50]. Subsequently, the WAI convened a working group on cognitive and learning disabilities [51] that meets regularly and has published several sets of recommendations related to cognitive web accessibility, such as (1) personalisation and preferences; (2) security and privacy technologies; (3) multimodal content; (4) the distractors; (5) voice menu systems; (6) online payments; (7) online safety; (8) the use of symbols for preverbal people, and (9) the use of numbers and mathematics. Consequently, it can be said that intellectual disabilities are sufficiently represented within this work group.

Regarding autism, representation within the World Wide Web Consortium has been very limited and restricted only to the working group related to cognitive accessibility, where such participation has not been documented. However, apart from these groups, there have been numerous advances to identify appropriate design guidelines [52–54]. Two recent works have studied this issue in depth and have published recommendation guides. On the one hand, Raymaker et al. [55], within the framework of the Academic Association for Research and Education on the Autism Spectrum (AASPIRE), used a community-based participatory research approach to create a pilot website to improve access to health care for autistic adults. This website was used to assess priorities, and its contents were refined and implemented live through successive iterations.[1] AASPIRE recommendations are structured around three main categories of accessibility: physical (related to sensory aspects, sources, etc.), cognitive (simplicity of content) and social (related to the use of language). On the other hand, in another work carried out in the United Kingdom commissioned by the National Autistic Society (NAS) for the renewal of its website,[2] Frankowska-Takhari et al. [56] obtained a set of 49 web design recommendations that can be implemented together with those of the WCAG to improve web accessibility for autistic people. This study integrated qualitative and quantitative methods in two parts: a first phase, in which documentary research and interviews with three accessibility experts were carried out, followed by a second phase with an online survey in which 398 autistic people participated, including 110 who also had intellectual disabilities, and a focus group study with 17 autistic users who regularly used the web. An interesting aspect of these recommendations is that they differentiate between the preferences that, according to their study, most autistic people share and another group of individual preferences (in which the opinions of the research participants were disparate and could not be unified). Thus, the following preferences shared by all or most autistic web users were identified: muted colours; non-distracting background images; symmetry in design; logical ordering and sizing of elements based on their importance or weight; preventing videos or other auto-playing animations; avoiding surprises,

---

[1] https://autismandhealth.org.
[2] https://www.autism.org.uk.

and provide customisation in terms of colours, fonts and other aspects of navigation. Regarding individual preferences, in which it was not possible to unify criteria, the following are found: the textual or non-textual format of the information; the use of light or dark backgrounds; the use of fonts with serifs or ornaments (serif) or without them (san serif); communication in real time (chats) or delayed (email), and various aspects related to the user's web experience [56].

4   Conclusions

This chapter has analysed how autistic people can be involved at every single stage of technology development and why it is necessary that they participate in this process as much as possible. Different approaches have been reviewed to support their participation, and different study designs have been considered to maximise the opportunities for their voices to be heard so that all of the autism spectrum is truly represented. Several technology development approaches have been considered to identify the most appropriate ones to obtain relevant results. An evaluative method that is flexible enough to consider a wide range of study designs has also been analysed, which is a crucial step for advancing towards a framework of evidence-based practices in technologies for autism.

Acknowledgements The research leading to these results is in the frame of the "EMPOWER. Design and evaluation of technological support tools to empower stakeholders in digital education" project, which has received funding from the European Union's Horizon Europe programme under grant agreement No. 101060918. However, the views and opinions expressed are those of the authors(s) only and do not necessarily reflect those of the European Union. Neither the European Union nor the granting authority can be held responsible for them.

References

1. Knoppers BM, Harris JR, Budin-Ljøsne I, Dove ES (2014) A human rights approach to an international code of conduct for genomic and clinical data sharing. Hum Genet 133:895–903. https://doi.org/10.1007/s00439-014-1432-6
2. Bury SM, Jellett R, Spoor JR, Hedley D (2023) "It defines who I am" or "It's something I have": what language do [autistic] Australian adults [on the autism spectrum] prefer? J Autism Dev Disord 53(2):677–687. https://doi.org/10.1007/s10803-020-04425-3
3. Vivanti G (2020) Ask the editor: What is the most appropriate way to talk about individuals with a diagnosis of autism? J Autism Dev Disord 50(2):691–693. https://doi.org/10.1007/s10803-019-04280-x
4. Botha M, Hanlon J, Williams GL (2021) Does language matter? Identity-first versus person-first language use in autism research: a response to Vivanti. J Autism Dev Disord 1–9. https://doi.org/10.1007/s10803-020-04858-w
5. Bottema-Beutel K, Kapp SK, Lester JN, Sasson NJ, Hand BN (2021) Avoiding ableist language: suggestions for autism researchers. Autism in Adulthood 3:18–29. https://doi.org/10.1089/aut.2020.0014

6. Kenny L, Hattersley C, Molins B, Buckley C, Povey C, Pellicano E (2016) Which terms should be used to describe autism? Perspectives from the UK autism community. Autism 20(4):442–462. https://doi.org/10.1177/1362361315588200
7. Keating CT, Hickman L, Leung J, Monk R, Montgomery A, Heath H, Sowden S (2023) Autism-related language preferences of English-speaking individuals across the globe: a mixed methods investigation. Autism Res 16(2):406–428. https://doi.org/10.1002/aur.2864
8. Singer A, Lutz A, Escher J, Halladay A (2023) A full semantic toolbox is essential for autism research and practice to thrive. Autism Res 16(3):497–501. https://doi.org/10.1002/aur.2876
9. Robison JE (2019) Talking about autism-thoughts for researchers. Autism Res 12(7):1004–1006. https://doi.org/10.1002/aur.2119
10. Dwyer P, Ryan JG, Williams ZJ, Gassner DL (2022) First do no harm: suggestions regarding respectful autism language. Pediatrics 149(Suppl 4):e2020049437N. https://doi.org/10.1542/peds.2020-049437N
11. Taboas A, Doepke K, Zimmerman C (2023) Preferences for identity-first versus person-first language in a US sample of autism stakeholders. Autism 27(2):565–570. https://doi.org/10.1177/13623613221130845
12. Buijsman R, Begeer S, Scheeren AM (2023) 'Autistic person' or 'person with autism'? Person-first language preference in Dutch adults with autism and parents. Autism 27(3):788–795. https://doi.org/10.1177/13623613221117914
13. Bosman R, Thijs J (2023) Language preferences in the Dutch autism community: a social psychological approach. J Autism Dev Disord 1–13. https://doi.org/10.1007/s10803-023-05903-0
14. Bury SM, Jellett R, Haschek A, Wenzel M, Hedley D, Spoor JR (2023) Understanding language preference: autism knowledge, experience of stigma and autism identity. Autism 27(6):1588–1600. https://doi.org/10.1177/13623613221142383
15. Cascio MA, Weiss JA, Racine E, Autism Research Ethics Task Force (2020) Person-oriented ethics for autism research: creating best practices through engagement with autism and autistic communities. Autism: Int J Res Pract 24(7):1676–1690. https://doi.org/10.1177/1362361320918763
16. Cascio MA, Racine E (2018) Person-oriented research ethics: integrating relational and everyday ethics in research. Account Res 25(3):170–197. https://doi.org/10.1080/08989621.2018.1442218
17. Cicchetti DV (2011) On the reliability and accuracy of the evaluative method for identifying evidence-based practices in autism. In: Reichow B, Doehring P, Cicchetti DV, Volkmar FR (eds) Evidence-based practices and treatments for children with autism, pp 41–51. https://doi.org/10.1007/978-1-4419-6975-0_3
18. Kratochwill TR, Hitchcock J, Horner RH, Levin JR, Odom SL, Rindskopf DM, Shadish WR (2010) Single-case designs technical documentation. What Works Clearinghouse website. http://ies.ed.gov/ncee/wwc/pdf/reference_resources/wwc_scd.pdf
19. Pérez-Fuster P, Sevilla J, Herrera G (2019) Enhancing daily living skills in four adults with autism spectrum disorder through an embodied digital technology-mediated intervention. Res Autism Spectr Disord 58:54–67. https://doi.org/10.1016/j.rasd.2018.08.006
20. Pérez-Fuster P, Herrera G, Kossyvaki L, Ferrer A (2022) Enhancing joint attention skills in children on the autism spectrum through an augmented reality technology-mediated intervention. Children 9(2):258. https://doi.org/10.3390/children9020258
21. Pérez-Fuster P, Herrera G (2023) Implementing intervention studies with autistic people and digital technologies in natural settings: a guide to best practice. In: Sousa C, Tkaczyk AH (eds) Media literacy and assistive technologies for empowerment in autism. Edições Universitárias Lusófonas, pp 158–166. https://www.doi.org/https://doi.org/10.24140/asdigital.v1.p02.10
22. Barker D, McElduff P, D'Este C, Campbell MJ (2016) Stepped wedge cluster randomised trials: a review of the statistical methodology used and available. BMC Med Res Methodol 16(1):69. https://doi.org/10.1186/s12874-016-0176-5
23. Leppink J (2019) Statistical methods for experimental research in education and psychology. Springer, Cham Switzerland. https://doi.org/10.1007/978-3-030-21241-4

24. Maric M, Van der Werff V (2020) Single case experimental designs in clinical intervention research. In: Van de Schoot R, Miocevic M (eds) Small sample size solutions: a guide for applied researchers and practitioners (Chapter 7). Routledge, New York
25. Leppink J, Pérez-Fuster P (2019) Mental effort, workload, time on task, and certainty: beyond linear models. Educ Psychol Rev 31(2):421–438. https://doi.org/10.1007/s10648-018-09460-2
26. Horner RH, Carr EG, Halle J, McGee G, Odom S, Wolery M (2005) The use of single-subject research to identify evidence-based practice in special education. Except Child 71(2):165–179. https://doi.org/10.1177/001440290507100203
27. Romeiser Logan L, Hickman RR, Harris SR, Heriza CB (2008) Single-subject research design: recommendations for levels of evidence and quality rating. Dev Med Child Neurol 50:99–103. https://doi.org/10.1111/j.1469-8749.2007.02005.x
28. Reichow B, Volkmar FR, Cicchetti DV (2008) Development of the evaluative method for evaluating and determining evidence-based practices in autism. J Autism Dev Disord 38(7):1311–1319. https://doi.org/10.1007/s10803-007-0517-7
29. Reichow B (2011) Development, procedures, and application of the evaluative method for determining evidence-based practices in autism. In: Reichow B, Doehring P, Cicchetti DV, Volkmar FR (eds) Evidence-based practices and treatments for children with autism. Springer, New York, NY, pp 25–39. https://doi.org/10.1007/978-1-4419-6975-0_2
30. Gevarter C, Bryant DP, Bryant B, Watkins L, Zamora C, Sammarco N (2016) Mathematics interventions for individuals with autism spectrum disorder: a systematic review. Rev J Autism Dev Disord 3:224–238. https://doi.org/10.1007/s40489-016-0078-9
31. Reichow B, Volkmar FR (2010) Social skills interventions for autistic individuals: evaluation for evidence-based practices within a best evidence synthesis framework. J Autism Dev Disord 40:149–166. https://doi.org/10.1007/s10803-009-0842-0
32. Hughes EM, Yakubova G (2019) Addressing the mathematics gap for students with ASD: an evidence-based systematic review of video-based mathematics interventions. Rev J Autism Dev Disord 1–12. https://doi.org/10.1007/s40489-019-00160-3
33. Watkins L, O'Reilly M, Kuhn M, Gevarter C, Lancioni GE, Sigafoos J, Lang R (2015) A review of peer-mediated social interaction interventions for students with autism in inclusive settings. J Autism Dev Disord 45:1070–1083. https://doi.org/10.1007/s10803-014-2264-x
34. Whalon KJ, Conroy MA, Martinez JR, Werch BL (2015) School-based peer-related social competence interventions for children with autism spectrum disorder: a meta-analysis and descriptive review of single case research design studies. J Autism Dev Disord 45:1513–1531. https://doi.org/10.1007/s10803-015-2373-1
35. Cascio MA, Weiss JA, Racine E (2021) Empowerment in decision-making for autistic people in research. Disabil Soc 36(1):100–144. https://doi.org/10.1080/09687599.2020.1712189
36. Benton L, Johnson H, Ashwin E, Brosnan M, Grawemeyer B (2012) Developing IDEAS: supporting children with autism within a participatory design team. In: CHI '12 proceedings of the SIGCHI conference on human factors in computing systems. https://doi.org/10.1145/2207676.2208650
37. Kitchenham BA, Dyba T, Jorgensen M (2004) Evidence-based software engineering. In: Proceedings of the 26th international conference on software engineering. IEEE Computer Society, pp 273–281. https://doi.org/10.1109/ICSE.2004.1317449
38. Jordan PW (2003) Designing pleasurable products: an introduction to the new human factors. CRC press Londres (Reino Unido)
39. Brosnan M, Ashwin E, Johnson H, Grawemeyer B, Benton L (2012) Demonstrating a computer-based mathematics tutor specifically designed for learners with autism spectrum disorder. Speech presented at ITASD 2012
40. Druin A (1999) Cooperative inquiry: developing new technologies for children with children. In: Proceedings of the CHI. ACM Press, pp 595–599. https://doi.org/10.1145/302979.303166
41. Kientz JA, Hayes GR, Goodwin MS, Gelsomini M, Abowd GD (2020) Interactive technologies and autism. In: Synthesis lectures on assistive, rehabilitative, and health-preserving technologies, 2nd edn., vol 9, pp i–229

42. Richard A. Krueger, Mary Anne Casey (2000) Focus groups. A practical guide for applied research. Forum Qualitative Sozialforschung/Forum: Qual Soc Res 3(4)
43. Hasson F, Keeney S, McKenna H (2000) Research guidelines for the Delphi survey technique. J Adv Nurs 32(4):1008–1015. https://doi.org/10.1046/j.1365-2648.2000.t01-1-01567.x
44. Trevelyan EG, Robinson N (2015) Delphi methodology in health research: how to do it? Euro J Integr Med 7(4):423–428. https://doi.org/10.1016/j.eujim.2015.07.002
45. Ager A, Stark L, Akesson B, Boothby N (2010) Defining best practice in care and protection of children in crisis affected settings: a delphi study. Child Dev 81(4):1271–1286. https://doi.org/10.1111/j.1467-8624.2010.01467.x
46. Herrera G, Sevilla J, Vera L, Portalés C, Casas S (2018) On the development of VR and AR learning contents for children on the autism spectrum: from real requirements to virtual scenarios. In: Augmented reality for enhanced learning environments, pp 106–141
47. Al-Azawi R, Ayesh A, Al-Obaidy M (2014) Towards agent-based agile approach for game development methodology. In: Proceeding of the 2014 World Congress on computer applications and information systems (WCCAIS). https://doi.org/10.1109/WCCAIS.2014.6916626
48. Camargo MC, Barros RM, Brancher JD, Barros VT, Santana M (2019) Designing gamified interventions for autism spectrum disorder: a systematic review. In: Entertainment computing and serious games: first IFIP TC 14 joint international conference, ICEC-JCSG 2019, Arequipa, Peru, Proceedings 1. Springer International Publishing, pp 341–352. https://doi.org/10.1007/978-3-030-34644-7_28
49. Valencia K, Rusu C, Quiñones D, Jamet E (2019) The impact of technology on people with autism spectrum disorder: a systematic literature review. Sensors 19(20):4485. https://doi.org/10.3390/s19204485
50. Sevilla J, Herrera G, Martínez B, Alcantud F (2007) Web accessibility for individuals with cognitive deficits: a comparative study between an existing commercial Web and its cognitively accessible equivalent. ACM Trans Comput-Hum Interact 14(3):12. https://doi.org/10.1145/1279700.1279702
51. W3C Web Accessibility Initiative (2018) Cognitive and learning disabilities accessibility task force (Cognitive A11Y TF). https://www.w3.org/WAI/PF/cognitive-a11y-tf/
52. Biever C (2007) Web removes social barriers for those with autism. New Sci 2610:26–27
53. Jordan C (2010) Evolution of autism support and understanding via the world wide web. Intellect Dev Disabil 48(3):220–227. https://doi.org/10.1352/1934-9556-48.3.220
54. Britto T, Pizzolato E (2016) Towards web accessibility guidelines of interaction and interface design for people with autism spectrum disorder. In: Speech presented at international conference on advances in computer-human interactions, Venecia (Italia)
55. Raymaker DM, Kapp SK, McDonald KE, Weiner M, Ashkenazy E, Nicolaidis C (2019) Development of the AASPIRE web accessibility guidelines for autistic web users. Autism in Adulthood: Chall Manag 1(2):146–157. https://doi.org/10.1089/aut.2018.0020
56. Frankowska-Takhari S, Hassell J (2020) Autism accessibility guidelines research project. https://www.autism.org.uk/what-we-do/website/accessibility

The Utility of Biomarkers for Assessment and Intervention in Neurodevelopmental Disorders

Stella Guldner, Julia Ernst, Frauke Nees, and Nathalie Holz

Abstract

The inherent heterogeneity of neurodevelopmental disorders (NDDs) such as attention deficit hyperactivity disorders (ADHD) and autism spectrum disorder (ASD) underscores a challenge, where heterogeneous clinical, neurocognitive and neurobiological traits defy consistent characterization across diagnoses. Therefore, the field of neurodevelopmental research has undergone strong advances with the aim to provide evidence on the underlying mechanisms of neurodevelopmental disorders. In the present chapter, we will provide an overview on the current state of knowledge on identified underlying biomarkers, elaborating on different types of biomarkers, the neural and neurophysiological, genetic, epigenetic and metabolic correlates of ADHD and ASD and discussing their potential for diagnostic and therapeutic strategies. Despite advancements in the field, the search for a single biomarker meeting the optimal standards of sensitivity and specificity remains unfulfilled. The chapter therefore also discusses potential needs for developmentally informed research strategies to address the dynamic nature of NDDs. This includes innovations in machine learning, which may offer promising biomarker discovery approaches in the spirit of precision

S. Guldner · J. Ernst · N. Holz (✉)
Department of Child and Adolescent Psychiatry and Psychotherapy, Central Institute of Mental Health, Medical Faculty Mannheim, University of Heidelberg, Mannheim, Germany
e-mail: nathalie.holz@zi-mannheim.de

S. Guldner
e-mail: stella.guldner@zi-mannheim.de

J. Ernst
e-mail: julia.ernst@zi-mannheim.de

F. Nees (✉)
Institute of Medical Psychology and Medical Sociology, University Medical Center Schleswig-Holstein, Kiel University, Kiel, Germany
e-mail: frauke.nees@uksh.de

medicine. Addressing these complexities and the ethical considerations, particularly the risk of discrimination and stigmatization, is imperative for future research.

> **Keywords**
>
> Neurodevelopmental disorders (NDDs) • Diagnostic biomarkers for NDDs • Neural correlates of ADHD and ASD • Genetic biomarkers in ADHD and ASD • Epigenetic correlates in NDDs

Introduction

In the field of neurodevelopmental research, a notable contradiction currently exists. While the vast majority of experts acknowledge the clinical and etiological diversity inherent to most neurodevelopmental disorders—and the notable overlap among them—it is evident that those diagnosed with a broad clinical label might not exhibit consistent neurocognitive or neurobiological traits [1]. This understanding has sparked a surge of enthusiasm in unearthing biomarkers, aiming to refine patient categorization and embrace precision medicine [2]. It has highlighted the nascence of a biological understanding of NDD, however, the prevailing methodological approaches typically contrasts a specific clinical group with a set of "neurotypical" individuals.

Such a methodology stems from a categorical perspective on psychiatry, which implies that particular disorders are characterized by unique and consistent neurocognitive or neurobiological features. In the present chapter, we will introduce the biomarker concept, its link to clinical symptoms and related assessments and interventions and also highlight respective potentials and pitfalls.

1 What Are Biomarkers?

At its core, a biomarker is an objectively measurable trait that serves as an indicator of typical biological activities, disease-related processes, or reactions to therapeutic treatments [3]. The rising emphasis on biomarker identification is driven by their proven clinical efficacy across various medical domains, offering a more precise and consistent means for diagnosing ailments or forecasting individualized responses to treatments [4, 5].

Fundamentally, a biomarker might manifest as any definitive attribute or result from genetic evaluations, chemical tests, neuroimaging analyses, ocular tracking, or cognitive assessments that can provide trustworthy forecasts about a person. This might materialize as the following scores: a consistent score that assumes clinical significance beyond a designated threshold, a distinct score—such as the presence or lack of a specific genetic marker—that hints at the likelihood of a distinct condition or variant, or an aggregate score synthesized from multiple indicators [6]. Even though universally agreed standards for diagnostic biomarkers are lacking, an acceptable biomarker can classify a condition with around 80% sensitivity and 80% specificity (with a Cohen's d value of 1.66; [7, 8]).

1.1 Diagnostic Biomarker

A diagnostic biomarker is essentially a distinguishable attribute signaling the presence of a general medical condition, providing a clear route to accurate diagnosis. If a condition displays consistency across its affected population, the biomarker in question should be broadly applicable. This means it should exhibit high sensitivity, ensure accurate detection of true cases and have high specificity, in order to allow for effective identification of those without the condition [3]. Additionally, like all types of biomarkers, diagnostic biomarkers should demonstrate strong positive and negative predictive capacities.

1.2 Stratification Biomarker

When a clinical condition varies across its population, we reference stratification biomarkers. This is a discernible feature that assists in pinpointing more uniform biological clusters either within a specific diagnostic group or spanning multiple diagnoses [9]. Essentially, these stratification biomarkers facilitate in identifying a particular subset of individuals within a broader condition. They can help professionals understand an individual's potential disease trajectory or predict their likely response to certain treatments or interventions [10].

These more defined groups might emerge based on certain individual attributes like gender or age. However, they might also arise due to unique neurobiological factors, such as distinct neurocognitive patterns or particular brain deviations [10]. The challenge lies in determining the number of these subsets, gauging their size, and establishing the thresholds that are clinically pertinent.

1.3 Prognostic Biomarkers

Within clinical research, when examining the potential trajectory of a disease, we utilize prognostic biomarkers. This is a distinct and measurable attribute that provides insights into the likely evolution of a disease in an individual, regardless of the received treatment. In essence, prognostic biomarkers shed light on the natural course of a condition, offering a glimpse into an individual's future health status [6]. Such biomarkers are pivotal in assessing the probable trajectory of a disease, whether it is likely to advance aggressively, remain stable, or even regress. They aid healthcare professionals in tailoring management plans, setting patient expectations, and making informed decisions about treatment aggressiveness. While diagnostic biomarkers identify diseases and stratification biomarkers categorize patients, prognostic biomarkers offer insight into the disease's progression.

1.4 Predictive Biomarker

When assessing a disease's response to treatment, we turn to predictive biomarkers. These are tangible and measurable attributes that can forecast how an individual's disease will react to a given therapeutic approach. While prognostic biomarkers give insights into the likely course of a disease, predictive biomarkers focus exclusively on forecasting how a disease might respond to particular treatments [6]. For instance, with a predictive biomarker, doctors can determine a patient's potential response or the side effects caused by a given medication. This vital insight allows medical practitioners to personalize treatments, balancing the best possible outcomes against any potential hazards. In essence, while diagnostic biomarkers identify the presence of a disease and prognostic biomarkers indicate its potential progression, predictive biomarkers guide treatment choices based on expected responses.

1.5 Risk/Likelihood Biomarker

A risk or likelihood biomarker is a scientifically validated metric that quantifies an individual's predisposition to developing a specific condition or disease in the future. Distinct from predictive or prognostic biomarkers, which focus on treatment responses or disease progression respectively, risk biomarkers emphasize the probabilistic onset of a disease based on genetic, environmental, or lifestyle factors. By understanding these probabilities, clinicians and researchers can strategize preventative interventions, recommend specific monitoring protocols, and emphasize lifestyle or genetic counseling, thereby mitigating potential health risks [11].

In summary, different types of biomarkers can offer implications for diagnostic, treatment-related, prognostic and risk-related aspects of NDDs. Importantly, biomarkers can be situated at any level of observation from genes to behavior, and correspondingly, a large variety of assessment tools are used in order to obtain biomarkers and associated indices for investigation (see Fig. 1 for an overview of assessment tools for biomarkers). What do biomarkers have to offer for NDDs in research and clinical practice?

2 Biomarkers as Assessment Tools in NDD

Neurodevelopmental disorders comprise a group of disorders characterized by their early onset and chronicity, with core impairments in a range of functions including intellectual, motor, cognitive or social functions that deviate from typical development (e.g. [12]). NDDs are very heterogeneous and evolve dynamically. As

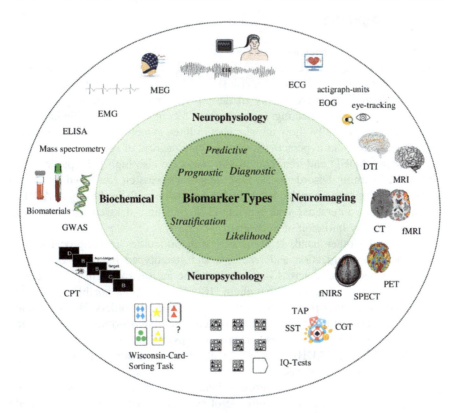

Fig. 1 Overview on the types of biomarkers and associated assessment tools. *Note* **Neurophysiology**: *EEG* = electroencephalography; *MEG* = magnetoencephalography; *ECG* = electrocardiography; *EMG* = electromiography; *EOG* = electrooculography (e.g. acoustic startle reflex). **Neuroimaging**: *MRI* = magnetic resonance imaging; *fMRI* = functional magnetic resonance imaging; *DTI* = diffusion tensor imaging; *fNIRS* = functional near-infrared spectroscopy; *CT* = computed tomography; *SPECT* = single-photon emission computed tomography; *PET* = positron emission tomography. **Neuropsychology**: *IQ-Tests* = intelligence quotient-tests; *TAP* = test of attentional performance; *CPT* = continuous performance task; *SST* = stop signal task; *CGT* = cambridge gambling task. **Biochemical**: *GWAS* = genome-wide association studies; *ELISA* = enzyme-linked immunosorbent assay

such, they present a challenge to diagnostic and treatment related clinical decision-making, as well as monitoring. Although this group of impairments encompasses multiple disorders, here we will focus on Attention Deficit Hyperactivity Disorder (ADHD) and Autism Spectrum Disorder (ASD). While previous versions of the prevalent classification systems have allocated ADHD and ASD into different categories, this has now been changed in the current 11th version of the International Statistical Classification of Diseases and Related Health Problems (ICD-11; [13]), reflecting the accumulated evidence.

2.1 Diagnostics

Presently, neurodevelopmental disorders—such as ADHD and ASD—are determined based on diagnostic criteria defined in prevalent classification systems, such as the ICD-10 or 11. While these criteria are based on scientific evidence and systematic evaluation, they are mostly of descriptive nature. ADHD is one of the most common NDDs, affecting approximately 5% of children worldwide [14]. ADHD children typically show impairments in three symptom clusters: attention, impulse inhibition and hyperactivity, with varying degrees of severity and impairment. Among ADHD children, comorbidity rates are also high [15], particularly with ASD, Learning Disorders, Tic Disorders or Depression (reviewed by [16]). Accordingly, the heterogeneity in clinical presentation both in ASD and ADHD is vast, complex, interactive and dynamic [12], causing a delayed diagnosis and impeding a timely initiation of treatment.

ASD, on the other hand, is associated with difficulties in reciprocal social interactions, communication and repetitive and stereotyped interests. Beyond a substantial heterogeneity across individuals on the autism spectrum [17], including variability along a severity continuum [18], there is also a notable amount of comorbidity with other psychiatric, somatic and genetic disorders. While current estimates suggest that there are about 1% of autistic children worldwide [19], up to 70% of these children show at least one comorbid psychiatric and language impairment [20]. Moreover, ADHD was one of the three most prevalent co-occurring diagnosis in about 28% of cases [20].

While diagnostic criteria are aimed at being non-overlapping and specific, in reality, patients often present a multitude of symptoms that are non-specific and dynamic, that are therefore often better captured by dimensional approaches or evolve over time. Moreover, there is a naturally occurring variation in development across children and adolescents, such that a deviation from normative developmental is a key objective that is at times hard to determine based on descriptive criteria. Given these challenges, biomarkers could help to identify or stratify affected individuals and offer probabilistic information regarding progression, outcome, and risk. Together, this can potentially lead to individualized treatment approaches [1, 21] to enhance efficacy, effectiveness and efficiency of available treatments and support systems. First, biomarkers could inform different stages of the diagnostic process, as well as support the development of tools that enhance quantification of otherwise qualitative data or data lacking normative comparisons. Machine learning approaches based on normative modelling could be one example, which determines when development deviates significantly from a typically developing population. Moreover, these approaches could help to deal with a second diagnostic challenge, which is the high heterogeneity of NDDs. While being standard assessments for development regarding body height, or weight, recent efforts aim to develop comparable models for structural brain development as a biomarker for specific psychiatric disorders [10, 22–25]. Here, biomarkers might be helpful to identify subgroups of patients with particular difficulties or progressions, based on underlying biological characteristics. This type of stratification might allow more customized treatment possibilities and determine suitable timing of interventions [21]. Third, as mentioned above, diagnostic criteria are currently descriptive and thus do not rely on or imply a specific etiology. Biomarker research could be helpful to inform etiological models of NDDs on the full scope of levels—from genes to behavior—to enhance prevention, treatment, positively influence progression and enhance adaptation to difficulties associated with the disorder on the level of the family or system. Lastly, biomarkers could also help early, or very early, detection when existing behavioral measures might still not be sensitive enough. This early detection can facilitate personalized, adequate interventions and preventional measures to avoid secondary difficulties and suffering. Thus, together with risk, prognostic and predictive biomarkers, there is the opportunity to help ascertain diagnoses to kick-off individualized supportive measures.

2.2 Treatment Monitoring

From the standpoint of treatment monitoring, the goal of biomarker development is to monitor the treatment response, treatment engagement and predict outcomes. Repeated biomarker assessments before and after treatment have to be sensitive to meaningful clinical changes and reflect treatment mechanisms. This helps us understand clinical response differences, guiding treatment and optimizing clinical trials [9]. Such biomarkers may also play a role in allowing treatment switching or continuance basing on the evidence of a response or so-called "target engagement" [26]. Therefore, is important to further investigate potential candidate biomarkers that may aid future monitoring of treatment effects and point to mechanistic targets for novel treatments. The current state of research and evidence on treatment monitoring in ADHD and ASD is summarized in this chapter.

3 State of Research on Biomarkers in ADHD and ASD

3.1 Magnetic Resonance Imaging

In this section, we present a concise overview of recent research employing both functional and structural magnetic resonance imaging (MRI) for ADHD and ASD. Considering the vast literature in this field, we concentrate on meta-analyses, which combine data from multiple individual studies, and mega-analyses, which pool raw data from multiple studies to conduct a large-scale analysis, to decipher the links between brain structure and function and NDD in a complex dimensional context.

ADHD. MRI studies highlight ADHD-associated changes in brain structure and function in particular within the reward system centered around the basal ganglia, comprising the caudate nucleus, putamen, pallidum, nucleus accumbens [27, 28]. These regions crucially process rewards, regulate motor activities and form habits. ADHD individuals often show altered dopamine transmission here, resulting in atypical reward sensitivity [29]. Such irregularities can lead to a preference for immediate over delayed rewards (known as "delay discounting"). Moreover, dysfunctions within the basal ganglia and its subcomponents can contribute to the impulsivity and inattention characteristic of ADHD. Many ADHD treatments target dopamine modulation in the basal ganglia to address these reward system dysfunctions and ameliorate symptoms. Likewise, inhibition—the brain's ability to suppress irrelevant or interfering stimuli and responses—is frequently compromised in ADHD individuals [30]. Deficits in inhibitory control could lead to hallmark ADHD symptoms like impulsivity, difficulty waiting one's turn, and interrupting others. On a neural level, this is often linked to irregularities in the prefrontal cortex, such as the inferior frontal gyrus (IFG), and its associated pathways, which are crucial for executive functions and self-control. Therapies and interventions for ADHD often focus on enhancing inhibitory control to help individuals manage impulsive behaviors and improve attention regulation. Indeed, disruptions in the fronto-cortical and fronto-subcortical networks [31] have been noted and meta-analyses on task-fMRI experiments identified aberrant activity patterns in the left pallidum/putamen together with a decrease in activity in the left Inferior Frontal Gyrus (IFG) during processing of neutral stimuli [32], especially among male subjects. The ventral putamen—rich in dopamine—receives signals from both the medial orbitofrontal cortex and the IFG. Studies have demonstrated that abnormalities in these regions correlate with ADHD symptoms like hyperactivity, impulsivity, disinhibition and inattention [33, 34]. Despite this convergence seen with respect to neutral stimuli processing, no conclusive aberrant activation related to ADHD was found with respect to inhibitory control, attention, or other cognitive tasks such as memory, timing and reasoning [32], which casts doubts on these domains as presenting markers for ADHD.

Resting-state functional connectivity (rsFC) techniques are increasingly used to investigate ADHD's assumed disruptions in major brain networks related to attention and cognition. This non-invasive method has revealed consistent anomalies in ADHD, notably in the Frontoparietal Network (FPN), central to cognitive control and information integration. A meta-analysis confirmed disrupted connectivity between the FPN, the introspective Default Mode Network (DMN), and the stimulus-responsive Ventral Attention Network (VAN), supporting the triple-network dysfunction model seen in ADHD and other disorders [35]. Further, alterations were found in the Somatosensory Network (SSN) and Affective Network (AN), linked to ADHD's hyperactive and impulsive symptoms. Leveraging rsFC techniques, a study synthesized data from 20 sources (944 ADHD patients, 1121 controls) revealing connectivity disruptions within the DMN with reduced connectivity in the posterior cingulate cortex, as well as increased connectivity in the dorsal medial prefrontal cortex and the cognitive control network. In children and adolescents, connectivity between the DMN and both the cognitive control and affective/motivational networks was decreased, supporting the idea that such alterations underlie pediatric ADHD manifestations [36]. However, these meta-analytic findings have to be considered with caution, given that these patterns were not observed in two other meta-analyses [32, 37].

Utilizing ENIGMA ADHD Working Group's resources, an international research effort aimed at understanding brain diseases and genetic causes, pooled and compared brain scans from 1713 ADHD patients and 1529 controls worldwide across 23 sites. ADHD was associated with reduced volumes in key subcortical brain regions, including the accumbens, amygdala, caudate, hippocampus, and putamen, potentially underlying emotion- and motivation-related differences. Notably, it suggested a brain maturation delay in ADHD individuals, with pronounced structural variations in children under 15 compared to adults [38]. Expanding on this knowledge, a subsequent ENIGMA-ADHD study revealed diminished surface area in frontal, cingulate, and temporal regions in ADHD children with areas, like the fusiform gyrus exhibiting a thinner cortex. Remarkably, these structural differences subsided in adolescents and adults. Additionally, familial influences on surface area disparities were identified in certain regions. Moreover, an analysis from the Generation-R study uncovered correlations between attention-related problems and reduced surface areas in regions coinciding with those identified in the ADHD study, further enriching the understanding of structural nuances in attention-related challenges [39]. In essence, the detailed examination of the ENIGMA-ADHD consortium data highlights specific structural brain differences in ADHD children and these differences tend to evolve or diminish as individuals progress into adolescence and adulthood, emphasizing the dynamic nature of ADHD's neurobiological profile across the lifespan.

MRI-based treatment monitoring in ADHD. Functional MRI can be used to examine treatment related changes in brain networks in ADHD, for instance during medical treatment with Methylphenidate (MPH; [40]). For instance, Liddle et al. [41] showed that MPH improved deactivation of default mode network in the ADHD group during the stop task. Among different neuroimaging biomarkers, the striatum was the most extensively studied region, with a change of signalling at the level of the ventral striatum and an increase in the release of dopamine after MPH somministration [42]. Moreover, improvements in ADHD symptoms over 2 weeks were observed in a group exposed to fMRI neurofeedback of the right IFG, which correlated with clinical improvements [43]. Alegria et al. [44] reported increased activation at the level of the left insula, IFG and putamen during error trials, which was associated with improvements in ADHD symptoms after neurofeedback of the right IFG. Further, left IFG, insula and dACC were upregulated by MPH and this was also associated with changes in inattention symptoms [45]. Moreover, imaging markers related to DMN-striatum connectivity might have a significant role to predict treatment response in adult ADHD [46]. Changes in structural neuroimaging markers following treatment with MPH have also been studied, showing increases in fractional anisotropy and cortical thickness among medicated children [47, 48].

ASD. Functional neuroimaging has been a pivotal tool in the exploration of Autism Spectrum Disorder (ASD) biomarkers. Sensory abnormalities often emerge as early markers in infants who are later diagnosed with ASD, with some differences detectable as early as six months of age [49]. Despite the varied sensory attributes linked to ASD, dysregulated sensory processing emerges as a common trait, possibly exacerbating autism's prevalent social challenges. Key neurobiological insights suggest functional and anatomical disparties in the thalamus, a primary relay for most senses, which might be central to these sensory irregularities in ASD [50]. Additionally, abnormalities in areas like the ACC, insula, and superior temporal cortex (STC) suggest a connection between sensory processing and social cognition [50].

Many studies have investigated tasks related to biological motion analysis and social psychological evaluations, such as making nonverbal judgments after observing certain scenarios or games. Interestingly, task activations closely related to ASD severity were commonly observed in areas such as the superior temporal sulcus, parieto-temporal junction, and medial and inferior prefrontal cortices [51, 52]. Task activations in the superior temporal sulcus underline potential challenges autistic individuals may have with social cues, while alterations in the parieto-temporal junction suggest difficulties in perspective taking. Disruptions in the medial prefrontal cortex indicate issues understanding emotional states, whereas changes in the inferior prefrontal cortex hint at challenges with emotion-based decisions. Collectively, these findings spotlight profound disruptions in autistic individuals' social-emotional understanding and processing.

Another notable focus in investigating ASD biomarkers is reward processing. Reduced ventral striatum activity during reward anticipation, consistent for both social and monetary rewards, has been observed in autistic individuals [53]. This challenges the social motivation deficit hypothesis, suggesting a broader reward-processing anomaly in ASD, not just limited to social rewards.

In the vast landscape of ASD biomarker research, studies focusing on functional connectivity—how various brain regions interact—have provided interesting insights. These studies, while varying in methods, are crucial in understanding the neural dynamics of ASD. For instance, the discovery of weaker connections within the perceptual and motor networks suggests potential difficulties in integrating sensory input with motor actions [54]. On the other hand, stronger connections with association networks might imply that these individuals rely more on higher-order brain regions responsible for complex cognitive processes, possibly as a compensatory mechanism [54]. Reduced connectivity between the medial prefrontal cortex and posterior cingulate cortex within the default mode network is consistently observed across studies. This may underpin social and introspective challenges in ASD, potentially explaining difficulties in understanding one's own emotions, grasping others' feelings or navigating social contexts [52].

Differences between the brain's left and right sides—known as hemispheric asymmetry—have recently caught the attention of researchers, offering a new perspective on understanding ASD. A recent meta-analysis reported that structural differences in lateralization are more widespread than functional differences, with a strong relationship between structural and functional lateralization changes, indicating that structural deviations may be a primary feature of atypical asymmetry in autism, while functional differences are highly variable among individuals [55].

Comparing gray matter in autistic individuals to a normative pattern of brain lateralization, indicates that individuals on the autism spectrum displayed unique right- or left-brain deviations, especially in language, motor, and spatial processing areas, which correlated with symptom severity [56]. Notably, language delay was related to more pronounced right-brain deviations. These findings emphasize the importance of considering autism's diverse neuroanatomy and suggest that unusual brain lateralization could be a potential stratifying factor in autism treatments.

From a developmental perspective, studies have unveiled aberrant trajectories of brain development in ASD [57]. As such, a thicker cortex during childhood has been shown, which may result from excess of neurons (possibly due to migration or pruning deficits), together with a greater dendritic spine density and an increased number of synapses and neuronal size [58, 59]. In contrast, accelerated cortical thinning from adolescence onwards has been suggested to result from an initial delay in synaptic and axonal pruning, which is thought to lead to a subsequent greater-than-normal neural loss [59, 60]. With respect to brain surface area, an unusual expansion of the cortical surface in autism has been revealed, potentially attributed to irregularities in white matter growth and synaptic pruning [59].

MRI-based treatment monitoring in ASD. Activation of regions in the medial prefrontal cortex and the parieto-temporal junction are found across different study designs and show changes that correlate with ASD symptoms in clinical trials [51]. Functional connectivity analyses show consistent decreased connectivity between the medial prefrontal cortex and posterior cingulate cortex within the default mode network and some correlation with ASD symptoms [61]. Furthermore, amygdala volume and functional connectivity within the default mode network have shown to have a potential role in treatment monitoring [62]. Strong associations have been noted between pre-treatment brain activation to biological motion and behavioral change in the treatment target, suggesting that brain response is tapping into neurobiological readiness to respond to treatment [63]. Concurrent changes in brain structural connectivity associated with improvements in social and communicative functioning have been found [64].

3.2   Electroencephalography

Electroencephalography (EEG) is a valuable tool for studying neurodevelopmental disorders, as it allows researchers and clinicians to observe and analyze the electrical activity of the brain (for a review see [65]). EEG results provide information about the electrical activity of the brain and have provided valuable insights into the neural underpinnings of these conditions, revealing abnormal patterns that may be associated with certain neurodevelopmental disorders (reviewed by [1, 66]). EEG-studies focus on the examination of frequency bands within the EEG signal or Event-Related Potentials (ERP) in response to particular stimuli or task-demands.

ADHD. EEG studies in ADHD individuals indicated differences in brainwave patterns. For instance, studies have shown that ADHD children may exhibit differences in the theta and beta brainwave frequencies, which are related to attention and focus [67–69], specifically increased theta (4–8 Hz) and decreased beta (13–30 Hz) activity have been reported in some resting state studies (for meta-analytic evidence see [67]). Increased theta power has been associated with inattention, while reduced beta power has been linked to hyperactivity. There are notable gender differences observed in these studies. Males exhibited globally increased theta activity, while females only showed increased frontal theta activity compared to gender-matched controls. Females also had reduced posterior beta activity which was, however, not found in males [70]. An EEG study in boys by Hobbs et al. [71] showed global differences in adolescent boys with combined type and inattentive type ADHD using resting-state EEG with closed eyes. The ADHD group had higher absolute delta and theta activity and an elevated theta/beta ratio compared to the controls. ADHD participants also exhibited a reduction in relative beta activity in lateral frontal regions. Significant deviations from normal CNS development were noted in the participants, which did not suggest a delay in maturation.

Moreover, also age-related changes from childhood to adolescence have been investigated. For example, Kamida et al. [72] found that, with increasing age, both ADHD and control participants showed decreased absolute occipital alpha and frontal beta activity. However, while 10 year-old ADHD children showed significantly reduced occipital alpha compared to controls, this difference was not oberserved in children over 10 years of age. Instead, beta activity in the ADHD group was elevated compared to controls at both age stages. The result for the alpha band was considered indicative of maturation delay, while the beta band findings were interpreted as developmental deviations. Along with frequency analyses, ERPs such as the P300, N2, and N3 components, have been investigated in ADHD individuals (e.g. [73, 74]), showing that differences in the timing and amplitude of these components may provide insights into attention and inhibitory control deficits seen in ADHD.

Finally, EEG can also be used to assess neural activity during tasks that require sustained attention, such as the Continuous Performance Test (CPT) or the Go/No-Go task. A longitudinal EEG study, in which the trajectory of impaired cognitive functions in ADHD has been examined, yielded interesting results; all ERP components such as Cue P3, NoGo P3 and Contingent Negative Variation (CNV) developed without significant time-group interactions [75]. Only CNV remained reduced in the ADHD group from childhood to adulthood. This suggests that attention and preparation deficits in ADHD persist into adulthood, with a diminished CNV reflecting a particularly stable marker of ADHD. Further longitudinal studies are needed to confirm these findings [75].

Together, many existing ADHD models have undergone testing and been either refuted, revised, or considered too simplistic to capture the intricate symptom interactions in the disorder. Arousal seems to play a role in all ADHD children, regardless of their EEG profile. While we observe significant EEG maturation from childhood to adulthood, the delayed maturation model remains largely untested in the literature. One challenge for all these models has been studies showing that the EEG profile of ADHD individuals does not represent a single homogeneous type, and ADHD can be attributed to a range of different CNS functional abnormalities (for a review see [76]). Finally, for EEG results also the effects of ADHD medications on brain activity needs to be considered. Stimulant medications, such as methylphenidate and amphetamines, have been found to influence EEG patterns in ADHD individuals [77–80]. These effects can help researchers to better understand the neurobiological mechanisms of these medications.

EEG-based treatment monitoring in ADHD. In ADHD, EEG biomarkers related to theta/beta ratio (TBR), event-related potentials (ERPs) and alpha peak frequency (APF) have demonstrated sensitivity to treatment response [81]. Attentional (cue P3) and preparatory (contingent negative variation) brain activity and performance non specifically reduced after treatment [82]. Increases in N2 and P3 amplitudes in the ADHD group have been reported after MPH adminstration [83]. Moreover, modulation of TBR by increasing beta power and decreasing theta power respectively have been reported as a response to MPH [84]. Additionally, quantitative EEG (qEEG) measures can provide valuable information about neurofeedback-based interventions [52].

ASD. In ASD, studies using EEG measurement have reported variable results. Research has shown that there may be differences in EEG patterns, such as increased high-frequency oscillations in autistic individuals compared to typically developing individuals (e.g. [85]), but some individuals on the autism spectrum may show increased high-frequency oscillations or abnormalities in specific brain regions (e.g. [86]). Moreover, abnormalities in resting-state EEG, such as altered power spectra and reduced complexity, have been reported in individuals on the autism spectrum (e.g. [87]). Resting-state EEG recordings are captured when an individual on the autism spectrum is awake but in a state of rest with their eyes closed. For eyes closed, however, no significant difference between the ASD group and the control group in resting-state EEG have been reported [88]. With eyes open it was shown that delta, theta, beta, and gamma energy in autistic patients are higher, whereas alpha energy is lower than in the control group [89–97]. Here, the severity of ASD symptoms—as well as gender—are yet to be considered as critical factors. The energy of gamma, delta, theta, and alpha seem to be even smaller as the severity of ASD increases. This deviates somewhat from the conclusions mentioned before. Moreover, as men age, gamma energy has been shown to decrease, and the stronger the social interaction abilities of men on the autism spectrum, the lower the theta and alpha energies have been found, and this was not observed in women [88]. Interestingly, however, in the general population, associations between resting state oscillations (e.g., gamma) and autistic traits have not always been observed [98]. This suggests biomarker validity to depend on symptomatology and developmental processes.

ERP studies, on the other hand, showed atypical processing of social and emotional stimuli in individuals on the autism spectrum [99, 100]. For example, the P300 component is often studied in the context of attention and memory processing in autism (e.g. [101, 102], for review see [103]), but also the N1, N170, P1 and mismatch negativity (MMN) waves has undergone intensive testing in ASD (for review see [66]). However, the experimenters did not reach a consistent conclusion regarding the patterns of abnormal amplitude and latency in ASD. Some studies suggest that autistic patients are insensitive to stimuli, meaning that the amplitude decreases and latency increases. This leads to the conclusion that patients on the autism spectrum have poor ability to process faces [104–109]. Others also indicated that autistic patients exhibit abnormal gaze direction [110]. Different types of stimuli also yield different results, and the outcome within the ASD group itself differs from that between ASD and the control group [111]. These inconclusive findings might partly be due to the range of individuals that have been investigated across the existing studies. Finally, EEG studies in individuals on the autism spectrum have identified differences in brain connectivity and synchronization [112, 113]. Some research showed increased local connectivity (short-range connections) and reduced long-range connectivity in certain brain regions [114], suggesting disrupted neural communication, which can impact information processing and integration.

EEG-based treatment monitoring in ASD. In autism, EEG markers such as atypical gamma oscillations and aberrant sensory processing patterns are under investigation. Children on the autism spectrum exposed to a high-intensity program of the Early Start Denver Model (ESDM), which is a comprehensive early intervention approach for autism, exhibited greater cortical activation and normalized neural signatures associated with fewer social problems and better social communication [115] together with better neurophysiological response. Possible association of M50—latency of a response elicited by simple auditory stimulation—with GABA signaling has been reported as a possible prediction of treatment response [116]. Several case-control studies assessed the fixation time as monitoring response to intervention, showing a correlation with symptom severity. Finally, eye-tracking measures of social attention have been discussed as powerful indicators of treatment response, especially related with social engagement and motivation [115, 117, 118].

3.3 Genetics

Neurodevelopmental disorders have a multifactorial etiology, involving both genetic and environmental factors [119]. In conditions like ASD and ADHD, there is evidence of a strong genetic predisposition and substantial evidence from twin, family, and adoption studies indicates a high heritability ([120, 121], for review see [122, 123]). On the level of genetics, research has focused mainly on the identification of candidate genes, such as specific genetic variants (e.g., single nucleotide polymorphisms, SNPs, copy number variations, CNV).

ADHD. In ADHD, researchers have focused on candidate genes known to be involved in neurotransmitter regulation, neural development, and executive function. Recent molecular genetic studies on ADHD have however shown that it is highly polygenic—its genetic architecture is explained by an enormous number of common gene variants, but each of which has shown to have a small effect size [124]. Also rare mutations have been found, some of which with much larger effect sizes (e.g., Chromosome 16p13.11 duplication; [125]). Genes involved in the regulation of dopamine and norepinephrine neurotransmitter systems are of particular interest. Variations in genes related to dopamine receptors (e.g., DRD4, DRD5, COMT), dopamine transporters (DAT1/SLC6A3), and enzymes involved in dopamine synthesis have been associated with ADHD (for a review see e.g. [126]; see [123, 127]). Genes related to the serotonin neurotransmitter system have also been investigated in ADHD. Serotonin plays a role in mood regulation and impulse control, and genetic variations in serotonin-related genes may contribute to ADHD risk [128, 129]. However, ADHD also demonstrates significant genetic correlations with a much larger group of neuropsychiatric disorders (for example Tourette syndrome, schizophrenia and, interestingly, non-psychiatric conditions). Thus, an important next step is investigating potential explanations for these associations (for a review see [130]). This also relates to the rather inconclusive findings that stem from GWAS studies in ADHD, which also provided mainly non-overlapping findings with candidate gene approaches. The recent ADHD GWAS including 20,183 ADHD cases and 35,191 controls, revealed significant effects on 12 independent genomic loci [124], including one containing the FOXP2 gene, previously associated with severe speech and language difficulties [131]. None of the genome-wide significant loci included any of the candidate genes previously implicated in ADHD (e.g., dopamine-related genes). It is possible that with larger GWAS samples, evidence may emerge implicating some of these genes, as effect sizes are small, and ADHD GWASs are still underexplored. Therefore, it is premature to dismiss these findings. However, in the meantime, caution should be exercised regarding earlier findings on candidate genes and studies utilizing them.

However, an interesting finding that stems from ADHD GWAS studies, refers to the prediction of ADHD trait levels in the general population. Here, two studies utilized an independent ADHD GWAS discovery dataset to generate ADHD polygenic risk scores (PRS)—the relative burden of common ADHD genetic variant risk alleles carried by an individual—in population cohorts the Netherlands [132] and in the United Kingdom [133]. In a third British study [134], it was also observed that deriving PRS for an ADHD trait measure from a population cohort predicted ADHD diagnosis in an independent sample of patients. Even further went the largest and most recent ADHD GWAS [124]. In this study, the genetic correlation between ADHD diagnosis and a large GWAS meta-analysis of ADHD trait measures was tested in 17,666 European individuals from the EAGLE Consortium [135]. The results are noteworthy in that researchers observed a genetic correlation of 0.94 between ADHD diagnosis in patients and ADHD traits in population-based cohorts. The overall genetic findings suggest that ADHD diagnosis lies at the extreme end of a quantitative trait. However, the genetic risk for ADHD diagnosis is not solely associated with a single continuously distributed trait measure for ADHD.

Interestingly, several recently conducted longitudinal studies have adopted a developmental life course perspective to assess ADHD and have identified an apparent "late-onset" form of ADHD, where ADHD symptoms were not reported in childhood but emerged later in adolescence or adulthood [136]. If their age of onset were known, these individuals would not have met current diagnostic criteria for ADHD. Thus, the discovery of this group challenges the conceptualization of ADHD as a neurodevelopmental disorder. In three studies examining "late-onset" ADHD, no associations with ADHD PRS were observed, although these findings were limited in their interpretability due to sample size constraints [137–139]. Therefore, the genetic similarity suggested for childhood-onset ADHD and persistent ADHD appears not to be the case for "late-onset" ADHD. Further research is thus needed on this late-onset group.

Genetic-based treatment monitoring in ADHD. A recent systematic review [140] showed that only the single nucleotide polymorphism (SNP) on the SYT1 gene related to the SNARE complex was associated with clinical amelioration by treatment, specifically in the domains of inattention and hostility. Alterations in the gene encoding dopamine transporter 1 (DAT1) and the gene encoding the alpha-2-adrenergic receptor (ADRA2A) have also been considered as potential relevant biomarkers for monitoring treatment response.

ASD. In ASD, numerous candidate genes have been identified, such as genes involved in synaptic function and neural development. Examples include genes like SHANK3, NLGN3, NLGN4X, and CHD8 (reviewed by [122, 141]) as well as so-called homeobox genes: a large and highly specialized group of closely related genes that drive the development and formation of the bilateral body plan, including the brain (e.g., GeneCards [142, 143]). There is evidence that certain homeobox genes could be associated with the onset of ASD, due to their encoding of homeodomain transcription factors that largely regulate gene expression in cell clusters, tissue arrays, and organ systems. Most of the homebox genes interact with the transcription factor SP1 (Genome Browser [144, 145]), for which it is known that it regulates several autism candidate genes (e.g. [146]), and that SP1 proteins are significantly elevated in the anterior cingulate gyrus (ACG) of autistic patients [147]. This might also come into play because of evidence that the ACG extend into the neural areas of the amygdala and the orbitofrontal cortex, both of which are brain networks shown that underlie the nosology of ASD [147]. Some rare variants of identified genes are de novo mutations, meaning they occur spontaneously and are not inherited from parents (e.g. [148], reviewed by [149]). While these studies have identified some genetic loci of interest, the effects of individual common variants are generally small, and the genetic architecture of autism is highly heterogeneous. Finally, there is evidence to suggest that the genetic architecture of autism may differ between males and females. Males are more commonly affected by autism than females, and some genetic factors may contribute to this gender bias [150, 151].

Genetic-based treatment monitoring in ASD. Glutathione has been found to be a potential marker of a positive clinical response to treatment with methylcobalamin in a recent systematic review and meta-analysis [152]. Furthermore, studies focused on sulforaphane—a supplement with indirect antioxidant effects—reported improvements in behavior and social responsiveness [153]. Moreover, intravenous somministration of immunoglobulin (IL-6) has been found to lead to significant improvements in clinical measurements of stereotyped behaviors and repetitive interests [154] and in distinguishing between specific subgroups. One study reported that heart rate variability predicted treatment response to propranolol [155]. Intranasal dose of oxytocin was followed by improvement in ADOS scores, which was also correlated with greater resting state connectivity [156]. Structural DNA alterations, single nucleotide polymorphisms (SNPs) and CYP2D6 polymorphism influences the response on risperidone treatment, predicting the dosage and improving clinical outcomes. A medium-sized open-label, prospective, baseline-controlled cohort study found that the anti-dopamine D2L receptor and anti-tubulin autoantibodies predicted treatment response to intravenous immunoglobulin [157]. Moreover, FRAA has been shown to predict response to leucovorin treatment in a recent double-blind placebo-controlled trial [158].

3.4 Epigenetics

Epigenetics is a field of study that examines changes in gene expression or cellular phenotype that do not involve alterations to the underlying DNA sequence. These changes can also be influenced by various environmental factors (toxins, stress, nutrition, and other factors) in critical periods of brain development, including prenatal and early postnatal stages [159, 160]. Epigenetic changes play a significant role in the development and progression of neurodevelopmental disorders, by affecting brain function (for review see [161, 162]). DNA methylation is one of the most well-studied epigenetic mechanisms affecting gene expression [163, 164], while another important mechanism influencing gene expression is histone modification, such as acetylation and methylation of histones, which influence packaging and regulate access to DNA.

ADHD. In ADHD research, alterations in DNA methylation patterns in specific genes (for example related to dopamine receptors (e.g., DRD4), dopamine transporters (DAT1/SLC6A3) have been investigated (see also above). Associations between DNA methylation and clinical symptoms have also been described for ADHD, particularly during the period from birth to school age [165]. Such associations may need to be considered in the context of environmental factors, such as maternal smoking during pregnancy, which has been linked to DNA methylation changes in offspring related to ADHD risk [166], or childhood adversity, which has been found to interact for example with COMT, BDNF and MAOA polymorphisms and affect sublinical ADHD symptoms in generally healthy youth [167]. Regarding histone modification, studies suggested a critical role of histone modifications in intellectual disability and deficits of cognition [168–170].

Existing research has also focused on potential effects of medication on epigenetic marks [171]. These medications can affect gene expression and neurotransmitter systems, and understanding their epigenetic effects may provide insights into their mechanisms of action. In this respect, it is important to proceed in investigations that consider an overlap between with genetics and EEG indicators of potential intermediate phenotypes for ADHD in the domains of quantitative EEG indices of arousal and intraindividual variability, as well as functional investigations of inhibition and error processing using ERP techniques. Examining the genetic and environmental contributions to EEG/ERP and the shared genetic overlap with ADHD can enhance molecular genetic studies and provide new insights into etiology. Such research will aid in precisely characterizing the clinical deficits observed in ADHD and guide the development of new interventions and prevention strategies for at-risk individuals (see [172]).

ASD. For ASD, researchers have observed differences in DNA methylation patterns in individuals on the autism spectrum compared to typically developing individuals. Here, the CpG dinucleotide sequence of the PPP2R2C gene is hypermethylated, according to analysis of DNA methylation across the autism genome, and has also been shown to be associated with ASD [173–175]. In addition, primarily animal and in vitro studies suggest that deacetylation of histone 3 proteins at lysine residues (h3k27ac), which results in abnormal transcription of candidate genes also implicated in ASD [176, 177]. Additionally, changes in DNA methylation at the promoter regions of genes like SHANK3, OXTR (oxytocin receptor), and MECP2 (associated with Rett syndrome) have been reported in individuals on the autism spectrum [178, 179]. Regarding histone modifications, allele-specific mutations of genes coding for histone-modifying proteins such as KMT2C, KDM5B and ASH1L, which may lead to structural brain anomalies such as micro-/macrocephaly and cortical malformation, have been found [180–182]. Lastly, some subtypes of ASD may arise from the maternal duplication of imprinted domains on Chromosome 15q11-13 [183]. Another monoallelically inherited gene believed to be a risk factor for ASD is Autism Susceptibility Candidate 2 (AUTS2). This gene is also shown to be duplicated in lymphoblastoid cell lines of autistic patients [184].

3.5 Metabolism

Metabolism is a fundamental biological process that involves the conversion of nutrients into energy and the building blocks necessary for the growth, maintenance, and function of cells and tissues. As such, metabolic processes are crucial for the synthesis, release, and reuptake of neurotransmitters relevant to NDDs, such as dopamine and norepinephrine. The metabolism can be influenced by several factors, including mitochondrial dysfunction, nutrition, inflammation, physical activity, sleep and the gut microbiome. Metabolomics are discussed as one of the key players on the stage of precision medicine, reflecting the interplay of genetics and environment [185], to stratifiy patient groups based on their metabotype.

ADHD. Some studies have examined the role of diet and nutrition in ADHD. Certain dietary patterns, such as those high in sugar or processed foods, have been associated with ADHD-like behaviors and worsening ADHD symptoms in some individuals (e.g. [186], for review see [187]). Additionally, specific nutrients like omega-3 fatty acids and iron may play a role in brain function and have been investigated in relation to ADHD as well (for overview see [188, 189]). Other studies have suggested a potential association between ADHD and an increased risk of obesity and metabolic syndrome in adulthood (e.g. [190–192]). These conditions involve metabolic disturbances, such as insulin resistance and dyslipidemia, which can have long-term health implications.

Emerging research also suggests a potential link between the gut microbiome and ADHD. The gut microbiome influences metabolic processes and can produce or metabolize compounds that may affect brain function. Alterations in the gut microbiota composition have been observed in some ADHD individuals as well as ASD, but the exact mechanisms are still being explored (e.g. [190, 193]). The fact that ADHD individuals, but also ASD individuals, often suffer from gastrointestinal (GI) alterations, including chronic constipation, diarrhea, and abdominal pain, underscores the possibility that the gut microbiome could play a role in this condition [194]. In a recent study [195], production rates of dopamine and serotonin precursors and the major short-chain fatty acids that influence health have been determined based on three diets (Western, Atkins, Vegan) and compared to those of healthy individuals. The calculation of elasticities has been used to understand the sensitivity of exchange fluxes to changes in diet and bacterial abundance at the species level. This revealed potential indicators of the gut microbiota of ADHD indicated by the presence of Bacillota (genus Coprococcus and Subdoligranulum), Actinobacteria (genus Collinsella) and Bacteroidetes (genus Bacteroides). Although further studies are required, this recent research offers evidence for comprehending the gastrointestinal mechanisms underlying ADHD and may contribute to identifying ways to enhance patients' quality of life. In a systematic review of maternal inflammatory states during pregnancy and neurodevelopmental disorders (NDDs), it was found that maternal conditions such as obesity, pre-eclampsia, smoking, low socioeconomic status (SES), stress, autoimmune diseases, and asthma were associated with an increased risk of ADHD in offspring. This suggests a potential link between maternal inflammation and the development of ADHD [204].

Lastly, sleep disturbances are common in ADHD individuals, and sleep plays a critical role in metabolism and overall health. Sleep problems can affect energy metabolism, mood regulation, and cognitive function, all of which may influence ADHD symptoms ([196], for a review [197]). Regular physical activity can have a positive impact on metabolism and overall well-being. Exercise has been shown to improve attention and impulse control, which can benefit ADHD individuals. Sleep problems in ADHD children have also shown to affect the family functioning. Parents specifically felt impairments in daily life and well-being putting a strain on children-spouse relationships [198].

ASD. Some individuals on the autism spectrum have been found to have nutritional deficiencies influencing metabolic functions. These deficiencies can result from selective eating patterns, food aversions, or limited diets often seen in individuals on the autism spectrum [199, 200]. In this respect, some studies have also explored the impact of dietary interventions on ASD symptoms. For example, gluten-free and casein-free (GFCF) diets have been tried by some individuals on the autism spectrum based on the belief that dietary changes may reduce symptoms ([201], for a review see [202]). Research on the effectiveness of such diets is ongoing. Metabolic and immune system dysregulation can lead to chronic inflammation in some individuals on the autism spectrum [203]. Inflammation is thus increasingly recognized as a potential contributor to neurological and behavioral symptoms in ASD. It has also been shown that even maternal acute and chronic inflammation in pregnancy is associated with ASD, and also ADHD, in the offspring [204].

4 Critical View and Future Directions

There is substantial hope for biomarkers to support diagnostics, treatment, monitoring and etiological understanding of NDDs and psychiatric disorders of childhood and adolescence. We have seen in the previous sections of this chapter, that reliable biomarkers would be of great value to enhance clinical decision-making processes in the face of inherent issues of heterogeneity and variability. Although a substantial amount of resources is directed to the identification of potential biomarkers, only few fulfill criteria that would be necessary for them to be useful in clinical practice [205]. Why have biomarkers not fulfilled their promise so far?

For biomarkers to be translatable and useful in clinical practice, they should fulfill specific criteria [9], as outlined by American Psychiatric Association (APA): demonstrate a high enough level of sensitivity and specificity (approx. 80%) regarding their identification of true positive and true negative cases, respectively, across multiple well-powered studies. Additionally, they should be internally and externally valid markers for the disorder and be reliable across time and varying examiners. Moreover, biomarkers should be sensitive to change, for instance in response to the progression of the disorder over time. Besides, the clinical usefulness and practicability should be reflected in added benefit in comparison to state-of-the-art practices and be ecologically sensible. Given these criteria, Cortese and colleagues [205] come to the sober conclusion, that presently, these criteria are not fulfilled by any of the prevalent biomarker candidates in NDD. Although this seems relatively somber, there are also clear implications to be drawn for future studies, for instance, being well-powered, replicating previous findings, examining and reporting relevant indices (e.g., effect-sizes or number needed to treat, NNT), investigating aspects of cost-effectiveness, controlling for confounding factors systematically, applying longitudinal assessments and using standardized assessments (e.g., in neuroimaging studies; see Fig. 1).

Beside the quality related criteria for biomarker validation, research on biomarkers is complicated by the fact, that it relies on hypotheses and theories that are based on the current descriptive classification systems, and are also tested on populations which have been stratified using these systems. The Research Domain

Criteria initiative [RDoC; 206] aimed to offer alternative criteria for classification of (mental) disorders based on a biological system level approach, reaching from genetic aspects to behaviour. Although this approach might be helpful to advance the field of biomarker research, it is also problematic in its own right [207, 208]. One critical aspect of note is that while NDDs are thought to arise from biological factors, such as genetic, metabolic or neural abnormalities, biological systems interact with each other and with external, environmental, social or psychological factors, which can in turn influence, exacerbate or intercept disorder specific impairments (see e.g. [209, 210]). Factors that might influence NDDs are for instance, environmental exposures (such as toxins or living evnironments), comorbidities, access to help systems and health services as well as societal resource, familial coping strategies and resources, cultural and societal requirements and definitions of healthy functioning, in addition (see e.g. [211, 212]). That is, biological mechanisms associated with NDDs interact dynamically with each other and within a psychosocial context. Future research will need to consider the dynamic interplay between biological (brain and body) and social mechanisms (such as stress and stigma) when exploring the origins of NDD in specific conditions and contexts. This approach calls for closer collaboration with patients to improve the relevance of concepts and methodologies, the development of tools for assessing social and biological factors in diverse naturalistic settings, innovative analytical methods to study these interactions (including emergent properties), and cross-condition designs to identify mechanisms that are common across various conditions or specific to particular subgroups.

Understandably, the idea of an objectively measureable factor in the face of complex, multifaceted etiology of NDD is attractive, but as of now, the predictive power of genetic or neuroimaging based evidence is small [205]. To complicate things, particularly neuroimaging and neurophysiological measures are not only influenced by heterogeneity within and across NDDs, but also by factors such as age and sex (e.g. [96]) or the method used (neuroimaging protocols, tasks or comparison group). Moreover, each individual may have a unique profile of biomarkers (a particular challenge for group-level research methods [6]), and a multidisciplinary approach might be required for comprehensive assessment and treatment planning. Lastly, it must be noted that biomarkers together with multifaceted data—such as risk and resilience factors—can only inform of the probability with which a disorder might develop or be present, while a thorough clinical assessment with standard diagnostic tools is indispensable.

Research into biomarkers as a field is relatively young, and has focused largely on identification of mechanisms underlying disorders [213]. Yet there are diagnostic biomarkers that are promising candidates for future investigations. As previously discussed, for biomarkers to contribute valuable information to the clinical decision-making process, they should meet various criteria, including objective and reliable measurability, quantifiability, and scalability [11, 213, 214] (see Fig. 2 for a summary of promises and challenges related to biomarker research). Quantifiable and objective measures have another important aspect: they might contribute to access of individuals to societal support systems through clear-cut criteria, rather

Fig. 2 Biomarkers between promises and pitfalls

than subjective evaluations, making it easier and timelier for children and families to arrive at helpful and specialized schools, care, jobs or living arrangements in later life. The hope is that, as our understanding of these biomarkers continues to advance, so too will our ability to provide targeted and effective interventions for neurodiverse individuals.

Ethical aspects. So far, we have reviewed scientific advantages and disadvantages regarding research into biomarkers to NDDs. Beyond scientific evaluation, there are also ethical aspects to be considered (see e.g. [215–217]). One marked argument is that biomarker for NDD might lead to discrimination and stigmatization. Particularly, risk biomarkers aim to identify affected individuals early, at best before disorders become apparent. There are at least two implications to be considered: one the one hand, biomarkers are probabilistic and thus, will produce a section of false positive and false negative cases, on the other, implication for clinical practice have to be discussed and outlined. That is, in case a biomarker for ADHD or ASD is present and identified early in a child, there have to be implications as to which measures should be taken next. For instance, if a child were to be identified at high risk for ADHD at an early age, would this imply earlier treatment? Which nature of treatment should then be taken? Moreover, it is questionable what kind of effect this would have on the micro and macro systems in which the child develops (care-takers, teachers, family), their behaviour towards the child, or the child itself. On the one hand, this might lead to stigmatization and isolation (e.g. [218]), potentially (premature or preventional) medication or other treatments, an identification with an at-risk personality, such as beliefs in self-efficacy [219, 220]. On the other hand, it might lead to timely and targeted medical and societal support, attention and societal ressources, or positive and empowering identification in later life (celebrating neurodiversity and positive aspects of ASD and ADHD).

Another issue, which we have briefly touched upon previously, is the translation of biomarker research outside the clinical realm, for instance, into law. This is important because, translation into medical or social practice is dependent on scientific and political decisions and available laws to guide these practices and make societal ressources available where needed. Therefore, there is a responsibility of scientists to communicate biomarker research intricately and accurately to avoid overgeneralization and simplification during the process of translation from science into public opinion. Lastly, commercialization of biomarkers must be observed carefully (e.g. www.23andme.com; [221]).

At face value, the promise of biomarkers as single facets being able to determine the presence or absence of disorders, such as NDDs, with high certainty, might suggest that biological factors by themselves are able to explain the multifaceted presentation of NDDs. While this is not the current scientific opinion, reductionist approaches must be avoided and research approaches including the examination of multiple factors must be weighted carefully: "biology is not destiny: biology provides information about potentials" [216].

5 Final Conclusion

In conclusion, methodological challenges in neuroimaging biomarker discovery include a predominant focus on identifying brain alterations rather than pinpointing actionable biomarkers. While understanding biological mechanisms behind biomarkers is ideal, validation should take precedence, akin to how some effective drugs were used before fully understanding their mechanics [213]. Due to NDD's heterogeneous nature, no biomarker currently achieves the 80% sensitivity and 80% specificity standard. Challenges such as varied imaging techniques, the disorder's complexity, and confounding factors like comorbidities hinder the identification of a definitive biomarker. Further, different developmental presentations such as of ADHD emerge over the lifespan: in ADHD adults, the symptom landscape shifts with inattention persists, hyperactivity diminishing, and mood disorders becoming more prevalent [222]. This evolution suggests that for instance while there is a foundational neural framework for ADHD, specific affected brain regions may differ between children and adults. Historically, research has primarily focused on either childhood or adult ADHD, rarely bridging the two. As a result, even with numerous studies, clear markers for both age groups remain elusive. To truly grasp for instance the neurobiological underpinnings of NDD, it is imperative to delineate both shared and age-specific neural patterns. Additionally, the variability in brain development complicates case-control comparisons, especially during youth, making it difficult to decipher if observed patterns signal delays or accelerations in neurodevelopment [25, 223]. Recent machine learning advances help chart normal development trajectories and offer more predictive individual-level statistics akin to growth charts as used in pediatrics [10]. Such techniques also assist in combining multi-faceted biological data, which might expedite biomarker identification [24].

References

1. Buitelaar J, Bölte S, Brandeis D, Caye A, Christmann N, Cortese S, Coghill D, Faraone SV, Franke B, Gleitz M, Greven CU, Kooij S, Leffa DT, Rommelse N, Newcorn JH, Polanczyk GV, Rohde LA, Simonoff E, Stein M, Vitiello B, Yazgan Y, Roesler M, Doepfner M, Banaschewski T (2022) Toward precision medicine in ADHD. Front Behav Neurosci 16:900981. https://doi.org/10.3389/fnbeh.2022.900981
2. Loth E, Spooren W, Ham LM, Isaac MB, Auriche-Benichou C, Banaschewski T, Baron-Cohen S, Broich K, Bölte S, Bourgeron T, Charman T, Collier D, de Andres-Trelles F, Durston S, Ecker C, Elferink A, Haberkamp M, Hemmings R, Johnson MH, Jones EJH, Khwaja OS, Lenton S, Mason L, Mantua V, Meyer-Lindenberg A, Lombardo MV, O'Dwyer L, Okamoto K, Pandina GJ, Pani L, Persico AM, Simonoff E, Tauscher-Wisniewski S, Llinares-Garcia J, Vamvakas S, Williams S, Buitelaar JK, Murphy DGM (2016) Identification and validation of biomarkers for autism spectrum disorders. Nat Rev Drug Discov 15:70–73. https://doi.org/10.1038/nrd.2015.7
3. Biomarkers Definitions Working Group (2001) Biomarkers and surrogate endpoints: preferred definitions and conceptual framework. Clin Pharmacol Ther 69:89–95. https://doi.org/10.1067/mcp.2001.113989
4. Insel T, Cuthbert B, Garvey M, Heinssen R, Pine DS, Quinn K, Sanislow C, Wang P (2010) Research domain criteria (RDoC): toward a new classification framework for research on mental disorders. Am J Psychiatr 167:748–751. https://doi.org/10.1176/appi.ajp.2010.09091379
5. Stephenson D, Hill D, Cedarbaum JM, Tome M, Vamvakas S, Romero K, Conrado DJ, Dexter DT, Seibyl J, Jennings D, Nicholas T, Matthews D, Xie Z, Imam S, Maguire P, Russell D, Gordon MF, Stebbins GT, Somer E, Gallagher J, Roach A, Basseches P, Grosset D, Marek K (2019) The qualification of an enrichment biomarker for clinical trials targeting early stages of Parkinson's disease. J Park Dis 9:553–563. https://doi.org/10.3233/JPD-191648
6. Loth E, Ahmad J, Chatham C, López B, Carter B, Crawley D, Oakley B, Hayward H, Cooke J, San José Cáceres A, Bzdok D, Jones E, Charman T, Beckmann C, Bourgeron T, Toro R, Buitelaar J, Murphy D, Dumas G (2021) The meaning of significant mean group differences for biomarker discovery. PLoS Comput Biol 17:e1009477. https://doi.org/10.1371/journal.pcbi.1009477
7. English PA, Williams JA, Martini J-F, Motzer RJ, Valota O, Buller RE (2016) A case for the use of receiver operating characteristic analysis of potential clinical efficacy biomarkers in advanced renal cell carcinoma. Future Oncol Lond Engl 12:175–182. https://doi.org/10.2217/fon.15.290
8. Geomini P, Kruitwagen R, Bremer GL, Cnossen J, Mol BWJ (2009) The accuracy of risk scores in predicting ovarian malignancy: a systematic review. Obstet Gynecol 113:384–394. https://doi.org/10.1097/AOG.0b013e318195ad17
9. McPartland JC (2016) Considerations in biomarker development for neurodevelopmental disorders. Curr Opin Neurol 29:118–122. https://doi.org/10.1097/WCO.0000000000000300
10. Marquand AF, Kia SM, Zabihi M, Wolfers T, Buitelaar JK, Beckmann CF (2019) Conceptualizing mental disorders as deviations from normative functioning. Mol Psychiatr 24:1415–1424. https://doi.org/10.1038/s41380-019-0441-1
11. García-Gutiérrez MS, Navarrete F, Sala F, Gasparyan A, Austrich-Olivares A, Manzanares J (2020) Biomarkers in psychiatry: concept, definition, types and relevance to the clinical reality. Front Psychiatr 11:432. https://doi.org/10.3389/fpsyt.2020.00432
12. Thapar A, Cooper M, Rutter M (2017) Neurodevelopmental disorders. Lancet Psychiatr 4:339–346
13. World Health Organization (2019) International classification of diseases, Eleventh Revision (ICD-11). Available Rom Httpsicd Who Intbrowse11

14. Polanczyk GV, Willcutt EG, Salum GA, Kieling C, Rohde LA (2014) ADHD prevalence estimates across three decades: an updated systematic review and meta-regression analysis. Int J Epidemiol 43:434–442. https://doi.org/10.1093/ije/dyt261
15. Gillberg C, Gillberg IC, Rasmussen P, Kadesjö B, Söderström H, Råstam M, Johnson M, Rothenberger A, Niklasson L (2004) Co-existing disorders in ADHD—Implications for diagnosis and intervention. Eur Child Adolesc Psychiatr 13(Suppl 1):I80-92. https://doi.org/10.1007/s00787-004-1008-4
16. Gnanavel S, Sharma P, Kaushal P, Hussain S (2019) Attention deficit hyperactivity disorder and comorbidity: a review of literature. World J Clin Cases 7:2420–2426. https://doi.org/10.12998/wjcc.v7.i17.2420
17. Jacob S, Wolff JJ, Steinbach MS, Doyle CB, Kumar V, Elison JT (2019) Neurodevelopmental heterogeneity and computational approaches for understanding autism. Transl Psychiatr 9:63. https://doi.org/10.1038/s41398-019-0390-0
18. Lord C, Elsabbagh M, Baird G, Veenstra-Vanderweele J (2018) Autism spectrum disorder. Lancet Lond Engl 392:508–520. https://doi.org/10.1016/S0140-6736(18)31129-2
19. Zeidan J, Fombonne E, Scorah J, Ibrahim A, Durkin MS, Saxena S, Yusuf A, Shih A, Elsabbagh M (2022) Global prevalence of autism: a systematic review update. Autism Res 15:778–790. https://doi.org/10.1002/aur.2696
20. Simonoff E, Pickles A, Charman T, Chandler S, Loucas T, Baird G (2008) Psychiatric disorders in children with autism spectrum disorders: prevalence, comorbidity, and associated factors in a population-derived sample. J Am Acad Child Adolesc Psychiatr 47:921–929. https://doi.org/10.1097/CHI.0b013e318179964f
21. Fernandes BS, Williams LM, Steiner J, Leboyer M, Carvalho AF, Berk M (2017) The new field of 'precision psychiatry.' BMC Med 15:80. https://doi.org/10.1186/s12916-017-0849-x
22. Bethlehem RAI, Seidlitz J, White SR, Vogel JW, Anderson KM, Adamson C, Adler S, Alexopoulos GS, Anagnostou E, Areces-Gonzalez A, Astle DE, Auyeung B, Ayub M, Bae J, Ball G, Baron-Cohen S, Beare R, Bedford SA, Benegal V, Beyer F, Blangero J, Blesa Cábez M, Boardman JP, Borzage M, Bosch-Bayard JF, Bourke N, Calhoun VD, Chakravarty MM, Chen C, Chertavian C, Chetelat G, Chong YS, Cole JH, Corvin A, Costantino M, Courchesne E, Crivello F, Cropley VL, Crosbie J, Crossley N, Delarue M, Delorme R, Desrivieres S, Devenyi GA, Di Biase MA, Dolan R, Donald KA, Donohoe G, Dunlop K, Edwards AD, Elison JT, Ellis CT, Elman JA, Eyler L, Fair DA, Feczko E, Fletcher PC, Fonagy P, Franz CE, Galan-Garcia L, Gholipour A, Giedd J, Gilmore JH, Glahn DC, Goodyer IM, Grant PE, Groenewold NA, Gunning FM, Gur RE, Gur RC, Hammill CF, Hansson O, Hedden T, Heinz A, Henson RN, Heuer K, Hoare J, Holla B, Holmes AJ, Holt R, Huang H, Im K, Ipser J, Jack CR, Jackowski AP, Jia T, Johnson KA, Jones PB, Jones DT, Kahn RS, Karlsson H, Karlsson L, Kawashima R, Kelley EA, Kern S, Kim KW, Kitzbichler MG, Kremen WS, Lalonde F, Landeau B, Lee S, Lerch J, Lewis JD, Li J, Liao W, Liston C, Lombardo MV, Lv J, Lynch C, Mallard TT, Marcelis M, Markello RD, Mathias SR, Mazoyer B, McGuire P, Meaney MJ, Mechelli A, Medic N, Misic B, Morgan SE, Mothersill D, Nigg J, Ong MQW, Ortinau C, Ossenkoppele R, Ouyang M, Palaniyappan L, Paly L, Pan PM, Pantelis C, Park MM, Paus T, Pausova Z, Paz-Linares D, Pichet Binette A, Pierce K, Qian X, Qiu J, Qiu A, Raznahan A, Rittman T, Rodrigue A, Rollins CK, Romero-Garcia R, Ronan L, Rosenberg MD, Rowitch DH, Salum GA, Satterthwaite TD, Schaare HL, Schachar RJ, Schultz AP, Schumann G, Schöll M, Sharp D, Shinohara RT, Skoog I, Smyser CD, Sperling RA, Stein DJ, Stolicyn A, Suckling J, Sullivan G, Taki Y, Thyreau B, Toro R, Traut N, Tsvetanov KA, Turk-Browne NB, Tuulari JJ, Tzourio C, Vachon-Presseau É, Valdes-Sosa MJ, Valdes-Sosa PA, Valk SL, van Amelsvoort T, Vandekar SN, Vasung L, Victoria LW, Villeneuve S, Villringer A, Vértes PE, Wagstyl K, Wang YS, Warfield SK, Warrier V, Westman E, Westwater ML, Whalley HC, Witte AV, Yang N, Yeo B, Yun H, Zalesky A, Zar HJ, Zettergren A, Zhou JH, Ziauddeen H, Zugman A, Zuo XN, Bullmore ET, Alexander-Bloch AF (2022) Brain charts for the human lifespan. Nature 604:525–533. https://doi.org/10.1038/s41586-022-04554-y

23. Rutherford S, Barkema P, Tso IF, Sripada C, Beckmann CF, Ruhe HG, Marquand AF (2023) Evidence for embracing normative modeling. eLife 12:e85082. https://doi.org/10.7554/eLife.85082
24. Holz NE, Floris DL, Llera A, Aggensteiner PM, Kia SM, Wolfers T, Baumeister S, Böttinger B, Glennon JC, Hoekstra PJ, Dietrich A, Saam MC, Schulze UME, Lythgoe DJ, Williams SCR, Santosh P, Rosa-Justicia M, Bargallo N, Castro-Fornieles J, Arango C, Penzol MJ, Walitza S, Meyer-Lindenberg A, Zwiers M, Franke B, Buitelaar J, Naaijen J, Brandeis D, Beckmann C, Banaschewski T, Marquand AF (2023) Age-related brain deviations and aggression. Psychol Med 53:4012–4021. https://doi.org/10.1017/S003329172200068X
25. Holz NE, Zabihi M, Kia SM, Monninger M, Aggensteiner P-M, Siehl S, Floris DL, Bokde ALW, Desrivières S, Flor H, Grigis A, Garavan H, Gowland P, Heinz A, Brühl R, Martinot J-L, Martinot M-LP, Orfanos DP, Paus T, Poustka L, Fröhner JH, Smolka MN, Vaidya N, Walter H, Whelan R, Schumann G, Meyer-Lindenberg A, Brandeis D, Buitelaar JK, Nees F, Beckmann C, Banaschewski T, Marquand AF (2023) A stable and replicable neural signature of lifespan adversity in the adult brain. Nat Neurosci 1–10. https://doi.org/10.1038/s41593-023-01410-8
26. Sahin M, Jones SR, Sweeney JA, Berry-Kravis E, Connors BW, Ewen JB, Hartman AL, Levin AR, Potter WZ, Mamounas LA (2018) Discovering translational biomarkers in neurodevelopmental disorders. Nat Rev Drug Discov. https://doi.org/10.1038/d41573-018-00010-7
27. Bos DJ, Oranje B, Achterberg M, Vlaskamp C, Ambrosino S, de Reus MA, van den Heuvel MP, Rombouts SARB, Durston S (2017) Structural and functional connectivity in children and adolescents with and without attention deficit/hyperactivity disorder. J Child Psychol Psychiatr 58:810–818. https://doi.org/10.1111/jcpp.12712
28. de Lacy N, Kodish I, Rachakonda S, Calhoun VD (2018) Novel in silico multivariate mapping of intrinsic and anticorrelated connectivity to neurocognitive functional maps supports the maturational hypothesis of ADHD. Hum Brain Mapp 39:3449–3467. https://doi.org/10.1002/hbm.24187
29. Plichta MM, Scheres A (2014) Ventral-striatal responsiveness during reward anticipation in ADHD and its relation to trait impulsivity in the healthy population: a meta-analytic review of the fMRI literature. Neurosci Biobehav Rev 38:125–134. https://doi.org/10.1016/j.neubiorev.2013.07.012
30. Hart H, Chantiluke K, Cubillo AI, Smith AB, Simmons A, Brammer MJ, Marquand AF, Rubia K (2014) Pattern classification of response inhibition in ADHD: toward the development of neurobiological markers for ADHD. Hum Brain Mapp 35:3083–3094. https://doi.org/10.1002/hbm.22386
31. Rubia K, Alegria A, Brinson H (2014) Imaging the ADHD brain: disorder-specificity, medication effects and clinical translation. Expert Rev Neurother 14:519–538. https://doi.org/10.1586/14737175.2014.907526
32. Samea F, Soluki S, Nejati V, Zarei M, Cortese S, Eickhoff SB, Tahmasian M, Eickhoff CR (2019) Brain alterations in children/adolescents with ADHD revisited: a neuroimaging meta-analysis of 96 structural and functional studies. Neurosci Biobehav Rev 100:1–8. https://doi.org/10.1016/j.neubiorev.2019.02.011
33. Itami S, Uno H (2002) Orbitofrontal cortex dysfunction in attention-deficit hyperactivity disorder revealed by reversal and extinction tasks. NeuroReport 13:2453–2457. https://doi.org/10.1097/00001756-200212200-00016
34. Max JE, Fox PT, Lancaster JL, Kochunov P, Mathews K, Manes FF, Robertson BAM, Arndt S, Robin DA, Lansing AE (2002) Putamen lesions and the development of attention-deficit/hyperactivity symptomatology. J Am Acad Child Adolesc Psychiatr 41:563–571. https://doi.org/10.1097/00004583-200205000-00014
35. Gao Y, Shuai D, Bu X, Hu X, Tang S, Zhang L, Li H, Hu X, Lu L, Gong Q, Huang X (2019) Impairments of large-scale functional networks in attention-deficit/hyperactivity disorder: a meta-analysis of resting-state functional connectivity. Psychol Med 49:2475–2485. https://doi.org/10.1017/S003329171900237X

36. Sutcubasi B, Metin B, Kurban MK, Metin ZE, Beser B, Sonuga-Barke E (2020) Resting-state network dysconnectivity in ADHD: a system-neuroscience-based meta-analysis. World J Biol Psychiatry Off J World Fed Soc Biol Psychiatr 21:662–672. https://doi.org/10.1080/15622975.2020.1775889
37. Cortese S, Aoki YY, Itahashi T, Castellanos FX, Eickhoff SB (2021) Systematic review and meta-analysis: resting-state functional magnetic resonance imaging studies of attention-deficit/hyperactivity disorder. J Am Acad Child Adolesc Psychiatr 60:61–75. https://doi.org/10.1016/j.jaac.2020.08.014
38. Hoogman M, Bralten J, Hibar DP, Mennes M, Zwiers MP, Schweren LSJ, van Hulzen KJE, Medland SE, Shumskaya E, Jahanshad N, de Zeeuw P, Szekely E, Sudre G, Wolfers T, Onnink AMH, Dammers JT, Mostert JC, Vives-Gilabert Y, Kohls G, Oberwelland E, Seitz J, Schulte-Rüther M, Ambrosino S, Doyle AE, Høvik MF, Dramsdahl M, Tamm L, van Erp TGM, Dale A, Schork A, Conzelmann A, Zierhut K, Baur R, McCarthy H, Yoncheva YN, Cubillo A, Chantiluke K, Mehta MA, Paloyelis Y, Hohmann S, Baumeister S, Bramati I, Mattos P, Tovar-Moll F, Douglas P, Banaschewski T, Brandeis D, Kuntsi J, Asherson P, Rubia K, Kelly C, Martino AD, Milham MP, Castellanos FX, Frodl T, Zentis M, Lesch K-P, Reif A, Pauli P, Jernigan TL, Haavik J, Plessen KJ, Lundervold AJ, Hugdahl K, Seidman LJ, Biederman J, Rommelse N, Heslenfeld DJ, Hartman CA, Hoekstra PJ, Oosterlaan J, von Polier G, Konrad K, Vilarroya O, Ramos-Quiroga JA, Soliva JC, Durston S, Buitelaar JK, Faraone SV, Shaw P, Thompson PM, Franke B (2017) Subcortical brain volume differences in participants with attention deficit hyperactivity disorder in children and adults: a cross-sectional mega-analysis. Lancet Psychiatr 4:310–319. https://doi.org/10.1016/S2215-0366(17)30049-4
39. Hoogman M, Muetzel R, Guimaraes JP, Shumskaya E, Mennes M, Zwiers MP, Jahanshad N, Sudre G, Wolfers T, Earl EA, Soliva Vila JC, Vives-Gilabert Y, Khadka S, Novotny SE, Hartman CA, Heslenfeld DJ, Schweren LJS, Ambrosino S, Oranje B, de Zeeuw P, Chaim-Avancini TM, Rosa PGP, Zanetti MV, Malpas CB, Kohls G, von Polier GG, Seitz J, Biederman J, Doyle AE, Dale AM, van Erp TGM, Epstein JN, Jernigan TL, Baur-Streubel R, Ziegler GC, Zierhut KC, Schrantee A, Høvik MF, Lundervold AJ, Kelly C, McCarthy H, Skokauskas N, O'Gorman Tuura RL, Calvo A, Lera-Miguel S, Nicolau R, Chantiluke KC, Christakou A, Vance A, Cercignani M, Gabel MC, Asherson P, Baumeister S, Brandeis D, Hohmann S, Bramati IE, Tovar-Moll F, Fallgatter AJ, Kardatzki B, Schwarz L, Anikin A, Baranov A, Gogberashvili T, Kapilushniy D, Solovieva A, El Marroun H, White T, Karkashadze G, Namazova-Baranova L, Ethofer T, Mattos P, Banaschewski T, Coghill D, Plessen KJ, Kuntsi J, Mehta MA, Paloyelis Y, Harrison NA, Bellgrove MA, Silk TJ, Cubillo AI, Rubia K, Lazaro L, Brem S, Walitza S, Frodl T, Zentis M, Castellanos FX, Yoncheva YN, Haavik J, Reneman L, Conzelmann A, Lesch K-P, Pauli P, Reif A, Tamm L, Konrad K, Oberwelland Weiss E, Busatto GF, Louza MR, Durston S, Hoekstra PJ, Oosterlaan J, Stevens MC, Ramos-Quiroga JA, Vilarroya O, Fair DA, Nigg JT, Thompson PM, Buitelaar JK, Faraone SV, Shaw P, Tiemeier H, Bralten J, Franke B (2019) Brain imaging of the cortex in ADHD: a coordinated analysis of large-scale clinical and population-based samples. Am J Psychiatry 176:531–542. https://doi.org/10.1176/appi.ajp.2019.18091033
40. Hodgkins P, Shaw M, Coghill D, Hechtman L (2012) Amfetamine and methylphenidate medications for attention-deficit/hyperactivity disorder: complementary treatment options. Eur Child Adolesc Psychiatr 21:477–492. https://doi.org/10.1007/s00787-012-0286-5
41. Liddle EB, Hollis C, Batty MJ, Groom MJ, Totman JJ, Liotti M, Scerif G, Liddle PF (2011) Task-related default mode network modulation and inhibitory control in ADHD: effects of motivation and methylphenidate: default mode network modulation in ADHD. J Child Psychol Psychiatr 52:761–771. https://doi.org/10.1111/j.1469-7610.2010.02333.x
42. Duval F, Erb A, Mokrani M, Weiss T, Carcangiu R (2021) First-dose methylphenidate-induced changes in the anti-saccade task performance and outcome in adults with attention-deficit/hyperactivity disorder. Psychiatr Res Clin Pract 3:146–152. https://doi.org/10.1176/appi.prcp.20210010

43. Rubia K, Halari R, Cubillo A, Mohammad A-M, Brammer M, Taylor E (2009) Methylphenidate normalises activation and functional connectivity deficits in attention and motivation networks in medication-naïve children with ADHD during a rewarded continuous performance task. Neuropharmacology 57:640–652. https://doi.org/10.1016/j.neuropharm.2009.08.013
44. Alegria AA, Wulff M, Brinson H, Barker GJ, Norman LJ, Brandeis D, Stahl D, David AS, Taylor E, Giampietro V, Rubia K (2017) Real-time f MRI neurofeedback in adolescents with attention deficit hyperactivity disorder. Hum Brain Mapp 38:3190–3209. https://doi.org/10.1002/hbm.23584
45. Alyagon U, Shahar H, Hadar A, Barnea-Ygael N, Lazarovits A, Shalev H, Zangen A (2020) Alleviation of ADHD symptoms by non-invasive right prefrontal stimulation is correlated with EEG activity. NeuroImage Clin 26:102206. https://doi.org/10.1016/j.nicl.2020.102206
46. Cubillo A, Smith AB, Barrett N, Giampietro V, Brammer M, Simmons A, Rubia K (2014) Drug-specific laterality effects on frontal lobe activation of atomoxetine and methylphenidate in attention deficit hyperactivity disorder boys during working memory. Psychol Med 44:633–646. https://doi.org/10.1017/S0033291713000676
47. Bouziane C, Filatova OG, Schrantee A, Caan MWA, Vos FM, Reneman L (2019) White matter by diffusion MRI following methylphenidate treatment: a randomized control trial in males with attention-deficit/hyperactivity disorder. Radiology 293:186–192. https://doi.org/10.1148/radiol.2019182528
48. Michelini G, Norman LJ, Shaw P, Loo SK (2022) Treatment biomarkers for ADHD: taking stock and moving forward. Transl Psychiatry 12:444. https://doi.org/10.1038/s41398-022-02207-2
49. Clifford SM, Hudry K, Elsabbagh M, Charman T, Johnson MH, BASIS Team (2013) Temperament in the first 2 years of life in infants at high-risk for autism spectrum disorders. J Autism Dev Disord 43:673–686. https://doi.org/10.1007/s10803-012-1612-y
50. Thye MD, Bednarz HM, Herringshaw AJ, Sartin EB, Kana RK (2018) The impact of atypical sensory processing on social impairments in autism spectrum disorder. Dev Cogn Neurosci 29:151–167. https://doi.org/10.1016/j.dcn.2017.04.010
51. Moessnang C, Baumeister S, Tillmann J, Goyard D, Charman T, Ambrosino S, Baron-Cohen S, Beckmann C, Bölte S, Bours C, Crawley D, Dell'Acqua F, Durston S, Ecker C, Frouin V, Hayward H, Holt R, Johnson M, Jones E, Lai M-C, Lombardo MV, Mason L, Oldenhinkel M, Persico A, Cáceres ASJ, Spooren W, Loth E, Murphy DGM, Buitelaar JK, Banaschewski T, Brandeis D, Tost H, Meyer-Lindenberg A, EU-AIMS LEAP group (2020) Social brain activation during mentalizing in a large autism cohort: the Longitudinal European Autism Project. Mol Autism 11:17. https://doi.org/10.1186/s13229-020-0317-x
52. Parellada M, Andreu-Bernabeu Á, Burdeus M, San José Cáceres A, Urbiola E, Carpenter LL, Kraguljac NV, McDonald WM, Nemeroff CB, Rodriguez CI, Widge AS, State MW, Sanders SJ (2023) In search of biomarkers to guide interventions in autism spectrum disorder: a systematic review. Am J Psychiatr 180:23–40. https://doi.org/10.1176/appi.ajp.21100992
53. Baumeister S, Moessnang C, Bast N, Hohmann S, Aggensteiner P, Kaiser A, Tillmann J, Goyard D, Charman T, Ambrosino S, Baron-Cohen S, Beckmann C, Bölte S, Bourgeron T, Rausch A, Crawley D, Dell'Acqua F, Dumas G, Durston S, Ecker C, Floris DL, Frouin V, Hayward H, Holt R, Johnson MH, Jones EJH, Lai M-C, Lombardo MV, Mason L, Oakley B, Oldehinkel M, Persico AM, Cáceres ASJ, Wolfers T, Loth E, Murphy DGM, Buitelaar JK, Tost H, Meyer-Lindenberg A, Banaschewski T, Brandeis D, Group the E-AL (2023) Processing of social and monetary rewards in autism spectrum disorders. Br J Psychiatry 1–12. https://doi.org/10.1192/bjp.2022.157
54. Tang S, Sun N, Floris DL, Zhang X, Di Martino A, Yeo BTT (2020) Reconciling dimensional and categorical models of autism heterogeneity: a brain connectomics and behavioral study. Biol Psychiatr 87:1071–1082. https://doi.org/10.1016/j.biopsych.2019.11.009
55. Li Q, Zhao W, Palaniyappan L, Guo S (2023) Atypical hemispheric lateralization of brain function and structure in autism: a comprehensive meta-analysis study. Psychol Med 1–12. https://doi.org/10.1017/S0033291723000181

56. Floris DL, Wolfers T, Zabihi M, Holz NE, Zwiers MP, Charman T, Tillmann J, Ecker C, Dell'Acqua F, Banaschewski T, Moessnang C, Baron-Cohen S, Holt R, Durston S, Loth E, Murphy DGM, Marquand A, Buitelaar JK, Beckmann CF, EU-AIMS Longitudinal European Autism Project Group (2021) Atypical brain asymmetry in autism-a candidate for clinically meaningful stratification. Biol Psychiatr Cogn Neurosci Neuroimaging 6:802–812. https://doi.org/10.1016/j.bpsc.2020.08.008
57. Pretzsch CM, Ecker C (2023) Structural neuroimaging phenotypes and associated molecular and genomic underpinnings in autism: a review. Front Neurosci 17:1172779. https://doi.org/10.3389/fnins.2023.1172779
58. Khundrakpam BS, Lewis JD, Kostopoulos P, Carbonell F, Evans AC (2017) Cortical thickness abnormalities in autism spectrum disorders through late childhood, adolescence, and adulthood: a large-scale MRI study. Cereb Cortex N Y N 27:1721–1731. https://doi.org/10.1093/cercor/bhx038
59. Tang G, Gudsnuk K, Kuo S-H, Cotrina ML, Rosoklija G, Sosunov A, Sonders MS, Kanter E, Castagna C, Yamamoto A, Yue Z, Arancio O, Peterson BS, Champagne F, Dwork AJ, Goldman J, Sulzer D (2014) Loss of mTOR-dependent macroautophagy causes autistic-like synaptic pruning deficits. Neuron 83:1131–1143. https://doi.org/10.1016/j.neuron.2014.07.040
60. Lewis JD, Elman JL (2008) Growth-related neural reorganization and the autism phenotype: a test of the hypothesis that altered brain growth leads to altered connectivity. Dev Sci 11:135–155. https://doi.org/10.1111/j.1467-7687.2007.00634.x
61. Neufeld J, Kuja-Halkola R, Mevel K, Cauvet É, Fransson P, Bölte S (2018) Alterations in resting state connectivity along the autism trait continuum: a twin study. Mol Psychiatr 23:1659–1665. https://doi.org/10.1038/mp.2017.160
62. Jensen AR, Lane AL, Werner BA, McLees SE, Fletcher TS, Frye RE (2022) Modern biomarkers for autism spectrum disorder: future directions. Mol Diagn Ther 26:483–495. https://doi.org/10.1007/s40291-022-00600-7
63. Yang D, Pelphrey KA, Sukhodolsky DG, Crowley MJ, Dayan E, Dvornek NC, Venkataraman A, Duncan J, Staib L, Ventola P (2016) Brain responses to biological motion predict treatment outcome in young children with autism. Transl Psychiatr 6:e948–e948. https://doi.org/10.1038/tp.2016.213
64. Carpenter KLH, Major S, Tallman C, Chen LW, Franz L, Sun J, Kurtzberg J, Song A, Dawson G (2019) White matter tract changes associated with clinical improvement in an open-label trial assessing autologous umbilical cord blood for treatment of young children with autism. Stem Cells Transl Med 8:138–147. https://doi.org/10.1002/sctm.18-0251
65. Ewen JB, Sweeney JA, Potter WZ (2019) Conceptual, regulatory and strategic imperatives in the early days of EEG-based biomarker validation for neurodevelopmental disabilities. Front Integr Neurosci 13:45. https://doi.org/10.3389/fnint.2019.00045
66. Shan J, Gu Y, Zhang J, Hu X, Wu H, Yuan T, Zhao D (2023) A scoping review of physiological biomarkers in autism. Front Neurosci 17:1269880. https://doi.org/10.3389/fnins.2023.1269880
67. Arns M, Conners CK, Kraemer HC (2013) A decade of EEG theta/beta ratio research in ADHD: a meta-analysis. J Atten Disord 17:374–383. https://doi.org/10.1177/1087054712460087
68. Cowley BU, Juurmaa K, Palomäki J (2022) Reduced power in fronto-parietal theta EEG linked to impaired attention-sampling in adult ADHD. eNeuro 9:ENEURO.0028-21.2021. https://doi.org/10.1523/ENEURO.0028-21.2021
69. Hale TS, Smalley SL, Walshaw PD, Hanada G, Macion J, McCracken JT, McGough JJ, Loo SK (2010) Atypical EEG beta asymmetry in adults with ADHD. Neuropsychologia 48:3532–3539. https://doi.org/10.1016/j.neuropsychologia.2010.08.002
70. Hermens DF, Kohn MR, Clarke SD, Gordon E, Williams LM (2005) Sex differences in adolescent ADHD: findings from concurrent EEG and EDA. Clin Neurophysiol Off J Int Fed Clin Neurophysiol 116:1455–1463. https://doi.org/10.1016/j.clinph.2005.02.012

71. Hobbs MJ, Clarke AR, Barry RJ, McCarthy R, Selikowitz M (2007) EEG abnormalities in adolescent males with AD/HD. Clin Neurophysiol Off J Int Fed Clin Neurophysiol 118:363–371. https://doi.org/10.1016/j.clinph.2006.10.013
72. Kamida A, Shimabayashi K, Oguri M, Takamori T, Ueda N, Koyanagi Y, Sannomiya N, Nagira H, Ikunishi S, Hattori Y, Sato K, Fukuda C, Hirooka Y, Maegaki Y (2016) EEG power spectrum analysis in children with ADHD. Yonago Acta Med 59:169–173
73. Chen C, Yang H, Du Y, Zhai G, Xiong H, Yao D, Xu P, Gong J, Yin G, Li F (2021) Altered functional connectivity in children with ADHD revealed by scalp EEG: an ERP study. Neural Plast 2021:6615384. https://doi.org/10.1155/2021/6615384
74. Shahaf G, Fisher T, Aharon-Peretz J, Pratt H (2015) Comprehensive analysis suggests simple processes underlying EEG/ERP—demonstration with the go/no-go paradigm in ADHD. J Neurosci Methods 239:183–193. https://doi.org/10.1016/j.jneumeth.2014.10.016
75. Doehnert M, Brandeis D, Schneider G, Drechsler R, Steinhausen H-C (2013) A neurophysiological marker of impaired preparation in an 11-year follow-up study of attention-deficit/hyperactivity disorder (ADHD). J Child Psychol Psychiatr 54:260–270. https://doi.org/10.1111/j.1469-7610.2012.02572.x
76. Clarke AR, Barry RJ, Johnstone S (2020) Resting state EEG power research in attention-deficit/hyperactivity disorder: a review update. Clin Neurophysiol 131:1463–1479. https://doi.org/10.1016/j.clinph.2020.03.029
77. Kean JD, Kaufman J, Lomas J, Goh A, White D, Simpson D, Scholey A, Singh H, Sarris J, Zangara A, Stough C (2015) A randomized controlled trial investigating the effects of a special extract of bacopa monnieri (CDRI 08) on hyperactivity and inattention in male children and adolescents: BACHI study protocol (ANZCTRN12612000827831). Nutrients 7:9931–9945. https://doi.org/10.3390/nu7125507
78. Loo SK, Hopfer C, Teale PD, Reite ML (2004) EEG correlates of methylphenidate response in ADHD: association with cognitive and behavioral measures. J Clin Neurophysiol Off Publ Am Electroencephalogr Soc 21:457–464. https://doi.org/10.1097/01.wnp.0000150890.14421.9a
79. Rubinson M, Horowitz I, Naim-Feil J, Gothelf D, Levit-Binnun N, Moses E (2019) Effects of methylphenidate on the ERP amplitude in youth with ADHD: a double-blind placebo-controlled cross-over EEG study. Plos One 14:e0217383. https://doi.org/10.1371/journal.pone.0217383
80. Sari Gokten E, Tulay EE, Beser B, Elagoz Yuksel M, Arikan K, Tarhan N, Metin B (2019) Predictive value of slow and fast EEG oscillations for methylphenidate response in ADHD. Clin EEG Neurosci 50:332–338. https://doi.org/10.1177/1550059419863206
81. Kaiser A, Aggensteiner P-M, Baumeister S, Holz NE, Banaschewski T, Brandeis D (2020) Earlier versus later cognitive event-related potentials (ERPs) in attention-deficit/hyperactivity disorder (ADHD): a meta-analysis. Neurosci Biobehav Rev 112:117–134. https://doi.org/10.1016/j.neubiorev.2020.01.019
82. Aggensteiner P-M, Albrecht B, Strehl U, Wörz S, Ruckes C, Freitag CM, Rothenberger A, Gevensleben H, Millenet S, Hohmann S, Banaschewski T, Legenbauer T, Holtmann M, Brandeis D (2021) Can neurophysiological markers of anticipation and attention predict ADHD severity and neurofeedback outcomes? Biol Psychol 165:108169. https://doi.org/10.1016/j.biopsycho.2021.108169
83. Groom MJ, Liddle EB, Scerif G, Liddle PF, Batty MJ, Liotti M, Hollis CP (2013) Motivational incentives and methylphenidate enhance electrophysiological correlates of error monitoring in children with attention deficit/hyperactivity disorder. J Child Psychol Psychiatry 54:836–845. https://doi.org/10.1111/jcpp.12069
84. Schrantee A, Mutsaerts H, Bouziane C, Tamminga H, Bottelier M, Reneman L (2017) The age-dependent effects of a single-dose methylphenidate challenge on cerebral perfusion in patients with attention-deficit/hyperactivity disorder. NeuroImage Clin 13:123–129. https://doi.org/10.1016/j.nicl.2016.11.021

85. Orekhova EV, Stroganova TA, Nygren G, Tsetlin MM, Posikera IN, Gillberg C, Elam M (2007) Excess of high frequency electroencephalogram oscillations in boys with autism. Biol Psychiatry 62:1022–1029. https://doi.org/10.1016/j.biopsych.2006.12.029
86. Buard I, Rogers SJ, Hepburn S, Kronberg E, Rojas DC (2013) Altered oscillation patterns and connectivity during picture naming in autism. Front Hum Neurosci 7:742. https://doi.org/10.3389/fnhum.2013.00742
87. Manyukhina VO, Prokofyev AO, Galuta IA, Goiaeva DE, Obukhova TS, Schneiderman JF, Altukhov DI, Stroganova TA, Orekhova EV (2022) Globally elevated excitation-inhibition ratio in children with autism spectrum disorder and below-average intelligence. Mol Autism 13:20. https://doi.org/10.1186/s13229-022-00498-2
88. Mathewson KJ, Jetha MK, Drmic IE, Bryson SE, Goldberg JO, Schmidt LA (2012) Regional EEG alpha power, coherence, and behavioral symptomatology in autism spectrum disorder. Clin Neurophysiol Off J Int Fed Clin Neurophysiol 123:1798–1809. https://doi.org/10.1016/j.clinph.2012.02.061
89. Brito NH, Elliott AJ, Isler JR, Rodriguez C, Friedrich C, Shuffrey LC, Fifer WP (2019) Neonatal EEG linked to individual differences in socioemotional outcomes and autism risk in toddlers. Dev Psychobiol 61:1110–1119. https://doi.org/10.1002/dev.21870
90. Chan AS, Sze SL, Cheung M-C (2007) Quantitative electroencephalographic profiles for children with autistic spectrum disorder. Neuropsychology 21:74–81. https://doi.org/10.1037/0894-4105.21.1.74
91. Chan AS, Cheung M, Han YMY, Sze SL, Leung WW, Man HS, To CY (2009) Executive function deficits and neural discordance in children with autism spectrum disorders. Clin Neurophysiol Off J Int Fed Clin Neurophysiol 120:1107–1115. https://doi.org/10.1016/j.clinph.2009.04.002
92. Coben R, Clarke AR, Hudspeth W, Barry RJ (2008) EEG power and coherence in autistic spectrum disorder. Clin Neurophysiol Off J Int Fed Clin Neurophysiol 119:1002–1009. https://doi.org/10.1016/j.clinph.2008.01.013
93. Klimesch W, Sauseng P, Hanslmayr S (2007) EEG alpha oscillations: the inhibition-timing hypothesis. Brain Res Rev 53:63–88. https://doi.org/10.1016/j.brainresrev.2006.06.003
94. Mably AJ, Colgin LL (2018) Gamma oscillations in cognitive disorders. Curr Opin Neurobiol 52:182–187. https://doi.org/10.1016/j.conb.2018.07.009
95. Murias M, Webb SJ, Greenson J, Dawson G (2007) Resting state cortical connectivity reflected in EEG coherence in autistic individuals. Biol Psychiatry 62:270–273. https://doi.org/10.1016/j.biopsych.2006.11.012
96. Neuhaus E, Lowry SJ, Santhosh M, Kresse A, Edwards LA, Keller J, Libsack EJ, Kang VY, Naples A, Jack A, Jeste S, McPartland JC, Aylward E, Bernier R, Bookheimer S, Dapretto M, Van Horn JD, Pelphrey K, Webb SJ, and the ACE GENDAAR Network (2021) Resting state EEG in youth with ASD: age, sex, and relation to phenotype. J Neurodev Disord 13:33. https://doi.org/10.1186/s11689-021-09390-1
97. Wang J, Barstein J, Ethridge LE, Mosconi MW, Takarae Y, Sweeney JA (2013) Resting state EEG abnormalities in autism spectrum disorders. J Neurodev Disord 5:24. https://doi.org/10.1186/1866-1955-5-24
98. De Groot K, Van Strien JW (2018) Spontaneous resting-state gamma oscillations are not predictive of autistic traits in the general population. Eur J Neurosci 48:2928–2937. https://doi.org/10.1111/ejn.13973
99. Benning SD, Kovac M, Campbell A, Miller S, Hanna EK, Damiano CR, Sabatino-DiCriscio A, Turner-Brown L, Sasson NJ, Aaron RV, Kinard J, Dichter GS (2016) Late positive potential ERP responses to social and nonsocial stimuli in youth with autism spectrum disorder. J Autism Dev Disord 46:3068–3077. https://doi.org/10.1007/s10803-016-2845-y
100. Fan Y-T, Chen C, Chen S-C, Decety J, Cheng Y (2014) Empathic arousal and social understanding in individuals with autism: evidence from fMRI and ERP measurements. Soc Cogn Affect Neurosci 9:1203–1213. https://doi.org/10.1093/scan/nst101

101. Chien Y-L, Hsieh MH, Gau SS-F (2018) Mismatch negativity and P3a in adolescents and young adults with autism spectrum disorders: behavioral correlates and clinical implications. J Autism Dev Disord 48:1684–1697. https://doi.org/10.1007/s10803-017-3426-4
102. Wang S, Yang C, Liu Y, Shao Z, Jackson T (2017) Early and late stage processing abnormalities in autism spectrum disorders: an ERP study. Plos One 12:e0178542. https://doi.org/10.1371/journal.pone.0178542
103. Cui T, Wang PP, Liu S, Zhang X (2017) P300 amplitude and latency in autism spectrum disorder: a meta-analysis. Eur Child Adolesc Psychiatry 26:177–190. https://doi.org/10.1007/s00787-016-0880-z
104. Jeste SS, Hirsch S, Vogel-Farley V, Norona A, Navalta M-C, Gregas MC, Prabhu SP, Sahin M, Nelson CA (2013) Atypical face processing in children with tuberous sclerosis complex. J Child Neurol 28:1569–1576. https://doi.org/10.1177/0883073812465122
105. McPartland JC, Dawson G, Webb SJ, Panagiotides H, Carver LJ (2004) Event-related brain potentials reveal anomalies in temporal processing of faces in autism spectrum disorder. J Child Psychol Psychiatr 45:1235–1245. https://doi.org/10.1111/j.1469-7610.2004.00318.x
106. McPartland JC, Wu J, Bailey CA, Mayes LC, Schultz RT, Klin A (2011) Atypical neural specialization for social percepts in autism spectrum disorder. Soc Neurosci 6:436–451. https://doi.org/10.1080/17470919.2011.586880
107. O'Connor K, Hamm JP, Kirk IJ (2007) Neurophysiological responses to face, facial regions and objects in adults with Asperger's syndrome: an ERP investigation. Int J Psychophysiol Off J Int Organ Psychophysiol 63:283–293. https://doi.org/10.1016/j.ijpsycho.2006.12.001
108. Tye C, Mercure E, Ashwood KL, Azadi B, Asherson P, Johnson MH, Bolton P, McLoughlin G (2013) Neurophysiological responses to faces and gaze direction differentiate children with ASD, ADHD and ASD+ADHD. Dev Cogn Neurosci 5:71–85. https://doi.org/10.1016/j.dcn.2013.01.001
109. Webb SJ, Dawson G, Bernier R, Panagiotides H (2006) ERP evidence of atypical face processing in young children with autism. J Autism Dev Disord 36:881–890. https://doi.org/10.1007/s10803-006-0126-x
110. Senju A, Tojo Y, Yaguchi K, Hasegawa T (2005) Deviant gaze processing in children with autism: an ERP study. Neuropsychologia 43:1297–1306. https://doi.org/10.1016/j.neuropsychologia.2004.12.002
111. Brandwein AB, Foxe JJ, Butler JS, Frey H-P, Bates JC, Shulman LH, Molholm S (2015) Neurophysiological indices of atypical auditory processing and multisensory integration are associated with symptom severity in autism. J Autism Dev Disord 45:230–244. https://doi.org/10.1007/s10803-014-2212-9
112. Desaunay P, Clochon P, Doidy F, Hinault T, Lambrechts A, Wantzen P, Wallois F, Mahmoudzadeh M, Guile J-M, Guénolé F, Baleyte J-M, Eustache F, Bowler DM, Guillery-Girard B (2023) Intact memory storage but impaired retrieval in visual memory in autism: new insights from an electrophysiological study. Autism Res Off J Int Soc Autism Res 16:99–105. https://doi.org/10.1002/aur.2838
113. Kang J, Xie H, Mao W, Wu J, Li X, Geng X (2023) EEG connectivity diversity differences between children with autism and typically developing children: a comparative study. Bioeng Basel Switz 10:1030. https://doi.org/10.3390/bioengineering10091030
114. Ghanbari Y, Bloy L, Christopher Edgar J, Blaskey L, Verma R, Roberts TPL (2015) Joint analysis of band-specific functional connectivity and signal complexity in autism. J Autism Dev Disord 45:444–460. https://doi.org/10.1007/s10803-013-1915-7
115. Dawson G, Bernier R, Ring RH (2012) Social attention: a possible early indicator of efficacy in autism clinical trials. J Neurodev Disord 4:11. https://doi.org/10.1186/1866-1955-4-11
116. Port RG, Anwar AR, Ku M, Carlson GC, Siegel SJ, Roberts TPL (2015) Prospective MEG biomarkers in ASD: pre-clinical evidence and clinical promise of electrophysiological signatures. Yale J Biol Med 88:25–36
117. Murias M, Major S, Davlantis K, Franz L, Harris A, Rardin B, Sabatos-DeVito M, Dawson G (2018) Validation of eye-tracking measures of social attention as a potential biomarker for autism clinical trials. Autism Res 11:166–174. https://doi.org/10.1002/aur.1894

118. Umbricht D, Del Valle RM, Hollander E, McCracken JT, Shic F, Scahill L, Noeldeke J, Boak L, Khwaja O, Squassante L, Grundschober C, Kletzl H, Fontoura P (2017) A single dose, randomized, controlled proof-of-mechanism study of a novel vasopressin 1a receptor antagonist (RG7713) in high-functioning adults with autism spectrum disorder. Neuropsychopharmacology 42:1914–1923. https://doi.org/10.1038/npp.2016.232
119. Pietropaolo S, Crusio WE, Feldon J (2017) Gene-environment interactions in neurodevelopmental disorders. Neural Plast 2017:9272804. https://doi.org/10.1155/2017/9272804
120. Taylor SC, Steeman S, Gehringer BN, Dow HC, Langer A, Rawot E, Perez L, Goodman M, Smernoff Z, Grewal M, Eshraghi O, Pallathra AA, Oksas C, Mendez M, Gur RC, Rader DJ, Bucan M, Almasy L, Brodkin ES (2021) Heritability of quantitative autism spectrum traits in adults: a family-based study. Autism Res Off J Int Soc Autism Res 14:1543–1553. https://doi.org/10.1002/aur.2571
121. Uchida M, DiSalvo M, Walsh D, Biederman J (2023) The heritability of ADHD in children of ADHD parents: a post-hoc analysis of longitudinal data. J Atten Disord 27:250–257. https://doi.org/10.1177/10870547221136251
122. Genovese A, Butler MG (2023) The autism spectrum: behavioral, psychiatric and genetic associations. Genes 14:677. https://doi.org/10.3390/genes14030677
123. Kranz TM, Grimm O (2023) Update on genetics of attention deficit/hyperactivity disorder: current status 2023. Curr Opin Psychiatr 36:257–262. https://doi.org/10.1097/YCO.0000000000000852
124. Demontis D, Walters RK, Martin J, Mattheisen M, Als TD, Agerbo E, Belliveau R, Bybjerg-Grauholm J, Bækvad-Hansen M, Cerrato F, Chambert K, Churchhouse C, Dumont A, Eriksson N, Gandal M, Goldstein J, Grove J, Hansen CS, Hauberg ME, Hollegaard MV, Howrigan DP, Huang H, Maller J, Martin AR, Moran J, Pallesen J, Palmer DS, Pedersen CB, Pedersen MG, Poterba T, Poulsen JB, Ripke S, Robinson EB, Satterstrom KF, Stevens C, Turley P, Won H, ADHD Working Group of the Psychiatric Genomics Consortium (PGC) EL &amp, Genetic Epidemiology (EAGLE) Consortium 23andMe Research Team, Andreassen OA, Burton C, Boomsma D, Cormand B, Dalsgaard S, Franke B, Gelernter J, Geschwind D, Hakonarson H, Haavik J, Kranzler H, Kuntsi J, Langley K, Lesch K-P, Middeldorp C, Reif A, Rohde LA, Roussos P, Schachar R, Sklar P, Sonuga-Barke E, Sullivan PF, Thapar A, Tung J, Waldman I, Nordentoft M, Hougaard DM, Werge T, Mors O, Mortensen PB, Daly MJ, Faraone SV, Børglum AD, Neale BM (2017) Discovery of the first genome-wide significant risk loci for ADHD, 145581
125. Williams NM, Zaharieva I, Martin A, Langley K, Mantripragada K, Fossdal R, Stefansson H, Stefansson K, Magnusson P, Gudmundsson OO, Gustafsson O, Holmans P, Owen MJ, O'Donovan M, Thapar A (2010) Rare chromosomal deletions and duplications in attention-deficit hyperactivity disorder: a genome-wide analysis. Lancet Lond Engl 376:1401–1408. https://doi.org/10.1016/S0140-6736(10)61109-9
126. Ribasés M, Mitjans M, Hartman CA, Soler Artigas M, Demontis D, Larsson H, Ramos-Quiroga JA, Kuntsi J, Faraone SV, Børglum AD, Reif A, Franke B, Cormand B (2023) Genetic architecture of ADHD and overlap with other psychiatric disorders and cognition-related phenotypes. Neurosci Biobehav Rev 153:105313. https://doi.org/10.1016/j.neubiorev.2023.105313
127. Green A, Baroud E, DiSalvo M, Faraone SV, Biederman J (2022) Examining the impact of ADHD polygenic risk scores on ADHD and associated outcomes: a systematic review and meta-analysis. J Psychiatr Res 155:49–67. https://doi.org/10.1016/j.jpsychires.2022.07.032
128. Coray R, Quednow BB (2022) The role of serotonin in declarative memory: a systematic review of animal and human research. Neurosci Biobehav Rev 139:104729. https://doi.org/10.1016/j.neubiorev.2022.104729
129. Dinu LM, Phattharakulnij N (1996) Dommett EJ (2022) Tryptophan modulation in individuals with attention deficit hyperactivity disorder: a systematic review. J Neural Transm Vienna Austria 129:361–377. https://doi.org/10.1007/s00702-022-02478-5

130. Thapar A (2018) Discoveries on the genetics of ADHD in the 21st century: new findings and their implications. Am J Psychiatry 175:943–950. https://doi.org/10.1176/appi.ajp.2018.180 40383
131. Vernes SC, Newbury DF, Abrahams BS, Winchester L, Nicod J, Groszer M, Alarcón M, Oliver PL, Davies KE, Geschwind DH, Monaco AP, Fisher SE (2008) A functional genetic link between distinct developmental language disorders. N Engl J Med 359:2337–2345. https://doi.org/10.1056/NEJMoa0802828
132. Groen-Blokhuis MM, Middeldorp CM, Kan K-J, Abdellaoui A, van Beijsterveldt CEM, Ehli EA, Davies GE, Scheet PA, Xiao X, Hudziak JJ, Hottenga J-J, Psychiatric Genomics Consortium ADHD Working Group, Neale BM, Boomsma DI (2014) Attention-deficit/hyperactivity disorder polygenic risk scores predict attention problems in a population-based sample of children. J Am Acad Child Adolesc Psychiatr 53:1123–1129.e6. https://doi.org/10.1016/j.jaac.2014.06.014
133. Martin J, Hamshere ML, Stergiakouli E, O'Donovan MC, Thapar A (2014) Genetic risk for attention-deficit/hyperactivity disorder contributes to neurodevelopmental traits in the general population. Biol Psychiatr 76:664–671. https://doi.org/10.1016/j.biopsych.2014.02.013
134. Stergiakouli E, Martin J, Hamshere ML, Langley K, Evans DM, Pourcain PSt, Timpson NJ, owen MJ, O'Donovan M, Thapar A, Smith GD (2015) Shared genetic influences between attention-deficit/hyperactivity disorder (ADHD) traits in children and clinical ADHD. J Am Acad Child Adolesc Psychiatr 54:322–327. https://doi.org/10.1016/j.jaac.2015.01.010
135. Middeldorp CM, Hammerschlag AR, Ouwens KG, Groen-Blokhuis MM, Pourcain BS, Greven CU, Pappa I, Tiesler CMT, Ang W, Nolte IM, Vilor-Tejedor N, Bacelis J, Ebejer JL, Zhao H, Davies GE, Ehli EA, Evans DM, Fedko IO, Guxens M, Hottenga J-J, Hudziak JJ, Jugessur A, Kemp JP, Krapohl E, Martin NG, Murcia M, Myhre R, Ormel J, Ring SM, Standl M, Stergiakouli E, Stoltenberg C, Thiering E, Timpson NJ, Trzaskowski M, van der Most PJ, Wang C, EArly Genetics and Lifecourse Epidemiology (EAGLE) Consortium, Psychiatric Genomics Consortium ADHD Working Group, Nyholt DR, Medland SE, Neale B, Jacobsson B, Sunyer J, Hartman CA, Whitehouse AJO, Pennell CE, Heinrich J, Plomin R, Smith GD, Tiemeier H, Posthuma D, Boomsma DI (2016) A genome-wide association meta-analysis of attention-deficit/hyperactivity disorder symptoms in population-based pediatric cohorts. J Am Acad Child Adolesc Psychiatr 55:896–905.e6. https://doi.org/10.1016/j.jaac.2016.05.025
136. Asherson P, Agnew-Blais J (2019) Annual research review: does late-onset attention-deficit/hyperactivity disorder exist? J Child Psychol Psychiatr 60:333–352. https://doi.org/10.1111/jcpp.13020
137. Manfro AG, Santoro M, Polanczyk GV, Gadelha A, Pan PM, Bressan RA, Brietzke E, Talarico F, Belangero S, Rohde LA, Salum GA (2019) Heterotypic trajectories of dimensional psychopathology across the lifespan: the case of youth-onset attention deficit/hyperactivity disorder. J Child Psychol Psychiatr 60:533–544. https://doi.org/10.1111/jcpp.12987
138. Moffitt TE, Houts R, Asherson P, Belsky DW, Corcoran DL, Hammerle M, Harrington H, Hogan S, Meier MH, Polanczyk GV, Poulton R, Ramrakha S, Sugden K, Williams B, Rohde LA, Caspi A (2015) Is adult ADHD a childhood-onset neurodevelopmental disorder? Evidence from a four-decade longitudinal cohort study. Am J Psychiatr 172:967–977. https://doi.org/10.1176/appi.ajp.2015.14101266
139. Riglin L, Collishaw S, Thapar AK, Dalsgaard S, Langley K, Smith GD, Stergiakouli E, Maughan B, O'Donovan MC, Thapar A (2016) Association of genetic risk variants with attention-deficit/hyperactivity disorder trajectories in the general population. JAMA Psychiatr 73:1285–1292. https://doi.org/10.1001/jamapsychiatry.2016.2817
140. Capuzzi E, Caldiroli A, Auxilia AM, Borgonovo R, Capellazzi M, Clerici M, Buoli M (2022) Biological predictors of treatment response in adult attention deficit hyperactivity disorder (ADHD): a systematic review. J Pers Med 12:1742. https://doi.org/10.3390/jpm12101742
141. Fang Y, Cui Y, Yin Z, Hou M, Guo P, Wang H, Liu N, Cai C, Wang M (2023) Comprehensive systematic review and meta-analysis of the association between common genetic variants and autism spectrum disorder. Gene 887:147723. https://doi.org/10.1016/j.gene.2023.147723

142. Stelzer G, Rosen N, Plaschkes I, Zimmerman S, Twik M, Fishilevich S, Stein TI, Nudel R, Lieder I, Mazor Y, Kaplan S, Dahary D, Warshawsky D, Guan-Golan Y, Kohn A, Rappaport N, Safran M, Lancet D (2016) The genecards suite: from gene data mining to disease genome sequence analyses. Curr Protoc Bioinforma 54:1.30.1–1.30.33. https://doi.org/10.1002/cpbi.5
143. (2023) autism genes related genes—GeneCards search results. https://www.genecards.org/Search/Keyword?queryString=autism%20genes. Accessed 10 Oct 2023
144. Kent WJ, Sugnet CW, Furey TS, Roskin KM, Pringle TH, Zahler AM, Haussler D (2002) The human genome browser at UCSC. Genome Res 12:996–1006. https://doi.org/10.1101/gr.229102
145. (2023) UCSC genome browser gene interaction graph. https://genome.ucsc.edu/cgi-bin/hgGeneGraph?gene=ZEB1&1=OK&supportLevel=text&geneCount=25. Accessed 10 Oct 2023
146. Kolesnikoff N, Attema JL, Roslan S, Bert AG, Schwarz QP, Gregory PA, Goodall GJ (2014) Specificity protein 1 (Sp1) maintains basal epithelial expression of the miR-200 family: implications for epithelial-mesenchymal transition. J Biol Chem 289:11194–11205. https://doi.org/10.1074/jbc.M113.529172
147. Thanseem I, Anitha A, Nakamura K, Suda S, Iwata K, Matsuzaki H, Ohtsubo M, Ueki T, Katayama T, Iwata Y, Suzuki K, Minoshima S, Mori N (2012) Elevated transcription factor specificity protein 1 in autistic brains alters the expression of autism candidate genes. Biol Psychiatr 71:410–418. https://doi.org/10.1016/j.biopsych.2011.09.020
148. Tang X, Feng C, Zhao Y, Zhang H, Gao Y, Cao X, Hong Q, Lin J, Zhuang H, Feng Y, Wang H, Shen L (2023) A study of genetic heterogeneity in autism spectrum disorders based on plasma proteomic and metabolomic analysis: multiomics study of autism heterogeneity. MedComm 4:e380. https://doi.org/10.1002/mco2.380
149. Alonso-Gonzalez A, Rodriguez-Fontenla C, Carracedo A (2018) De novo mutations (DNMs) in autism spectrum disorder (ASD): pathway and network analysis. Front Genet 9:406. https://doi.org/10.3389/fgene.2018.00406
150. Calderoni S (2023) Sex/gender differences in children with autism spectrum disorder: a brief overview on epidemiology, symptom profile, and neuroanatomy. J Neurosci Res 101:739–750. https://doi.org/10.1002/jnr.25000
151. Li Y, Li R, Wang N, Gu J, Gao J (2023) Gender effects on autism spectrum disorder: a multi-site resting-state functional magnetic resonance imaging study of transcriptome-neuroimaging. Front Neurosci 17:1203690. https://doi.org/10.3389/fnins.2023.1203690
152. Frye RE, Vassall S, Kaur G, Lewis C, Karim M, Rossignol D (2019) Emerging biomarkers in autism spectrum disorder: a systematic review. Ann Transl Med 7:792–792. https://doi.org/10.21037/atm.2019.11.53
153. Bjørklund G, Doşa MD, Maes M, Dadar M, Frye RE, Peana M, Chirumbolo S (2021) The impact of glutathione metabolism in autism spectrum disorder. Pharmacol Res 166:105437. https://doi.org/10.1016/j.phrs.2021.105437
154. Melamed IR, Heffron M, Testori A, Lipe K (2018) A pilot study of high-dose intravenous immunoglobulin 5% for autism: impact on autism spectrum and markers of neuroinflammation. Autism Res 11:421–433. https://doi.org/10.1002/aur.1906
155. Quintana DS, Guastella AJ, Outhred T, Hickie IB, Kemp AH (2012) Heart rate variability is associated with emotion recognition: direct evidence for a relationship between the autonomic nervous system and social cognition. Int J Psychophysiol 86:168–172. https://doi.org/10.1016/j.ijpsycho.2012.08.012
156. Fathabadipour S, Mohammadi Z, Roshani F, Goharbakhsh N, Alizadeh H, Palizgar F, Cumming P, Michel TM, Vafaee MS (2022) The neural effects of oxytocin administration in autism spectrum disorders studied by fMRI: a systematic review. J Psychiatr Res 154:80–90. https://doi.org/10.1016/j.jpsychires.2022.06.033
157. Connery K, Tippett M, Delhey LM, Rose S, Slattery JC, Kahler SG, Hahn J, Kruger U, Cunningham MW, Shimasaki C, Frye RE (2018) Intravenous immunoglobulin for the treatment of autoimmune encephalopathy in children with autism. Transl Psychiatr 8:148. https://doi.org/10.1038/s41398-018-0214-7

158. Rose S, Bennuri SC, Davis JE, Wynne R, Slattery JC, Tippett M, Delhey L, Melnyk S, Kahler SG, MacFabe DF, Frye RE (2018) Butyrate enhances mitochondrial function during oxidative stress in cell lines from boys with autism. Transl Psychiatr 8:42. https://doi.org/10.1038/s41398-017-0089-z
159. Mareckova K, Pacinkova A, Marecek R, Sebejova L, Izakovicova Holla L, Klanova J, Brazdil M, Nikolova YS (2023) Longitudinal study of epigenetic aging and its relationship with brain aging and cognitive skills in young adulthood. Front Aging Neurosci 15:1215957. https://doi.org/10.3389/fnagi.2023.1215957
160. Nazzari S, Cagliero L, Grumi S, Pisoni E, Mallucci G, Bergamaschi R, Maccarini J, Giorda R, Provenzi L (2023) Prenatal exposure to environmental air pollution and psychosocial stress jointly contribute to the epigenetic regulation of the serotonin transporter gene in newborns. Mol Psychiatr. https://doi.org/10.1038/s41380-023-02206-9
161. Roth TL, Sweatt JD (2011) Annual research review: epigenetic mechanisms and environmental shaping of the brain during sensitive periods of development. J Child Psychol Psychiatr 52:398–408. https://doi.org/10.1111/j.1469-7610.2010.02282.x
162. Yeshurun S, Hannan AJ (2019) Transgenerational epigenetic influences of paternal environmental exposures on brain function and predisposition to psychiatric disorders. Mol Psychiatr 24:536–548. https://doi.org/10.1038/s41380-018-0039-z
163. Bacon ER, Brinton RD (2021) Epigenetics of the developing and aging brain: mechanisms that regulate onset and outcomes of brain reorganization. Neurosci Biobehav Rev 125:503–516. https://doi.org/10.1016/j.neubiorev.2021.02.040
164. Shirvani-Farsani Z, Maloum Z, Bagheri-Hosseinabadi Z, Vilor-Tejedor N, Sadeghi I (2021) DNA methylation signature as a biomarker of major neuropsychiatric disorders. J Psychiatr Res 141:34–49. https://doi.org/10.1016/j.jpsychires.2021.06.013
165. Neumann A, Walton E, Alemany S, Cecil C, González JR, Jima DD, Lahti J, Tuominen ST, Barker ED, Binder E, Caramaschi D, Carracedo Á, Czamara D, Evandt J, Felix JF, Fuemmeler BF, Gutzkow KB, Hoyo C, Julvez J, Kajantie E, Laivuori H, Maguire R, Maitre L, Murphy SK, Murcia M, Villa PM, Sharp G, Sunyer J, Raikkönen K, Bakermans-Kranenburg M, IJzendoorn M van, Guxens M, Relton CL, Tiemeier H (2020) Association between DNA methylation and ADHD symptoms from birth to school age: a prospective meta-analysis. Transl Psychiatr 10:398. https://doi.org/10.1038/s41398-020-01058-z
166. Sengupta SM, Smith AK, Grizenko N, Joober R (2017) Locus-specific DNA methylation changes and phenotypic variability in children with attention-deficit hyperactivity disorder. Psychiatry Res 256:298–304. https://doi.org/10.1016/j.psychres.2017.06.048
167. Tsai M-C, Jhang K-J, Lee C-T, Lin Y-F, Strong C, Lin Y-C, Hsieh Y-P, Lin C-Y (2020) Effects of childhood adversity and its interaction with the MAOA, BDNF, and COMT polymorphisms on subclinical attention deficit/hyperactivity symptoms in generally healthy youth. Child Basel Switz 7:122. https://doi.org/10.3390/children7090122
168. Kim S, Kaang B-K (2017) Epigenetic regulation and chromatin remodeling in learning and memory. Exp Mol Med 49:e281–e281. https://doi.org/10.1038/emm.2016.140
169. Parkel S, Lopez-Atalaya JP, Barco A (2013) Histone H3 lysine methylation in cognition and intellectual disability disorders. Learn Mem Cold Spring Harb N 20:570–579. https://doi.org/10.1101/lm.029363.112
170. Peixoto L, Abel T (2013) The role of histone acetylation in memory formation and cognitive impairments. Neuropsychopharmacol Off Publ Am Coll Neuropsychopharmacol 38:62–76. https://doi.org/10.1038/npp.2012.86
171. Samadzadeh S, Kruschel T, Novak M, Kallenbach M, Hefter H (2022) Different response behavior to therapeutic approaches in homozygotic wilson's disease twins with clinical phenotypic variability: case report and literature review. Genes 13:1217. https://doi.org/10.3390/genes13071217
172. Tye C, McLoughlin G, Kuntsi J, Asherson P (2011) Electrophysiological markers of genetic risk for attention deficit hyperactivity disorder. Expert Rev Mol Med 13:e9. https://doi.org/10.1017/S1462399411001797

173. Harvey ZH, Chen Y, Jarosz DF (2018) Protein-based inheritance: epigenetics beyond the chromosome. Mol Cell 69:195–202. https://doi.org/10.1016/j.molcel.2017.10.030
174. Hwang J-Y, Aromolaran KA, Zukin RS (2017) The emerging field of epigenetics in neurodegeneration and neuroprotection. Nat Rev Neurosci 18:347–361. https://doi.org/10.1038/nrn.2017.46
175. Jeffries MA (2020) The development of epigenetics in the study of disease pathogenesis. Adv Exp Med Biol 1253:57–94. https://doi.org/10.1007/978-981-15-3449-2_2
176. Bekiesinska-Figatowska M, Mierzewska H, Jurkiewicz E (2013) Basal ganglia lesions in children and adults. Eur J Radiol 82:837–849. https://doi.org/10.1016/j.ejrad.2012.12.006
177. Smith DM, Torregrossa MM (2021) Valence encoding in the amygdala influences motivated behavior. Behav Brain Res 411:113370. https://doi.org/10.1016/j.bbr.2021.113370
178. Stoccoro A, Conti E, Scaffei E, Calderoni S, Coppedè F, Migliore L, Battini R (2023) DNA methylation biomarkers for young children with idiopathic autism spectrum disorder: a systematic review. Int J Mol Sci 24:9138. https://doi.org/10.3390/ijms24119138
179. Yasuda Y, Matsumoto J, Miura K, Hasegawa N, Hashimoto R (2023) Genetics of autism spectrum disorders and future direction. J Hum Genet 68:193–197. https://doi.org/10.1038/s10038-022-01076-3
180. Cederquist GY, Tchieu J, Callahan SJ, Ramnarine K, Ryan S, Zhang C, Rittenhouse C, Zeltner N, Chung SY, Zhou T, Chen S, Betel D, White RM, Tomishima M, Studer L (2020) A multiplex human pluripotent stem cell platform defines molecular and functional subclasses of autism-related genes. Cell Stem Cell 27:35-49.e6. https://doi.org/10.1016/j.stem.2020.06.004
181. Ciptasari U, van Bokhoven H (2020) The phenomenal epigenome in neurodevelopmental disorders. Hum Mol Genet 29:R42–R50. https://doi.org/10.1093/hmg/ddaa175
182. Krumm N, O'Roak BJ, Shendure J, Eichler EE (2014) A de novo convergence of autism genetics and molecular neuroscience. Trends Neurosci 37:95–105. https://doi.org/10.1016/j.tins.2013.11.005
183. Butler MG (2017) Clinical and genetic aspects of the 15q11.2 BP1-BP2 microdeletion disorder. J Intellect Disabil Res JIDR 61:568–579. https://doi.org/10.1111/jir.12382
184. Sanchez-Jimeno C, Blanco-Kelly F, López-Grondona F, Losada-Del Pozo R, Moreno B, Rodrigo-Moreno M, Martinez-Cayuelas E, Riveiro-Alvarez R, Fenollar-Cortés M, Ayuso C, Rodríguez de Alba M, Lorda-Sanchez I, Almoguera B (2021) Attention deficit hyperactivity and autism spectrum disorders as the core symptoms of AUTS2 syndrome: description of five new patients and update of the frequency of manifestations and genotype-phenotype correlation. Genes 12:1360. https://doi.org/10.3390/genes12091360
185. Siracusano M, Arturi L, Riccioni A, Noto A, Mussap M, Mazzone L (2023) Metabolomics: perspectives on clinical employment in autism spectrum disorder. Int J Mol Sci 24:13404. https://doi.org/10.3390/ijms241713404
186. Kang J, Park M, Oh C-M, Kim T (2023) High-fat diet-induced dopaminergic dysregulation induces REM sleep fragmentation and ADHD-like behaviors. Psychiatr Res 327:115412. https://doi.org/10.1016/j.psychres.2023.115412
187. Lange KW, Lange KM, Nakamura Y, Reissmann A (2023) Nutrition in the management of ADHD: a review of recent research. Curr Nutr Rep 12:383–394. https://doi.org/10.1007/s13668-023-00487-8
188. Cascone AD, Calabro F, Foran W, Larsen B, Nugiel T, Parr AC, Tervo-Clemmens B, Luna B, Cohen JR (2023) Brain tissue iron neurophysiology and its relationship with the cognitive effects of dopaminergic modulation in children with and without ADHD. Dev Cogn Neurosci 63:101274. https://doi.org/10.1016/j.dcn.2023.101274
189. Liu T-H, Wu J-Y, Huang P-Y, Lai C-C, Chang JP-C, Lin C-H, Su K-P (2023) Omega-3 polyunsaturated fatty acids for core symptoms of attention-deficit/hyperactivity disorder: a meta-analysis of randomized controlled trials. J Clin Psychiatr 84:22r14772. https://doi.org/10.4088/JCP.22r14772

190. Bundgaard-Nielsen C, Lauritsen MB, Knudsen JK, Rold LS, Larsen MH, Hindersson P, Villadsen AB, Leutscher PDC, Hagstrøm S, Nyegaard M, Sørensen S (2023) Children and adolescents with attention deficit hyperactivity disorder and autism spectrum disorder share distinct microbiota compositions. Gut Microbes 15:2211923. https://doi.org/10.1080/19490976.2023.2211923
191. di Girolamo G, Bracco IF, Portigliatti Pomeri A, Puglisi S, Oliva F (2022) Prevalence of metabolic syndrome and insulin resistance in a sample of adult ADHD outpatients. Front Psychiatr 13:891479. https://doi.org/10.3389/fpsyt.2022.891479
192. Wynchank D, Bijlenga D, Lamers F, Kooij JJS, Bron TI, Beekman ATF, Penninx BWJH (2018) The association between metabolic syndrome, obesity-related outcomes, and ADHD in adults with comorbid affective disorders. J Atten Disord 22:460–471. https://doi.org/10.1177/1087054716659137
193. Cickovski T, Mathee K, Aguirre G, Tatke G, Hermida A, Narasimhan G, Stollstorff M (2023) Attention deficit hyperactivity disorder (ADHD) and the gut microbiome: an ecological perspective. Plos One 18:e0273890. https://doi.org/10.1371/journal.pone.0273890
194. Pan P-Y, Taylor MJ, Larsson H, Almqvist C, Lichtenstein P, Lundström S, Bölte S (2023) Genetic and environmental contributions to co-occurring physical health conditions in autism spectrum condition and attention-deficit/hyperactivity disorder. Mol Autism 14:17. https://doi.org/10.1186/s13229-023-00548-3
195. Taş E, Ülgen KO (2023) Understanding the ADHD-Gut axis by metabolic network analysis. Metabolites 13:592. https://doi.org/10.3390/metabo13050592
196. González-Safont L, Rebagliato M, Arregi A, Carrasco P, Guxens M, Vegas O, Julvez J, Estarlich M (2023) Sleep problems at ages 8–9 and ADHD symptoms at ages 10–11: evidence in three cohorts from INMA study. Eur J Pediatr. https://doi.org/10.1007/s00431-023-05145-3
197. Marten F, Keuppens L, Baeyens D, Boyer BE, Danckaerts M, Cortese S, Van der Oord S (2023) Sleep parameters and problems in adolescents with and without ADHD: a systematic review and meta-analysis. JCPP Adv 3:e12151. https://doi.org/10.1002/jcv2.12151
198. French B, Quain E, Kilgariff J, Lockwood J, Daley D (2023) The impact of sleep difficulties in children with attention deficit hyperactivity disorder on the family: a thematic analysis. J Clin Sleep Med JCSM Off Publ Am Acad Sleep Med 19:1735–1741. https://doi.org/10.5664/jcsm.10662
199. Alibrandi A, Zirilli A, Loschiavo F, Gangemi MC, Sindoni A, Tribulato G, Lo Giudice R, Famà F (2023) Food selectivity in children with autism spectrum disorder: a statistical analysis in Southern Italy. Child Basel Switz 10:1553. https://doi.org/10.3390/children10091553
200. Harris HA, Derks IPM, Prinzie P, Louwerse A, Hillegers MHJ, Jansen PW (2023) Interrelated development of autism spectrum disorder symptoms and eating problems in childhood: a population-based cohort. Front Pediatr 11:1062012. https://doi.org/10.3389/fped.2023.1062012
201. Acosta A, Khokhlovich E, Reis H, Vyshedskiy A (2023) Dietary factors impact developmental trajectories in young autistic children. J Autism Dev Disord. https://doi.org/10.1007/s10803-023-06074-8
202. Akhter M, Khan SM, Firdous SN, Tikmani P, Khan A, Rafique H (2022) A narrative review on manifestations of gluten free casein free diet in autism and autism spectrum disorders. JPMA J Pak Med Assoc 72:2054–2060. https://doi.org/10.47391/JPMA.3971
203. Harutyunyan AA, Harutyunyan HA, Yenkoyan KB (2021) Novel probable glance at inflammatory scenario development in autistic pathology. Front Psychiatr 12:788779. https://doi.org/10.3389/fpsyt.2021.788779
204. Han VX, Patel S, Jones HF, Nielsen TC, Mohammad SS, Hofer MJ, Gold W, Brilot F, Lain SJ, Nassar N, Dale RC (2021) Maternal acute and chronic inflammation in pregnancy is associated with common neurodevelopmental disorders: a systematic review. Transl Psychiatr 11:71. https://doi.org/10.1038/s41398-021-01198-w
205. Cortese S, Solmi M, Michelini G, Bellato A, Blanner C, Canozzi A, Eudave L, Farhat LC, Højlund M, Köhler-Forsberg O, Leffa DT, Rohde C, de Pablo GS, Vita G, Wesselhoeft R,

Martin J, Baumeister S, Bozhilova NS, Carlisi CO, Leno VC, Floris DL, Holz NE, Kraaijenvanger EJ, Sacu S, Vainieri I, Ostuzzi G, Barbui C, Correll CU (2023) Candidate diagnostic biomarkers for neurodevelopmental disorders in children and adolescents: a systematic review. World Psychiatr 22:129–149. https://doi.org/10.1002/wps.21037
206. Cuthbert BN, Insel TR (2010) Toward new approaches to psychotic disorders: the NIMH Research Domain Criteria project. Schizophr Bull 36:1061–1062. https://doi.org/10.1093/schbul/sbq108
207. Kirmayer LJ, Crafa D (2014) What kind of science for psychiatry? Front Hum Neurosci 8
208. Peterson BS (2015) Editorial: Research Domain Criteria (RDoC): a new psychiatric nosology whose time has not yet come. J Child Psychol Psychiatr 56:719–722. https://doi.org/10.1111/jcpp.12439
209. Boksa P (2013) A way forward for research on biomarkers for psychiatric disorders. J Psychiatr Neurosci JPN 38:75–77. https://doi.org/10.1503/jpn.130018
210. De Felice A, Ricceri L, Venerosi A, Chiarotti F, Calamandrei G (2015) Multifactorial origin of neurodevelopmental disorders: approaches to understanding complex etiologies. Toxics 3:89–129. https://doi.org/10.3390/toxics3010089
211. Kim JH, Kim JY, Lee J, Jeong GH, Lee E, Lee S, Lee KH, Kronbichler A, Stubbs B, Solmi M, Koyanagi A, Hong SH, Dragioti E, Jacob L, Brunoni AR, Carvalho AF, Radua J, Thompson T, Smith L, Oh H, Yang L, Grabovac I, Schuch F, Fornaro M, Stickley A, Rais TB, Salazar de Pablo G, Shin JI, Fusar-Poli P (2020) Environmental risk factors, protective factors, and peripheral biomarkers for ADHD: an umbrella review. Lancet Psychiatr 7:955–970. https://doi.org/10.1016/S2215-0366(20)30312-6
212. Uher R, Zwicker A (2017) Etiology in psychiatry: embracing the reality of poly-gene-environmental causation of mental illness. World Psychiatr 16:121–129. https://doi.org/10.1002/wps.20436
213. Abi-Dargham A, Horga G (2016) The search for imaging biomarkers in psychiatric disorders. Nat Med 22:1248–1255. https://doi.org/10.1038/nm.4190
214. First M, Botteron K, Carter C, Castellanos FX, Dickstein DP, Drevets W, Kim KL, Pescosolido MF, Rausch S, Seymour KE, Sheline Y (2012) Consensus report of the APA work group on neuroimaging markers of psychiatric disorders. Am Psychiatr Assoc
215. Glannon W (2022) Biomarkers in psychiatric disorders. Camb Q Healthc Ethics 31:444–452. https://doi.org/10.1017/S0963180122000056
216. Singh I, Rose N (2009) Biomarkers in psychiatry. Nature 460:202–207. https://doi.org/10.1038/460202a
217. Walsh P, Elsabbagh M, Bolton P, Singh I (2011) In search of biomarkers for autism: scientific, social and ethical challenges. Nat Rev Neurosci 12:603–612. https://doi.org/10.1038/nrn3113
218. Speerforck S, Stolzenburg S, Hertel J, Grabe HJ, Strauß M, Carta MG, Angermeyer MC, Schomerus G (2019) ADHD, stigma and continuum beliefs: a population survey on public attitudes towards children and adults with attention deficit hyperactivity disorder. Psychiatry Res 282:112570. https://doi.org/10.1016/j.psychres.2019.112570
219. Link BG, Struening EL, Neese-Todd S, Asmussen S, Phelan JC (2001) Stigma as a barrier to recovery: the consequences of stigma for the self-esteem of people with mental illnesses. Psychiatr Serv 52:1621–1626. https://doi.org/10.1176/appi.ps.52.12.1621
220. Phelan JC (2002) Genetic bases of mental illness—A cure for stigma? Trends Neurosci 25:430–431
221. Dunn LB (2018) Biomarkers in psychiatry: ethical issues. Focus 16:179–182. https://doi.org/10.1176/appi.focus.20180006
222. Faraone SV, Biederman J (2016) Can attention-deficit/hyperactivity disorder onset occur in adulthood? JAMA Psychiat 73:655–656. https://doi.org/10.1001/jamapsychiatry.2016.0400
223. Holz NE, Berhe O, Sacu S, Schwarz E, Tesarz J, Heim CM, Tost H (2023) Early social adversity, altered brain functional connectivity, and mental health. Biol s 93:430–441. https://doi.org/10.1016/j.biopsych.2022.10.019

Digital Biomarkers in Neurodevelopmental Health: Current Status, Promises, and Perils

Wamuyu Owotoki, Anninka Enseroth, Ruth Njeri Mbugua, and Peter Owotoki

Abstract

A digital biomarker is a quantifiable characteristic obtained from a digital device which serves as an indicator of a biological process. This includes both normal and pathological processes as well as responses to an exposure, for example to a treatment. There has been a surge of research interest on digital biomarkers in neurodevelopmental health. Persisting challenges in the field such as long waiting times for diagnoses have led to the exploration of novel technologies to address these problems. In this chapter, we provide an overview of recent advances in the development of digital biomarkers for neurodevelopmental health. We further discuss the potential improvements these new technologies can bring about as well as the associated risks and ethical challenges.

Keywords

Digital biomarkers • Neurodevelopmental conditions • Computer-aided diagnosis • Artificial intelligence in clinical trials • Artificial intelligence ethics

---

W. Owotoki · A. Enseroth (✉) · R. N. Mbugua · P. Owotoki
Vitafluence.ai, Kronberg im Taunus, Germany
e-mail: anninka.enseroth@vitafluence.ai

W. Owotoki
e-mail: wamuyu.owotoki@vitafluence.ai

R. N. Mbugua
e-mail: ruth.mbugua@vitafluence.ai

P. Owotoki
e-mail: peter.owotoki@vitafluence.ai

1 Introduction

Recent advances in computer science and data analytics have impacted nearly all areas of human societies, including healthcare. New technologies are transforming how health conditions are diagnosed, managed, and understood.

One of these novel technologies is digital biomarkers. This relatively new term describes a diverse array of quantitative measures derived from individuals' interactions with digital devices and platforms. In the realm of neurodevelopmental health, several pressing challenges persist. The timely and accurate diagnosis of conditions such as autism spectrum disorder (ASD) and attention-deficit/hyperactivity disorder (ADHD) remains challenging due to a shortage of specialists trained in complex diagnostic procedures and a lack of definitive biomarkers. Disparities in access to specialized care and diagnostic resources further compound the issue, disproportionately affecting underserved populations.

Digital biomarkers have been proposed as one measure to mitigate these shortcomings. The following chapter will introduce digital biomarkers in general and in neurodevelopmental health specifically. Clinical examples will reveal the current status of digital biomarkers in neurodevelopmental health. Finally, this chapter will outline the potential benefits and some of the ethical challenges associated with digital biomarkers and discuss ethical frameworks that can guide the development of ethical, representative digital biomarkers.

1.1 Digital Biomarkers—Definitions

1.1.1 Biomarkers

A biomarker is an objectively measurable, quantifiable characteristic which serves as an indicator of a biological process. This includes both normal and pathological processes as well as responses to an exposure, for example to a treatment [1, 2]. Biomarkers can be described based on their two components: the measurement and the clinical outcome [3]. There are different types of biomarkers which can be distinguished by their purpose and the associated clinical outcome. For instance, diagnostic biomarkers are used to detect or confirm a condition or to determine a disease subtype [2]. For example, a low level of the neuropeptide orexin-A measured in a patient's cerebrospinal fluid is a diagnostic biomarker for narcolepsy type I [4]. Conversely, monitoring biomarkers allow conclusions about disease status through repeated measurement. An example of this is measuring prostate-specific antigen in post-surgical prostate cancer patients to determine whether the disease is recurring [5]. Further types include susceptibility, prognostic, predictive, safety, and response biomarkers [2]. Biomarkers should be distinguished from clinical outcome assessments (COA), which are measures of how a patient feels, functions, or survives, thus representing outcomes of direct importance for the patient [1, 2, 6]. COAs can be obtained from patient self-report, a clinician's report, observations, or performance on a standardized test [7].

Revisiting the example provided above, a patient reports experiencing sleep attacks and cataplexy (COA). To confirm the diagnosis of narcolepsy type I (clinical outcome), the treating clinician orders a lumbar puncture to measure CSF orexin-A (measurement).

Leveraging biomarkers in neurodevelopmental health is an area that has drawn increasing interest from researchers and clinicians in recent years.

1.1.2 Digital Biomarkers

Recent technological advancements and increasing interdisciplinary research between computer and medical sciences led to the development of digital biomarkers. The key difference to traditional biomarkers is that they are collected using digital devices which can be portable (e.g. smartphones, tablets), wearable (e.g. smartwatches, rings, hats, or bracelets with sensors) or even implantable [8]. The latter however is the exception as most digital biomarkers are derived from non-invasive technologies. Currently, most of the research on digital biomarkers is on data obtained from wearables [9].

Digital biomarkers typically represent a fusion of multiple software (e.g., operating system, algorithm, user interface) and hardware elements (e.g., devices, sensors). When interoperable they can be combined as modules across different providers [10]. Take, for instance, a research group dedicated to enhancing autism detection in children. They have crafted a software-based eye tracker tailored for this purpose and a user interface to communicate the results to healthcare professionals (HCP). They run this on a third-party hardware, such as a smartphone which includes a camera (the sensor) and an operating system.

The individual components of a digital biomarker have been described with differing terminology but represent similar concepts. Babrak and colleagues describe biomarkers—both digital and traditional—using two components: measurement and clinical outcome [3]. Coravos and colleagues describe three components: an input layer, a signal processing layer, and an actionable metric. The signal processing layer is typically an artificial intelligence (AI) algorithm which converts the input into the actionable metrics. It often consists of multiple layers, especially in more complex cases. There is typically a layer for signal data processing to transform the raw data into certain metrics and a layer which connects the data to an outcome of interest [10]. In the example of eye tracking for autism detection there would be a layer for signal data processing (capturing different metrics such as saccades from the camera recording) and an algorithm to connect the processed data to a clinical outcome, the likelihood of a diagnosis. It should be noted that there can be multiple inputs as composite biomarkers incorporate multiple sources [10].

For this chapter, we will refer to the components as measurement (representing the input layer), signal processing layer, and clinical outcome (representing the output layer). Besides these, the context should also be considered, especially in the field of neurodevelopmental health, where measurements are often obtained in response to certain stimuli to elicit a response of interest (Fig. 1). For example, images with or without social scenes which subjects view while their eye

Fig. 1 Components of digital biomarkers [3, 10]

movements are tracked to determine the looking time at social versus non-social scenes.

The definition of digital biomarkers remains a topic of debate. One key question, as posed by Montag and colleagues, is the level of connection to biology required for a digital biomarker. They differentiate between a narrow and a broad definition [11]. The narrow definition entails a direct link to a biological signal, like heart rate data from a wearable device used to assess cardiovascular disease risk [12]. Conversely, the broader definition also encompasses digital biomarkers based on behavioural input data, such as phone and app usage data, or which link to clinical outcomes representing psychological variables such as stress or depression [13, 14]. If the latter is the case, the distinction between COAs and digital biomarkers can be challenging. Montag et al. argue that outcome variables, such as affective states, should be referred to as clinical outcome assessments rather than linked to the term digital biomarkers. If termed digital biomarkers, they would fall under a significantly broad definition. According to Montag et al., legitimate digital biomarkers are associated with the underlying biological processes of a condition. Here, it is noteworthy that research shows how several metrics of interest in neurodevelopmental health have been shown to correlate with biological processes or states. For example, the duration of the longest look to faces, an eye tracking metric, is associated with polygenic scores for ADHD [15] and pupil diameter is associated with neuronal activation in the Locus Coeruleus [16]. However, this biological link is not established for all neurodevelopmental health metrics of interest, warranting further research.

This ongoing discourse underscores the evolving nature of the field and the need for further clarification and consensus. When reviewing current literature from the field, it is important to note that not all authors have the same definition of digital biomarkers. Some articles might describe what would fall under the narrow definition of a digital biomarker but not use the term. Others might use the digital biomarker label for something that falls under a broad definition of the term [11].

Digital biomarkers must undergo a multistep evaluation, including verification and validation. Verification is used to test the accurate measurement and storage of data [10]. In our eye tracking example, this would mean ensuring that the fixation time captured by a software-based gaze tracker is the actual time an individual spent fixating an area of interest. In other words, the raw video data, as obtained from the camera, was transformed into an accurate measurement of fixation time.

The goal for validation is to determine whether a digital biomarker is fit for purpose. As its performance might vary across different populations, validation is necessary to ensure that a digital biomarker works accurately for the intended population [10]. For example, an eye tracking metric developed for toddlers might not work in teenagers, and a vocal biomarker developed for a non-tonal language such as English might not work on a tonal language like Mandarin. This is now also being reflected in regulatory processes: In their guidance on AI-based Medical Devices, the Food and Drug Authority of Saudia Arabia (SFDA) requires that datasets used for validation must align with the demographic, socio-economic attributes, and fundamental health indicators of the population in the target region [17].

Biomarkers can be classified into three categories: approved, original, and novel [3]. The basis of this classification is the evaluation status of their components, the measurement and the clinical outcome. The biomarker is approved when the measurement and the outcome are known and validated. An example for this would be the previous example of heart rate obtained from a wearable and its association to cardiovascular disease risk. Here, the digital measurement replaces another measurement form, while the association between the measurement and the clinical outcome is well-established. When one of the components is novel and the other is known, the biomarker is original. Finally, when both are novel, then the biomarker is novel. In the area of neurodevelopmental health, almost all biomarkers, digital and traditional, are either original or novel.

In the upcoming subchapters we will give a high-level overview of research advances in digital biomarkers and explore one example—eye tracking—in greater detail.

2 Current Status

Digital biomarkers for neurodevelopmental health have received increasing interest from researchers, but to date there has been little transfer into clinical practice. The main reason for this is that, for many metrics, the relationship to an existing clinical endpoint cannot be reliably established. Simply put, more research is needed. To the best of our knowledge, no company using digital biomarkers in neurodevelopmental health has received approval by a regulatory body and achieved full commercialization. However, there have been meaningful developments for software as a medical device. There is one product authorized by the US Food and Drug Administration (FDA) that leverages machine learning to assist autism screening: Canvas Dx can be prescribed for use in children ages 1.5–6 years [18]. The product combines data from questionnaires, clinician observation, and short videos of the child. A human rater codes the videos then machine learning is used to integrate the information from these three sources into an output that the HCP receives to support their diagnostic decision [19]. Furthermore, diaMentis, a company using retina imaging to assist the diagnosis of schizophrenia, bipolar disorder, and major depression is in the final phase of validation with the FDA and has previously received the agency's Breakthrough Designation for major scientific advances [20].

2.1 Wearable Technologies

Arguably, the most widely known digital biomarkers are those derived from wearable technology such as smartwatches and smart rings. The number of connected wearable devices rose to 1.1 billion in 2022 [21]. The information gathered from these devices ranges from heart rate to sleep patterns, subsequently used for purposes such as health monitoring, diagnosis, and management of chronic diseases [22]. Many of these devices are designed for personal use to help the wearers make healthier choices. However, they can also be used in collaboration with a HCP by sharing the measurements. Several insurance companies have encouraged the use of wearables, and multiple healthcare institutions have begun the integration of wearable device data into electronic health records [23].

Researchers have recently begun exploring the potential of wearable technology in neurodevelopmental health. One group developed wearable movement sensors to capture spontaneous limb movements in babies to assist the detection of neurodevelopmental conditions. The movement sensors could be worn on the wrists and ankles. The same group also developed a cap with multiple embedded sensors to capture how children oriented towards different stimuli [24]. Another researcher used a commercially available wearable wristband to detect anxiety in autistic adults based on heart rate measures [25].

2.2 Eye Tracking

Eye tracking is a frequently used method in psychological research. It helps determine the pupil's position in relation to an external stimulus. That is usually achieved by capturing the eye's position every few milliseconds using a camera, calculating the pupil's position and relating it to the spatial coordinates of the viewed visual stimulus [26]. This process is usually preceded by a calibration procedure [27]. Eye movements have typically been measured using specific hardware. However, recent computer science developments allow for fully software-based solutions using a smartphone or tablet camera. Technically, these software-based solutions for eye tracking involve a high-definition (HD) camera. The camera captures images of a user's interaction with the device screen. Stimuli are presented on the screen to catch the user's attention.

Image processing techniques such as thresholding, edge detection, and blob analysis are applied to the captured images to extract various eye features such as the pupil's position, centre of the eye, iris, and the eyelids' position. Thresholding for example is a technique where pixels of an image are classified as dark or light [28].

Once these features have been extracted, various machine learning algorithms are employed to process and analyse the gathered data, yielding a diverse set of eye-tracking metrics. Among these algorithms, Convolutional Neural Networks (CNNs) have emerged as a popular choice [29, 30]. Inspired by the way our brains process visual information, CNNs are designed to learn and comprehend visual data, similar to our brain's ability to identify patterns, objects or faces in what we observe. CNNs are structured with multiple layers that specialise in recognising different visual patterns, such as edges, shapes, textures, and even more complex features. This capability allows them to categorise images into distinct categories, making them an invaluable tool for identifying emotional responses within facial expressions, tracking eye movements, and detecting various visual cues.

The calibration process accurately maps the eye's movements to specific screen coordinates. This involves the user following predefined points on the screen while their gaze data is recorded, allowing the software to create a personalized mapping of the eye movements. Machine learning models are customized to adapt to individual characteristics and conditions, resulting in more accurate eye-tracking solutions. Next we will cover several eye tracking metrics relevant to neurodevelopmental health and represent potential digital biomarkers.

2.2.1 Fixation Duration

Fixation duration is the time a subject spends looking at an area of interest (AOI), either in total or proportional to the overall viewing time. The duration of the longest look at one AOI can also be of interest. In autism research, the AOIs are often social stimuli—such as faces or scenes of people interacting—and non-social stimuli—such as objects or geometric shapes. The two are often presented next to each other to determine visual preference. A meta-analysis from 2016 found that autistic individuals spent less time looking at social stimuli than their typically developing peers. The resulting effect size, Cohen's $d = 0.5$ indicates a medium effect. However, the literature on this is inconsistent. While multiple recently published studies showed significant differences in looking time towards social AOIs between children on the autism spectrum and children that are not on the autism spectrum [29, 31, 32], some found none [33, 34]. One study even found an effect in the opposite direction, where autistic children watched more social elements [35]. Studies on the topic are heterogeneous for both proband and stimulus characteristics [36]. The stimuli used include static ones, such as images [33, 34], dynamic ones, such as videos or avatars [29], and even virtual reality environments [35]. There are also vast differences in the age range. How these factors influence eye tracking metrics is described in more detail below.

In research on ADHD, the AOIs can be a target stimulus, which an individual is asked to focus on or is associated with a task. They are distinguishable from areas irrelevant to the task, such as distractors. Through calculating different eye tracking metrics in relation to these AOIs and feeding them into a logistic regression model, Lee and colleagues were able to obtain high sensitivity (0.73) and specificity (0.86) [37]. However, social stimuli are also used as AOIs in ADHD research. Airdrie et al. [38] investigated eye movements in ADHD adolescents or with conduct disorder, or both conditions co-occurring, as well as in typically developing youth. They presented a facial emotion recognition task, during which they also tracked eye movements. The proportion of time spent looking at the eyes was significantly lower in ADHD participants, both with and without co-occurring conduct disorder.

2.2.2 Saccade Profiles

A saccade is a rapid, abrupt eye movement to change the viewer's point of fixation. Just before a saccade and throughout its duration, saccadic suppression occurs, a phenomenon where visual perception, especially vision sensitivity, is suppressed. There is a distinction between voluntary and involuntary or reflexive saccades [39].

Different tasks can be used to assess saccades, most notably the prosaccade and antisaccade task [40]. During both tasks, a target stimulus (such as a dot) is displayed at the center of the screen. Another stimulus then appears in the periphery. The subject is instructed to either follow the movement with the eyes (prosaccade task) [41] or respond with an eye movement in the opposite direction (antisaccade task). Humans would typically make a reflexive saccade to the new stimulus location. The antisaccade task requires humans to inhibit this reflexive saccade and instead make a voluntary saccade in the opposite direction. Research shows that error rates in this task, i.e. failing to inhibit the reflexive saccade, are higher in several disorders including schizophrenia [42].

The analysis of saccades has been applied frequently to research on ADHD. It has been shown that on the antisaccade task, ADHD children make significantly more direction errors than their typically developing peers [43, 44]. A variation of the antisaccade task is the memory-guided antisaccade task. During this task, subjects are shown a visual cue but asked not to make the saccade immediately. After a short period of time, the saccade is executed towards the memorised location of the target [45, 46]. ADHD participants have been shown to make more anticipatory errors in this task, meaning that they made a saccade to the cue before they were instructed to do so [43].

2.2.3 Smooth Pursuit Eye Movements

The goal of smooth pursuit movements is to continuously follow a moving stimulus with the eyes, thus keeping it on the fovea, an area on the retina where visual acuity is highest. Compared to saccades, these movements are much slower and require a moving target the observer can follow. In the absence of a stimulus, attempting the same movement would result in a saccade rather than a smooth pursuit [47]. To keep up with the moving stimulus, the movement needs to be carried out with a certain velocity. The ratio between this target velocity and the actual eye movement velocity, is called pursuit gain [48]. When the eye falls behind the target, it is necessary to correct the positional error by initiating a catch-up saccade [49, 50]. This catch-up saccade involves moving the eye in the direction of the target to align with the stimulus and minimize the positional discrepancy [48]. The ability to smoothly follow a target can be impaired in patients with disorders such as Parkinson's disease [51] and schizophrenia [52, 53]. Though research on this topic is limited, some differences in smooth pursuit eye movements have been associated with ADHD. Caldani and colleagues found that ADHD children exhibited a higher number of catch-up saccades and had lower pursuit gain than their typically developing peers. The most striking difference here is in the catch-up saccades: The average of catch-up saccades throughout the task was 22 in the TD group and 50 in the ADHD group. This measure also decreased significantly after a training session on visual attention, making it a possible response biomarker [48].

2.2.4 Factors Influencing Eye Tracking

Several factors have shown to impact eye tracking measures. They can be roughly divided into stimulus and viewer characteristics. Potential stimulus characteristics include threat, social content, and stimulus type. Crawford and colleagues hypothesized that the perceived threat of a stimulus could influence how much attention viewers pay to it. To test this, they presented stimuli—either non-social or social—that were either moving towards the viewer (threat condition) or past the viewer (non-threat condition). They drew a comparison between autistic adolescents and those with special education needs but not autistic. There was in fact a significant main effect for threat versus no-threat: Both groups spent a higher amount of time looking at stimuli in the threat condition. In the threat condition the proportion of looking at social stimuli was significantly lower in autism than controls while the difference was not significant in the non-threat condition [54].

Chita-Tegmark identified an effect for social content in a meta-analysis: When social stimuli had higher social content, i.e. showed more than one person, social attention in autism was most impacted [36]. Similarly, Chevallier and colleagues showed that the type of stimulus is important when attempting to classify autistic children and non-autistic children. Their study compared three groups of stimuli containing social and non-social stimuli, including static stimuli (photos of faces and objects), dynamic stimuli (videos of objects and of emotional faces), and interactive stimuli (videos of two children playing in parallel or together with objects around them). Group differences in eye movements were only found in response to interactive stimuli. Consistent with that, classification into an autism and non-autism group was only possible when tracking eye movements in response to the interactive stimuli [55]. It should be noted that the interactive stimuli also had a higher social content.

Different characteristics of the viewer must also be considered when developing digital biomarkers based on eye tracking. This includes factors such as age and medications. As Caldani et al. described in their study on pursuit eye movements, the number of catch-up saccades correlates significantly with age in typically developing children, where the number of catch-up saccades decreases with age. In ADHD children, however, this correlation does not exist: The number of catch-up saccades does not decrease with age [48]. Certain medications can also alter eye movement metrics. For example, benzodiazepines, anticonvulsants, and mood stabilizers can decrease the velocity of saccades and smooth pursuit movements [56].

2.2.5 Machine Learning Classification

While many of the previously described studies evaluate use of individual eye tracking metrics, machine learning studies on eye tracking data typically conduct multivariate analyses, integrating multiple metrics into one model. For example,

De Silva and colleagues integrated fixation and saccade-based features into their model for ADHD classification, obtaining 81% accuracy [57].

A recent systematic review and meta-analysis of 261 research articles aimed at distinguishing autistic from typically developing individuals through machine learning techniques showed promising results: For preschool-aged children, an overall accuracy of 88% across studies was achieved, while analyses on school-aged children exhibited a slightly lower accuracy of 79%. However, the authors underscored the significant heterogeneity across studies, stemming from differences in stimuli, algorithms, and performance evaluation methods, a notion supported by other researchers in the field [58, 59]. The issue of heterogeneity is also present in the autism diagnostic criteria serving as the ground truth in these studies: A systematic review assessing 11 studies showed that the criteria vary greatly across studies, spanning from unreported criteria to various diagnostic tools, including CARS, AQ-child, and ADOS [59]. This complicates direct comparisons and replicability. In conclusion, while eye tracking-based approaches hold great promise for autism research, it is currently characterized by significant heterogeneity, making it challenging to arrive at overarching conclusions.

2.3 Pupillometry

Pupillometry is a technique for measuring pupil diameter [60]. Pupils constrict when exposed to brightness or during fixation on nearby objects, whereas darkness, cognitive activity, or experiencing heightened autonomic arousal trigger dilation. Dilation is controlled by the iris dilator muscle which is innervated by the sympathetic nervous system, while contraction is controlled by the iris sphincter muscle which is innervated by the parasympathetic nervous system. This connection explains why pupils are smaller when at rest or even sleepy and larger when alert, aroused, and awake [61].

Recently, software-based solutions to pupillometry have emerged [62, 63, 64], opening promising new research avenues. In a preliminary study conducted in 2013, a smartphone-based pupillometry prototype was introduced. This system incorporated an optical setup featuring infrared and white LEDs affixed to a smartphone's camera [65]. In this design, infrared LEDs were utilized to capture pupil dilation images in low light conditions without influencing pupil size, while white LEDs induced pupil constriction. All captured images were subsequently processed through a proposed algorithm within the Android platform using Photoshop [66]. The findings demonstrated a high degree of accuracy ($97.7 \pm 1.3\%$), highlighting the promising potential of smartphone-based pupillometry for further exploration and development.

Another study by Piaggio et al. reinforced the concept of higher accuracy and significant correlations in comparison to commercially available solutions for all pupillometry-related metrics [67]. These collective studies underscore the potential of smartphone-based pupillometry as a reliable, user-friendly, portable, and cost-efficient method for pupil measurements, with relevance in resource-constrained settings. However, it is evident that further research and development efforts are necessary to fully unlock the capabilities of this innovative approach.

To date, there is one meta-analysis focusing specifically on pupil responses to light and visual stimuli in individuals on the autism spectrum, which has identified a distinctive characteristic: a notably prolonged latency in the pupil response. Latency here signifies the duration it takes for the pupil to either dilate or constrict following the presentation of a stimulus or light. The group difference here is substantial, denoted by a large effect size of $g = 1.03$. Despite these intriguing findings, no conclusive explanations for this group difference have emerged yet, but several authors have hypothesized an involvement of the locus coeruleus-norepinephrine system [68]. Pupil size and locus coeruleus activity are reliably associated [16] and the locus coeruleus is part of the pathway controlling pupil dilation [61]. A recently published study further found that autistic individuals showed a significantly lower pupillary response than their typically developing peers when watching videos displaying human interaction. Correspondingly, their pupillary response was significantly higher in videos without humans [69].

Using solely pupillometry data, authors Das and Khanna [70] created a tool based on a support vector machine (SVM) model with the purpose of assisting in the classification of ADHD. This tool achieved impressive results with a sensitivity of 0.77 and specificity of 0.75. SVM are mathematical models well suited for separating and classifying data into distinct groups, meaning it assesses the data and identifies a 'line' or 'hyperplane' (depending on the dimension or number of features of the data) that best distinguishes the data points. In the case of ADHD diagnosis, the SVM would analyse the pupillometry data and find the best 'boundary' that maximises the gap between the two groups of individuals with and without ADHD. To achieve this, the researchers utilised a variety of metrics, such as the rate of pupil-size dilation, to process the data. This innovative approach sheds light on the potential of utilising pupillometry as a valuable tool for diagnosing and understanding ADHD.

2.4 Vocal Biomarkers

Vocal biomarkers are advantageous for several reasons. They can be obtained in all ages, even from infants [71, 72]. Furthermore, voice analysis can shed a light on multiple conditions, including neurodegenerative [73, 74] and psychiatric [75], making it practical to obtain a high volume of information from one speech sample.

Voice recordings are captured using microphones, smartphones, or other specialized devices. The audio data is stored securely. Pre-processing is carried out to filter noise. Machine learning algorithms are then applied to extract acoustic features from the audio data. Multiple features can be extracted from a voice sample. An important feature is the fundamental frequency, also denoted as f0. This parameter represents the rate of vibration of the vocal folds and is measured in Hertz. Humans perceive this as pitch; how high or low a sound is. From the fundamental frequency, various metrics can be derived, including f0 mean, variance, standard deviation, and range. Pitch variance, standard deviation, and range are all measures of pitch variability, i.e. the changes in f0 over a certain time period. Another voice feature is intensity, quantified in decibels, which corresponds to our perception of loudness. Furthermore, measures related to pauses can be examined, such as the mean duration of pauses and the total duration of pauses in a speech sample [75, 76]. Voice duration represents a measure of the length of a vocal production, such as a baby's cry [72] or a word [77]. Besides these voice features, the content of spoken language can also be analysed. However, this subchapter's focus will be on non-language voice metrics.

Different tasks can be used for voice elicitation. Low and colleagues describe two main categories: constrained and free speech. A constrained task includes reading a passage or sustaining vowels. These tasks allow for a more controlled setting and are best for measuring source and respiration features. In free speech tasks, subjects might be asked to retell a memory or talk about a given topic. They can also include conversations. For example, speech recorded during a clinical interview or a simulated interaction task. Advantages are a higher ecological validity and social dynamics, such as taking turns in a dialogue being captured [75].

Most research in this area has been conducted on autism screening. Findings from meta-analyses indicated that autistic individuals exhibit a higher mean pitch, higher pitch variability—most often indicated by pitch range—[78, 79], and longer voice duration [78]. Howbeit, a number of factors can have an influence on these metrics, such as age [78], type of voice elicitation tasks [78], biological sex [80], and language [80–82]. How age and sex impact different voice metrics can also differ across languages [80]. For example, in their cross-linguistic investigation with Danish and US English voice samples Fusaroli et al. could only replicate findings of increased pitch variability in Danish but not English. Nevertheless, a distinct autism-associated acoustic pattern, characterised by higher pitch and longer pauses, was identified across the two languages. These group differences corresponded to a moderate effect size [80].

This research underscores the significance of considering language as a variable in voice analysis. This is particularly relevant in the context of tonal languages, in which the meaning of a word or syllable depends on the pitch or tone in which it is pronounced. In tonal languages, the pitch or tone can change the meaning of a word, even if the consonants and vowels are pronounced the same [83]. A study investigating voice markers in Mandarin and Cantonese found that in these languages, autistic children also exhibited a higher mean pitch, and in some tasks also a higher pitch variability [82]. Another study investigated differences between Cantonese and English in fundamental frequency contours, which show how f0 changes over an utterance, thus including multiple timepoints rather than a single metric. The authors found that a machine learning model based on f0 contours in Cantonese could not successfully classify subjects by autism diagnosis, whereas results for English were significant [81]. It should be noted that the two studies employed both different tasks and methods of analysis. The heterogeneity in the literature and inconsistent results lead to the question how well these models can be generalised when new data are fed into them. Rybner and colleagues tested this by testing several machine learning models for autism classification on different voice elicitation tasks and languages. They found generalisability to be very limited, especially with regard to various languages [84]. This represents a major challenge the field needs to overcome to make reliable vocal biomarkers for autism screening a reality.

Less research is available on other conditions, but initial results indicate the possibility of using vocal biomarkers to detect ADHD [85, 86].

2.5 Other Biomarkers

While giving a detailed description of all potential digital biomarkers is beyond the scope of this chapter, we want to provide a brief overview of additional metrics. Liao and colleagues investigated facial expressions in detecting autism and achieved 77.5% accuracy using a random forest solely based on facial expression data [87]. In a meta-analysis, researchers found a moderate effect size for the differences in facial expressions between autistic individuals and non-autistic individuals. One example of these differences is that individuals on the autism spectrum exhibit facial mimicry—meaning automatically imitating others' facial expressions—less frequently [88]. Blink rates are another metric that might be useful in detecting autism as autistic people tend to blink more than their typically developing peers [89].

2.6 Multimodal Biomarkers

Finally, it should be noted that where multiple biomarkers, digital or traditional, are relevant, they can be integrated into one model. This can be referred to as composite [10] or multimodal digital biomarkers. For example, De Silva and colleagues [90] combined eye movement and pupillometry data for ADHD classification. The highest-performing algorithm reached a maximum accuracy of 84%. Jiang et al. [91] combined eye tracking data with response times to an emotion recognition task, reaching a maximum accuracy of 86.2% in autism classification. They observed that the task features alone had very low sensitivity, which rose to 91.3% when combined with eye tracking features. Finally, Liao et al. combined data from facial expressions, eye movements, and EEG, reaching an accuracy of 87.5%, 10 percentage points more than facial expressions alone [87].

Research on precision health in other disciplines has shown that the fusion of multiple data types improves predictive performance with a mean accuracy increase of 6.4%. Nevertheless, this is also associated with the downside of reduced scalability as data fusion requires time intensive data transformations [92]. However with more scalable algorithms enabled by advances in AI, the benefits of multimodality can be secured. And use of multiple modalities in principle is expected to yield better accuracy results for most use cases.

3 Promises

The power and capabilities of digital technologies keep growing exponentially and doubling every 18–24 months, in line with the famed Moores law. Such that a standard mobile device of today is as capable as the most powerful supercomputer from 30 years ago and millions of times more capable than the Apollo 11 computer that took humanity to the moon. Also, costs have decreased exponentially. The cost of one megabyte of storage at the time of the moon landing was approximately 1 million USD and today it is less than 1 Cent.

Additionally, the capability to sense various modalities such as light, pressure, sound, taste, temperature, and even smell is expected to grow and improve over time. As indicated in Sect. 2.6, increased multimodality correlates with increased accuracy. And herein lies the **first promise** of digital biomarkers: the ability to measure a greater variety of biomarkers faster, cheaper, and more accurately. As digital health technologies increase exponentially in their raw hardware capabilities and their increasing modalities to sense and measure physiological processes, they are expected to pave the way for the increasing use of digital biomarkers to measure and capture rudimentary physiological data for various normal, pathological/pathogenic, and interventional processes.

The **second promise** is that of algorithmic sophistication. The advances of modern artificial intelligence, in particular, and of other machine learning and statistical analytics approaches enable new ways of analyzing large amounts of data and leveraging the underlying digital capabilities. As more data from various digital devices with increasing modalities are collected, the algorithmic sophistication makes it increasingly possible to understand the data and derive meaningful health insights from the digital biomarkers. Consequently, this leads to various healthcare use cases. We elaborate below on some of the use case cases that become possible because of this.

The **third promise**, and in our opinion of most significant impact, is the opportunity for bridging the access gap to healthcare, made achievable by the broad availability of digital tech across the globe. For illustration, there are ca. half a billion mobile subscriptions in Africa [93]. That is ten times more than just 10 years ago. Projecting at half the previous growth rate there will be more smartphones than humans in 10 years. The ubiquity of these devices, the increased capabilities at a reduced cost, obtained as a result of the first promise, and the various health-important use cases enabled by algorithmic sophistication, as a result of the second promise, provide a unique opportunity for achieving health equity globally.

This also provides a unique opportunity for low- and middle-income countries (LMICs) to leapfrog the development of their health systems and infrastructure to take advantage of the promises made possible due to the transformative power of digital biomarkers.To better illustrate the promises of digital biomarkers, we will elaborate on three categories of use cases demonstrating the utility of digital biomarkers to transform health delivery. We focus on the use case for (1) Screening and Diagnosis, (2) Health and Treatment Monitoring, and (3) Clinical Trials.

3.1 Screening and Diagnosis

There are currently immense challenges in adequate care for neurodiverse people. A study on outpatients in Italy found a median duration of untreated ADHD as high as 17 years [94]. A study from Bosnia and Herzegovina found that parents concerned with their child's development had an average of more than six visits with a professional for over a year before receiving a diagnosis [95]. Even in Switzerland, one of the most well-resourced health systems globally, it takes almost two years on average from the first observation of atypical development to an autism diagnosis [96]. Whereas these problems are complex, digital biomarkers have the potential to contribute to simplified screening by reducing the workload of human experts.

This effect is more pronounced in LMICs with more constrained resources and fewer trained specialists. For example, in Nairobi, a city of over five million, there are less than five paediatric neurodevelopmental specialists. Effective digital biomarkers could have an enormous impact to lead to timely and accurate earlier diagnoses paving the way for early intervention therapeutics that are crucial to positive outcomes.

The ability to continuously capture information is also invaluable when dealing with neurodevelopmental conditions, where the presentation of symptoms can notably be different in clinical settings compared to a more natural environment, like at home. For instance, selective mutism might manifest differently in a doctor's or therapist's office than in the familiarity of a child's home environment, which can lead to being misdiagnosed with autism. A possible solution to this is remote, home-based assessments based on digital biomarkers.

Additionally, digital biomarkers can provide more objective diagnostic outcomes by say, enabling the assessment of non-speaking patients, such as non-verbal autistic adults and young children.

3.2 Health and Treatment Monitoring

Digital biomarkers also offer profound advantages through their capacity for continuous measurement, effectively transcending the limitations of traditional snapshot assessments [3]. Given the shortage of specialists, many HCPs will only see their patients every few months. This places the burden of communicating relevant information on the patient or their caregivers, whereas digital biomarkers could enable a continuous data stream capturing different symptoms in between appointments. This becomes of greater value in resource and manpower-constrained settings of both the global South and the North.

In the global South, especially in remote settings with very limited access to specialist care, digital biomarkers for monitoring could play a significant role in monitoring health at the individual and the populational level, thus paving the way for optimal, telemedical approaches and planning of limited specialist resources to address the needs of the population. The demographic transition in the North leading to a more elderly population with fewer caregivers could benefit significantly from digital biomarkers for monitoring. There are already multiple instances of smart wearables and other digital biomarkers providing early intervention signals and saving lives, such that the Defense Department of the United States is consolidating these capabilities into a Rapid Assessment of Threat Exposure project or the RATE program [97]. Such programs are expected to increase.

3.3 Clinical Trials

Digital biomarkers also hold immense promise for clinical trials as they enable the decentralization of studies through remote measurements [10]. Many of the metrics we discussed in this chapter can be obtained using just a smartphone or tablet which makes it possible for participants to easily record and share their data with researchers. With the adoption of digital biomarkers, participants do not necessarily have to travel to a study site. Where site visits are necessary, the data collected there can be enriched by data obtained from remote measurements. This shift can reduce the burden on trial participants but also opens the door to a more diverse and geographically widespread participant pool. Moreover, it introduces the potential for continuous, real-time measurements, allowing researchers to gather more data points over longer durations, leading to richer insights and a more comprehensive understanding of treatment efficacy. There is also the potential to reduce costs from reimbursing proband travel costs, making cutting-edge research more accessible and affordable.

4 Perils

The promise of digital biomarkers is that they will become better, smarter, and cheaper and will enable new use cases that help to achieve global health equity. According to the WHO, AI healthcare tools, at the heart of digital biomarkers, have enormous potential to strengthen the delivery of healthcare and medicine and to help all countries achieve universal health coverage. They can empower patients and communities to assume control of their healthcare and better understand their evolving needs. In essence, they create unique opportunities to accelerate access to health and prosperity across the globe with immediate potential for triple billions of US dollars of impact in the short term [98].

As the proverbial double-edged sword, these promises come with key considerations that must be addressed as they are developed, to contain certain perils. If unaddressed, there is a real risk of further exacerbating and amplifying global inequities. We summarize the perils to watch out for as follows using our framework of three double As (1) Accuracy and Authenticity (2) Autonomy and Agency and (3) Access and Availability.

4.1 Accuracy and Authenticity

Mental health conditions are multifactorial disorders that require a comprehensive understanding of not only measurable biometric data but also the complex social and historical context that also contributes heavily to outcomes [99]. Capturing and combining these biomarkers are non-trivial and need to be implemented with scientific rigor and discipline to measure their impact, accuracy, specificity, and sensitivity.

There are reported but non-reproducible claims of digital biomarkers apps that can accurately measure blood pressure using the smartphone camera [100], or of cities banning facial recognition tools that have proven to not meet the bar of repeatability and consistency of accuracy of the results [101]. Health regulators must maintain due diligence regarding the accuracy of digital biomarker solutions that get to patients.

Performance also needs to be robust in one-off scenarios as well as longitudinally. One could mitigate the one-moment-in-time data collection for example of a voice sample by including patient histories in the training data. The creation of safe spaces for innovation could help to create this balance. Use cases that retain the human in the loop of decision-making should be encouraged to enable the generation of sufficient validation data to improve the accuracy of results [102].

As such, we recommend that digital biomarkers be initially implemented in clinical settings to triage and ease the workload for HCPs. In other scenarios, digital biomarkers show acceptable accuracy performance within a narrow test band but fail to generalize within the general population. An example of this are AI skin lesion detection tools not trained on darker skin tones that fail to generalize to a more representative population [103, 104].

Users should have transparency on the capabilities and limitations of the AI tools to make informed decisions [105] . If the dataset used for training an algorithm was only tested on a subset of the population, HCPs should be informed so that they can only use these tools accurately for that cohort. The goal however is to ensure that tools have been robustly trained and validated on representative data to avoid or minimize bias in an increasingly globalised world.

Accuracy is very much dependent on data quality. Training, validating, and testing datasets should be of high quality. This requires developers to implement data governance measures that ensure the accuracy, reliability, and relevance of the data used. In addition, AI systems should include proper human oversight mechanisms to prevent or minimize risks for example ability for human operators to intervene and override decisions made by AI tools. For digital biomarkers to be effective, existing biases based on race, ethnicity, age, and gender, that are encoded in data used to train algorithms, must be overcome. Algorithmic bias may creep into AI systems used for the biomarkers via flawed or incomplete data sampling leading to harmful outcomes. Bias increases the risk of vulnerable populations becoming distrustful of participating in research which then negatively impacts the robustness of such tools, resulting in a vicious circle.

4.2 Autonomy and Agency

Digital biomarkers' currency is data collected in the very private space of humans and as such consists of information that is very sensitive and mostly personal and private. Needless to note, the importance of the highest standards of cybersecurity concerning the collection, transmission, usage, and storage of personal data. Humans should have full agency and control of their data to avoid leakages and other dire consequences resulting from loss of control over the data.

AI research is qualitatively more different than research on human participants as regulated by existing clinical research guidelines. This has raised novel questions for researchers/developers as using existing rules for example, does using anonymized data discount the need for informed consent? There is a need for all stakeholders to be invested in updated ethical and regulatory frameworks for AI healthcare tools used on humans, but that also does not hinder the speed and growth of new technologies. The proposed EU's AI Act could provide comprehensive guardrails on transparency, quality, human oversight, robustness, and accuracy of AI tools among others [105]. A laissez-faire approach on matters of privacy and informed consent may frustrate innovation and growth in AI technologies if a lack of trust and unchecked risks were to lead to a backlash by the public or potential research participants [99, 101]. Other frameworks in discussion worldwide include the Rome Call for AI Ethics (Rome Call for AI Ethics), the EU Assessment List for Trustworthy AI (HLEG), the AI Bill of Rights (AIBoR) and the Further Advancing Racial Equity and Support for Underserved Communities Through the Federal Government (EO 14091) executive order. The perceived need for speed, which is rightfully encouraged by the increased capabilities of these tools, may hinder efforts to put adequate guardrails in place.

Another peril is the loss of autonomy and personal agency over what one chooses to reveal. Controlling that AI tools do not take personal agency away for instance the right of using or revealing information about a person without their consent is vital. Autonomy for humans means that they remain in full control of their healthcare and medical decisions. This is undermined when decisions that should be made by humans are transferred to machines as the former may not understand how an AI technology arrives at a decision, nor be able to negotiate with a technology to reach a shared decision [98].

4.3 Access and Availability

Even before the advent of AI, there was already a pre-existing digital divide of access and use of information and communication technologies between high and low-income populations, within and between countries. AI tools have the potential to address cost and access barriers by positively impacting individual and populational health. We propose that AI tools should be developed using standard devices such as smartphones as opposed to specialized gadgets that may only be available to high-income communities. Further, more stakeholders such as clinicians and patients should be involved at the design phase and not only seen as end-users.

Whereas the proliferation of digital devices is expected to continue to grow even in low and middle-income settings as described under the third promise of digital biomarkers, there are some indications of a digital divide [106], as well as a gender divide in those settings and these need to be addressed to ensure that the solutions do not exacerbate the inequality. In conclusion, ethical considerations and human rights must be placed at the center of the design, development, and deployment of AI technologies for health.

5 Conclusion

Digital biomarkers and the AI methods used to create them have immense potential to improve healthcare in neurodevelopmental health. They can enable decentralized clinical trials, support continuous monitoring, and reduce HCP workloads, thus contributing to earlier assessments. In recent years, research has been conducted on potential digital biomarkers based on eye tracking, voice metrics, pupillometry, and data obtained from wearables, among others. Promising results from various studies have emerged, but this is a highly complex topic. Individual differences such as different languages, ages, gender, medications, and co-occurring conditions must be taken into account when developing, using, and interpreting digital biomarkers.

Digital biomarkers, due to the advances in the underlying digital technology, are poised to get better at collecting data from increasing multiplicities of modality and to enable even more impactful use cases that contribute to increased global access to healthcare. However, they face challenges that could peril their successful adoption if not addressed adequately. The biomarkers need to be consistently accurate and provide predictably authentic readings of the underlying condition. They need to be developed to fully respect human agency and autonomy and to ensure that the solutions foster access and availability in all markets to claim the promise of enabling more equitable access to healthcare.

Furthermore, to fully harness the potential of digital biomarkers, more research on large, representative datasets is needed to reliably establish the relationship between the gathered metrics and clinical endpoints. The diversity within the population, including individuals with various neurodevelopmental conditions and backgrounds, must be taken into account to ensure that the findings can be applied broadly in healthcare settings. This emphasis on data diversity and the nuanced understanding of individual factors will be essential for the successful integration of digital biomarkers into neurodevelopmental healthcare practices.

References

1. European Medicines Agency (n.d.) Biomarker. In: European medicines agency glossary of regulatory terms. https://www.ema.europa.eu/en/glossary/biomarker. Accessed 21 Aug 2023
2. FDA-NIH Biomarker Working Group (2016) BEST (Biomarkers, EndpointS, and other Tools) Resource. Food and Drug Administration (US), Silver Spring (MD)
3. Babrak LM, Menetski J, Rebhan M, Nisato G, Zinggeler M, Brasier N, Baerenfaller K, Brenzikofer T, Baltzer L, Vogler C, Gschwind L, Schneider C, Streiff F, Groenen PMA, Miho E (2019) Traditional and digital biomarkers: two worlds apart? Digit Biomark 3:92–102. https://doi.org/10.1159/000502000
4. Barateau L, Pizza F, Plazzi G, Dauvilliers Y (2022) Narcolepsy. J Sleep Res 31:e13631. https://doi.org/10.1111/jsr.13631
5. Sandler HM, Eisenberger MA (2007) Assessing and treating patients with increasing prostate specific antigen following radical prostatectomy. J Urol 178:S20-24. https://doi.org/10.1016/j.juro.2007.04.034
6. Califf RM (2018) Biomarker definitions and their applications. Exp Biol Med (Maywood) 243:213–221. https://doi.org/10.1177/1535370217750088
7. FDA Center for Devices and Radiological Health (2023) Clinical outcome assessments (COAs) in medical device decision making. https://www.fda.gov/about-fda/cdrh-patient-science-and-engagement-program/clinical-outcome-assessments-coas-medical-device-decision-making. Accessed 14 Sep 2023
8. Piau A, Wild K, Mattek N, Kaye J (2019) Current state of digital biomarker technologies for real-life, home-based monitoring of cognitive function for mild cognitive impairment to mild Alzheimer disease and implications for clinical care: systematic review. J Med Internet Res 21:e12785. https://doi.org/10.2196/12785
9. Motahari-Nezhad H, Fgaier M, Mahdi Abid M, Péntek M, Gulácsi L, Zrubka Z (2022) Digital biomarker-based studies: scoping review of systematic reviews. JMIR Mhealth Uhealth 10:e35722. https://doi.org/10.2196/35722
10. Coravos A, Khozin S, Mandl KD (2019) Developing and adopting safe and effective digital biomarkers to improve patient outcomes. NPJ Digit Med 2:1–5. https://doi.org/10.1038/s41746-019-0090-4
11. Montag C, Elhai JD, Dagum P (2021) On blurry boundaries when defining digital biomarkers: how much biology needs to be in a digital biomarker? Front Psych 12. https://doi.org/10.3389/fpsyt.2021.740292
12. Bent B, Lu B, Kim J, Dunn JP (2021) Biosignal compression toolbox for digital biomarker discovery. Sensors (Basel) 21:516. https://doi.org/10.3390/s21020516
13. Aalbers G, Hendrickson AT, Vanden Abeele MM, Keijsers L (2023) Smartphone-tracked digital markers of momentary subjective stress in college students: idiographic machine learning analysis. JMIR Mhealth Uhealth 11:e37469. https://doi.org/10.2196/37469
14. Saeb S, Zhang M, Karr CJ, Schueller SM, Corden ME, Kording KP, Mohr DC (2015) Mobile phone sensor correlates of depressive symptom severity in daily-life behavior: an exploratory study. J Med Internet Res 17:e175. https://doi.org/10.2196/jmir.4273
15. Gui A, Mason L, Gliga T, Hendry A, Begum Ali J, Pasco G, Shephard E, Curtis C, Charman T, Johnson MH, Meaburn E, Jones EJH, BASIS-STAARS team (2020) Look duration at the face as a developmental endophenotype: elucidating pathways to autism and ADHD. Dev Psychopathol 32:1303–1322. https://doi.org/10.1017/S0954579420000930
16. Joshi S, Li Y, Kalwani RM, Gold JI (2016) Relationships between pupil diameter and neuronal activity in the locus coeruleus, colliculi, and cingulate cortex. Neuron 89:221–234. https://doi.org/10.1016/j.neuron.2015.11.028
17. Saudi Food and Drug Authority (2022) Guidance on artificial intelligence (AI) and machine learning (ML) technologies based medical devices. https://www.sfda.gov.sa/sites/default/files/2023-01/MDS-G010ML.pdf. Accessed 14 Oct 2023

18. FDA (2021) FDA authorizes marketing of diagnostic aid for autism spectrum disorder. In: FDA news release. https://www.fda.gov/news-events/press-announcements/fda-authorizes-marketing-diagnostic-aid-autism-spectrum-disorder. Accessed 9 Oct 2023
19. Cognoa Inc. (2023) Canvas DxTM and supporting software user guide for healthcare providers (HCPs). https://cognoa-production-cms.s3.amazonaws.com/documents/CanvasDxLBL-001-HCPPortal-Instructions-for-Use-v6.pdf
20. diaMentis (2022) Press release September 22 2022. https://diamentis.com/en/. Accessed 12 Oct 2023
21. Laricchia F (2023) Global connected wearable devices 2019–2022. In: Statista. https://www.statista.com/statistics/487291/global-connected-wearable-devices/. Accessed 8 Sep 2023
22. Lu L, Zhang J, Xie Y, Gao F, Xu S, Wu X, Ye Z (2020) Wearable health devices in health care: narrative systematic review. JMIR Mhealth Uhealth 8:e18907. https://doi.org/10.2196/18907
23. Dinh-Le C, Chuang R, Chokshi S, Mann D (2019) Wearable health technology and electronic health record integration: scoping review and future directions. JMIR Mhealth Uhealth 7:e12861. https://doi.org/10.2196/12861
24. Campolo D, Taffoni F, Schiavone G, Laschi C, Keller F, Guglielmelli E (2008) A novel technological approach towards the early diagnosis of neurodevelopmental disorders. In: Annual international conference of the IEEE engineering in medicine and biology society 2008, pp 4875–4878. https://doi.org/10.1109/IEMBS.2008.4650306
25. Kerns A (2020) Using fitbits to assess anxiety in adults with autism and intellectual disability. University of North Carolina at Chapel Hill
26. Krummenacher J, Müller HJ (2022) Blickbewegungsmessung. In: Dorsch Lexikon der Psychologie. https://dorsch.hogrefe.com/stichwort/blickbewegungsmessung. Accessed 31 Aug 2023
27. Harezlak K, Kasprowski P, Stasch M (2014) Towards accurate eye tracker calibration—Methods and procedures. Procedia Comput Sci 35:1073–1081. https://doi.org/10.1016/j.procs.2014.08.194
28. Bradley D, Roth G (2007) Adaptive thresholding using the integral image. J Graph Tools 12(2):13–21. https://doi.org/10.1080/2151237X.2007.10129236
29. Wen TH, Cheng A, Andreason C, Zahiri J, Xiao Y, Xu R, Bao B, Courchesne E, Barnes CC, Arias SJ, Pierce K (2022) Large scale validation of an early-age eye-tracking biomarker of an autism spectrum disorder subtype. Sci Rep 12:4253. https://doi.org/10.1038/s41598-022-08102-6
30. Birawo B, Kasprowski P (2022) Review and evaluation of eye movement event detection algorithms. Sensors (Basel) 22:8810. https://doi.org/10.3390/s22228810
31. Shic F, Barney EC, Naples AJ, Dommer KJ, Chang SA, Li B, McAllister T, Atyabi A, Wang Q, Bernier R, Dawson G, Dziura J, Faja S, Jeste SS, Murias M, Johnson SP, Sabatos-DeVito M, Helleman G, Senturk D, Sugar CA, Webb SJ, McPartland JC, Chawarska K, Autism Biomarkers Consortium for Clinical Trials (2023) The Selective Social Attention task in children with autism spectrum disorder: results from the Autism Biomarkers Consortium for Clinical Trials (ABC-CT) feasibility study. Autism Research. https://doi.org/10.1002/aur.3026
32. Camero R, Gallego C, Martínez V (2023) Gaze following as an early diagnostic marker of autism in a new word learning task in toddlers. J Autism Dev Disord. https://doi.org/10.1007/s10803-023-06043-1
33. Frost-Karlsson M, Galazka MA, Gillberg C, Gillberg C, Miniscalco C, Billstedt E, Hadjikhani N, Åsberg Johnels J (2019) Social scene perception in autism spectrum disorder: an eye-tracking and pupillometric study. J Clin Exp Neuropsychol 41:1024–1032. https://doi.org/10.1080/13803395.2019.1646214
34. Elsabbagh M, Gliga T, Pickles A, Hudry K, Charman T, Johnson MH (2013) The development of face orienting mechanisms in infants at-risk for autism. Behav Brain Res 251:147–154. https://doi.org/10.1016/j.bbr.2012.07.030

35. Alcañiz M, Chicchi-Giglioli IA, Carrasco-Ribelles LA, Marín-Morales J, Minissi ME, Teruel-García G, Sirera M, Abad L (2022) Eye gaze as a biomarker in the recognition of autism spectrum disorder using virtual reality and machine learning: a proof of concept for diagnosis. Autism Res 15:131–145. https://doi.org/10.1002/aur.2636
36. Chita-Tegmark M (2016) Social attention in ASD: a review and meta-analysis of eye-tracking studies. Res Dev Disabil 48:79–93. https://doi.org/10.1016/j.ridd.2015.10.011
37. Lee DY, Shin Y, Park RW, Cho S-M, Han S, Yoon C, Choo J, Shim JM, Kim K, Jeon S-W, Kim S-J (2023) Use of eye tracking to improve the identification of attention-deficit/hyperactivity disorder in children. Sci Rep 13:14469. https://doi.org/10.1038/s41598-023-41654-9
38. Airdrie JN, Langley K, Thapar A, van Goozen SHM (2018) Facial emotion recognition and eye gaze in attention-deficit/hyperactivity disorder with and without comorbid conduct disorder. J Am Acad Child Adolesc Psychiatr 57:561–570. https://doi.org/10.1016/j.jaac.2018.04.016
39. Heuer H (2016) Sakkade. In: Dorsch Lexikon der Psychologie. https://dorsch.hogrefe.com/stichwort/sakkade. Accessed 1 Sep 2023
40. Hallett PE (1978) Primary and secondary saccades to goals defined by instructions. Vision Res 18:1279–1296. https://doi.org/10.1016/0042-6989(78)90218-3
41. Zhou J (2021) Differences on prosaccade task in skilled and less skilled female adolescent soccer players. Front Psychol 12. https://doi.org/10.3389/fpsyg.2021.711420
42. Levy DL, Mendell NR, Holzman PS (2004) The antisaccade task and neuropsychological tests of prefrontal cortical integrity in schizophrenia: empirical findings and interpretative considerations. World Psychiatr 3:32–40
43. Goto Y, Hatakeyama K, Kitama T, Sato Y, Kanemura H, Aoyagi K, Sugita K, Aihara M (2010) Saccade eye movements as a quantitative measure of frontostriatal network in children with ADHD. Brain Develop 32:347–355. https://doi.org/10.1016/j.braindev.2009.04.017
44. Huang J-H, Chan Y-S (2020) Saccade eye movement in children with attention deficit hyperactivity disorder. Nord J Psychiatr 74:16–22. https://doi.org/10.1080/08039488.2019.1666919
45. Mostofsky SH, Lasker AG, Cutting LE, Denckla MB, Zee DS (2002) Oculomotor abnormalities in attention deficit hyperactivity disorder. Am J Ophtamol 133:P176. https://doi.org/10.1016/S0002-9394(01)01348-4
46. Sherigar SS, Gamsa AH, Srinivasan K (2023) Oculomotor deficits in attention deficit hyperactivity disorder: a systematic review and meta-analysis. Eye 37:1975–1981. https://doi.org/10.1038/s41433-022-02284-z
47. Purves D, Augustine GJ, Fitzpatrick D, Katz LC, LaMantia A-S, McNamara JO, Williams SM (2001) Types of eye movements and their functions. In: Neuroscience, 2nd edn. Sinauer Associates
48. Caldani S, Delorme R, Moscoso A, Septier M, Acquaviva E, Bucci MP (2020) Improvement of pursuit eye movement alterations after short visuo-attentional training in ADHD. Brain Sci 10:816. https://doi.org/10.3390/brainsci10110816
49. Krauzlis RJ, Lisberger SG (1994) A model of visually-guided smooth pursuit eye movements based on behavioral observations. J Comput Neurosci 1:265–283. https://doi.org/10.1007/BF00961876
50. Nachmani O, Coutinho J, Khan AZ, Lefèvre P, Blohm G (2020) Predicted position error triggers catch-up saccades during sustained smooth pursuit. eNeuro 7. https://doi.org/10.1523/ENEURO.0196-18.2019
51. Frei K (2021) Abnormalities of smooth pursuit in Parkinson's disease: a systematic review. Clin Park Relat Disord 4:100085. https://doi.org/10.1016/j.prdoa.2020.100085
52. Morita K, Miura K, Kasai K, Hashimoto R (2020) Eye movement characteristics in schizophrenia: a recent update with clinical implications. Neuropsychopharmacol Rep 40:2–9. https://doi.org/10.1002/npr2.12087
53. Jacobsen LK, Hong WL, Hommer DW, Hamburger SD, Castellanos FX, Frazier JA, Giedd JN, Gordon CT, Karp BI, McKenna K, Rapoport JL (1996) Smooth pursuit eye movements in

childhood-onset schizophrenia: comparison with attention-deficit hyperactivity disorder and normal controls. Biol Psychiatr 40:1144–1154. https://doi.org/10.1016/S0006-3223(95)00630-3
54. Crawford H, Moss J, Oliver C, Elliott N, Anderson GM, McCleery JP (2016) Visual preference for social stimuli in autistic individuals or neurodevelopmental disorders: an eye-tracking study. Mol Autism 7:24. https://doi.org/10.1186/s13229-016-0084-x
55. Chevallier C, Parish-Morris J, McVey A, Rump KM, Sasson NJ, Herrington JD, Schultz RT (2015) Measuring social attention and motivation in autism spectrum disorder using eye-tracking: Stimulus type matters. Autism Res 8:620–628. https://doi.org/10.1002/aur.1479
56. Reilly JL, Lencer R, Bishop JR, Keedy S, Sweeney JA (2008) Pharmacological treatment effects on eye movement control. Brain Cogn 68:415–435. https://doi.org/10.1016/j.bandc.2008.08.026
57. De Silva S, Dayarathna S, Ariyarathne G, Meedeniya D, Jayarathna S, Michalek AMP (2021) Computational decision support system for ADHD identification. Int J Autom Comput 18:233–255. https://doi.org/10.1007/s11633-020-1252-1
58. Mastergeorge AM, Kahathuduwa C, Blume J (2021) Eye-tracking in infants and young children at risk for autism spectrum disorder: a systematic review of visual stimuli in experimental paradigms. J Autism Dev Disord 51:2578–2599. https://doi.org/10.1007/s10803-020-04731-w
59. Minissi ME, Chicchi Giglioli IA, Mantovani F, Alcañiz Raya M (2022) Assessment of the autism spectrum disorder based on machine learning and social visual attention: a systematic review. J Autism Dev Disord 52:2187–2202. https://doi.org/10.1007/s10803-021-05106-5
60. Pupillometrie. In: Spektrum Lexikon der Psychologie. https://www.spektrum.de/lexikon/psychologie/pupillometrie/12270. Accessed 10 Oct 2023
61. Mathot S (2018) Pupillometry: psychology, physiology, and function. J Cogn 1:16. https://doi.org/10.5334/joc.18
62. Barry C, de Souza J, Xuan Y, Holden J, Granholm E, Wang EJ (2022) At-home pupillometry using smartphone facial identification cameras. In: Proceedings of the 2022 CHI conference on human factors in computing systems. Association for Computing Machinery, New York, NY, USA, pp 1–12
63. Neice AE, Fowler C, Jaffe RA, Brock-Utne JG (2021) Feasibility study of a smartphone pupillometer and evaluation of its accuracy. J Clin Monit Comput 35:1269–1277. https://doi.org/10.1007/s10877-020-00592-x
64. Calandra DM, Di Martino S, Riccio D, Visconti A (2017) Smartphone based pupillometry: an empirical evaluation of accuracy and safety. In: Battiato S, Gallo G, Schettini R, Stanco F (eds) Image analysis and processing—ICIAP 2017. Springer International Publishing, Cham, pp 433–443
65. Kim T-H, Youn J-I (2013) Development of a smartphone-based pupillometer. J Opt Soc Korea, JOSK 17:249–254
66. Adobe Inc. (2019) Adobe photoshop
67. Piaggio D, Namm G, Melillo P, Simonelli F, Iadanza E, Pecchia L (2021) Pupillometry via smartphone for low-resource settings. Biocybern Biomed Eng 41:891–902. https://doi.org/10.1016/j.bbe.2021.05.012
68. de Vries L, Fouquaet I, Boets B, Naulaers G, Steyaert J (2021) Autism spectrum disorder and pupillometry: a systematic review and meta-analysis. Neurosci Biobehav Rev 120:479–508. https://doi.org/10.1016/j.neubiorev.2020.09.032
69. Bast N, Mason L, Ecker C, Baumeister S, Banaschewski T, Jones EJH, Murphy DGM, Buitelaar JK, Loth E, Pandina G, EU-AIMS LEAP Group, Freitag CM (2023) Sensory salience processing moderates attenuated gazes on faces in autism spectrum disorder: a case-control study. Mol Autism 14:5. https://doi.org/10.1186/s13229-023-00537-6
70. Das W, Khanna S (2021) A robust machine learning based framework for the automated detection of ADHD using pupillometric biomarkers and time series analysis. Sci Rep 11:16370. https://doi.org/10.1038/s41598-021-95673-5

71. Sheinkopf SJ, Iverson JM, Rinaldi ML, Lester BM (2012) Atypical cry acoustics in 6-month-old infants at risk for autism spectrum disorder. Autism Res 5:331–339. https://doi.org/10.1002/aur.1244
72. Unwin LM, Bruz I, Maybery MT, Reynolds V, Ciccone N, Dissanayake C, Hickey M, Whitehouse AJO (2017) Acoustic properties of cries in 12-month old infants at high-risk of autism spectrum disorder. J Autism Dev Disord 47:2108–2119. https://doi.org/10.1007/s10803-017-3119-z
73. Liu N, Luo K, Yuan Z, Chen Y (2022) A transfer learning method for detecting Alzheimer's disease based on speech and natural language processing. Front Public Health 10. https://doi.org/10.3389/fpubh.2022.772592
74. Arora S, Visanji NP, Mestre TA, Tsanas A, AlDakheel A, Connolly BS, Gasca-Salas C, Kern DS, Jain J, Slow EJ, Faust-Socher A, Lang AE, Little MA, Marras C (2018) Investigating voice as a biomarker for leucine-rich repeat kinase 2-associated Parkinson's disease. J Parkinsons Dis 8:503–510. https://doi.org/10.3233/JPD-181389
75. Low DM, Bentley KH, Ghosh SS (2020) Automated assessment of psychiatric disorders using speech: a systematic review. Laryngoscope Investigative Otolaryngol 5:96–116. https://doi.org/10.1002/lio2.354
76. Cummins N, Scherer S, Krajewski J, Schnieder S, Epps J, Quatieri TF (2015) A review of depression and suicide risk assessment using speech analysis. Speech Commun 71:10–49. https://doi.org/10.1016/j.specom.2015.03.004
77. Parish-Morris J, Liberman M, Ryant N, Cieri C, Bateman L, Ferguson E, Schultz R (2016) Exploring autism spectrum disorders using HLT. In: Proceedings of the third workshop on computational linguistics and clinical psychology. Association for Computational Linguistics, San Diego, CA, USA, pp 74–84
78. Asghari SZ, Farashi S, Bashirian S, Jenabi E (2021) Distinctive prosodic features of people with autism spectrum disorder: a systematic review and meta-analysis study. Sci Rep 11:23093. https://doi.org/10.1038/s41598-021-02487-6
79. Fusaroli R, Lambrechts A, Bang D, Bowler DM, Gaigg SB (2017) Is voice a marker for Autism spectrum disorder? A systematic review and meta-analysis": vocal production in ASD. Autism Res 10:384–407. https://doi.org/10.1002/aur.1678
80. Fusaroli R, Grossman R, Bilenberg N, Cantio C, Jepsen JRM, Weed E (2022) Toward a cumulative science of vocal markers of autism: a cross-linguistic meta-analysis-based investigation of acoustic markers in American and Danish autistic children. Autism Res 15:653–664. https://doi.org/10.1002/aur.2661
81. Lau JCY, Patel S, Kang X, Nayar K, Martin GE, Choy J, Wong PCM, Losh M (2022) Cross-linguistic patterns of speech prosodic differences in autism: a machine learning study. Plos One 17:e0269537. https://doi.org/10.1371/journal.pone.0269637
82. Chen F, Cheung CC-H, Peng G (2022) Linguistic tone and non-linguistic pitch imitation in children with autism spectrum disorders: a cross-linguistic investigation. J Autism Dev Disord 52:2325–2343. https://doi.org/10.1007/s10803-021-05123-4
83. Yip MJW (2002) Tone. Cambridge University Press
84. Rybner A, Jessen ET, Mortensen MD, Larsen SN, Grossman R, Bilenberg N, Cantio C, Jepsen JRM, Weed E, Simonsen A, Fusaroli R (2022) Vocal markers of autism: assessing the generalizability of machine learning models. Autism Res 15:1018–1030. https://doi.org/10.1002/aur.2721
85. Breznitz Z (2003) The speech and vocalization patterns of boys with ADHD compared with boys with dyslexia and boys without learning disabilities. J Genet Psychol 164:425–452. https://doi.org/10.1080/00221320309597888
86. Hamdan A-L, Deeb R, Sibai A, Rameh C, Rifai H, Fayyad J (2009) Vocal characteristics in children with attention deficit hyperactivity disorder. J Voice 23:190–194. https://doi.org/10.1016/j.jvoice.2007.09.004
87. Liao M, Duan H, Wang G (2022) Application of machine learning techniques to detect the children with autism spectrum disorder. J Healthc Eng 2022:9340027. https://doi.org/10.1155/2022/9340027

88. Trevisan DA, Hoskyn M, Birmingham E (2018) Facial expression production in autism: a meta-analysis. Autism Res 11:1586–1601. https://doi.org/10.1002/aur.2037
89. Krishnappa Babu PR, Aikat V, Di Martino JM, Chang Z, Perochon S, Espinosa S, Aiello R, L. H. Carpenter K, Compton S, Davis N, Eichner B, Flowers J, Franz L, Dawson G, Sapiro G (2023) Blink rate and facial orientation reveal distinctive patterns of attentional engagement in autistic toddlers: a digital phenotyping approach. Sci Rep 13:7158. https://doi.org/10.1038/s41598-023-34293-7
90. De Silva S, Dayarathna S, Ariyarathne G, Meedeniya D, Jayarathna S, Michalek AMP, Jayawardena G (2019) A rule-based system for ADHD Identification using eye movement data. In: 2019 Moratuwa engineering research conference (MERCon), pp 538–543
91. Jiang M, Francis SM, Srishyla D, Conelea C, Zhao Q, Jacob S (2019) Classifying individuals with ASD through facial emotion recognition and eye-tracking. 2019 41st annual international conference of the IEEE engineering in medicine and biology society (EMBC). IEEE, Berlin, Germany, pp 6063–6068
92. Kline A, Wang H, Li Y, Dennis S, Hutch M, Xu Z, Wang F, Cheng F, Luo Y (2022) Multimodal machine learning in precision health: a scoping review. NPJ Digit Med 5:1–14. https://doi.org/10.1038/s41746-022-00712-8
93. Taylor (2023) Sub Saharan Africa: smartphone subscriptions 2011–2028. In: Statista. https://www.statista.com/statistics/1133777/sub-saharan-africa-smartphone-subscriptions/. Accessed 15 Oct 2023
94. Oliva F, Malandrone F, Mirabella S, Ferreri P, di Girolamo G, Maina G (2021) Diagnostic delay in ADHD: duration of untreated illness and its socio-demographic and clinical predictors in a sample of adult outpatients. Early Interv Psychiatr 15:957–965. https://doi.org/10.1111/eip.13041
95. Pistoljevic N, Dzanko E, Ghaziuddin M (2021) Practice patterns and potential barriers to early diagnosis of autism in Bosnia and Herzegovina: a preliminary study. J Autism Dev Disord 51:4447–4455. https://doi.org/10.1007/s10803-021-04875-3
96. Schaefer C, Schneider N, Jenni O, von Rhein M (2018) Frühe Fördermassnahmen für Kinder mit Autismus-Spektrum-Störung. Schweizerische Zeitschrift für Heilpädagogik 24:14–19
97. Conroy B, Silva I, Mehraei G, Damiano R, Gross B, Salvati E, Feng T, Schneider J, Olson N, Rizzo AG, Curtin CM, Frassica J, McFarlane DC (2022) Real-time infection prediction with wearable physiological monitoring and AI to aid military workforce readiness during COVID-19. Sci Rep 12(1). https://doi.org/10.1038/s41598-022-07764-6
98. World Health Organization (2021) Ethics and governance of artificial intelligence for health. https://www.who.int/publications-detail-redirect/9789240029200. Accessed 15 Oct 2023
99. Villongco C, Khan F (2020) "Sorry I Didn't Hear You". The ethics of voice computing and AI in high risk mental health populations. AJOB Neurosci 11:105–112. https://doi.org/10.1080/21507740.2020.1740355
100. Wetsman N (2021) WHO outlines principles for ethics in health AI. In: The Verge. https://www.theverge.com/2021/6/30/22557119/who-ethics-ai-healthcare. Accessed 15 Oct 2023
101. Chen A. Why San Francisco's ban on face recognition is only the start of a long fight. In: MIT technology review. https://www.technologyreview.com/2019/05/16/135339/facial-recognition-ban-san-francisco-surveillance-privacy-private-corporate-interests/. Accessed 15 Oct 2023
102. Kassam I, Ilkina D, Kemp J, Roble H, Carter-Langford A, Shen N (2023) Patient perspectives and preferences for consent in the digital health context: state-of-the-art literature review. J Med Internet Res 25:e42507. https://doi.org/10.2196/42507
103. Aggarwal P, Papay FA (2022) Artificial intelligence image recognition of melanoma and basal cell carcinoma in racially diverse populations. J Dermatol Treat 33:2257–2262. https://doi.org/10.1080/09546634.2021.1944970
104. Liu Y, Primiero CA, Kulkarni V, Soyer HP, Betz-Stablein B (2023) Artificial intelligence for the classification of pigmented skin lesions in populations with skin of color: a systematic review. Dermatology 239:499–513. https://doi.org/10.1159/000530225

105. European Commission, Directorate-General for Communications Networks, Content and Technology (2021) Proposal for a Regulation laying down harmonised rules on artificial intelligence
106. Taylor K, Silver L (2019) Smartphone ownership is growing rapidly around the world, but not always equally. Pew Research Center
107. Wei Q, Cao H, Shi Y, Xu X, Li T (2023) Machine learning based on eye-tracking data to identify Autism Spectrum disorder: a systematic review and meta-analysis. J Biomed Inform 137:104254. https://doi.org/10.1016/j.jbi.2022.104254

Support, But Do Not Replace, Human Expertise: A Few Considerations for the Deployment of Machine Learning in Support of Neurodiverse Children and Adolescents

Serge Thill

Abstract

Machine learning and artificial intelligence currently see rapid developments and growth. In this chapter, we discuss some of the implications of the increasing ubiquitousness of resulting algorithms in technology used to support neurodiverse children in various contexts. The focus is less on discussing specific methods, given the rapid pace at which they currently evolve, and more on an attempt to highlight general principles and concerns. We highlight in particular that although algorithmic approaches can support various stakeholders, such as parents, therapists, teachers, and the children themselves, they cannot and should not replace them. More generally, we will distinguish between different uses of algorithms, namely the description of observable data and the interpretation thereof. We also discuss some of the fundamental challenges, for example in assessing vaguely-defined mental states. Overall, the purpose of this chapter is to create an awareness of the potentials, but also the limitations of machine learning approaches to supporting neurodiverse children in various contexts.

Keywords

Machine learning · Descriptive versus interpretative algorithms · Overt and covert signals · Stakeholder support

---

S. Thill (✉)
Donders Institute for Brain, Cognition, and Behaviour, Radboud University Nijmegen, Nijmegen, Netherlands
e-mail: serge.thill@donders.ru.nl

1 Introduction

With advances in artificial intelligence and machine learning comes a corresponding desire to apply the resulting algorithms in societally relevant applications, in the hope that they can meet and resolve some current challenges faced by practitioners in this area. Many such applications are in the healthcare domain, for a number of reasons, such as its societal relevance, the potential benefits, and a corresponding focus from funding agencies. With respect to supporting neurodiverse children, a prominent example in research has been the development of so-called robot-assisted therapy for children on the autism spectrum (ASD) [16, 30]. This use case also demonstrates a relevance to machine learning research: its specific therapeutic needs and requirements can drive the development of novel algorithms that can deliver on these [33].

At the same time, while there is thus significant symbiotic potential between algorithmic development and deployment in healthcare and other societally relevant domains, there are also a few caveats. For developers of algorithms, this can be a lack of understanding of actual end user requirements. When it comes to companion robots for the elderly, for example, it has been shown that what robotics researchers consider to be appropriate platforms does not align well with end user desires [12], and even the potential ethical concerns identified by end users differ from those discussed in ethics research [13].

This is not to say that one perspective is more or less important than the other, it merely illustrates the importance of involving all stakeholders in the design of novel solutions to a perceived issue. When this is not done, significant efforts can potentially be spent in vain. There is, for example, work to design autonomous wheelchairs whose purpose it is to help humans arrive at some destination with little to no intervention required. Human wheelchair users, however, want to be active rather than passive [17], and this has significant consequences for algorithmic design [18]. In the afore mentioned use case of robot-assisted therapy for children on the autism spectrum, there is a vast literature of exploratory studies; however, a meta-analysis a few years ago showed that of 861 papers considered, only 12 satisfied the inclusion criteria to assess their psychotherapeutic relevance [19].

Conversely, it might be that stakeholders in application areas overestimate or misjudge the possibilities or limitations of algorithmic solutions. A recent example is the use of algorithmic means to detect aspects such as trustworthiness in a person. In principle, this amounts to physiognomy [31], but when it is presented in the form of a machine learning innovation, the pseudo-scientific status might not be readily apparent. Deploying algorithms to automate, amongst others, such aspects has been shown repeatedly to exacerbate rather than reduce societal challenges [8].

This chapter discusses some of the issues that one should be aware of when attempting algorithmic solutions to support neurodiverse children through novel technological means. Although we will touch upon some of the state-of-the-art methods that currently exist, the point is less to provide a review of such approaches and more to distill the lessons that one can learn. While we will touch on large language models, for example, there is little point in discussing the precise ramifications of the current version of chatGPT because such a text is likely to be obsolete by the time the chapter has gone from being written to being published. We will also not discuss in detail specifics such as legal and ethical concerns because this is again an evolving landscape, and the interested reader is better served perusing the relevant output from the appropriate legal and ethical authorities. Rather, the remainder of the chapter will instead discuss some of the application areas, possibilities, and limitations of machine learning algorithms and the caveats that accompany them (such as the above-mentioned issues of forays into pseudo-scientific territory).

2 Uses of Machine Learning in Supporting Neurodiverse Children

Technology can be deployed in a number of different ways in therapeutic contexts. This can, for example, be the introduction of new tools into therapy, such as the recent aforementioned use of robots in therapy. In some instances, these tools require the development of machine learning algorithms: robots, if they are to operate, at least to some degree, autonomously, need algorithms to assess the appropriate course of actions to take [16].

Another, potentially complementary, role concerns the support of various care takers, such as therapists, teachers, parents or legal guardians. This can be done, for example, by collecting descriptive statistical data on specific aspects of interaction with technology. Such abilities can be complementary with the previous approach because sometimes the necessary information is the same—for example, the next exercise in an intervention could be co-determined by the level of engagement shown by a child while, therapeutically, information about engagement can also be relevant. Similarly, this can also concern the development of novel sensors, such as new eye trackers, and the corresponding algorithms to interpret the measures taken from these sensors [14, 15].

Lastly, for the present purposes, there is the potential to deploy technology directly to support children. This concerns any technology that is meant to be used directly by the children to support them or facilitate aspects in their daily lives. As with the above, machine learning can be needed here to provide analyses of some kind, for example, to help them understand their own affective states. It can also concern algorithms that are necessary for the technology to function. For example, the automated wheelchair example from the introduction requires an interpretation of the intentions of its users in order to assist them in navigation [18] along their own chosen trajectory. If the wheelchair was fully autonomous, this would not be needed as it could simply plan its own trajectory.

Regardless of the specific application, we can note two major roles for machine learning. One concerns the gathering and analysis of data of some kind to provide descriptions thereof. The other concerns some sort of interpretation of this data in order to achieve some tasks, for example the control of a robot. In the brief discussion here, we have also seen two different types of constructs that one might want such algorithms to operate on. One concerns overt aspects, that is, anything that is directly perceivable, such as the direction of gaze, while the other concerns covert aspects, which are not necessarily directly perceivable, such as the level of engagement of a child. The latter thus tend to involve some level of interpretation. In most therapeutic contexts, covert aspects play a significant role. A recent study [4] assessed what kind of data would be necessary to address DSM-5 criteria for ASD diagnosis [1] and found that these are largely covert aspects. At the same time, some aspects are clearly overt, and there is a utility in providing objective measures thereof. In the following, we will therefore briefly discuss specific considerations for overt and covert constructs in the context of algorithmic development.

3 Interpretation of Covert Constructs

As noted above, a significant portion of the use cases for machine learning algorithms in supporting neurodiverse children involves an attempt to assess aspects that are not immediately and directly perceivable. Ready examples of this include affective states, levels of engagement, valence of an interaction, and the like. In all these cases, the main assumption is that it is possible to measure some variable which is, in turn, indicative of the actual variable of interest; in other words, it is possible to infer the hidden variable from what can be seen. This is possible because some variables can be correlated such as heart rate and level of excitement, but it is not unambiguous because heart rate, for example, can also vary for other reasons. For other aspects, the observable correlates of a variable of interest are not as readily apparent—engagement is an instance of this.

One aspect that is often overlooked in the development of algorithms that are to measure such hidden variables is the question of how well defined the underlying concepts really are, and, somewhat relatedly, how humans perform on such tasks. When interventions are coded by therapists, interrater agreements are computed to validate the assessments and it is readily apparent in the literature that these are usually above chance, but nearly never close to perfect alignment. In a non-therapeutic context, a study assessed the degree to which variables such as engagement and valence are apparent to humans from observation of children playing freely [5]. The main purpose was to assess the degree to which algorithms can perform similar assessments. Of interest here, however, is that interrater agreements, in this case using Krippendorff's alpha, were computed for each item on the assessment of these videos. The largest value found was 0.463, which is above the chance level of 0 (all values were above this, though some only marginally so) but still far from the usual 2/3 threshold usually expected. Importantly, this concerns level of agreement between non-experts. In clinical studies, the level of agreement tends to be higher because coding is done by trained experts. What this demonstrates, however, is that the hidden constructs we refer to are not well-defined given the low level of agreement between arbitrary humans. When experts are specifically trained and the agreement is higher, this is to some degree also a choice of what to focus on and what to disregard.

Overall, this sets some baselines for what one can expect from algorithms. Since there is going to be some amount of disagreement even between humans as to what is observed, it seems futile to assume that an algorithm can be used to provide some accurate, objective measurement. A more subtle point in all of this concerns the nature of ground truth. For the type of classification that is implied in this kind of work, supervised approaches are typically employed, which means that a training and test set have to be provided that contain not just the stimuli—whatever measures signal is expected to correlate with the hidden variable of interest—but also a "correct", or at least expected output—what it is that we ought to see in this data. However, as just discussed, such information can rarely be accurately provided, since the actual variable of interest is, by definition, not directly observable, and even humans do not fully align on estimating it from what they can perceive. For example, with respect to emotion or affect, whatever ground truth exists is known, at best, only to the person experiencing it. The only way to access it is by asking them, but there is no guarantee that the answer will be accurate or that the mere process of asking will not influence the result.

At the same time, especially in therapeutic contexts, this is not necessarily the end of the road. After all, therapies are successful despite the fact that some of the relevant variables are unknowable. What that illustrates is that the criterion for success is not necessarily accurate identification of something that cannot always be reliably assessed such as affective states—rather, it is the degree to which the interpretation that is made, irrespective of its accuracy with respect to some unattainable ground truth, helps to achieve the desired support. In other words, success is defined in terms of the quality of interaction between the technology and whoever is using it as judged by the relevant experts (such as therapists) [32]. While this seems like a natural observation from a more psychotherapeutic perspective, it has consequences for the design of algorithms that go against standard practice in supervised learning. Essentially, there is no longer a direct relationship between some observable state of a human and a "correct" classification thereof; rather whether any such classifications are successful can only be known after some time of using the candidate algorithm. Problems for which a positive or negative assessment of performance can only be given post-hoc are typically solved with reinforcement learning (RL) [27]. In this approach, the assumption is that a system will eventually receive a reward signal of some kind, indicating whether or not it is performing well. The algorithmic challenge, solved by a variety of different approaches depending on the exact nature of the problem, is figuring out how to improve a system given a history of actions it has undertaken and a reward signal that was eventually received.

It can be shown that the problems of interest in the context of this chapter are also amenable to a RL formulation [32], however implementing such a solution in practice is challenging as RL remains hard to deploy in real-world scenarios for a number of reasons; for example, because reward signals are often sparse (in the sense that the system does not receive enough to have enough information on how to improve) [29].

At this point, it is fair to ask about the obvious missing aspect in this entire section: not all internal states of humans are always hidden. Emotions, for example, also have a clear social role and it is often the case that humans simply communicate, verbally or not, regarding their internal states. When this is the case, we are no longer dealing with a covert signal; after all, it is now out in the open. From an algorithmic perspective, we move from the problematic issue of estimating the likely state of something internal to having to recognise, and possibly classify, explicit overt signals.

4   Recognizing and Describing Overt Signals

Interpreting internal states of other humans seems, at first glance, fundamental to our social interactions, and this ability is studied in Psychology as Theory of Mind [21]. There is, however, no agreement on how precisely humans achieve this; the main candidate theories either posit that humans have some model of other humans (Theory theory), or that they can make use of their own experience as a human to interpret actions of others (Simulation theory). However, it is disputed whether such a conceptualization is the appropriate way to think about these human abilities [2, 3, 22, 23]. Recent studies from vision science also suggest that at least some aspects of social interaction might be directly perceivable and not dependent on mentalizing [28]. The exact mechanisms underlying the human ability to infer mental states of others, and to some degree even the question of what is directly perceivable and what requires interpretation, still require further study.

Nonetheless, it is clear that some aspects are directly perceivable because humans, consciously or not, explicitly communicate these as noted above. Such overt signals can be observed with appropriate sensors and can be summarised for various stakeholders. The earlier-mentioned study [4] that found a large part of DSM-5 diagnostic criteria for ASD to be covert also notes that some are, in fact, directly perceivable and can be appropriately summarised to support therapists in their decision making (while at the same time clearly not allowing for an automated diagnosis). In a sense, this is less of a machine learning challenge and more a question of what kind of information is useful to a therapist, caretaker, or child and what sensors can be used to perceive these. It is also relevant to note that these sensors are not restricted to the equivalent of human senses. On-body sensors can be used to identify heart-rate variability, galvanic skin response, and the like. It may not always be appropriate to rely on on-body sensors; for example, children on the autism spectrum can be hypersensitive to such invasions [33] but increased availability of off-the-shelf gadgets such as smart watches make obtaining such signals feasible. Off-body sensors are also possible and can reveal more than human senses. Cameras, including relatively cheap options such as the front camera on a smartphone for example, can also detect heart rate variability [25]. The challenges here are thus more related to the availability of sensors, their practicality, and legal and ethical concerns around their deployment (continuously recording from cameras and microphones can have important privacy implications for example) than they are with machine learning algorithms themselves.

The main point to make is thus less to do with the feasibility of acquiring overt signals and more with the limitations of what can be achieved with them. Historically, attempts at correlating measurable aspects with mental ones are abound and almost always problematic. Phrenology, for example, was the attempt at determining character traits and/or mental abilities from the shape of the skull. Similarly, physiognomy denotes attempts at judging such features from facial features and expressions. Neither can be considered scientific since there is ample evidence that none of the measured features are actually indicative of any such variable of interest. It is nonetheless the case that a number of algorithmic attempts are currently made to achieve similar goals. Notably, most of these attempts are not in a therapeutic context—rather, they constitute, for example, attempts at predicting trustworthiness, criminality, and similar. That these attempts cannot work is well documented [31], as is the fact that they consistently and disproportionately affect minorities in a negative manner [8].

Overall, this reinforces the notion that collaboration with relevant experts such as teachers and therapists is essential when developing technological solutions in therapeutic contexts. Algorithmic solutions can be very effective in supporting their work through the provision of quantified data—eye tracking data, for example, is useful in supporting diagnosis and being able to automatically quantify regions of gaze rather than relying on several human annotators laboring through videos can significantly lessen the burden on human therapists [7]. However, it does not follow from this that diagnosis can consequently be automated. Diagnosis not only depends on more than one criterion; not all human expertise—or human cognition in general for that matter—can be reduced to solving classification problems in the way that current machine learning approaches do [20].

Lastly, this also highlights the responsibility that machine learning researchers have in accurately describing the potential and limitations of their algorithms, even in situations where these are co-developed with relevant experts from psychotherapy, education, or similar. One well-lnown perceived weakness of current approaches is that they depend to some degree on the specific experts involved, attempts to strengthen confidence in the result through constructs such as inter-rater agreements non withstanding. There is thus a natural desire to reduce this dependency and make processes more "objective" (which is one of the motivations for asking to what degree aspects of diagnosis can be automated [4]). Machine learning can provide the illusion of objectivity since it can be perceived as calculations (which are the same for everyone) carried out to achieve some objective success criterion. However, this is not the case: where algorithms are trained on data sets, they will be subjective in the sense that they reflect all the biases that exist in that data set [9] and claims that larger data sets will eventually solve this are shown to be misguided [11].

When developing algorithms specifically for applications that involve vulnerable populations, such as neurodiverse human beings, the opposite problem can exist: there may not exist enough data to train on. This leads, for example, to studies that are underpowered by necessity [6]. While this is not a problem in itself, overly strong statements regarding the conclusions obtained from such studies can lead to a false impression with respect to the abilities of the system studied. This has been particularly visible in the afore-mentioned use case of robots for therapy for autistic children: as mentioned earlier, among all the papers that were written on the subject, only very few satisfied the inclusion criteria for a systematic metaanalysis [19]. Using modern machine learning approaches on very small data sets can also lead to problems of overfitting—here, the algorithm is sufficiently powerful to memorise the data it is being trained on, leading to impressive results in single studies that, however, typically do not generalise well [35].

All in all, machine learning approaches can give the appearance of being very successful where, in fact, they are not. This leads to a temptation to use them beyond what they reasonably can do and apply them to problems that they cannot solve. When working with vulnerable populations, this is clearly problematic. More generally, it leads to issues of algorithmic injustice [8], of which recent cases include the use of proctoring software that discriminated against students with black skin or crime detection software that included biases against racial minorities picked up from the data sets (which are built by humans) on which it was trained.

To conclude this section, algorithmic solutions to quantifying and describing overt behaviour are possible and useful. Most of the technical challenges are less to do with algorithms themselves and more to do with building and (safely, legally, ethically) deploying the resulting platform. The aspect that is relevant for algorithmic design is that these algorithms may lead to temptations to move beyond such quantifications and descriptions and towards algorithms trusted with making decisions that have consequences for humans. Such situations can occur for legitimate intentions, such as unburdening expert stakeholders, but that does not mean that the algorithms are suitable for such a task. Essentially, such endeavours lead us into similar territory as discussed above when we considered explicitly covert constructs, and, as before, algorithms cannot replace expert judgment, they can merely support it. In this kind of setting, the role of algorithmic implementations is not—and should not be—to make decisions about mental abilities or states of children, neurodiverse or not.

5   Limitations of Generative AI

In the above, we highlighted the danger of ascribing to current machine learning algorithms more abilities than they have. Our final consideration therefore needs to be about a specific class of algorithms that is currently particularly popular, generative AI in general and Large Language Models (LLMs) in particular. These reated using a particular type of neural network called a transformer [34] and are capable of generating plausible-looking responses to questions provided as an input, or, more generally, to provide a plausible output given some input. They are trained, in a self-supervised manner, on very large amounts of textual data to produce a plausible token to follow a sequence of given tokens. This is somewhat akin to asking the model to "fill in the blank" in a sentence such as *"The boy kicks the..."*, with the blank always being at the end of the sentence. The self-supervised part of the training means that the model can pick an example sentence from the training set by itself, blank out the last word, then try to guess a reasonable candidate and verify whether it makes sense by comparing with similar sentences in the training set.

This turns out to be a powerful way of generating novel outputs even when given a previously unseen sentence. In particular, it is possible to apply this technique repeatedly to partial answers in order to extend them. When a LLM is given a prompt, that prompt is treated as the initial incomplete sequence of tokens (that normally happens to be a complete sentence, often a question) and an answer is then generated iteratively until the model outputs an "end" token. A direct consequence of this is that the way the initial question is phrased matters, and this is why certain instructions (for example, to ask the model to adopt a certain type of persona) can change the result significantly. Prompt engineering is then the skill of crafting the prompt such that a high quality output is obtained.

LLMs, and generative AI more generally, are currently at the center of significant debates covering abilities and limitations, ethical concerns, and more [10]. For the purposes of the present chapter, we do not need to address all of them, but limitations should be flagged because, while it may be tempting to think that generative approaches can overcome some of the fundamental limitations we have discussed in this chapter, this is currently not the case. First and foremost, given how generative AI functions, it should be clear that there cannot be a guarantee that it produces correct output. This can be seen from the basic training approach—it rewards finding the next word in a sequence of words; the actual use case of LLMs later on, however, is not to replicate sentences from the training set by completing them, it is to generate novel sentences. The very notion of a *generative* model implies that it will *generate* content, so it is not feasible to guarantee that each creation will be correct. This also follows from the fact that the prompt of the user is part of the generative process and significantly co-determines the final output.

Next, one could ask where the "ground truth" for evaluating the output would come from. This raises the follow-up question of what exactly the training set actually is, and this is not known for all LLMs at present. In particular, offerings by for-profit companies tend to be closed in that respect, although it is likely that the training set contains most of what can be scraped from the internet as well as other sources. One issue with this is that these data are known to be biased in several significant ways, and, as discussed earlier in the chapter, that this bias does not go away with scale. In other words, even if it was possible to use the training set as some "ground truth" to ensure correctness of the output, the lack of transparency around the included sources makes it impossible to verify this, and in any case, this would then include the biases that exist in this data set. Additionally, current LLMs are fine-tuned using human input following initial training. This can be from feedback on actual performance "in the wild" provided by users, but it also involves humans who are paid to evaluate responses to prompts and provide feedback. This technique is called "reinforcement learning with human feedback" [24]. Here sits another source of uncertainty as it is not known for all models to what degree this is employed nor what the criteria are that these humans use to provide feedback.

To sum up, it cannot be guaranteed that the output of LLMs is always correct. It might already be challenging to define what "correct" even means in certain circumstances, but even if it is possible to define clearly, it does not follow that each prompt will necessarily lead to this output. It is more accurate to think of LLMs as being trained to generate compelling, plausible-looking output. While the hope is that compelling and plausible output also turns out to be correct, it should be clear that this is not guaranteed. One of the skills in prompt engineering is to reduce the gap between the two. This often requires expert knowledge of the topic in question, sometimes even of the answer being sought.

To summarise, while it may be tempting to use LLMs to "solve" some of the limitations of machine learning that we have noted above, their fundamental design means they cannot do so. Rather, as with the other approaches we have discussed in this chapter, there is a danger that LLMs are perceived as being able to solve problems they cannot actually solve. There is again a need to be clear about these limitations when they are to be deployed in contexts of interest to this book. At first glance, they offer attractive abilities since they can, if nothing else, easily power a chatbot. Efforts to deploy such chatbots in healthcare, medical, or therapeutic contexts can readily be found but readily demonstrate that these also pose important challenges [26].

6 Conclusions

The conclusion of this chapter is fairly straightforward: machine learning and artificial intelligence are powerful tools that will enable a plethora of new societally relevant applications. Some of these are going to be new technologies that support the neurodiverse population. With increased talk of success of algorithms in other domains, it may become tempting to fully replace human expertise in such scenarios with algorithmic solutions. At the time of writing, for example, it is claimed on social media that LLMs may one day replace a human therapist. Earlier, the CEO of OpenAI similarly argued that LLMs could remove the need to visit a doctor when seeking medical advice. In this chapter, we have seen that such claims cannot be supported by what algorithms are currently capable of. Rather than working to replace humans, whether generally or in any context of this book, we should rather develop solutions that support humans, whether these are therapists, caretakers, teachers, or neurodiverse children and adolescents themselves.

Acknowledgements This chapter is in part of the "EMPOWER. Design and evaluation of technological support tools to empower stakeholders in digital education" project (https://www.project-empower.eu), which has received funding from the European Union's Horizon Europe programme under grant agreement No. 101060918. Views and opinions expressed are however those of the authors(s) only and do not necessarily reflect those of the European Union. Neither the European Union nor the granting authority can be held responsible for them.

References

1. American Psychiatric Association (2022) Diagnostic and statistical manual of mental disorders, 5th edn. (text rev). https://doi.org/10.1176/appi.books.9780890425787
2. Baggs E (2020) Book review: action and interaction. Front Psychol 11
3. Barnby JM, Bellucci G, Alon N, Schilbach L, Bell V, Frith C, Dayan P (2023) Beyond theory of mind: a formal framework for social inference and representation. https://doi.org/10.31234/osf.io/cmgu7. https://osf.io/preprints/psyarxiv/cmgu7/
4. Bartlett M, Costescu C, Baxter P, Thill S (2020) Requirements for robotic interpretation of social signals "in the wild": insights from diagnostic criteria of autism spectrum disorder. Information 11(2). https://doi.org/10.3390/info11020081
5. Bartlett ME, Edmunds CER, Belpaeme T, Thill S, Lemaignan S (2019) What can you see? Identifying cues on internal states from the movements of natural social interactions. Front Robot AI 6:49. https://doi.org/10.3389/frobt.201900049
6. Bartlett ME, Edmunds CER, Belpaeme T, Thill S (2022) Have I got the power? Analysing and reporting statistical power in HRI. ACM Trans Hum-Robot Interact 11(2). https://doi.org/10.1145/3495246
7. Billing E, Belpaeme T, Cai H, Cao HL, Ciocan A, Costescu C, David D, Homewood R, Garcia DH, Esteban PG, Liu H, Nair V, Matu S, Mazel A, Selescu M, Senft E, Thill S, Vanderborght B, Vernon D, Ziemke T (2020) The DREAM dataset: supporting a data-driven study of autism spectrum disorder and robot enhanced therapy. Plos One 15(8). https://doi.org/10.1371/journal.pone.0236939
8. Birhane A (2021) Algorithmic injustice: a relational ethics approach. Patterns 2(2). https://doi.org/10.1016/j.patter.2021.100205
9. Birhane A, PrabhuVU (2021) Large image datasets: a pyrrhic win for computer vision? In: 2021 IEEE winter conference on applications of computer vision (WACV), pp 1536–1546. https://doi.org/10.1109/WACV48630.2021.00158. ISSN: 2642-9381
10. Birhane A, Kasirzadeh A, Leslie D, Wachter S (2023) Science in the age of large language models. Nat Rev Phys 5(5):277–280. https://doi.org/10.1038/s42254-023-00581-4
11. Birhane A, Prabhu V, Han S, Boddeti VN (2023) On hate scaling laws for data-swamps. https://doi.org/10.48550/arXiv.2306.13141. http://arxiv.org/abs/2306.13141
12. Bradwell HL, Edwards KJ, Winnington R, Thill S, Jones RB (2019) Companion robots for older people: importance of user-centred design demonstrated through observations and focus groups comparing preferences of older people and roboticists in south west england. BMJ Open 9(9). https://doi.org/10.1136/bmjopen-2019-032468
13. Bradwell HL, Winnington R, Thill S, Jones RB (2020) Ethical perceptions towards real-world use of companion robots with older people and people with dementia: survey opinions among younger adults. BMC Geriatr 20(1):244. https://doi.org/10.1186/s12877-020-01641-5
14. Cai H, Liu B, Ju Z, Thill S, Belpaeme T, Vanderborght B, Liu H (2018) Accurate eye center localization via hierarchical adaptive convolution. In: Proceedings of the 2018 British machine vision conference (BMVC)
15. Cai H, Fang Y, Ju Z, Costescu C, David D, Billing E, Ziemke T, Thill S, Belpaeme T, Vanderborght B, Vernon D, Richardson K, Liu H (2019) Sensingenhanced therapy system for assessing children with autism spectrum disorders: a feasibility study. IEEE Sens J 19(4):1508–1518. https://doi.org/10.1109/JSEN.2018.2877662

16. Cao H, Esteban PG, Bartlett M, Baxter P, Belpaeme T, Billing E, Cai H, Coeckelbergh M, Costescu C, David D, De Beir A, Hernandez D, Kennedy J, Liu H, Matu S, Mazel A, Pandey A, Richardson K, Senft E, Thill S, Van de Perre G, Vanderborght B, Vernon D, Wakanuma K, Yu H, Zhou X, Ziemke T (2019) Robot-enhanced therapy: development and validation of supervised autonomous robotic system for autism spectrum disorders therapy. IEEE Robot Autom Mag 26(2):49–58. https://doi.org/10.1109/MRA.2019.2904121
17. Carlson T, Demiris Y (2008) Human-wheelchair collaboration through prediction of intention and adaptive assistance. In: 2008 IEEE international conference on robotics and automation, pp 3926–3931. https://doi.org/10.1109/ROBOT.2008.4543814. ISSN: 1050-4729
18. Carlson T, Demiris Y (2012) Collaborative control for a robotic wheelchair: evaluation of performance, attention, and workload. IEEE Trans Syst Man Cybern Part B (Cybernetics) 42(3):876–888. https://doi.org/10.1109/TSMCB.2011.2181833
19. Costescu CA, Vanderborght B, David DO (2014) The effects of robot-enhanced psychotherapy: a meta-analysis. Rev General Psychol 18(2):127–136 (SAGE Publications Inc.). https://doi.org/10.1037/gpr0000007
20. Edelman S (2016) The minority report: some common assumptions to reconsider in the modelling of the brain and behaviour. J Exp Theor Artif Intell 28(4):751–776. https://doi.org/10.1080/0952813X.2015.1042534
21. Frith C, Frith U (2005) Theory of mind. Curr Biol 15(17):R644–R645
22. Gallagher S (2001) The practice of mind: theory, simulation or primary interaction? J Conscious Stud 8(5–7):83–108
23. Gallagher S (2020) Action and interaction. Oxford University Press, Oxford, United Kingdom
24. Griffith S, Subramanian K, Scholz J, Isbell CL, Thomaz AL (2013) Policy shaping: integrating human feedback with reinforcement learning. In: Advances in neural information processing systems, curran associates, vol 26
25. Huynh S, Balan RK, Ko J, Lee Y (2019) VitaMon: measuring heart rate variability using smartphone front camera. In: Proceedings of the 17th conference on embedded networked sensor systems, association for comreferee's puting machinery, New York, NY, USA, SenSys '19, pp 1–14, https://doi.org/10.1145/3356250.3360036
26. Jo E, Epstein DA, Jung H, Kim YH (2023) Understanding the benefits and challenges of deploying conversational AI leveraging large language models for public health intervention. In: Proceedings of the 2023 CHI conference on human factors in computing systems, association for computing machinery, New York, NY, USA, CHI '23, pp 1–16. https://doi.org/10.1145/3544548.3581503
27. Kaelbling LP, Littman ML, Moore AW (1996) Reinforcement learning: a survey. J Artif Intell Res 4:237–285. https://doi.org/10.1613/jair.301
28. McMahon E, Isik L (2023) Seeing social interactions. Trends Cogn Sci. https://doi.org/10.1016/j.tics.2023.09.001
29. Nair A, McGrew B, Andrychowicz M, Zaremba W, Abbeel P (2018) Overcoming exploration in reinforcement learning with demonstrations. In: 2018 IEEE international conference on robotics and automation (ICRA), pp 6292–6299, https://doi.org/10.1109/ICRA.2018.8463162. ISSN: 2577-087X
30. Scassellati B, Admoni H, Matarić M (2012) Robots for use in autism research. Ann Rev Biomed Eng 14:275–294. https://doi.org/10.1146/annurev-bioeng-071811-150036
31. Spanton RW, Guest O (2022) Measuring Trustworthiness or Automating Physiognomy? A comment on Safra, Chevallier, Gr\ezes, and Baumard (2020). https://doi.org/10.48550/arXiv.2202.08674
32. Thill S, Vernon D (2016) How to design emergent models of cognition for application-driven artificial agents. In: Twomey K, Westermann G, Monaghan P, Smith A (eds) Neurocomputational models of cognitive development and processing: proceedings of the 14th neural computation and psychology workshop. World Scientific Publishing, Singapore, pp 115–129. https://doi.org/10.1142/97898146993410008

33. Thill S, Pop C, Belpaeme T, Ziemke T, Vanderborght B (2012) Robot assisted therapy for autism spectrum disorders with (partially) autonomous control: challenges and outlook. Paladyn 3(4):209–217. https://doi.org/10.2478/s13230-013-0107-7
34. Vaswani A, Shazeer N, Parmar N, Uszkoreit J, Jones L, Gomez AN, Kaiser L, Polosukhin I (2017) Attention is all you need. In: Advances in neural information processing systems., vol 30. Curran Associates, Inc.
35. Ying X (2019) An overview of overfitting and its solutions. J Phys: Conf Ser 1168(2):022022. https://doi.org/10.1088/1742-6596/1168/2/022022

Social Robotics in Psychological Interventions for Children

Anouk Neerinex, Joana Brito, Marta Couto, Joana Campos, Maartje de Graaf, Judith Masthoff, and Ana Paiva

Absract

Social Robotics is focused on designing robots that interact with humans naturally, aligning with social norms. Interaction with Social Robots shows significant benefits across diverse domains, such as education, health or general well-being due to its physical embodiment and social features. The chapter offers a succinct review of recent research in child-robot interaction studies, presenting a framework for designing psychological interventions involving children and Social Robots. We focus on interventions in the domain of therapy, general mental well-being and education. The proposed framework guides researchers and practitioners, highlighting recent studies and providing insights

---

Ana Paiva—This author ceased her activities on this project on April 4th, 2024.

A. Neerinex · M. de Graaf · J. Masthoff
Utrecht University, Utrecht, The Netherlands
e-mail: a.neerincx@uu.nl

M. de Graaf
e-mail: m.m.a.degraaf@uu.nl

J. Masthoff
e-mail: j.f.m.masthoff@uu.nl

J. Brito · M. Couto · J. Campos (✉) · A. Paiva
INESC-ID, Instituto Superior Técnico, University of Lisbon, Lisbon, Portugal
e-mail: joana.campos@tecnico.ulisboa.pt

J. Brito
e-mail: joana.b.brito@tecnico.ulisboa.pt

M. Couto
e-mail: marta.couto@gaips.inesc-id.pt

A. Paiva
e-mail: ana.paiva@inesc-id.pt

© The Author(s), under exclusive license to Springer Nature Switzerland AG 2024
C. Costescu (ed.), *Digital Technologies for Learning and Psychological Interventions*,
Integrated Science 33, https://doi.org/10.1007/978-3-031-76414-1_6

for designing future interventions aligned with the most current research. The three main components of the framework are the robot, the child, and the intervention context. We delve into the features of these 3 dimensions and illustrate in two Case Studies how child-robot interactions are designed to create interesting and meaningful interactive experiences in educational and therapeutic settings.

1 Introduction

Social Robotics is a multidisciplinary field at the intersection of computer science, artificial intelligence, engineering, and psychology, primarily concerned with designing and developing robots that are able to interact with humans in a natural way. More specifically, Social Robots (SR) refers to robots that are equipped to interact with humans in a manner compatible with social norms and expectations. SR have been shown to play a beneficial role in education, health, quality of life, entertainment, communication, and collaborative teamwork [13].

With children in particular, SRs have a compelling effect attributed to their physical embodiment and social features.

Due to the nature of SRs, their use for assisting and delivering psychological interventions for children is a growing field, with evidence of psychotherapeutic [26] and learning [8] benefits. The key factor that facilitates positive outcomes in these types of interactions is the robot's capability to communicate both verbally and non-verbally, enabling it to establish and maintain a relationship with the child.

This social dimension, which includes perception of the environment, building rapport, socially appropriate decision-making mechanisms, and expression of affective behaviours, plays a central role in creating a conducive environment for interesting and meaningful interventions. However, all these aspects pose a critical challenge when developing technology that seamlessly operates in both the physical and social space, especially in unconstrained domains with a specific intent by design [8].

Psychological interventions are designed to bring change in people and encompass a variety of approaches designed to modify behaviors, emotions, or cognitive processes, all with the aim of enhancing individuals' functional outcomes and mental well-being [74, 94]. When designing child-robot interactions to augment traditional intervention modes it is necessary to carefully consider the robot's appearance, capabilities, role (e.g., peer, tutor, novice), modes of interaction, and expectations of its users, because all wield substantial influence over the effectiveness of such interventions. In addition, integrating robots into these intervention

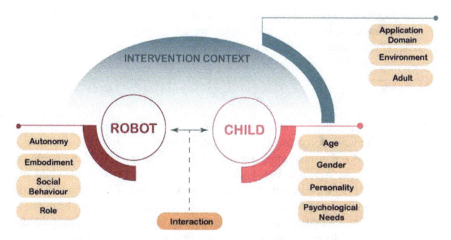

Fig. 1 A framework for designing psychological interventions for children with social robots. Focused on the child-robot interaction, this figure highlights three pivotal elements—the robot, the child and the intervention context

contexts demands tackling a range of technical challenges interwoven with established practices,[1] making it a complex and multidisciplinary endeavor. Moreover, technological progress has not been equal in all domains, and an intervention designer must be aware of existing technical constraints.

In this chapter, we highlight those issues and present current alternatives in a brief review of recent research in child-robot interaction studies. We do this while considering a framework for designing psychological interventions involving children and SR, in the context of robot-mediated therapy for children on the Autism Spectrum (ASD), or overall mental-wellbeing and education. The proposed framework aims to guide both researchers and practitioners in understanding the requirements and technical challenges to design SRs for psychological interventions in these application domains. Our goal is to highlight aspects that have been studied recently and offer guidance for designing future interventions that align with the most current research. The framework comprises three main components to be taken into account when designing psychological interventions: the robot, the child, and the intervention context. Together, these elements influence how child-robot interactions are designed for psychological interventions (see Fig. 1) and affect the key features of SR: autonomy, embodiment, and social behaviour, in different ways.

In the following, we delve into the dimensions of the framework and its features, presenting examples of how researchers have designed robots to create meaningful interactions. Then, we present two case studies where we designed child-robot interactions with different interaction goals to illustrate the robot's

---

[1] Conventional intervention modes are intentionally structured to ensure specific anticipated outcomes.

varying affordances and the resulting interaction, as well as its impact on the interaction outcomes. At the end of the chapter, we add a brief discussion and reflect on some ethical issues of child-robot interaction.

2 Framework

To better understand the various elements that must be considered when designing child-robot interactions for psychological interventions, we start by proposing a framework organized around three main axes: the Robot, the Child, and the Intervention Context. As shown in Fig. 1, the whole interaction between the child and the robot, which is at the center of the framework, is shaped by the intervention context given by the specific situation, both social and environmental. Features of the robot, such as its embodiment, also need to be considered depending on the intervention type. Moreover, the whole interaction will be tailored to the child's capabilities and psychological needs.

The framework builds upon prior research in the field of human-robot interaction, identifying features considered highly relevant to the design of social robots [6]. As illustrated in Fig. 1, each main component has a set of features that create a multitude of unique interactions between the child and the robot. The robot can be characterized in terms of autonomy, embodiment, social behaviour and role. The age, gender, personality and psychological needs of the child are amongst the features deemed important to consider in these scenarios. The intervention context depends on the application domain (therapeutic, educational, or focused on general mental well-being), the environment where it takes place (at home, school, the hospital, or the therapist's office). Finally, when designing robots for psychological interventions, it is important to understand the role of the "adult in the room", i.e., the role in the interaction of the caretaker, educator, or therapist during the intervention, and to consider how can technology support their functions.

2.1 The Robot

In this section, we discuss the features of SRs that can be leveraged in the particular context of designing and deploying psychological interventions for children. These characteristics include embodiment, autonomy, social behaviour, and role.

The embodiment is important in how children and robots interact. There is a distinct contrast between using virtual character robots—i.e. robots lacking tangible and physical form—and physical embodiment, which encompasses a large range of robots. Different types of embodiment offer different interaction opportunities that influence how children respond to them; for instance, more anthropomorphic robots, featuring eyes and fingers, facilitate pointing and gazing, providing effective affordances for shared attention during interventions. According to Fong et al. [35], the physical embodiment of a robot can be classified in (i) functional, machine-like robots with a functional design; (ii) caricatured robots with exaggerated toy-like features; (iii) zoomorphic robots that resemble pets; and (iv) anthropomorphic or humanoid robots. In Fig. 2, examples of SR with various embodiments and features are depicted.

Robots vary greatly in how autonomous they are. From a robot that can operate fully autonomously to a remote controlled one, there are diverse types and degrees of autonomy. Humans become autonomous as the grow up and small steps in autonomy often include starting to eat by themselves, riding a bike, or being able to go to school by themselves. In the case of machines, and specifically robots, as defined by Castelfranchi [21], we consider "executive autonomy", to be the ability to move, act, and make decisions without being explicitly helped by a humans to do so. This requires the ability to perceive the environment, i.e. the situation in which the robot is, respond to it, and assess the outcome of its own actions, and adjust them to achieve the best outcomes. To allow for a higher degree of autonomy, the robot requires a range of features, including speech recognition, facial and spatial recognition, and the integration of sensor data, such as tactile and ground sensors, in an automated manner. Yet, in many scenarios for SRs in

Fig. 2 Examples of SRs with various embodiments and affordances that create unique social experiences. **a** EMYS (EMotive headY System) robotic head developed for human companionship. The three discs of the head, along with the movable eyes, eyelids, and neck enable emotional expression. An internal speaker enables verbal communication, and a camera and kinetic sensors the perception of its surroundings. **b** ASTRO [46] (left) and Pepper2 (right). ASTRO's features are provided in Sect. 3.1. Pepper is a humanoid robot capable of facial, emotion and speech recognition as well as navigation and perception, allowing it to perceive the environment and establish natural dialogue. **c** NAO [76], a humanoid robot with the appearance of a toddler. Its features include high mobility, text-to-speech functionality, and sound localization

complex domains, achieving a high degree of autonomy is extremely challenging. For instance, ensuring proper language education with the generation of accurate feedback to a learner would require precise speech recognition [70]. Although speech recognition tools have become increasingly powerful, child speech recognition is not meeting performance expectations [9, 98]. Additionally, ethical concerns related to child safety come to the forefront (further discussed in Sect. 4). As highlighted by Belpaeme et al. [7] another aspect underlying autonomy is the robot's ability to choose the appropriate action (speech, non-verbal behaviour, movement, etc.) at the right time. This is a difficult task in well-defined domains and becomes an impossible challenge in open domains. To overcome the technical challenges and study specific aspects of the interactions, researchers have pursued the "Wizard of Oz" technique. This is largely used in Human-Robot Interaction studies, as a response to the perception bottleneck [7]. In these scenarios, the adult participating in the intervention (or the researcher) assumes control of the robot's actions from a distant corner of the dedicated intervention room or operates the robot "behind-the-scenes" in another room through remote control or programmed commands. This allows a human to perceive the environment and make decisions for the robot about what action to take. Nevertheless, more empirical studies in the literature are incorporating autonomous and semi-autonomous mechanisms to enhance interactions, due to the importance of testing the technology in real-world situations.

One main aspect that makes robots so appealing is humans' ability to anthropomorphize them, which is particularly the case for children, leading to the attribution of social attributes to the interaction. This makes robots a great tool for researchers to design effective interventions due to the importance of socialization in learning and therapeutic settings. That means that there is a necessity to equip the robot with some degree of social behaviour. This entails the ability to perceive, interpret, and respond in an appropriate and empathetic manner to the child's mental or emotional state. The degree of social behaviour impacts the quality of the social interaction. The adequacy of this response implies that the robot itself is able to convey emotional expressions, a fundamental element of social interaction. Emotions in robots are expressed through various means, primarily via speech and non-verbal behaviors, including eye gaze and head movements. This interplay between perceiving and conveying emotions underpins the potential of SR to emotionally resonate with children.

Finally, depending on the type of the intervention the robot may take different roles. In mental-wellbeing domains, the robot frequently takes the role of a companion or mediator that offers support during and after the interventions. In education settings, robots can be teachers, tutors, or peers, making the child engage in peer-to-peer interaction and supporting skill consolidation where the child acts as an expert and the robot as a novice [8]. All these different roles provide different benefits.

2.2 The Child

When implementing new, technological solutions such as SRs, it is necessary to design them with the end user in mind [69]. Children are a specific target group with their own specific needs [63]. When designing SR interventions for children, it is necessary to take their individual characteristics into account [32], such as age and gender [80], as well as personality [68]. Since we are looking at psychological interventions, it is especially relevant to include specific psychological needs of children when designing SR implementations for this purpose.

SRs have successfully been used for children in various settings. This is due to several reasons. Children show great acceptance of robots, and robots can capture children's attention and heighten their engagement [67] due to their (child-like) appearance. Children tend to look at a SR not as a machine, but more like a cute toy they can interact with by means of many interactive abilities (such as speech, sound, music or games, depending on the robot's design) [71]. Children generally view SRs as something in-between a companion and a pet, which creates a safe environment for the child to develop new skills [14].

Across ages and developmental levels, SRs have shown to be effective for a diverse set of implementations, such as supporting healthcare [29] and education [8]. However, the SR's embodiment as well as behavior should be adapted to the child's needs. For example, younger children tend to be more attracted to lights, movement, and sounds, while older children might be more interested in robots they can actually have a conversation with. Adolescents might enjoy programming and/or building the robots themselves. Also, gender plays a role when implementing SRs. For example, previous research has shown that girls tend to focus more on intimacy and alliance in their friendships. This is also reflected in child-robot interaction, with girls highlighting the social nature of the robot more compared to boys [96]. All these aspects need to be considered when deciding on the most suitable robot platform for the children involved in the intervention.

When designing psychological interventions, it is necessary to consider the children's specific psychological needs. For example, robots can be used to help children feel more comfortable in stressful situations, such as during hospital stays [48]. They have been proven to reduce anxiety and stress in some cases, for example by acting as a companion and/or distracting the child by means of a dance. In such cases, the child's psychological need can be described as "reducing anxiety", or "improving mood". By using the right tools and applications, such as a game that the child plays together with the robot, the child's mental well-being can be improved. SRs can increase children's engagement compared to other technological devices [65], which is useful for various types of psychological interventions such as in therapy settings and (psycho-)education. Children can for example learn about self-regulation and self-management together with robots [42], improving the quality of life of for example chronically ill children. It is expected that the positive effects of SR implementations can be increased by personalizing the robot's behavior towards the child's preferences, for example by matching the robot's personality to the child's [97]. Additionally, to stimulate long-term child-robot interaction, relationship building between the child and robot is beneficial, for which reciprocal self-disclosure is essential [17]. Self-disclosure is also dependent on a child's characteristics such as personality traits [68]. To further stimulate relationship building, the robot can for example be equipped with a mental model of the child, which is updated after each interaction. In other words, the SR creates memories of the child and the child-robot interactions that took place [56].

SRs have been implemented for more specific use cases. For example, SRs are quite often used for children on the autism spectrum and other developmental disorders [71]. One reason for this is that SRs show great potential in teaching children social skills. Autistic children generally enjoy communicating with SRs due to their clear and repetitive manner of communication, as well as their object-like tangible nature. SRs have been often used for physical therapy as well. The repetitive nature of movements that robots exhibit can be a great asset when carrying out different types of exercises with children, mentally and physically.

In summary, the child involved in the interaction has a great influence when designing appropriate SR behaviors for psychological interventions. Important child characteristics to consider are for example age and gender when selecting the right robot platform for the intervention (e.g., by supporting more complex verbal interactions for older children). Other relevant characteristics are the child's personality (e.g., children might prefer a robot that matches their own personality traits), as well as their psychological needs.

2.3 The Intervention Context

The intervention context, as one of the fundamental building blocks of our framework, plays a pivotal role shaping the characteristics of the interaction, encompassing the application domain and the environment. The adult participating in the intervention may take on a role as a parent, a teacher, or a therapist, and vary in their degree of involvement and control over the child-robot interactions, therefore shaping the intervention's environment.

This section is organized by application domain of the intervention, and we distinguish between three main domains of application: therapy, general mental well-being and education. Each of these domains reflect a unique environment in which children's psychological well-being is nurtured. We will explore related works in each of these areas, underlining how the robot's design has been tailored to the specific intervention context in those works.

2.3.1 Robot Mediated Therapy for Autism Spectrum Disorders

The relationship between technology and rehabilitation is long. Therefore, it comes with little surprise that SRs have emerged as a potential tool to aid in therapy with children. Amongst the many different therapies available and possible diagnoses for children, Autism Spectrum Disorders (ASD) is a particular area of interest for

Robot Mediated Therapy (RAT). ASD consists of persistent deficits in social communication and social interaction across multiple contexts and restricted, repetitive patterns of behaviour, interests, or activities [4]. Children on the autism spectrum have a range of occupational and performance problems that interfere with their full participation in social contexts [20], and have significant implications in adult independent life. These children often show more interest in objects than in social stimuli [30, 89] which led several researchers to evaluate the use of SRs to improve symptom severity due to the object-like nature of robot is an object, similar to a toy, but is able to be programmed to exhibit social behaviour and engage in social interaction. Some studies show that autistic children who interact very little with humans seem willing to engage with robots [28, 59, 95]. A recent review by Salimi et al. [79] investigated randomised controlled trials for RAT for ASD. Many studies focus on training one or two behaviours. Often, these behaviours are related to social communication, like producing and recognizing intransitive gestures [84–85], responding to joint attention [52, 84, 89, 100] or self-initiating questions [45].

Therapeutic contexts have certain specificities that are not shared by other contexts, like play, for example. In a therapeutic context, in many instances, clinicians want a significant behaviour change that corresponds to a more adapted behaviour. So, the engagement with the tool (in this case, the robot) is not sufficient. A certain quality of interaction is necessary that allows for changes in behaviour. Change often requires time, and in fact, many child-robot interactions in a therapeutic context are long-term interactions (between 3 and 12 weeks) [79]. Therapy is also usually conducted in a dedicated space, which, on the one hand, can pose a difficulty for researchers but, on the other hand, allows researchers to prepare the setting to receive this type of therapy. In many instances, researchers want to record the interaction to spot target behaviours like eye gaze, which is a frequent impairment in ASD [31], or the frequency and presence of social interaction initiations, another frequent impairment of autistic children [16].

RAT occurs in all ages, developmental stages and with children with different diagnoses. In the case of ASD interventions, researchers need to account not only for age but also for IQ and language development. Within the population on the autism spectrum, we see many different language abilities in different age groups; for example, researchers might be working with 8-year-old children who do not utter complete sentences, and this has an impact on the interaction with the robot as well as it might be incredibly challenging to have a robot that can accurately perceive the responses given by the participants. In all child-robot interaction, researchers face robot perception challenges, but these seem to be amplified when dealing with special needs children's groups.

Studies focusing on populations on the autism spectrum need to have special considerations about the robots that they want to use. For example, certain social stimuli can be overwhelming for autistic children, so if facial expressions are not of interest for the research, some researchers might opt not to have a face or facial expressions in their robot, for example, Huskens et al. [45] used a NAO robot but simplified the face to avoid over stimulation. NAO robot (in Fig. 2c) seems to be particularly popular for ASD randomised controlled trials (see [79]). Nevertheless, several projects have developed robots specifically for RAT (for example, the INSIDE project described in Sect. 3.1). Given the sensory difficulties of many autistic children, personalization becomes essential. For example, sound feedback might trigger the child, depending on the sound, the volume and, of course, the child. It is also important that the stimuli provided to the child do not promote unwanted behavior (for example, repeatedly doing something wrong to listen to the corrective feedback).

2.3.2 Mental Well-Being

SRs show potential in supporting children's overall mental well-being [63]. Children tend to respond positively to robots in general, and SRs show potential in diverse settings. This is due to several benefits of SRs. First of all, SRs can cause increased engagement in children, which can be beneficial in various (e.g., therapeutic, educational, medical) settings. Second, children as well as other stakeholders involved in the interaction (e.g., parents, healthcare professionals) tend to evaluate SRs positively. It is therefore not surprising that SRs are implemented in a diverse range of pediatric settings [54]. For example, they can offer essential mental support in times of need [64]. Most SR interventions for mental well-being take place in medical settings. Medical interventions can be stressful for children, and SRs have the potential to alleviate their stress levels [10, 57, 92]. The presence of a SR in a hospital setting can promote positive emotions and increased (social) engagement [48, 93]. SRs can also offer distraction (e.g., [10]), relaxation, and enhanced communication, for instance, by mediating between children and therapists [60]. Additionally, in such mediator role, SRs can facilitate connections among children, healthcare professionals, and parents, especially in cases where communication is challenging [36]. Furthermore, SRs can boost engagement and motivation during physical rehabilitation therapy sessions [18] and enhance a child's self-discipline and awareness during treatment sessions for pediatric disorders [42]. These aspects play a vital role in child development and care, making SRs an important asset.

Particularly in the realm of mental healthcare interventions, children show a preference for digital features such as videos, minimal text content, personalization options, social connectivity, and text message reminders [57]. The multi-modal nature of most SR platforms could easily incorporate all these preferred features. When supporting child's mental well-being, many studies including humanoid robots use the NAO robot (in Fig. 2c), which is a small child-size robot with arms, legs and a head. Humanoid robots usually communicate by means of speech and gestures (e.g., [10, 67]) with the child. Sometimes, the robot is equipped with a screen, which is used to for example show videos to the child (e.g., [65, 68, 99]), or to play an interactive game with the child [66]. In a verbal interaction, the robot might e.g., ask questions to the child, or inform them about a medical procedure [65]. Quite often, a Wizard-of-Oz set-up is used in these cases, to ensure a satisfactory verbal interaction between child and robot. Recent advancements in speech recognition causes that sometimes-automatic speech recognition can be used. However, especially for children, automatic speech recognition often still has many shortcomings. Pet-like robots are usually employed in free interactions, where the child can for example pet the robot to help them relax, and where the robot will respond by means of animal-like sounds and gestures (e.g., [27]). An example of a commonly used zoomorphic robot to reduce anxiety in children is PARO, a robot shaped like a seal. Also, robots with a more dog-like or cat-like embodiment are used quite often [50]. Sometimes, the robot has a soft, plush embodiment, which helps reducing stress and anxiety in children by means of physical touch [48]. Functional and caricatured robots are less common, but sometimes used to play games.

SR interventions to improve general mental well-being in children occur in all age groups, for children with diverse psychological needs. A child-centric approach is needed when designing the appropriate SR intervention, since the robot embodiment as well as type of intervention should match the child's needs. Also, when improving general mental well-being, the type of psychological needs as well as other child's characteristics are important. It is necessary to pre-define the children's specific psychological needs. For e.g., SRs are particularly effective in immediately improving children's mental well-being during stressful situations, such as hospital settings. Often in such situations, the end goal is to reduce stress, pain, and anxiety, or to increase positive mood and engagement in children [92].

Most studies on SR to improve children's mental well-being are carried out in the healthcare field, for example before or during vaccinations. Here, SRs can act as a distraction, reducing pain and distress (e.g., [10, 67]). However, SRs are also used to reduce other types of mental distress, such as social stress, depression, or loneliness (e.g., [3]). These symptoms can occur in medical settings as well, for example during cancer treatment, but also in other settings such as school settings (e.g., bullying), or in the home. SRs also show great potential in stimulating child's self-management and self-regulation [42], which could help preventing more severe mental health problems. However, due to high hardware costs, the use of a virtual robot might be more feasible in some cases, for example at home. Even though people generally prefer physically-present robots compared to virtual ones [55], virtual robots can be just as effective as physical embodied ones when supporting children in their development [34].

2.3.3 Education

SRs are emerging as powerful educational tools, offering tremendous potential for the intellectual development of children. Substantial evidence supports their effectiveness, as exemplified by the results of post-learning language examinations in a study by Han et al. [37] and the consistent engagement of students, as observed in a similar task by the same authors [38]. These findings underscore that SRs outperform traditional learning resources such as books and audio materials.

One of the key strengths of SRs in the educational context is their innate appeal to children, i.e. the fact that children find robots "fun". By eliciting their endearment and enthusiasm, these robots boost children's motivation to complete learning tasks. Moreover, SRs hold a distinct advantage in comparison to conventional educational tools in their capacity to foster a social bond with the child. As emphasized by Bergin and Bergin [11], establishing a social bond between the tutor and the child is a pivotal factor for academic success. Robots have the capacity to elicit a range of emotions such as sympathy for instance, in a scenario where the child learns by teaching a robot-peer who is falling behind in class [91], or pride in a different context where the robot takes on the role of a "cheerleading" teaching assistant, praising the child's good performance in a specific task [23]. Studies have shown that children prefer to interact with robots that maintain social human-like behaviours during the interaction [49, 70, 78, 83]. This social behaviour implies that the robot itself is able to convey some form of affective state. Many educational robots studies adopt these practises, encompassing a spectrum of approaches, from equipping robots with typical children's idle behaviour i.e. playing rock-paper-scissors or hugging [51], to a socially supportive robot-tutor that dynamically expresses verbal and non-verbal cues of personal commitment towards its students' outcomes [78]. In a survey conducted by Shin and Kim [83], which sought to gain insight into children's own perspectives regarding the utilization of SRs in their education, a number of children expressed enthusiasm for the integration of affective elements into robots. One child went so far as to suggest that if robots could exhibit emotions, like humor in the classroom and a friendly demeanor toward students, "then I would likely regard them as teachers." The integration of robots into education goes beyond merely enhancing the engagement of the learning process. By virtue of their tangible nature, robots provide students with the means to manipulate and experiment, empowering them to be active participants in their educational journey. Robots introduce a shift in the learning paradigm, fostering a "bottom-up" approach to learning, where students actively engage in hands-on experimental activities to seek knowledge [25]. This approach stands in contrast to traditional didactic methods, where knowledge is predominantly transmitted from teacher to student. Robots such as LEGO Mindstorm are particularly instrumental in this shift in educational dynamics, especially for older children and have been used for subjects such as robotics [44], robot-interaction language [61], physics [24] and engineering [15].

SRs interventions in education address a wide age range of students, spanning from preschool years, with children as young as 3 or 4 years old, to high school students. The studies we present in this section of the chapter primarily cater to neurotypical children who follow standard education curricula. The type of robot utilized in these interventions is intricately linked to the child's age, ensuring that the educational intervention is not only engaging but also developmentally appropriate [62].

Two primary characteristics are important in an educational robot: (i) its embodiment, ranging from a virtual character [49] to diverse forms of physical representation, and (ii) the educational role it takes on as a mere tool, a peer for the child or a tutor. The selection of the robot's embodiment is thoughtfully aligned with the learning subject and the age of the students, optimizing the educational impact of these interventions. Functional robots, often machine-like and exemplified by robotic kits like LEGO Mindstorm or Parallax Scribbler [5] predominantly serve as educational tools tailored for the teaching of technical subjects. These functional tools are typically geared towards older children, typically over 12 years old [62]. Conversely, robots with anthropomorphic [23, 38, 40, 47, 51, 70, 82, 91], caricatured [43] or zoomorphic [41, 78] embodiment are commonly employed in educating younger children. The latter, beyond their physical appearance, possess a distinct capacity to convey emotional expressions, which allows them to establish a unique social bond with the child, transcending their role as mere teaching tools. Additionally, their" cute" appearance increased the toddlers engagement and motivation towards completion of the learning task. In many instances, these robots take on the roles of peers or tutors, facilitating a dynamic and interactive educational journey. In a study by Saerbeck et al. [78], the iCat toy-cat robot takes on the role of a tutor in a language learning task under two distinct conditions: one in which it exhibits rich social behaviour through detailed facial expressions, speech and gestures; and an other where it refrains from such expressions. The outcomes of this study reveal that children's learning efficacy as measured through a post-learning task is increased when the robot exhibits supportive social behaviour.

As previously mentioned, the choice of learning subject plays a crucial role in the educational context of these interventions. In the literature, there is a clear division between technological and non-technological subjects. In technological subjects, robots teach students about themselves, serving as learning tools on complex subjects such as robotics or programming [5, 15, 61, 75]. In the realm of non-technological subjects, robots have educational potential at explaining challenging and often abstract concepts in science topics like physics [24], engineering [15] and music [39] due to their tangible nature, allowing for three-dimensional visualizations within a "real-world" framework. In the topic of language learning, robots provide consistent and tireless repetition, ensuring that students receive extensive practice without fatigue or variation in tone [9, 38, 70, 83]. In a particular study by Chandra et al. [22], a robot is used as a tutor that supervises feedback provided by young children (5–6 years old) to their peers on a handwriting task.

Additionally, to the content that children are learning, the timing of when they learn it holds its own significance. There is a distinction between educational interventions integrated into the curriculum of specific courses and those that are offered as extracurricular activities, even when conducted within school hours. Extracurricular activities offer the advantage of being more straightforward to organize, as they typically don't require extensive curriculum adjustments or specialized staff training. However, these interventions often tend to be sporadic in nature, and their long-term impact on children is questionable.

In terms of the adult present, the literature commonly presents a few recurring scenarios. One prevalent approach involves a researcher who is responsible for controlling the robot stationed in a discreet corner of the room or in another room using a monitor. In this "wizard-of-oz" setup, the researcher is responsible for controlling the robot [40, 47, 70]. Alternatively, the adult may only supervise the child-robot interaction or even exit the room once the intervention starts, allowing the child and robot to engage more independently [78, 82]. Another common scenario entails the robot serving as a teaching assistant or learning tool, while a teacher remains in the room. In the last scenario we have total autonomy, with children taking home robots, as is often the case with robotics kits [5, 24]. In this case, there is typically less direct supervision, with children either engaging with the robot autonomously or with the guidance of a parent. In one study by Han et al. [38], the IROBI home robot is adapted for e-learning. This particular study stands out for its emphasis on a take-home humanoid emotion-displaying robot, fostering autonomous interactions with children.

In conclusion, the SRs interventions in education hold significant promise in enhancing the learning experience. This form of digital education brings about numerous benefits, enabling more interactive and engaging educational practices. However, it is imperative to acknowledge the challenges associated with the integration of educational robots. Namely, these tools are very costly encompassing both financial investment and allocation of resources, both physical spaces and personnel. Future work should focus on a compromise between educational robots with higher interaction capabilities such as emotion-displaying, that are affordable and portable, striving to make advanced educational technology accessible to a broader range of educational institutions and learners, thereby realizing the full potential of SRs in education. In Sect. 3.2 we present a case study of a direct educational intervention using Elmo, a desk robot that is affordable and use its emotion-displaying abilities to improve children's emotional competence skills.

3 Case Studies

In this section, we describe two case studies that illustrate the design of the interaction given the intervention goals, modes of interaction and the impact of social robots in psychological interventions for children. The first case study presents a series of small yet targeted interventions within the therapy domain, strategically designed to address key impairments in children on the autism spectrum. The second intervention happens in the educational domain, delving into the integration of an educational robot designed to teach neurotypical children emotional competence skills. These cases will be analyzed within the structure of the framework described previously, describing each case study in terms of the component features of this framework.

(a) The Obstacle task with the robot asking the child for help

(b) The Tangram game.

Fig. 3 Illustration of two of the training tasks that the team designed for child-robot interaction focused on the therapeutic goals of the activities

3.1 Project INSIDE: Towards Autonomous Semi-unstructured Human-Robot Social Interaction in Autism Therapy

The INSIDE PROJECT [58] gathered a team of engineers, psychologists, occupational therapists and physicians to create a small therapy session addressing key impairments of Autism Spectrum Disorders (ASD).

The sessions were conducted in a room at a school in Portugal[2] that was transformed to accommodate the sessions. The room was stripped of all previous equipment and a set of 3D cameras was set up on the ceiling, and each of the 7 activities took place in a dedicated space inside the room (for details of the room set up please refer to Fig. 3). Aside from the cameras the therapist had a microphone to provide verbal inputs for the robot.

We recruited 15 children on the autism spectrum, aged between 3 and 7 years old. For the control group, 15 children from a local school without any diagnosis of developmental disorder and between the ages of 3 and 7 years old participated in the study.

The Astro robot used in this study, illustrated in Fig. 3, has a LED screen face that allowed us to create different facial expressions; a tablet on the chest area was used for the child to play games with the robot and a removable drawer with an RFID reader allowed the robot to count items that the children place there, in this case-colored balls. For more details on the technical setup refer to [58].

---

[2] Centro de Desenvolvimento da Crianca Professor Torrado da Silva, Almada.

The team designed 7 tasks for the robot, focusing on the therapeutic goals of the activities. The goal was to create tasks that allowed us to train commonly impaired skills in autistic children, but also allowed the robot to actively mediate the session, rather than being a mere tool or toy. The first task was Say hello. When the child entered the room, the robot said hello, introduced itself and asked for the child's name. This represented a well-known social routine, it allowed the child to get acquainted with the robot, and presented the robot as a social partner that can communicate with the child. Once the child responded by saying his/her name, the robot invited the child to play a game and waited for the reply. This introduced the purpose of the session—playing games with the robot. The second task was The ball game. In this task the robot asked the child to retrieve 6 colored balls and place them in the robot's belly. This trained the child's ability to follow simple instructions (search for the balls and give them to the robot) while at the same time promoted physical proximity to the robot. It also provided an opportunity for the child to explore the surroundings while looking for the balls. The therapist could use scaffolding[3] to support the child's accomplishments and help them. The third task was the Obstacle and is illustrated in Fig. 3a, where while moving towards one of the tasks the robot's found the path obstructed by an obstacle and asked the child for help. To successfully complete the task the child needed to understand that the robot wanted to pass but could not remove the obstacle on its own, which required the child's ability to understand the robot's perspective. It was the most challenging task within the session, whose goal was to improve social reciprocity and empathy.

In the Puzzle task, the child had to complete a puzzle. All the puzzle pieces were on the screen except one. When the penultimate piece was on the puzzle, the robot pointed out that there was still a piece missing and encouraged the child to ask for help. Once the child asked the robot for help, the robot displayed the missing piece on its tablet and encouraged the child to touch the piece. Once the child touched the piece, it moved to the screen and the child was able to complete the puzzle.

Bernardo et al. [12] developed a Tangram game to be used as a turn-taking game for autistic children. We used a version of the game for children to play with the robot. It was impossible for the child to play on the robot's turn, thus forcing them to wait their turn. During the game the robot asked for help placing a piece, providing another opportunity for the child to train social reciprocity and help the robot. This task is illustrated in Fig. 3b.

For the Blocks task we wanted to bring the therapist to the centre of the activity. We wanted the robot to have an important role and not be a mere toy to use in therapy, but at the same time it did not make sense to take children with difficulties engaging in social interaction and provide a machine that behaves socially as a substitute for human interaction. Inspired by the method used by [72], we created

---

[3] A process of adult support of a child's accomplishment beyond his or her abilities at the time, to build new skills [81].

a task where the therapist knocked down a tower of blocks and waited to see if the child spontaneously helped her rebuild the tower.

The last task was called Say goodbye. The robot ended the session by saying it was time to go, and as it approached the door, the robot asked the child's help one more time which provides another opportunity for the child to help the robot while also representing a known social routine where the robot thanks the child for his/her help and says goodbye before leaving the room.

The INSIDE project created a robot and a therapy session with seven tasks for a long-term child-robot interaction. The children were always accompanied by the parents/legal guardians who were instructed not to intervene unless the child shared something with them. The therapist also played a significant role helping the children and prompting the robot.

3.2 Design of a Storytelling Robot-Assisted Game for Improving Emotional Competence in Children

Emotional competence encompasses the set of interpersonal skills that include the ability to experience and recognize basic emotions, control one's emotions and expressions, and engage in self-disclosure about the subjective experience of emotion, as defined by Ekman [33], Sprung et al. [88], Saarni [77]. Emotional competence is greatly dependent on child's development [77], and underdevelopment of emotional competence in children can have far-reaching consequences for their mental health in later stages of life [2]. This work [66] introduces an educational tool in the form of a game designed to enhance emotional competence in children through one-on-one child-robot interactions. In this game, the children are learning about different emotional experiences, derived from stories told by a social robot. A social robot asking reflective questions on these emotional experiences is compared to a control condition (i.e. social robot not asking reflective questions). Concepts such as emotion expression recognition and game performance as well as child's engagement and self-disclosure (e.g., to help reflecting on their emotional experiences) are included as indications for successful implementation of this game. This educational tool was tested in a field study to assess its impact on children's emotional self-disclosure, in two private schools in Lisbon. We will characterize this work in the four dimensions of the framework defined in Sect. 2.

In the field study, the game was conducted as an extracurricular activity during school hours. A dedicated room was provided for the child to engage in the activity. During the game, the child interacted with it on a computer and the robot was positioned beside the computer. The child-robot interaction during the activity was recorded to afterwards obtain measures on the child's engagement. This arrangement is visually depicted in Fig. 4. To ensure the safety and support of the participants, two researchers were present in the room during the activity. They were positioned in a far corner, only intervening in case the child encountered doubts about the activity or if any unexpected issues arose.

Fig. 4 The figure illustrates the experimental setting used for the study. In the dedicated room, the child is observed engaging with the educational game on a computer, positioned alongside the robot. Additionally, a strategically placed video camera records the entire interaction to facilitate subsequent data analysis and assessment of the child's engagement during child-robot interaction. The adult was positioned behind the camera, in a far corner of the room

The children recruited to participate (n = 28) were neurotypical and in in their primary school years, with ages comprised between 6 and 10 years old. The robot used in this study was Elmo [46], a small desktop robot that can be seen in Fig. 5. Elmo's interaction with the child was facilitated through his head movements and by displaying facial expressions, possible through an LCD screen (Elmo's face), capable of displaying images. Elmo can also play speech through its internal speakers. Other characteristics of the robot are not relevant to this work.

The role was to tell a story and the child was tasked to identify the emotion that better fit the situation described in the story (there were six emotions in total). Elmo's default head movements aim for natural idle interaction. The robot's facial expressions change to match the emotion of the story (the association between the stories and the six emotions studied were validated in a pre-study). Participants played the game under two conditions of child-robot interaction: one without prompts, and the other with the robot encouraging them to reflect on and express emotions. Four different questions were used to prompt the child's self-disclosure: (i) the robot asks the child to explain the reasons behind their choice of emotion to match the story; (ii) the robot shares a "personal" experience hoping that the child will do the same by imitation; the robot directly asks the child to (iii) share a personal experience of theirs with that particular emotion or (iv) share the experience of a friend of theirs. Elmo's speech during the game was generated through text to speech. A prolonged silence from the child is recognized as a cue to allow the robot to continue speaking with the goal to simulate natural dialogue. Elmo provides some help with the child's decision by displaying a facial expression concordant with the emotion felt by the character in the story during storytelling. After the child makes their decision, Elmo provides encouraging verbal feedback on the match between emotion and story, with an accompanying facial expression (some stories might correctly be associated with two different emotions, depending on the subjectivity of the child, for e.g. if someone steals John's ball, he might be sad or angry).

Initial results from this study indicate that prompts from the robot increased the depth and breadth of children's self-disclosure and improved their perception of the robot. In the reflective condition, children perceived the robot as more human-like and smarter, reporting increased trust.

4 Final Remarks

Social robots show great potential as a tool for facilitating psychological interventions and augmenting education and general well-being, demonstrating particular efficacy with children. One of the main reasons is that children engage with robots socially and treat them like life-like agents more than adults do [7]. In education, child-robot interactions allow creating learning experiences tailored to the learner, challenging the child in an individualized form. Additionally, the robot offers a comprehensive and empathetic environment that is consistently available to respond to the child's needs. The physical embodiment of the robot also enhances the child's social behaviors towards it, which is highly beneficial for the learning process [8]. In therapeutic contexts robots have also proven to increase joy and motivation of children in stressful situations, mostly in hospital settings. It has also been suggested that robots, in the role of a companion, take part in conventional therapy approaches (e.g., social anxiety) due to their non-judgmental, flexible, predictable nature [73]. The embodiment, role and modes of interactions play an important role of adoption and effectiveness of the technology, in this domain. Another area of research intensely active in child-robot interaction is supporting children on the autism spectrum. Robots are predictable and consistent, two characteristics that motivate autistic children to interact with robots [1]. These types of interactions reduce complexities of human–human interactions but are designed to help the child learn to better communicate, express and perceive emotions, and develop social competencies in general [19].

However, as outlined in Sect. 2, it is currently impossible to definitively determine which aspect of the robot (such as appearance, autonomy, role, or social behavior) will consistently yield more positive results in an intervention. Nevertheless, it is evident that both age and personality significantly influence children's perceptions of the robot, and consequently impacting the outcomes of the intervention. Therefore, for successful child-robot interventions, it is crucial to design human-robot interactions with a human-centered approach making sure that the unfolding interactions are positive. The framework proposed in this chapter identifies the child as a central element and together with the context of the psychological intervention it shapes the robot's design. As illustrated in the Case Studies (see Sect. 3), the mode of interaction and the design characteristics of the social robot depend strongly on the application domain, goals of the interaction and the characteristics of the child.

With the increasing interest in child-robot interactions and the building evidence of benefits in education and therapy it is necessary to discuss and be aware of potentially unwanted effects of child-robot interactions. Children see robots as a friend or has a companion and have interesting ability to "excuse" the robot and fill in the "lacunas in the interaction" [7]. This can lead to high levels of trust in the technology, which is intended for positive outcomes, but leads to children confide more in the robot than they do with adults, as found in a recent study [90]. In addition, robots continuously monitor the interactions (with high fidelity sensors) and use that information to respond in a socially acceptable manner and offer more personalized experiences. Without storing and processing the child's data the robot cannot be social. Nevertheless, it is of paramount importance to develop methods that protect privacy and prevent this vulnerable population to follow unsafe instructions from a robot.

Another important point to consider is the uptake of this technology in the future. Currently, there are many technical challenges that do not make viable the continuous operation of a robot at home, school or at the therapist office. What if in the future caregivers, teachers, tutors trust more on the technology and delegate care and education to a machine? [53]. It is important to discuss the impact of trust on SRs and the link to child development and social well-being. Children physical and mental development is ongoing and these factors must influence the functioning of the robot, which should support the child development. A child-centered approach to the design of child-robot interactions is the approach that will create more robust technology that listen to children's voices. In addition, other stakeholders (caregivers, healthcare professional, policy makers) also need to provide their input and feedback.

Acknowledgements This work was supported by national funds through Fundacao para a Ciencia e Tecnologia (FCT) with reference UIDB/50021/2020, as well as the projects CRAI C628696807-00454142 (IAPMEI/PRR),TAILORH2020-ICT-48-2020/952215, and Humain E AI Network H2020-ICT-48-2020/952026 and EMPOWER, a project funded by the EU Horizon 2021 research and innovation programme under GA No. 101060918.

References

1. Alcorn AM, Ainger E, Charisi V, Mantinioti S, Petrovi´c S, Schadenberg BR, Tavassoli T, Pellicano E (2019) Educators' views on using humanoid robots with autistic learners in special education settings in england. Front Robot AI 6:107
2. Aldao A, Nolen-Hoeksema S, Schweizer S (2010) Emotion-regulation strategies across psychopathology: a meta-analytic review. Clin Psychol Rev 30(2):217–237. https://doi.org/10.1016/j.cpr.2009.11.004
3. Alemi M, Meghdari A, Ghanbarzadeh A, Moghadam LJ, Ghanbarzadeh A (2014) Impact of a social humanoid robot as a therapy assistant in children cancer treatment. In: Social robotics: 6th international conference, ICSR 2014, Sydney, NSW, Australia. Proceedings, 6. Springer, pp 11–22

4. American Psychiatric Association (2013) Diagnostic and statistical manual of mental disorders, 5th edn. American Psychiatric Publishing, Arlington, VA
5. Balch T, Summet J, Blank D, Kumar D, Guzdial M, O'Hara K, Walker D, Sweat M, Gupta C, Tansley S, Jackson J, Gupta M, Muhammad M, Prashad S, Eilbert N, Gavin A (2008) Designing personal robots for education: hardware, software, and curriculum. IEEE Pervasive Comput 7:5–9. https://doi.org/10.1109/MPRV.2008.29
6. Baraka K, Alves-Oliveira P, Ribeiro T (2020) An extended framework for characterizing social robots. In: Human-robot interaction: evaluation methods and their standardization, pp 21–64
7. Belpaeme T, Baxter P, De Greeff J, Kennedy J, Read R, Looije R, Neerincx M, Baroni I, Zelati MC (2013) Child-robot interaction: perspectives and challenges. In: Social robotics: 5th international conference, ICSR 2013, Bristol, UK, Proceedings 5, Springer, pp 452–459
8. Belpaeme T, Kennedy J, Ramachandran A, Scassellati B, Tanaka F (2018) Social robots for education: a review. Sci Robot 3(21):eaat5954
9. Belpaeme T, Vogt P, van den Berghe R, Bergmann K, Goksun T, de Haas M, Kanero J, Kennedy J, Küntay A, Oudgenoeg-Paz O, Papadopoulos F, Schodde T, Verhagen J, Wallbridge C, Willemsen B, de Wit J, Geckin V, Social Robotics in Psychological Interventions for Children 21 Kunold Née Hoffmann L, Kopp S, Pandey AK (2018) Guidelines for designing social robots as second language tutors. Int J Soc Robot 10. https://doi.org/10.1007/s12369-018-0467-6
10. Beran TN, Ramirez-Serrano A, Vanderkooi OG, Kuhn S (2013) Reducing children's pain and distress towards flu vaccinations: a novel and effective application of humanoid robotics. Vaccine 31(25):2772–2777
11. Bergin C, Bergin D (2009) Attachment in the classroom. Educ Psychol Rev 21:141–170. https://doi.org/10.1007/s10648-009-9104-0
12. Bernardo B, Alves-Oliveira P, Santos M, Melo F, Paiva A (2016) Me and you together: a study on collaboration in manipulation tasks. In: Proceedings of the 16th international conference on intelligent virtual agents, pp 472–475
13. Breazeal C, Dautenhahn K, Kanda T (2016) Social robotics. Springer International Publishing, Cham, pp 1935–1972
14. Breazeal C (2011) Social robots for health applications. In: 2011 Annual international conference of the IEEE engineering in medicine and biology society, IEEE, pp 5368–5371
15. Bredenfeld A, Leimbach T (2010) The roberta® initiative
16. Bryson S, Zwaigenbaum L, Brian J, RobertsW SP, Rombough V, Mc-Dermott C (2007) A prospective case series of high-risk infants who developed autism. J Autism Dev Disord 37(1):12–24
17. Burger F, Broekens J, Neerincx MA (2017) Fostering relatedness between children and virtual agents through reciprocal self-disclosure. In: BNAIC 2016: artificial intelligence: 28th Benelux conference on artificial intelligence, Amsterdam, The Netherlands, Revised Selected Papers 28. Springer, pp 137–154
18. Butchart J, Harrison R, Ritchie J, Martí F, McCarthy C, Knight S, Scheinberg A (2021) Child and parent perceptions of acceptability and therapeutic value of a socially assistive robot used during pediatric rehabilitation. Disabil Rehabil 43(2):163–170
19. Cabibihan JJ, Javed H, Ang M, Aljunied SM (2013) Why robots? A survey on the roles and benefits of social robots in the therapy of children with autism. Int J Soc Robot 5:593–618
20. Case-Smith J, Arbesman M (2008) Evidence-based review of interventions for autism used in or of relevance to occupational therapy. Am J Occup Therapy 62(4):416–429
21. Castelfranchi C (1994) Guarantees for autonomy in cognitive agent architecture. In: International workshop on agent theories, architectures, and languages, Springer, pp 56–70
22. Chandra S, Dillenbourg P, Paiva A (2017) Developing learning scenarios to foster children's handwriting skills with the help of social robots. In: Proceedings of the companion of the 2017 ACM/IEEE international conference on human-robot interaction, association for computing machinery, New York, NY, USA, HRI '17, pp 337–338. https://doi.org/10.1145/3029798.3034818

23. Chang CW, Lee JH, Chao PY, Wang CY, Chen GD (2010) Exploring the possibility of using humanoid robots as instructional tools for teaching a second language in primary school. Educ Technol Soc 13:13–24
24. Church W, Ford T, Perova N, Rogers C (2010) Physics with robotics—Using lego mindstorms in high school education
25. Cooper M, Keating DA, Harwin WS, Dautenhahn K (1999) Robots in the classroom: tools for accessible education. https://api.semanticscholar.org/CorpusID:14719907
26. Costescu CA, Vanderborght B, David DO (2014) The effects of robot-enhanced psychotherapy: a meta-analysis. Rev General Psychol 18(2):127–136
27. Crossman MK, Kazdin AE, Kitt ER (2018) The influence of a socially assistive robot on mood, anxiety, and arousal in children. Prof Psychol Res Pract 49(1):48
28. Dautenhahn K (2000) Design issues on interactive environments for children with autism. In: 3th international conference on disability, virtual reality and associated technologies, pp 153–162. https://doi.org/10.1.1.33.4997
29. Dawe J, Sutherland C, Barco A, Broadbent E (2019) Can social robots help children in healthcare contexts? A scoping review. BMJ Paediatr Open 3(1)
30. Dawson G, Meltzoff A, Osterling J, Rinaldi J, Brown E (1998) Children with autism fail to orient to naturally occurring social stimuli. J Autism Dev Disord 28(6):479–485. https://doi.org/10.1023/A:1026043926488
31. Dawson G, Toth K, Abbott R, Osterling J, Munson J, Estes A, Liaw J (2004) Early social attention impairments in autism: social orienting, joint attention, and attention to distress. Dev Psychol 40(2):271–283. https://doi.org/10.1037/0012-1649.40.2.271
32. Druin A (2002) The role of children in the design of new technology. Behav Inf Technol 21(1):1–25
33. Ekman P (1992) An argument for basic emotions. Cogn Emot 6(3–4):169–200
34. Encarnação P, Alvarez L, Rios A, Maya C, Adams K, Cook A (2014) Using virtual robot-mediated play activities to assess cognitive skills. Disabil Rehabil: Assist Technol 9(3):231–241
35. Fong T, Nourbakhsh I, Dautenhahn K (2003) A survey of socially interactive robots. Robot Autonom Syst 42(3):143–166. https://doi.org/10.1016/S0921-8890(02)00372-X. https://www.sciencedirect.com/science/article/pii/S092188900200372X
36. Giannopulu I, Pradel G (2012) From child-robot interaction to child-robottherapist interaction: a case study in autism. Appl Bionics Biomech 9(2):173–179
37. Han J, Jo M, Jones V, Jo J (2008) Comparative study on the educational use of home robots for children. JIPS 4:159–168. https://doi.org/10.3745/JIPS.2008.4.4.159
38. Han J, Jo M, Park S, Kim S (2005) The educational use of home robots for children. In: ROMAN 2005. IEEE international workshop on robot and human interactive communication, 2005, pp 378–383. https://doi.org/10.1109/ROMAN.2005.1513808
39. Han JH, Kim D, Kim JW (2009) Physical learning activities with a teaching assistant robot in elementary school music class. In: 2009 fifth international joint conference on INC, IMS and IDC, pp 1406–1410. https://api.semanticscholar.org/CorpusID:16785704
40. Hashimoto T, Kobayashi H, Polishuk A, Verner I (2013) Elementary science lesson delivered by robot, pp 133–134. https://doi.org/10.1109/HRI.2013.6483537
41. Heerink M, Díaz M, Albo-Canals J, Angulo C, Barco A, Casacuberta J, Garriga C (2012) A field study with primary school children on perception of social presence and interactive behavior with a pet robot. In: 2012 IEEE RO-MAN: the 21st IEEE international symposium on robot and human interactive communication, pp 1045–1050. https://doi.org/10.1109/ROMAN.2012.6343887
42. Henkemans OAB, Bierman BP, Janssen J, Looije R, Neerincx MA, van Dooren MM, de Vries JL, van der Burg GJ, Huisman SD (2017) Design and evaluation of a personal robot playing a self-management education game with children with diabetes type 1. Int J Hum Comput Stud 106:63–76
43. Highfield K, Mulligan J, Hedberg JG (2008) Early mathematics learning through exploration with programmable toys. https://api.semanticscholar.org/CorpusID:116119520

44. Hirst A, Johnson J, Petre M, Price B, Richards M (2003) What is the best programming environment/language for teaching robotics using lego mindstorms? Artif Life Robot 7:124–131. https://doi.org/10.1007/BF02481160
45. Huskens B, Verschuur R, Gillesen J, Didden R, Barakova E (2013) Promoting question-asking in school-aged children with autism spectrum disorders: effectiveness of a robot intervention compared to a human-trainer intervention. Dev Neurorehabil 16(5):345–356
46. IDMind (2000) Idmind: living robotics. URL idmind.pt. Accessed 15 Sep 2023
47. Janssen J, Wal C, Neerincx M, Looije R (2011) Motivating children to learn arithmetic with an adaptive robot game, pp 153–162
48. Jeong S, Breazeal C, Logan D, Weinstock P (2018) Huggable: the impact of embodiment on promoting socio-emotional interactions for young pediatric inpatients. In: Proceedings of the 2018 CHI conference on human factors in computing systems, pp 1–13
49. Johnson W, Rickel J, Lester J (2000) Animated pedagogical agents: Face-to-face interaction in interactive learning environments. Int J Artif Intell Educ 11:47–78
50. Kabacińska K, Prescott TJ, Robillard JM (2021) Socially assistive robots as mental health interventions for children: a scoping review. Int J Soc Robot 13:919–935
51. Kanda T, Hirano T, Eaton D, Ishiguro H (2004) Interactive robots as social partners and peer tutors for children: a field trial. Hum Comput Interact (Special issues on human-robot interaction) 19:61–84
52. Kumazaki H, Yoshikawa Y, Yoshimura Y, Ikeda T, Hasegawa C, Saito D, Tomiyama S, An K, Shimaya J, Ishiguro H et al (2018) The impact of robotic intervention on joint attention in children with autism spectrum disorders. Mol Autism 9(1):46
53. Kurian N (2023) Toddlers and robots? The ethics of supporting young children with disabilities with ai companions and the implications for children's rights. Int J Hum Rights Educ 7(1):9
54. Lewis TT, Kim H, Darcy-Mahoney A, Waldron M, Lee WH, Park CH (2021) Robotic uses in pediatric care: a comprehensive review. J Pediatr Nurs 58:65–75
55. Li J (2015) The benefit of being physically present: a survey of experimental works comparing copresent robots, telepresent robots and virtual agents. Int J Hum Comput Stud 77:23–37
56. Ligthart M, Hindriks K, Neerincx MA (2018) Reducing stress by bonding with a social robot: towards autonomous long-term child-robot interaction. In: Companion of the 2018 ACM/IEEE international conference on human-robot interaction, pp 305–306
57. Liverpool S, Mota CP, Sales CM, Čuš A, Carletto S, Hancheva C, Sousa S, Cerón SC, Moreno-Peral P, Pietrabissa G et al (2020) Engaging children and young people in digital mental health interventions: systematic review of modes of delivery, facilitators, and barriers. J Med Internet Res 22(6):e16317
58. Melo FS, Sardinha A, Belo D, Couto M, Faria M, Farias A, Gambôa H, Jesus C, Kinarullathil M, Lima P, Luz L, Mateus A, Melo I, Moreno P, Osório D, Paiva A, Pimentel J, Rodrigues J, Sequeira P, Solera-Ureña R, Vasco M, Veloso M, Ventura R (2019) Project inside: towards autonomous semi-unstructured human-robot social interaction in autism therapy. Artif Intell Med 96:198–216. https://doi.org/10.1016/j.artmed.2018.12.003. https://www.sciencedirect.com/science/article/pii/S0933365717305997
59. Michaud F, Théberge-Turmel C (2002) Mobile robotic toys and autism. In: K D, A B, L C, B E (eds) Socially intelligent agents. Multiagent systems, artificial societies, and simulated organizations, vol 3. Springer, Boston, MA, pp 125–132
60. Moerman CJ, van der Heide L, Heerink M (2019) Social robots to support children's well-being under medical treatment: a systematic state-of-the-art review. J Child Health Care 23(4):596–612
61. Mubin O, Bartneck C, Feijs L, Hooft van Huysduynen H, Hu J, Muelver J (2012) Improving speech recognition with the robot interaction language. Disrupt Sci Technol 1:79–88. https://doi.org/10.1089/dst.2012.0010
62. Mubin O, Stevens C, Shahid S, Mahmud A, Dong JJ (2013) A review of the applicability of robots in education. Technol Educ Learn 1. https://doi.org/10.2316/Journal.209.2013.1.209-0015

63. Neerincx A, Veldhuis D, Masthoff JM, de Graaf MM (2023) Co-designing a social robot for child health care. Int J Child-Comput Interact 38:100615
64. Neerincx A, Luijk A (2020) Social robot's processing of context-sensitive emotions in child care: a Dutch use case. In: Companion publication of the 2020 international conference on multimodal interaction, pp 503–505
65. Neerincx A, Hiwat T, De Graaf M (2021) Social robot for health check and entertainment in waiting room: child's engagement and parent's involvement. In: Adjunct proceedings of the 29th ACM conference on user modeling, adaptation and personalization, pp 120–125
66. Neerincx A, Brito J, Campos J, Paiva A (2023) Design of a storytelling robot assisted game for improving emotional competence in children
67. Neerincx A, Leven J, Wolfert P, de Graaf MM (2023) The effect of simple emotional gesturing in a socially assistive robot on child's engagement at a group vaccination day. In: Proceedings of the 2023 ACM/IEEE international conference on human-robot interaction, pp 162–171
68. Neerincx A, Li Y, van de Sande K, Broz F, Neerincx M, de Graaf M (2023) Child's personality and self-disclosures to a robot persona "in-the-wild". In: International conference on robot and human interactive communication (RO-MAN). IEEE
69. Norman DA (2013) The design of everyday things, revised and expanded edition ed. BB (AZ)
70. Okita S, Ng-Thow-Hing V, Sarvadevabhatla SRK (2009) Learning together: Asimo developing an interactive learning partnership with children, pp 1125–1130. https://doi.org/10.1109/ROMAN.2009.5326135
71. Papakostas GA, Sidiropoulos GK, Papadopoulou CI, Vrochidou E, Kaburlasos VG, Papadopoulou MT, Holeva V, Nikopoulou VA, Dalivigkas N (2021) Social robots in special education: a systematic review. Electronics 10(12):1398
72. Plötner M, Over H, Carpenter M, Tomasello M (2015) Young children show the bystander effect in helping situations. Psychol Sci 26(4):499–506
73. Rasouli S, Gupta G, Nilsen E, Dautenhahn K (2022) Potential applications of social robots in robot-assisted interventions for social anxiety. Int J Soc Robot 14(5):1–32
74. Ricou M, Marina S, Vieira PM, Duarte I, Sampaio I, Regalado J, Canário C (2019) Psychological intervention at a primary health care center: predictors of success. BMC Family Pract 20(1):1–8
75. Riedo F, Retornaz P, Bergeron L, Nyffeler N, Mondada F (2011) A two years informal learning experience using the thymio robot
76. Robotics A (2004) Nao. https://www.aldebaran.com/en. Accessed 15 Sep 2023
77. Saarni C (2000) Emotional competence: a developmental perspective
78. Saerbeck M, Schut T, Bartneck C, Janse M (2010) Expressive robots in education-varying the degree of social supportive behavior of a robotic tutor. In: 28th ACM conference on human factors in computing systems (CHI2010). ACM, Atlanta, pp 1613–1622. https://doi.org/10.1145/1753326.1753567
79. Salimi Z, Jenabi E, Bashirian S (2021) Are social robots ready yet to be used in care and therapy of autism spectrum disorder: a systematic review of randomized controlled trials. Neurosci Biobehav Rev 129:1–16
80. Sandygulova A, O'Hare GM (2018) Age-and gender-based differences in children's interactions with a gender-matching robot. Int J Soc Robot 10(5):687–700
81. Schaff RC, Roley SS (2006) Ensory integration: applying clinical reasoning to practice with diverse populations. PRO-ED, Incorporated
82. Serholt S, Barendregt W (2016) Robots tutoring children: longitudinal evaluation of social engagement in child-robot interaction. https://doi.org/10.1145/2971485.2971536
83. Shin N, Kim S (2007) Learning about, from, and with robots: students' perspectives, pp 1040–1045. https://doi.org/10.1109/ROMAN.2007.4415235
84. So WC, Cheng CH, Lam WY, Huang Y, Ng KC, Tung HC, Wong W (2020) A robot-based play-drama intervention may improve the joint attention and functional play behaviors of chinese-speaking preschoolers with autism spectrum disorder: a pilot study. J Autism Dev Disord 50:467–481

85. So WC, Wong MKY, Lam WY, Cheng CH, Ku SY, Lam KY, Huang Y, Wong WL (2019) Who is a better teacher for children with autism? Comparison of learning outcomes between robot-based and human-based interventions in gestural production and recognition. Res Dev Disabil 86:62–75
86. So WC, Wong MKY, Lam CKY, Lam WY, Chui ATF, Lee TL, Ng HM, Chan CH, Fok DCW (2018) Using a social robot to teach gestural recognition and production in children with autism spectrum disorders. Disabil Rehabil Assist Technol 13(6):527–539
87. So WC, Wong MKY, Lam WY, Cheng CH, Yang JH, Huang Y, Ng P, Wong WL, Ho CL, Yeung KL et al (2018) Robot-based intervention may reduce delay in the production of intransitive gestures in Chinese-speaking preschoolers with autism spectrum disorder. Mol Autism 9(1):1–16
88. Sprung M, Münch HM, Harris PL, Ebesutani C, Hofmann SG (2015) Children's emotion understanding: a meta-analysis of training studies. Dev Rev 37:41–65
89. Srinivasan SM, Eigsti IM, Neelly L, Bhat AN (2016) The effects of embodied rhythm and robotic interventions on the spontaneous and responsive social attention patterns of children with autism spectrum disorder (ASD): a pilot randomized controlled trial. Res Autism Spectr Disord 27:54–72
90. Stower R, Kappas A, Sommer K (2024) When is it right for a robot to be wrong? Children trust a robot over a human in a selective trust task. Comput Human Behav 157
91. Tanaka F, Matsuzoe S (2012) Children teach a care-receiving robot to promote their learning: field experiments in a classroom for vocabulary learning. J Hum-Robot Interact 1(1):78–95. https://doi.org/10.5898/JHRI.1.1.Tanaka
92. Trost MJ, Ford AR, Kysh L, Gold JI, Matarić M (2019) Socially assistive robots for helping pediatric distress and pain: a review of current evidence and recommendations for future research and practice. Clin J Pain 35(5):451
93. Trujillo K (2010) Developing emotional security among children who have been adopted. Ph.D. thesis, University of Denver
94. Turliuc MN, Candel OS (2019) Ethical issues in couple and family research and therapy. In: Ethics in research practice and innovation, IGI Global, pp 226–242
95. Werry I, Dautenhahn K (1999) Applying mobile robot technology to the rehabilitation of autistic children. In: Procs SIRS99, 7th symp on intelligent robotic systems, pp 265–272
96. Westlund JMK, Park HW, Williams R, Breazeal C (2018) Measuring young children's long-term relationships with social robots. In: Proceedings of the 17th ACM conference on interaction design and children, pp 207–218
97. Whittaker S, Rogers Y, Petrovskaya E, Zhuang H (2021) Designing personas for expressive robots: Personality in the new breed of moving, speaking, and colorful social home robots. ACM Trans Human-Robot Interact (THRI) 10(1):1–25
98. Wilpon J, Jacobsen C (1996) A study of speech recognition for children and the elderly. In: 1996 IEEE international conference on acoustics, speech, and signal processing conference proceedings, vol 1, pp 349–352. https://doi.org/10.1109/ICASSP.1996.541104
99. Yasemin M, Kasımoglu Y, Kocaaydın S, Karslı E, Ince EBT, Ince G (2016) Reduction of dental anxiety and pain in children using robots. In: Proceedings from the ninth international conference on advances in computer-human interactions
100. Zheng Z, Nie G, Swanson A, Weitlauf A, Warren Z, Sarkar N (2020) A randomized controlled trial of an intelligent robotic response to joint attention intervention system. J Autism Dev Disord 50:2819–2831

Part II
Applications of Technology Use for Interventions

The Use of Technological Tools for Autistic Children

7

Cristina Costescu

Abstract

This chapter summarizes the most used types of technological tools for clinical and educational interventions developed for autistic children. Since several studies emphasize the advantages and benefits of using technology for maximizing the learning process in autistic children, we provide o overview regarding the effectiveness of using virtual reality, robots, computer-based interventions and wearables in autism therapy. For each of the above-mentioned technologies there are several studies showing their effectiveness, however there are many aspects that studies should consider when designing and testing the use of technology for autistic people. The final part of this chapter summarizes some of those aspects that should be considered for the technology design such as co-design of the technological tool, gamification, technology integration and cognitive availability. Since there are some inconclusive and mixed results in some of the domains of technology for autism spectrum disorder (ASD), each study should consider testing the technology in a rigorous experimental study.

Keywords

Virtual reality in autism interventions • Robots in autism therapy • Computer-based interventions for autism • Wearable technology in autism treatment • Effectiveness of technology in autism

---

C. Costescu (✉)
Special Education Department, Faculty of Psychology and Educational Sciences, Babeș-Bolyai University, Cluj-Napoca, Romania
e-mail: cristina.costescu@ubbcluj.ro

1 Introduction

There are several advantages in the use of technological tools when working with autistic children, among which the most important relevant are: the fact that the information is displayed in a visual display, the interaction with the technological device is more predictive and less intimidating and offers stability and not exhibit emotional transitions like a human being does [1]. Moreover, when using digital devices the focus is mainly on establishing the interaction between the child and the technological tool, encouraging the user to get more engaged with the task and device and less focused on the human interaction, which can reduce the frequency of the maladaptive behaviors and allow the child to focus on the learning process [1].

Autistic children seem to be more involved and learn faster even if the contents are about human–human interactions or about emotions, which are specific to humans. For example, a group of children that played *Transporters*, a game that puts facial expressions of trains, did manage to recognize the emotions better than another group of children that did not play the game [2].

According to Kientz et. al. [3], who conducted a comprehensive review of technologies used in ASD there are six main emerging interactive technology platforms: computers, robots, virtual reality, sensors or sensing technologies, active surfaces and mobile phones. In this chapter we will describe the first three, which are the most used and studied ones: personal computers, robotics, and virtual reality. Moreover, we will briefly introduce a new category: wearables and we will present some applications for recently developed resource, namely the Superpower Glass, an artificial- intelligence-driven wearable.

2 Virtual Reality

Virtual reality (VR) is a relatively new technology that projects a scenario in which the children can immerse themselves. VR environments can provide simplified and realistic educational activities which are very engaging for the child and the 3D presentations of the images take place in real time [4]. There are either 3D presentations that are controlled through an electronic device or a joystick or a fully immersive environment that requires the use of a virtual cube, headset and/ or a body motion detector [5]. Usually through VR environments autistic children train the abilities that are needed for an independent life and employment [6, 7]. Therefore, VR environments were used to teach individuals to cross the street [8], to use public transportation and to behave appropriately when entering in a restaurant and looking for a table [9].

A recent study investigated the effectiveness of VR on the recognition of primary emotions involving 60 autistic children with a mean age of 9 years old. Frolli and his collaborators [10] compared a traditional emotional training with one obtained using a VR. The training consisted of 3D projections including 38 scenes illustrating and referring to primary and secondary emotions. The traditional training consisted in the same scenarios illustrated in photos using the same characters. Total duration of the training was 3 months and sessions were scheduled three times per week. Their results illustrated a significant difference between the two types of interventions, where the VR treatment revealed a greater effectiveness.

A systematic review conducted in 2021 showed that autistic individuals with undergoing both augmented reality (AR) and VR trainings have significant improvements with a relatively large effect size on cognitive skills, social and communication skills, emotion regulation and recognition and daily living skills [11]. Out of the four major outcomes the strongest effect was observed on daily living skills. Even if they analyzed only five studies that used AR, they identified promising results. Out of the 33 studies, only 9 of them that investigated VR used a rigorous controlled design, out of which 5 analyzed the impact on social communication skills, 2 on daily living skills, 3 emotion regulation skills and one cognitive skill. Also, at this level of analysis, the most significant results were found at daily living skills. Same results were obtained when analyzing the 9 uncontrolled trials that targeted daily living skills. Among the daily living skills targeted we mention bus routine, driving skills and attitudes towards driving, crossing the street and air travel skills.

The effectiveness of AR treatments was like VR interventions, even if the number of studies and participants was relatively small, the authors consider that the results can be reliable due to the low heterogeneity within the trials. This represents an important result because of the simplicity of the design and the accessibility of AR-enabled mobile phones.

Glasar and Schimidt [12] developed a systematic literature review in which they analyzed 82 articles. Their overall results suggested that there are some inconsistencies in how VR is conceptualized and that can impact greatly the possibilities for learner interactions and how the benefits can be interpreted. However, with their analysis they answered some important questions from the field. The first question they tried to answer was what kind of technologies (VR) are being used for training in autistic children. Desktop-based interfaces was the most used technology. This type of technology included keyboards, computer mice, joysticks, video games controllers, eye trackers, motion trackers and driving interfaces. The second most used technology was CAVE systems where different scenarios were projected on several screens and the users could interact through motion trackers or several types of controllers. There are several configurations when using CAVE systems, 4-walls CAVEs, 6-walls CAVEs, etc. and no differences were presented in terms of their effectiveness. The third most used technology were head mounted devices, where the users received wearable helmets and they used Google Cardboard, Google Daydream and Tzumi Dream Vision. Some studies included in the review and meta-analysis used mobile-based devices to connect to lightweight mobile head mounted devices or a projector-based system connected to a Kinect. Regarding the persons who benefit the most from this type of intervention, unfortunately most of the studies do not provide a clear characterization of the children and adolescents involved. The majority of the participants are children or adolescents aged between 4 and 19 years old. Also, according to the authors of the review the physical locations are not always mentioned in the studies description. The most targeted skills in the studies and described by the authors are similar to the ones mentioned in previous reviews: social skills, daily living skills, communication and emotional skills.

Therefore, one of the main advantages of VR is the fact that everyday life situations can be implemented in a controlled and safe environment. Even if there are several studies investigating the effectiveness of VR for autistic children and adolescents, we still need to use this technology with caution. Many of the studies did not include control groups and the use of VR was rarely compared to standard treatment, and if so, the sample size was relatively small. Another important issue that should be considered is the fact that the results are difficult to generalize and extrapolate since the majority of the studies include high-functioning autistic children and adolescents and the majority of them are boys [13]. Another important drawback is represented by the high heterogeneity in which VR systems are defined and the multiple systems that are being used.

3   Computer Based Interventions

Computer based interventions employ different types of methods, that are both accessible and cost-effective and include embedding photos or videos, combining interactive feedback systems that inform end-users about their progress and guide them through the games. There are computer-based interventions that target social and emotional skills by using narratives that vary in complexity from simplistic themes-based games to narrative implementing real life scenarios [14, 15]. More recently Serios Games design framework was proposed as a relevant framework for developing computer-based interventions in ASD [16]. This provides guidelines about the use of feedback, rewards, level of difficulty, the use of a story, monitoring, custom learning and includes elements about the user interface design, such as illustrations, photographs, text, use of colors, sound, voice and the use of video [17]. The use of Serios Games framework is likely to enhance the motivational aspects of the computer-based interventions and to maximize the learning opportunities an engaging environment [16].

Valencia and her collaborators [18] develop a systematic literature review in which they investigated how technology is used in educational contexts. The majority of the analyzed studies were case studies, and their outcomes were categorized into conceptual skills (e.g., language, math, colors, money), practical skills (e.g. daily living, transportation, healthcare), social skills (e.g. communication, emotions, interpersonal relationships) and general skills (e.g. pointing). Out of the four categories social skill were the most targeted by the studies (36%), which means that most of the computer-based interventions developed aim to improve social skills. Even if accessibility and user experience are considered fundamental aspects when developing computer-based interventions for autistic children, the authors revealed that only 23 studies out of 94 reviewed provided some details of the use of these concepts in their studies.

One of the most important studies in this field, with a sample of 154 autistic children, together with their teachers (59) investigated the effectiveness of a computer-assisted intervention on cognitive abilities and receptive and expressive language skills [19]. The children (aged between 5 and 9) were randomized to one of the groups: treatment as usual (70 children) or computer-based intervention with Teach Town (84 children). The computer-based intervention targeted 6 domains: cognitive skills, language development, mathematics, social and emotional skills, language arts and adaptive skills. The computerized lessons followed a discrete trial format where the child needs to follow several instructions and to select the correct response. Children's responses are reinforced using verbal praise, animated games or graphics. Students are expected to play the game on a computer or on a digital tablet 20 min per day either independently or assisted by their teachers for one academic year. All the measurements used to assess the children's outcomes were standardized, they used Differential Ability Scale, 2nd Edition [20], and Bracken Basic Concept Scale 3rd Edition [21]. Their findings showed that children who benefit from the intervention with Teach Town did not show greater gains neither in their cognitive skills nor in their expressive or receptive language compared to children from the waitlist. Considering these results, the authors advise to carefully analyze the possibility of implementing such programs on a large scale. Even though in a previous study with preschool-age children the results were different, showing improvements in receptive language, those finding did not replicate when assessing older children [22].

Sandgreen and her collaborators [23] analyzed in their meta-analysis 14 studies that used computer programs to improve autistic children social skills, developmental skills, cognitive skills (attention, memory, cognitive flexibility etc.) and others (anxiety). The mean age of children (815 participants analyzed) was 10.6 and their benefited by interventions that lasted 12.3 h. The majority of the studies included showed small to medium effects sizes, meaning that the targeted outcomes improved after the intervention compared to a group of control with a diagnosis of ASD. Among those interventions we mention: Brave Online, an anxiety treatment that is based on cognitive behavioral therapy; face recognition trainings with the use of a computer; Find me, an tablet app that trains social communication; emotion recognition training using The Transporters Interactive DVD's and Mind Reading computer program; emotional and facial recognition training FaceSay and Let's Face It!; BOOTS-A an online program that support the transitions from high schools; GOLIAH (Gaming Open Library for Intervention in Autism at home), a training in communication and social interaction, Braingame, a computer game for training working memory and cognitive flexibility; Toby the app for training developmental skills; for attention training they included in their review a study that used Computerized Progressive Attentional Training.

Even if the overall effect size of the intervention was positive (rather small), the majority of the studies raised some concerns about the risk of bias. For example, most of the studies did not present a detailed protocol, no information about the blinding of individuals who did the assessment, the randomization process was not fully explained, or the missing data were not considered. Their conclusion was that more randomized clinical trial is needed in order to test the effectiveness of computer-based intervention for autistic children. Moreover, the effects on long-term should be also considered and a more rigorous procedure for testing the existing games and computer-based intervention should be implemented.

4 Robot-Based Interventions

The domain of robot-based intervention has increased dramatically in the last decades especially for the specific area of developing social skills in autistic children. Particularly because it has the potential to reduce the workload of the specialists and hence the cost of the interventions [24]. Social robots are described as physically embodied agents that may communicate and engage with individuals fully or partially autonomous. Among the advantages in using social robots in the psychological interventions we mention the attractive way the information is presented to children, which leads to a better improvement. Social robots are predictable and consistent in their interaction, which can optimize the learning process [25]. Moreover, their simplified facial expressions, interaction and their gradual increase in the level of difficulty acts like an important feature in the skills development process [26–28].

A recent meta-analysis included 40 studies in their study from 2008 until 2020 [29]. According to their classification there were three types of robots used in the studies humanoid (the majority of the studies 27 out of 40), animal-like robot (11 studies of the 40) and other. Among the most used robots from the humanoid category was NAO, but there were also other robots, such as QTrobot, Toto, Caro, Keepon. Within the animal-like category, Probo was mentioned in 6 studies and other robots were Pleo, Zoomer or Pol. The remaining category of other included robots that looked like a plant or just a robotic arm. In regard to the settings where the interventions took place, the most common ones were specialized centers or private clinics rooms, followed by homes, school and lab settings. Meaning that robot-based intervention is delivered mainly in ecological settings (29 studies of out 40), which can represent an advantage of this type of intervention. The session did not last were much, the average reported in the meta-analysis is 33.5 min per session with a mean duration of the treatment of 8.4 sessions implemented once or twice per week. Considering the role of the robot during the interventions, there are several used in the studies, out of which we mention the mediator, the storytelling, the imitation agent and the intermediator role. The most used one is the mediator, where there is a triadic relation during the session, with the robot, the child and the therapist. The targeted abilities were social and communication skills, engagement, collaborative play, joint attention, imitation, emotional development, and motor skills. 72% of the studies reported positive outcomes, 10% reported no significant differences in the target skills and one study reported a decrease in the attention skill measured. One of the possible mediators that was found to be significant is age, meaning that younger children benefited most of the robot-assisted interventions.

Among the first studies that investigated the effects of robot-based interventions using a long-term in-home social robot was the one implemented by Scassellati and his collaborators in 2018 [30]. 12 autistic children aged between 6 and 12 years old played 30 min per day for 30 days in a triadic interaction setting meant to model social gaze behaviors and provide feedback in different interactive games. The games targeted were social and emotional understanding, and consisted in sequence games, perspective-taking activities, and joint attention games. Their results showed that the children kept their engagement throughout the intervention sessions and that the caregivers reported increased social skills, more eye contact, more attempts to initiate communication and more frequent responses with them and with other people at the end of the intervention sessions compared to the baseline. Another important aspect of this study was the fact that they demonstrated the possibility of using fully autonomous robot intervention in-home setting. Even if they used the robot for one month, which represents a long time for robot-based interventions, the time was limited to 30 min per day and the applications were limited, therefore future studies should try to generate engaging content that can be adapted to longer periods of time and more personalized.

Saleh and collaborators [31] included in their comprehensive review 166 studies with a total number of 1671 participant and investigated the use of robots for autistic children. The most used robot was Nao and the majority of the studies focused on social skills and stereotyped behaviors. Moreover, they classified the studies according to the purpose of the research conducted, out of 166 studies, 41 of the studies (28%) focus on modelling or skills practicing whereas 19% focus on testing or evaluation and 12% on providing feedback or encouragement. The rest of the studies aim on improving specific skills, such as imitation, turn taking, vocalization or emotion recognition. Therefore, the robots are used as promoters, mediators, analyzers or monitoring tools.

The high interest in robot-assisted therapy for autistic children leaded to a high number of papers in this domain, however when analyzing the quality of the studies the conclusion from several reviews is that most of them are not using a rigorous methodology. Salimi and his collaborators [32] conducted a systematic review of randomized clinical trials and they analyzed 16 studies. When considering training of joint attention, they concluded that from the analyzed studies the results are mixed, while some studies demonstrate the effectiveness of the robots in training joint attention, others did not come with positive results. The situation is similar when they analyzed the advantage of robots over human therapists. The results were mixed, for example when measuring the eye contact or the social behaviors oriented through the robot or the human therapists. Another interesting aspect that they investigated is the engagement in the presence of the robot. Some of the studies showed how the engagement is decreasing while the novelty effect disappears, but some studies on the contrary showed that if they are adding new systems on the robots, they do not lose their capability of engaging the children.

There are several important studies, that were not included in meta-analysis or systematic reviews that focus on randomized clinical trials due to their choice for the design of the study. For example, the use of single case experiments is proven to be very efficient when measuring the effectiveness of innovative interventions on special populations. David and his collaborators [33] investigated to what degree the social robot Nao can improve turn-taking skills on preschool aged autistic children. They enrolled 5 autistic children in a single case design study and each child received 20 intervention session, 8 robot-enhanced sessions, 8 standardized sessions and 4 more sessions with the most effective treatment out of the two. They measured their performance in a turn-taking tasks and their engagement in the task, their eye-contact, verbal utterances and adaptive behaviors. Their results showed that most children had similar levels of performance across standard treatment and robot-enhanced intervention. The conditions between the two types of intervention were very similar, the tasks and the setting were the same, they replaced only the interactional partners (robot vs. adult). However, children looked more at the robotic partner and seemed to enjoy more those sessions.

5   Wearables

In 2019 Voss and his colleagues published the first randomized clinical trial that demonstrated the efficacy of Superpower Glass, a computer vision system that runs on Google Glass, a wearable behavioral intervention for autistic children [34]. They included 71 children in their study (mean age 8.38) randomized in two groups 40 children to experimental group and 31 to control group. Both groups received applied behavior therapy at least twice per week at home, children from the experimental group wore the Superpower Glass, a system that tracks faces, classifies the emotions of the interactional partner, and provides cues in real time for the child. Children had to wear the glasses four times per week for 20 min. They used several standardized instruments to test the effectiveness of the intervention, Vineland Adaptive Behaviors Scale [35], The Developmental Neuropsychological Assessment, second edition [36] and Social Responsiveness Scale [37] and they found that children from the intervention group showed significant improvements on the social subscale compared to the control group. According to the authors, there are two potential underlying mechanisms of the wearable intervention: the reinforcement that the faces have variation in emotions and the training of how to differentiate between emotions.

Prior to the randomized clinical trial implemented by Voss and his colleagues, there were several studies measuring the use of Google Glasses for autistic children, but all of them were case studies or single-case experimental design [38–40]. Vahabzadeh and her colleagues [39] tested the efficacy of Empowered Brain, which represents a computerized smart glass intervention designed to improve children's social and emotional skills. Empowered Brain integrates Google Glasses and a wide range of educational modules, that were developed through a user-centered design and were previously tested with specialists and end-users. It is designed to be used 10 min per session, while the children receive pro-social cues and instructions by auditory (speaker) and visual feedback (optical display). Their study lasted in total 6 weeks, out of which 3 weeks was the feasibility study and 3 weeks the controlled efficacy study. In the second study children wore the Empowered Brain twice per day for 10 min while the facilitators engaged the children in natural conversation regarding academic topics. 4 autistic children with age between 6 and 8 years old participated in the study in a single-case experiment design and they were showed improvements in their irritability level, hyperactivity and social withdrawal after the intervention measured with Aberant Behavioral Checklist [41]. Their outcomes improved after one week of intervention and after two weeks of intervention as well.

Even if there are not enough studies to conduct a systematic review or a meta-analysis, the use of smart glasses was investigated in more studies, mostly conducted by the team of Keshav, Sahin, Vahabzadeh and Liu. The most used design is single case experiment, which can determine whether is a causal relationship between the intervention and the outcome. However, to fully understand the mechanism of change and decide if these wearables could represent reliable intervention tools randomized experimental designs are needed.

6 Conclusions

The use of technology for assessing and training autistic children represents a great opportunity nowadays. Even if there are mixed results in some of the fields and further investigations are needed, there are several rigorous studies in each type of the technology discussed in these chapter that allows us to conclude that the use of technological tools can improve the learning process for autistic children. Figure 1 summarizes some of the main points that we need to consider when developing technological tools for any type of neurodiverse people or other types of vulnerabilities.

Firstly, when designing any type of technological tools for autistic children one's should consider involving end-users and stakeholders in the development process. Their feedback is very useful and may increase their engagement in the tasks and motivation. Moreover, if in the development of the technological tool one's considers the users' needs and their cognitive capabilities this can lead to the maximization of the benefits of that tool.

Regarding the integration of the technology in the learning process, there are several models that try to explain how the integration process may occur. Two of those models are *Technology, Pedagogy and Content Knowledge Model* TPACK [42] and *Substitution, Augmentation, Modification and Redefinition Model* (SAMR) [43, 44]. The TPACK represents a model of integrating technology in the classroom and is focused on three types of knowledge: technological knowledge, pedagogical knowledge, and content knowledge. All the types of knowledge change the way teachers decide to use the technology and are influences by the contexts, training, experience and the institution. The SARM model illustrates the

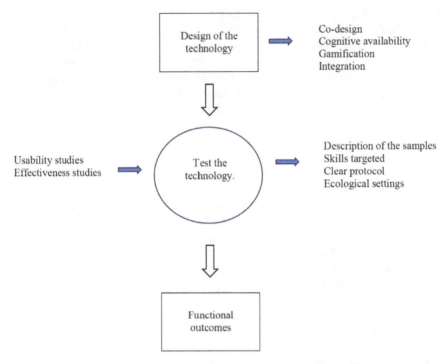

Fig. 1 Model of the design and use of technology for autistic children

way technology can be integrated into a learning activity so that it modifies the learning process by transforming it or by enhancing it. Each level of the four proposed in the model (substitution, augmentation, modification, and redefinition) has its own goal and the decision of the specialist (teacher or psychologist) regarding which level to choose depends on the learning outcomes and on the reason why they choose to integrate the technology in the first place. The models are complementary and can be used to integrate technology and support students' success and enhance their learning experience.

The gamification elements should also be considered when designing technology especially for children with special needs. Gamification of learning activities may boost the motivation, engagement, and enjoyment of the learners. Therefore, elements such as story or narrative of the activity, rewards, personalization, progression, use of avatars, different levels or monitorization of the progress should be considered when designing the technological tools [45].

Secondly when testing the efficacy of the technological tool there are some quality indicators that one needs to take into consideration: *description of the participants* (to provide sufficient details about the participants so that other researchers could replicate the study and to specify the inclusion and exclusion criteria), *the design used* (the most recommended ones are single case studies or randomized clinical studies), *the independent and the dependent variables* and the *description of the instruments used* to measure them (if the researchers use observation grids is very important to provide clear definitions of each behavior that they measure), the intervention protocol (with exact details about the implementation: duration, trials, description of each activity/game, performance, etc.), external validity and control of internal validity.

Thirdly when it comes to the outcomes of the studies, the social validity of their results needs to be addressed. Apart from the experimental results, the use of technology needs to be a way of helping people with different vulnerabilities to improve their abilities according to their needs. Aspects like cost-effectiveness and magnitude of change need to be considered when recommending the integration of a technological tool into an educational or clinical program.

References

1. Bauminger N, Goren-Bar D, Gal E, Weiss PL, Yifat R, Kupersmitt J, Pianesi F, Stock O, Zancanaro M (2007) Enhancing social communication in high-functioning children with autism through a co-located interface. In: 2007 IEEE 9th workshop on multimedia signal processing, pp 18–21. https://doi.org/10.1109/MMSP.2007.4412808
2. Boucenna S, Narzisi A, Tilmont E, Muratori F, Pioggia G, Cohen D, Chetouani M (2014) Interactive technologies for autistic children: a review. Cogn Comput 6:722–740. https://doi.org/10.1007/s12559-014-9276-x
3. Kientz JA, Goodwin MS, Hayes GR, Abowd GD (2014) Interactive technologies for autism. https://doi.org/10.1007/978-3-031-01604-2
4. Parsons S, Cobb S (2011) State-of-the-art of virtual reality technologies for children on the autism spectrum. Eur J Spec Needs Educ 26(3):355–366. https://doi.org/10.1080/08856257.2011.593831
5. Johnson-Glenberg MC (2018) Immersive VR and education: embodied design principles that include gesture and hand controls. Front Robot AI 5:81. https://doi.org/10.3389/frobt.2018.00081
6. Parsons S, Mitchell P, Leonard A (2004) The use and understanding of virtual environments by adolescents with autistic spectrum disorders. J Autism Dev Disord 34:449–466. https://doi.org/10.1023/B:JADD.0000037421.98517.8d
7. Standen PJ, Brown DJ (2005) Virtual reality in the rehabilitation of people with intellectual disabilities. Cyberpsychol Behav 8(3):272–282. https://doi.org/10.1089/cpb.2005.8.272
8. Saiano M, Pellegrino L, Casadio M, Summa S, Garbarino E, Rossi, V et al (2015) Natural interfaces and virtual environments for the acquisition of street crossing and path following skills in adults with Autism Spectrum Disorders: a feasibility study. J Neuroeng Rehabil 12:1–13. https://doi.org/10.1186/s12984-015-0010-z
9. Parsons S, Leonard A, Mitchell P (2006) Virtual environments for social skills training: comments from two adolescents with autistic spectrum disorder. Comput Educ 47(2):186–206. https://doi.org/10.1016/j.compedu.2004.10.003
10. Frolli A, Savarese G, Di Carmine F, Bosco A, Saviano E, Rega A et al (2022) Children on the autism spectrum and the use of virtual reality for supporting social skills. Children 9(2):181. https://doi.org/10.3390/children9020181
11. Karami B, Koushki R, Arabgol F, Rahmani M, Vahabie AH (2021) Effectiveness of virtual/augmented reality—Based therapeutic interventions on autistic individuals spectrum disorder: a comprehensive meta-analysis. Front Psychiatr 12:665326. https://doi.org/10.3389/fpsyt.2021.665326

12. Glaser N, Schmidt M (2022) Systematic literature review of virtual reality intervention design patterns for autistic individuals spectrum disorders. Int J Hum-Comput Interact 38(8):753–788. https://doi.org/10.1080/10447318.2021.1970433
13. Mesa-Gresa P, Gil-Gómez H, Lozano-Quilis JA, Gil-Gómez JA (2018) Effectiveness of virtual reality for children and adolescents with autism spectrum disorder: an evidence-based systematic review. Sensors 18(8):2486. https://doi.org/10.3390/s18082486
14. Faja S, Webb SJ, Jones E, Merkle K, Kamara D, Bavaro J, Aylward E, Dawson G (2012) The effects of face expertise training on the behavioral performance and brain activity of adults with high functioning autism spectrum disorders. J Autism Dev Disord 42:278–293. https://doi.org/10.1007/s10803-011-1243-8
15. Beaumont R, Sofronoff K (2008) A multi-component social skills intervention for children with Asperger syndrome: the junior detective training program. J Child Psychol Psychiatr 49(7):743–753. https://doi.org/10.1111/j.1469-7610.2008.01920.x
16. Whyte EM, Smyth JM, Scherf KS (2015) Designing serious game interventions for autistic individuals. J Autism Dev Disord 45:3820–3831. https://doi.org/10.1007/s10803-014-2333-1
17. Camargo A (2016) Fundamentals for applying gamification: a literature review (Doctoral dissertation, Verlag nicht ermittelbar)
18. Valencia K, Rusu C, Quiñones D, Jamet E ((2019) The impact of technology on people with autism spectrum disorder: a systematic literature review. Sensors 19(20):4485. https://doi.org/10.3390/s19204485
19. Pellecchia M, Marcus SC, Spaulding C, Seidman M, Xie M, Rump K et al (2020) Randomized trial of a computer-assisted intervention for children with autism in schools. J Am Acad Child Adolesc Psychiatr 59(3):373–380. https://doi.org/10.1016/j.jaac.2019.03.029
20. Elliot CD (1990) Differential ability scale administration and scoring manual. Psychological Corporation, San Antonio, TX
21. Bracken BA (1984). Bracken basic concept scale. Psychological Corporation
22. Whalen C, Moss D, Ilan AB, Vaupel M, Fielding P, Macdonald K et al (2010) Efficacy of teachtown: basics computer-assisted intervention for the intensive comprehensive autism program in Los Angeles unified school district. Autism 14(3):179–197. https://doi.org/10.1177/1362361310363282
23. Sandgreen H, Frederiksen LH, Bilenberg N (2021) Digital interventions for autism spectrum disorder: a meta-analysis. J Autism Dev Disord 51:3138–3152. https://doi.org/10.1007/s10803-020-04778-9
24. Thill S, Pop CA, Belpaeme T, Ziemke T, Vanderborght B (2012) Robot-assisted therapy for autism spectrum disorders with (partially) autonomous control: challenges and outlook. Paladyn 3:209–217. https://doi.org/10.2478/s13230-013-0107-7
25. van Straten CL, Smeekens I, Barakova E, Glennon J, Buitelaar J, Chen A (2018) Effects of robots' intonation and bodily appearance on robot-mediated communicative treatment outcomes for children with autism spectrum disorder. Pers Ubiquit Comput 22(2):379–390. https://doi.org/10.1007/s00779-017-1060-y
26. Begum M, Serna RW, Yanco HA (2016) Are robots ready to deliver autism interventions? A comprehensive review. Int J Soc Robot 8:157–181. https://doi.org/10.1007/s12369-016-0346-y
27. Diehl JJ, Schmitt LM, Villano M, Crowell CR (2012) The clinical use of robots for autistic individuals spectrum disorders: a critical review. Res Autism Spectr Disord 6(1):249–262. https://doi.org/10.1016/j.rasd.2011.05.006
28. Willemse C, Marchesi S, Wykowska A (2018) Robot faces that follow gaze facilitate attentional engagement and increase their likeability. Front Psychol 9:70. https://doi.org/10.3389/fpsyg.2018.00070
29. Kouroupa A, Laws KR, Irvine K, Mengoni SE, Baird A, Sharma S (2022) The use of social robots with children and young people on the autism spectrum: a systematic review and meta-analysis. Plos One 17(6):e0269800. https://doi.org/10.1371/journal.pone.0269800

30. Scassellati B, Boccanfuso L, Huang CM, Mademtzi M, Qin M, Salomons N, Ventola P, Shic F (2018) Improving social skills in children with ASD using a long-term, in-home social robot. Sci Robot 3(21):eaat7544. https://doi.org/10.1126/scirobotics.aat7544
31. Saleh MA, Hanapiah FA, Hashim H (2021) Robot applications for autism: a comprehensive review. Disabil Rehabil Assist Technol 16(6):580–602. https://doi.org/10.1080/17483107.2019.1685016
32. Salimi Z, Jenabi E, Bashirian S (2021) Are social robots ready yet to be used in care and therapy of autism spectrum disorder: a systematic review of randomized controlled trials. Neurosci Biobehav Rev 129:1–16. https://doi.org/10.1016/j.neubiorev.2021.04.009
33. David DO, Costescu CA, Matu S, Szentagotai A, Dobrean A (2020) Effects of a robot-enhanced intervention for children with ASD on teaching turn-taking skills. J Educ Comput Res 58(1):29–62. https://doi.org/10.1177/0735633119830344
34. Voss C, Schwartz J, Daniels J, Kline A, Haber N, Washington P et al (2019) Effect of wearable digital intervention for improving socialization in children with autism spectrum disorder: a randomized clinical trial. JAMA Pediatr 173(5):446–454. https://doi.org/10.1001/jamapediatrics.2019.0285
35. Sparrow SS, Cicchetti DV, Balla DA, Doll EA (2005) Vineland adaptive behavior scales: survey forms manual. American Guidance Service, Circle Pines MN
36. Brooks BL, Sherman EM, Strauss E (2009) Test review: NEPSY-II: a developmental neuropsychological assessment, second edition. Child Neuropsychol 16(1):80–101. https://doi.org/10.1080/09297040903146966
37. Constantino JN, Gruber CP (2012) Social responsiveness scale, 2nd edn (SRS-2). Western Psychological Services, Los Angeles, CA
38. Sahin NT, Keshav NU, Salisbury JP, Vahabzadeh A (2018) Second version of google glass as a wearable socio-affective aid: positive school desirability, high usability, and theoretical framework in a sample of children with autism. JMIR Hum Factors 5(1):e8785. https://doi.org/10.2196/humanfactors.8785
39. Vahabzadeh A, Keshav NU, Abdus-Sabur R, Huey K, Liu R, Sahin NT (2018) Improved socio-emotional and behavioral functioning in students with autism following school-based smartglasses intervention: multi-stage feasibility and controlled efficacy study. Behav Sci 8(10):85. https://doi.org/10.3390/bs8100085
40. Keshav NU, Salisbury JP, Vahabzadeh A, Sahin NT (2017) Social communication coaching smartglasses: well tolerated in a diverse sample of children and adults with autism. JMIR mHealth uHealth 5(9):e8534. https://doi.org/10.2196/mhealth.8534
41. Aman MG, Singh NN, Stewart AW, Field C (1985) The aberrant behavior checklist: a behavior rating scale for the assessment of treatment effects. Am J Ment Defic 89(5):485–491
42. Mishra P, Koehler MJ (2006) Technological pedagogical content knowledge: a framework for teacher knowledge. Teach College Record 108(6):1017–1054. https://journals.sagepub.com/doi/pdf/https://doi.org/10.1111/j.1467-9620.2006.00684.x
43. Puentedura RR (2013) SAMR model substitution, augmentation, modification, redefinition. https://d1pf6s1cgoc6y0.cloudfront.net/5fdcf2f73b804107b4fa3f2b6177affa.pdf
44. Arantes J (2022) The SAMR model as a framework for scaffolding online chat": a theoretical discussion of the SAMR model as a research method during these "interesting" times. Qual Res J. https://doi.org/10.1108/QRJ-08-2021-0088
45. Camargo MC, Barros RM, Brancher JD, Barros VT, Santana M (2019) Designing gamified interventions for autism spectrum disorder: a systematic review. In: Entertainment computing and serious games: first IFIP TC 14 joint international conference, ICEC-JCSG 2019, Arequipa, Peru, November 11–15 2019 Proceedings, vol 1. Springer International Publishing, pp 341–352. https://doi.org/10.1007/978-3-030-34644-7_28

Shaping Executive Functions of Neurodiverse Children Through Digital Technologies

Cristina Costescu, Carmen David, and Adrian Roșan

Abstract

Executive functions are critical for adaptive responses in new and complex contexts. However, research indicates the presence of deficits in executive functions neurodiverse children. In this chapter, we synthesize evidence on the current digital technologies employed in training executive functions in neurodiverse children, such as autistic individuals, intellectual disabled children, dyslexic children, and attention deficit hyperactivity disorder children. The chapter concludes considering some of the limitations in computerized trainings of executive functions, as well as some future directions of research on this topic.

Keywords

Executive functions · Neurodevelopmental disorders · Cognitive training · Technology use for executive functions

---

C. Costescu · C. David (✉) · A. Roșan
Special Education Department, Faculty of Psychology and Educational Sciences, Babeș-Bolyai University, Cluj-Napoca, Romania
e-mail: carmen.david@ubbcluj.ro

C. Costescu
e-mail: cristina.costescu@ubbcluj.ro

A. Roșan
e-mail: adrian.rosan@ubbcluj.ro

1 Executive Functions Training in Autistic Children

Executive functioning has been investigated extensively in the relation with a diagnosis of autism spectrum disorders (ASD) considering its proposed role in contributing to specific impairments ASD, such as theory of mind and social cognition, social impairment [1] restricted and repetitive behavior patterns [2] as well as broader impacts on quality of life [3]. Executive functions (EFs) are cognitive abilities that regulate thinking, feeling, and behavior to achieve goals, they encompass working memory, inhibitory control, and cognitive flexibility and are crucial for planning, reasoning, and integrating thought and action [4]. However, EFs have several definitions and subcomponents, and it is very difficult to draw a clear conclusion regarding the association between a specific EF and ASD symptoms. Another important aspect in EFs in ASD is the methods of assessment used because these measurements vary across studies. Moreover, most of the studies focused on a single cognitive domain, whereas other studies discuss about executive functioning as an umbrella construct.

A recent meta-analysis conducted by [5] on 75 studies with a combined sample of 3361 adults on the autism spectrum showed that the largest impairments in autistic adults were observed for processing speed, verbal learning and memory, and reasoning and solving problems. According to their analysis attention and working memory were the least impaired cognitive functions. On the other hand, Demetriou and his collaborators [6] concluded in their meta-analysis that no differences in effect sizes between specific domains of EFs were observed in their data. They included 235 studies comprising 14 081 participants, out of which 6818 were on the autism spectrum. Their aim was to analyze the association between EFs difficulties and ASD symptomatology, the differences across subdomains in executive functioning and to test the clinical utility and the impact that several moderators could have on the relationship between EFs and ASD severity. They reported a moderate overall effect, with similar effect sizes across different domains of EFs. Unlike the above-mentioned study, Demetriou and his collaborators concluded that we should address the executive functioning in ASD as a global impairment rather than trying to differentiate across the subdomains. All in all, people on the autism spectrum have poorer performances in EF compared with neurotypical population.

In this view the need of interventions that target EFs in autistic people increased dramatically. Along with behavior and cognitive based interventions, that are mainly used to improve executive functioning in neurodiverse children, the use of alternative technology-based strategies that may change the environment and facilitate the learning process were proven to increase the overall effectiveness of the intervention process [7]. O'Neill B and Gillespie [8] use the term "*assistive technologies for cognition*" and define it as technologies that can used to "*enable enhance or extend the cognitive functions.*" *(p. 1)*. There are several ways in which we can classify assistive technologies that can be used for autistic people. For example, Puentedura [9] developed the SAMR model for technology integration instructions SAMR (substitution, augmentation, modification and redefinition). In the first level, substitution, the technological device acts as a direct tool with no functional change, for example a textbook is replaced with a digital book or a computer to write some text instead of using the pen and the pencil. The substitution of the traditional delivery method with a technological way of delivery may not lead to improvements in their performance. The second level is similar with the first one, only that in the augmentation phase a slightly functional improvement may occur. For example, searching for an information using the computer and the internet resources compared to the traditional ways of searching in the library. In this situation improvements in students' performance can be seen. The modification phase implies that the technology allows for significant task redesign, whereas the aim of the task remains the same, the way the technology is used allows the student to illustrate their knowledge in a different way that will not be possible without the use of the technology. For example, videos that may illustrate abstract concepts or graphic organizers for planning that help students to organize their information and increase their performances. The last phase is redefinition where technology allows for the creation of new tasks, which are possible only with the use of technology. For example, using an application that can help the student express themselves though a digital story or through creating a digital book. The first two levels are called by the author enhancement and the last two transformation, because of the significant differentiation in the learning process. Even if we call them enhancement and transformation technologies, or low technology and high technology [10] several studies show that the second categories (i.e. transformation or high technologies) is more effective in enhancing the cognitive processes.

Regarding the definition of EFs or the cognitive processes that should be included in within the construct there is little consensus in the literature [11]. One of the most used classifications in the field is the one developed by Diamond [12]. Therefore, we will discuss in the following paragraphs about basic cognitive skills, such as working memory (WM), inhibitory control (IH) (including selective and executive attention) and cognitive flexibility (CF). We will discuss each of the above mentioned EFs considering the used technological based methods and techniques to enhance them.

Working memory is defined as a cognitive process responsible for temporarily maintaining and manipulating of the information during complex tasks, such as reasoning, comprehension, planning and other academic tasks. WM performance is highly predictive of individual differences in verbal and visuospatial memory span and reasoning, reading fluency and comprehensive and math. There are only a few studies that investigate the use of computerized WM training for autistic children. De Vries and Geurts [3] tested the efficacy of Braingame Brian, where they included a module for improving WM, for a sample of 121 autistic children aged between 8 and 12. Their results showed that there were no significant differences before and after the training, even if children that benefited from the WM training showed a trend toward improvement on near transfer. Moreover, the attrition rate was quite high, 26%, which may be due to lack of motivation to play the game. On the other hand, the *Caribbean Quest* serious game, which was played 12 h by autistic children aged between 6 and 13 years old, led to significant improvements in a small sample (N = 7) in their WM [13]. A more recent study tested the well-known platform for Cogmed for improving autistic children WM [14]. The training consisted of five web-based WM training sessions per week for 5 weeks, meaning 25 training sessions. Cogmed sessions are based on a robot theme and consist of tasks involving rotating displays, moving targets, reverse sequence tasks, numeric information to recall, and delayed responses. There were 26 autistic children, aged between 8 and 18 and they demonstrated improvements across the WM measurements from pre- to post-evaluations, showing evidence of near-transfer effects of the training. Moreover, training the WM conducted to improvements in behavioral measurements, not only in cognitive benefits, such as repetitive behaviors or off-task behaviors.

The use of the *Caribbean Quest* was also addressed by Macoun et al. [15] on 20 school-age children on the autism spectrum (6–12 years) who completed a 12 h of cognitive training, distributed over 8–10 weeks (24 sessions, 3 times/week, 30 min per session) in a school setting. Their results showed improvements both in WM and in selective attention. Project EVO app-based platform was also tested for autistic children with the aim of improve their cognitive control. Project EVO is a multi-tasking intervention that requires children to rapidly switch between a perceptual discrimination attention/memory task and a continuous visuomotor task. Significant improvements were found when using a standardized instrument for screening inhibitory control and attention, in the experimental group compared to the control condition involving an educational intervention.

Attention atypicality can be often seen in autistic children even from the first years of life, for example disengagement or joint attention deficits. Further in the development difficulties are also exhibited in sustained attention and selective attention. Sustained attention can be defined as the ability to maintain focus over extended periods of time, whereas selective attention is defined as a cognitive process that enhances processing of relevant information while suppressing distractors. This is very important because the attention capacity is linked with the learning process, as well as academic performance [16, 17]. Most of the training programs in ASD that target attention are developing joint attention skills, which are not necessarily relying in low-level attention functions [18]. One among the most investigated computerized trainings for improving attention in school aged children is the Computerized Progressive Attentional Training (CPAT) developed by [19] and tested on a sample of ADHD children. There are two main studies that investigated the effectiveness of the CPAT on improving autistic children school performance. Both were conducted by Spaniol et al. [20] from University of Sao Paulo in Brazil. In their first pilot study they enrolled 15 children on the autism spectrum aged between 6- and 10-year-old who were assigned to experimental and control group. The experimental group benefited by 8 weeks of training twice per week and the intervention consisted in three computerized tasks: sustained attention task (maintaining attention for a prolonged time), selective-spatial attention (focusing on relevant information while ignorant distractors) and executive attention (inhibition of irrelevant information). Each task had different levels of severity and were easy to understand and displayed visual and auditory feedback.

Their results showed that children from CPAT group improved reading comprehension, copying speed and did better in math tests. Moreover, their scores on Raven improved significantly following the training. Similar results were reported in their second study, when they assigned 26 autistic children to control and experimental group [21]. Apart from the measurements they used in the pilot study they also included behavioral measurements reported by parents and one attention cancellation task that was given to children in paper and pencil. No significant differences were found in terms of their behavioral outcomes reported by parents, but a significant difference was found in the score of the cancellation attention task in children that benefited from the training in post-intervention compared to those who didn't.

More recently a new computerized training was developed based on [22] named *Comprehensive attention training system* (CATS). Within this training children are asked to respond to dot stimuli that appear on the screen using assigned response keys. The difficulty of the tasks is controlled by the differences in the stimuli, which may change colors, locations and duration of appearance. CATS was developed by [23] and was tested in a clinical study with 25 children on the autism spectrum mean age 8.5 years. Their results revealed that CATS training may lead to improvements in shifting between different behavioral principals and an increase in forming abstract concepts and a decrease in incorrect perseverative behavior. However little improvements were seen on socialization or adaptative behaviors in the experimental group after the training compared to the control group.

Cognitive flexibility defined as the ability to adapt thinking and behavior to changing demands requires the interaction of several mechanisms, out of which we name attention shifting and perception, that are needed to respond to specific environmental demands in order to achieve flexible behaviors (for example to find a different response to a problem) [24]. Cognitive flexibility is linked with inhibitory control and working memory and allow switching from one task to another [25]. Probabilistic reversal learning (PRL) represents a direct assessment of direct flexible choice behaviors, as the information is presented and integrated over a number of trials in order to detect true changes and the trial-and-error learning is continually updated throughout the task and it was previously validated for use in ASD [26, 27]. Moreover, Schmitt et al. [27] examined the feasibility of the PRL as an outcome measurement following a group-based intervention for children and adolescents on the autism spectrum aged between 8 and 18 years old. 62 autistic children and adolescents participated in a 10-session intervention, 5-week group-based *Regulation Together* therapy. This type of therapy consists of multiple evidence-based strategies based on applied behavioral analysis, mindfulness, dialectical behavior intervention and cognitive-behavioral therapy [28]. Most of the participants demonstrated successful completion of PRL at the end of the intervention, namely children and adolescents needed fewer number of trials to reach the PRL criterion and sis less regressive errors in post intervention compared to pre intervention. Therefore, the authors concluded that PRL is sensitive to detect treatment-related change in cognitive and behavioral flexibility. Even though there are several studies showing that cognitive flexibility training intervention can be effective for autistic children [29, 30] and can even produce significant improvements in terms of perseverative responses, few studies tested that kind of effect after a cognitive computerized intervention. There are some digital games that were developed to train cognitive flexibility which seem to be very promising, but there were not tested yet in terms of their effectiveness for autistic children, such as *ASTRAS* [31] or *All you can eat* [32].

Considering all the above presented studies that aimed to improve EFs in autistic children, we can conclude that there are either mixed results or low efficacy compared to other types of training. These results were also found in a recent meta-analysis that investigated the effects of computer-based training on children's executive functioning [33]. One possible explanation could be the absence of human -to -human interaction and also their performance is also linked with their age. Previous studies suggested that younger children could benefit more from cognitive trainings due to their high brain plasticity [34, 35] however when designing computer-based trainings, there are some prerequisites that the child needs to have in order to be able to play the game.

2   Intellectual Disabilities (ID)

Intellectual disabilities (ID) are comprised of a heterogeneous group of various etiologies characterized by significant low intellectual and adaptive functioning that emerged in the developmental period. Studies addressing executive functioning in this population indicate that performance is consistently low as compared to typically developing. Regarding children with intellectual disabilities, research obtained mixed results when using comprehensive measures of executive functions. In a study by Danielsson et al. [36], the ID group performed similar to mental age matched group, on listening recall, verbal and non-verbal switching tasks, and on fluency tasks except for letter fluency, while it displayed a significantly lower performance on non-verbal odd one out, inhibition and planning tasks (whether verbal or non-verbal). A recent meta-analysis that synthesized studies comparing executive functions of intellectually disabled persons to mental aged matched, conducted by Spaniol and Danielsson [37], evidenced a significant effect size $g = -0,34$. This significant difference was present in syndromic ID such as Williams syndrome and Fragile-X, except for Down syndrome and ID nonspecific. On the other hand, in Tungate and Conners [38] a significant strong effect size emerged in the case of Down syndrome, when including short term memory in the analyses.

Research on cognitive training of executive functions is scarce in relation to children with intellectual disabilities. In a narrative review exploring executive functioning training in children with intellectual disabilities, Kirk et al. [39] identified mainly studies addressing working memory. Of the three, one addressed children with Down syndrome [40], and one comprised a group with mild intellectual disability and borderline [41]. Two of them employed a similar training program, JCWMT [40] and CWMT (used by [42]). The third, Van der Molen et al. [41] while based on the previously mentioned programs, used a main Odd one out task to train working memory. It used adaptive and non-adaptive memory training. Verbal short-term memory improved, as compared to the control, and in the follow up there was an effect on the visual spatial short-term memory, arithmetic and story recall in the Odd one out training, regardless of the adaptation. Participants in van de Molen et al. [41] were 5-year-old children with mild intellectual disability to borderline intelligence. In the case of Bennett et al. [40], near transfer effects were visible for visual spatial working memory, parent ratings of working memory, but not for verbal working memory or short term memory. There were no far transfer effects in inhibition, planning, emotional control, except for attention shifting measures through a parent rating instrument. In Söderqvist et al. [42] in the case of ID with ages between 6 and 12 years, near transfer effects emerged in the case of visual spatial and verbal working memory. No far transfer effects were apparent in reasoning and ADHD related behavior. The training was comprised of nonverbal reasoning tasks and visual spatial working memory tasks, and it was adapted. No studies addressing attention training in ID were identified.

In Van der Mole et al. [41] (training), an adaptive training was used that controlled for the number of sequences in a trial in relation to the child's performance. Also, the session duration was as long as 6 min, within the attention span of children with mild to borderline intellectual disabilities.

Bennett et al. [40] used a computerized training, Junior Cogmed working memory training for preschoolers. It is structured around the park theme; it addresses visual spatial working memory. It is an adaptable program, allowing for a change in the duration of tasks based on the player's performance. When the child gives a correct response, receives positive feedback and the interval between stimuli and recall is being increased [43].

Kirk et al. [40] drew attention to the importance of establishing the appropriate starting point. Many programs are too challenging. For instance, in [40], an initial pilot study indicated that CWMT was too difficult for children with Down Syndrome, ages 7–12, and that it took longer time to complete it. On the other hand, some programs may require a baseline level of skill to be effective [42].

Lanfranchi et al. [44] used computerized training. Participants were children and adolescents with Down syndrome, with a mean age 12.5 years old. The computerized training program was adapted from a program developed for typical developing children, by Mammarella et al. [45]. In this training, only the simultaneous spatial working memory tasks were kept. The training consisted of 8 sessions. It comprised: simple attention and spatial short term memory tasks, recalling simultaneous locations, recalling the position of a specific subject among many in a layout, choosing an image of the same setting of objects, placing the stimuli on the position after the presentation of the layout, spatial dual task. Direct effects on simultaneous working memory were obtained, that were kept 1 month after the training; near transfer effects on sequential and verbal working memory measures with active control were present. Participants that had lower scores in pre-test obtained better gains.

Pulina [46] used a similar spatial simultaneous working memory computerized training led by parents of children with Down syndrome. Participants were children and adolescents with DS, with a mean age of 12. Immediate improvements appeared on the active simultaneous task, for the parent led group. At the follow up, 1 month later, performance of the parent-led group improved on this measure. There were no differences between groups (parent led and expert led) in the active simultaneous task. Both groups improved performance immediately after the training and maintained the effect over a month. Also, near transfer effects were observed in both groups for sequential working memory, as well as far transfer to geometric puzzles activities. Transfer of skills to everyday activities were indicated by parents of children from the expert group, not from the parent-led group. This study supports the idea that computerized training are portable.

The content of working memory training is either visual spatial, or verbal or mixed. In a meta-analytic review Danilesson et al. [47] identified 10 studies addressing working memory training in individuals with intellectual disabilities. Of the 10 studies, 8 had participants with mean age ranging from 9.5 to 16.2. Half of these studies used a visual spatial working memory. The remaining four studies used a mixed working memory training (2 studies with the same first author), one study comprised verbal working memory content, and one study addressed verbal short-term memory.

Also, another point is addressing the issue of what to train. Kirk et al. [39] raised a point that given the mixed results on WM training efficacy as well as the lack of far transfer, to look into other executive functions [39]. They used TALI attention training program (The Training attention and learning initiative) which trains attention skills based on digital activities on a touch screen device [48]. Task difficulty is adjusted based on the performance on each level. The program contains four activities: one addressing sustained attention, one addressing selective attention, and 2 activities addressing executive attention, such as conflict resolution and response inhibition.

Cognitive flexibility is under addressed in cognitive training, and so is the case in computerized trainings. Even though, there is research addressing training in children with intellectual disabilities, it is scarce [49]. However, training cognitive flexibility in intellectually disabled adolescents seems to contribute to a reduction of cognitive impairments [50].

A complex cognitive training program by Orsolini et al. [51] comprised of attention, inhibition, switching, working memory and inferences, that combined repeated practice with adult interaction and strategy focus, lead to improvements in 6 out of 8 outcome measures in an adolescent with mild intellectual disability. The training combined activities presented on the computer with non-computerized activities. The training occurred in several phases, from a control condition, at home, on instrumental learning Feuerstein, to second phase in which attention and inhibition were trained, to switching and simple working memory tasks, and lastly, a phase in which complex working memory tasks were trained. The participant improved on complex dual task working memory, from not being able to perform the task, to performing close to normal scores of a 13-year-old boy (the participant was 15 years old at the time).

Wu et al. [52] conducted a randomized clinical trial in a sample of children with intellectual disabilities, with a multi-domain computerized cognitive training. The participants in this RCT were intellectually disabled children, aged between 4 and 6.5 years old. They employed the training in 5 sessions, 5 times per week, for 20 min. The training was administered on a tablet. The content addressed 4 domains: visual perception, attention, memory, and reasoning. Each domain included 2 trials. Each trial had three levels of difficulty and was adaptive. The training offers adaptation of the task based on the performance, gives immediate feedback, offers visual and verbal guidance, feedback after each trial with incentives. The content of the training is detailed further: perceptual speed trial and spatial perception trial for visual perception; select reaction time and space exploration for attention; memory span and visual memory for memory domain; deductive reasoning and figure recognition trail for the reasoning domain. The multi-domain training had an effect on intellectual and adaptive functioning, vocabulary and arithmetic of small intellectually disabled children.

Torra Moreno et al. [53] in a meta-analysis analyzed the effect of digital interventions on executive functions, as well as on other behavioral or basic cognitive functions. There aren't a lot of variations in digital technologies used for executive functions training. Even though technologies such as VR or handheld devices are promising, they are not as addressed in research studies. Computerized programs that are delivered through PCs are the most frequent. Mostly, these programs address working memory (8 out of 10 identified studies) and reasoning (4 of 10). Other executive functions are less represented in cognitive training with digital technologies. Few address inhibition and only one addressed planning. They indicated a great variability of the tasks used in research studies. However, when looking into the tasks addressing working memory, one can observe that mostly repeated sequences tasks are used. Cognitive training of working memory through repeated sequences seems to be effective, at least in post-test. The authors conclude that there is some effect on executive functions through digital interventions, but there is limited evidence on the lasting effect. Also, they underline some features of digital interventions found to be important for the success of the training: immediate feedback, rewards, and repetitions. There is not enough information on the effectiveness of such interventions in relation to intellectual deficit severity and comorbidities that are frequently encountered in this population. Also, there is not enough research of the effectiveness of cognitive training in the case of younger children with cognitive impairments, especially since we acknowledge the importance of early intervention, as well as the importance of basic executive functions such as inhibition, working memory for the development of more advanced ones, such as cognitive flexibility, cognitive control.

Bruttin [54] underlines the utility of touch screen technology for task engagement and attention allocation. Also, the author underlines the utility of touch screen in going about the motor difficulties often associated with intellectual disabilities. Also, technologies can afford for a better control of the cognitive load, while training reasoning strategies.

Ko et al. [55] used a tablet based computerized cognitive training in a randomized controlled trial design with children with cognitive impairment, with a cognitive age between 18 and 36 months. They developed 6 adaptive programs with 9 or 10 levels of difficulty, with 10 tasks each, addressing attentions, auditory and visual perception, memory and executive functions. They also developed 6 non-adaptive programs addressing the same abilities. Tasks in the adaptive program are hidden objects, puzzles, animal and pattern matching, identical images identification. The training was conducted twice a week, for 30 min, for 12 weeks. Both groups improved on all measures. However, compared to the active control group following a traditional rehabilitation program, the experimental group presented a greater change in social functioning, observation, manipulation, and attention measures.

Promising in terms of technology interaction, as well as of ecological validity are educational robotics solutions. In a study by Di Lieto et al. [56], they developed a program using Bee-bot to train executive functions in children with special education needs together with classmates. They proposed some adaptations to the tasks considering the special needs of the children. Improvements in inhibition skills were obtained, but not in working memory, even though this component was well represented in the content of the training. The results stress an important issue when addressing cognitive training in young children, which is the selection of the developmentally appropriate executive functions to address, such as inhibition.

Also, Beccaluva et al. [57] developed a tangible user interface to train memory skills in children with intellectual disabilities. It comprises digital enhanced cubes, a sensorized board and a mobile app. These combined devices allow for various configurations of memory tasks with cubes. The technology was tested for usability and preference, however, to our knowledge there is no study on its efficacy on training memory skills.

Overall, most of the computerized trainings address working memory, and a smaller number address other executive functions. As far as the content of working memory training with computerized programs is concerned, one can observe there is not a lot of variation. Many programs address visual spatial working memory. Most programs are built on a process-based paradigm, as opposed to a strategy based paradigm. Most programs address one component. Also, most of the programs are adaptable. Not all programs detail the game-effects or gamification strategy.

3   Executive Functions Training in Children with Specific Learning Disorders

Specific learning disorders are also a group of heterogeneous difficulties in the acquisition of reading or written expression, and/or Math skills, in the absence of other conditions, such as an intellectual deficit, a sensorial deficit, or a lack of learning opportunities. These difficulties affect the individuals on the functional level, in their daily activities, such as school performance. Specific learning disabilities and ADHD often co-occur. There are, however, differences in the estimated co-occurrence rate based on the specific type of LD, such as in the case of written expression type, between 55 and 64% [58] between dyslexia and ADHD, 25–40%, while between Math disabilities (MD) and ADHD, 11–30% [59]. Executive deficits have been identified in the case of children with specific learning disorders. However, results do not offer a clear picture of specific executive functions affected in this heterogeneous group. Barquero et al. [60] synthesized the research on the topic in the case of children with reading disabilities, scores on a semantic fluency task were significantly lower, as well as on measures of cognitive [61]. In Johnson et al. [62], the difference in scores on EF measures of planning, organizing, attention, when comparing RD with typically developing children, was of moderate size. Also, large effect sizes emerged in the case of verbal and visual spatial working memory. In the case of children with Math Disorder, a significant effect size emerged for EF of planning, organizing, strategizing, and WM. Written expression disorders are less researched in the case of EF. Hooper et al. [63] obtained significantly lower scores in the case of children with WD as compared to typical developed children, on measures of initiation and cognitive flexibility [60]. The deficits in EF in the case of individuals with dyslexia seem to vary along the lifespan [64]: there is evidence of executive deficits in dyslexic children, ages 6–12, on inhibition, working memory, shifting, attention, problem solving and planning; s dyslexic adolescent present lower scores in working memory and shifting; dyslexic adults present deficits in working memory, problem-solving and planning. Studies addressing executive deficits in dyslexic children, indicate difficulties with verbal working memory in dyslexia, while for dyscalculia, visual spatial working memory difficulties and central executive difficulties [65]. In a recent metanalysis, Lonergan et al. [66], evidenced deficits in inhibition, switching, and working memory in the case of dyslexic children, as compared to typically developed children. When comparing children with comorbid dyslexia and ADHD to TD, a similar profile of deficits emerged [66]. Agostini et al. [67] synthesized studies comparing children with MD to non-MD on domain-general cognitive measures. Significant differences were identified in visual search tasks, coding tasks, verbal and visual working memory, number inhibition tasks, stop signal tasks.

There aren't many studies on computerized intervention on executive functions in the case of children with specific learning disabilities. In a synthesis paper, Bombonato et al. [68] included 17 studies, of which 8 were computerized interventions. No intervention addressing attentional control or inhibition, working memory, cognitive flexibility was addressed to children with specific learning disorders. In the case of dyslexia, the most addressed executive functions through digital technologies are working memory and attention. Inhibition and cognitive flexibility training effects are scarce.

Pasqualotto et al. [69] used a combined intervention of phonological treatment and executive functions training for children with developmental dyslexia, from second and third grade (mean age of 9 years old). For the executive functions training they employed Brain-HQ [70], an online cognitive training system consisting of multiple short games with a mean duration of 5 min. From the pool of 29 exercises organized on 5 domains, the researchers extracted only games that addressed: attention, speed of visual processing, discrimination and processing of auditory stimuli, working memory (both verbal and visual), problem solving and inhibition. 25 children with DD followed the EF computerized training for 8 weeks, followed by the phonological training. 24 children with DD followed the phonological training throughout, for 24 weeks total. Children who participated in the combined group improved on visual spatial attention and working memory, as well as in reading accuracy and fluency. This program was designed for a multimodal approach to dyslexia.

Peijnenborgh et al. [71] in a meta-analytic study, analyzed the effect of working memory training in children with learning disabilities. However, most of the existing studies address ADHD. Of the thirteen studies that met the inclusion criteria, 10 had ADHD participants, 2 had LD non-specified, and one combined.

Nelwan et al. [72] used a working memory training, called Jungle Memory in combination with a math intervention on computerized format. The training was conducted with children from 4th to 6th grade, that had low performance in Math and attention difficulties. The 64 participants were randomly assigned to one of the three conditions: one that attended the working memory training and afterwards the Math training; a second condition, in which the order was reversed; a control condition that only received math training. Short term effects of Jungle memory were in relation with near transfer effects on verbal working memory, but not with visual working memory. The group that followed the domain general training first had better results after the Math intervention training.

Chen et al. [73] used an adaptive working memory training on updating with n-back type of tasks. The structure of the task was similar, the stimuli differed: animals, letters locations. The training was intensive, 20, 5 days per week, with 45 min sessions per day. However, the control group was passive. Each training task comprised 30 trials. The program was adaptive in terms of stimuli display time in response to performance. Participants were children with a mean age of approximately 10 years old. The performance in Working memory improved based on results on Backward digit span and updating. Also, results in non-verbal matrix reasoning improved. The effects were maintained 6 months after the training. No immediate effect after the training was observed for performance on Chinese and Math. However, 6 months after the training, the experimental group demonstrated increased performance.

Capodieci et al. [74] investigated the effect of a computerized cognitive training incorporated in RIDInet platform, MemoRan (Anastasis) cognitive skills and reading skills of children with language disorders and specific learning disorders (from kindergarten to 5th grade). The game consists of intermodal (visual-auditory) tasks, that exercise executive functions in integration tasks. After approximately three months of training, gains are visible in word dictation, speed and accuracy of reading, rapid lexical access, accuracy scores in inhibition, working memory scores. However, no significant differences emerged on the Brief assessment by parents. The results of this pilot study are to be seen with caution, as there was no passive control group. When comparing the MemoRAn training with Reading training from the same platform, a significant difference emerged in the speed of reading, for the group that followed the reading training. No other notable differences are reported. No information is provided on the Reading Trainer program, as far as duration, frequency, content.

Nazari et al. [75] used a process-based executive functions intervention in the case of children with developmental dyscalculia, aged 8–10 years old. The training lasted for three months. When compared to the control group, significant differences emerged for factual and procedural knowledge, that maintained within 3 months after the training. However, there were no differences in conceptual knowledge between groups.

Muñez et al. [76] investigated the effectiveness of a working memory training in children at risk for math learning disabilities. Four conditions were included and implemented within the classroom activities: an adaptive computerized game-based working memory training on updating paradigm, a combined condition, with updating tasks that used numerical stimuli; a numeracy intervention; an active control group that performed similar activities as the working memory group but were not required to memorize. After one year of training, no near and far transfer was observed for the WMT. The numerical training combined with working memory did not produce any working memory improvements. However, the numerical discrimination acuity improved, as well as performance on number line estimation (for some that had played longer). Numerical training induced similar results.

Di Giusto et al. [77] developed a Virtual reality rehabilitation program on executive functions, carried out over 6 weeks, with two weekly sessions of 45 min. The content of the games for VR addresses visual attention, inhibition, shifting/cognitive flexibility, working memory. After the training, visual attention, inhibition, flexibility, and planning scores increased and 6 weeks after, the effect was present for most of the outcomes. However, the study has some limitations, such as the lack of a control group, a small sample with an overrepresentation of boys, the lack of a working memory measure, and of academic. In the sample, the SLD types were variate, either only dyslexia, or dyslexia with dysorthographia, or dyslexia, dysorthographia, dysgraphia, dyscalculia etc.. Given the lack of a control group, the effect of the intervention may be overestimated. However, promising results are reflected in this study as far near effects. After 12 sessions, results show an effect on all four executive functions. In terms of preferred approach, all children completed the training session. A positive feedback was given to the VR training.

In research investigating the effects of AVG on attention and reading skills in children with developmental dyslexia, Bertoni et al. [78] trained attention mechanisms involved in reading, through action video-games. After the training phase, attention control efficacy increased in terms of response times and accuracy in the visual search task, and pseudoword decoding. Bertoni et al. [78] explain the results through some characteristics of action video games, such as the speed of events and moving objects, the elevated load of motor and perceptual items, the emphasis on peripheral processing may, in the opinion of the researchers, that tackle both attention networks. Training visual attention seems promising; however, no improvements were seen in word reading. This research, however, underlines the need to develop training content that is process-oriented.

4   Executive Functions Training in ADHD Children

Attention deficit hyperactivity disorder (ADHD) is a neurodevelopmental disorder that characterized by attention deficits, hyperactivity and impulsivity [79]. Even if ADHD is typically identified during school years, it developed in the preschool years and can persist during adolescence and adulthood [80]. In regard to the relationship between ADHD and executive functions, there is evidence showing that executive functions deficits at the age of 5 significantly predicted the presence of ADHD symptoms at the age of 7 and at the age of 13 [81–83]. The most consistent domains impaired in ADHD are according to a meta-analytic review [84] inhibitory control and working memory. Inhibitory controlled was linked with difficulties in emotion regulation, in self-directed speech and impaired allocation of attentional resources [85, 86]. Whereas deficits in working memory were strongly predictive for visual inattention, social impairment, and hyperactivity [87, 88]. Often difficulties in cognitive flexibility are linked with academic and problems solving problems in ADHD children [88, 89]. ADHD children also struggle to finish some tasks, because they get bored were bored [90].

Considering their difficulties to finish the tasks and their attention deficits, the majority of the studies focused on training their attention, working memory and inhibition. One of the largest studies in the field used a electroencephalogram-based brain computer technology to quantify one's attention level and the Cogoland game to train it [91]. 172 ADHD children aged between 6 and 12 years were randomized to intervention and waitlist. The intervention lasted 8 weeks, in which 3 sessions of training attention with the brain computer interface Cogoland were implemented followed by 3 training sessions in the next 12 weeks. Cogoland has three level of difficulty and in each level the aim of the child is to collect items from an island (e.g. fruits) situated in different positions along their way. The results show that the children improved their attention and reduced their inattentive symptoms, as well they reduced their internalization problems, as reported by children. Even if they used only a short training program of neurofeedback, there were some improvements (small to moderate). Future studies should increase their number of studies, because Cogoland was considered by children, parents and children as safe, engaging and well-tolerated.

Visual attention, cognitive flexibility, inhibition and working memory were also the target of a home-based computer training in which both short- and long-term effects were monitored [92]. 91 ADHD children were randomized to full-active condition, partially active condition and placebo condition. The difference between the two intervention groups that received training was that in the full-active condition the participants benefited from training on working memory, inhibition and cognitive flexibility, whereas in the partially active condition only inhibition and cognitive flexibility modules were on. Their results show that the improvements children made were specific to abilities that were trained, measured with specific executive functions tasks. No significant differences were identified on the parent and teachers reports on ADHD related symptoms between the three groups.

Peijnenborgh [71] in a meta-analytic study, analyzed the effect of working memory training in ADHD children. The researcher included 13 studies. The mostly use program for working memory training was Cogmed (10 studies). Jungle Memory (2 studies) and Braingame Brian (one study) were much less found. CogMed Working Memory Training (www.cogmed.com) is an adaptable model of training, intensive, with 25 sessions of 10–45 min each, for 5 weeks. It. Each session is comprised of 6 exercises that address visual and verbal working memory [93].

Braingame Brian [94] is a computerized training developed for ADHD children, addressing not only their executive function deficits, but also their motivational deficits. Similarly with the previous broadly used program, it consists of 25 sessions of 40–50 min (30 min of training per se and the rest for exploring the virtual worlds inside the game and reward himself/herself). For each session the child is to do two blocks of three EF tasks each. The first task is always a working memory task, while the second and third may be either inhibition or cognitive flexibility. By completing the task, the player receives rewards, extra powers and can improve the lives of the people living in the virtual worlds depicted in the game.

Jungle Memory [95] is a web-based instrument for training, addressed to children between 7 and 16 years old. It contains 3 games that address different aspects of working memory, each game having around 30 levels of difficulty: Quicksand (verbal working memory with word endings), Code Breaker (mental rotation of letters), and River crossing (sequential memory for math solutions). The program offers formative feedback and summative feedback. It has many motivational features, such as it provides verbal feedback, it shows the best scores of the player, it shows scores in percentile rankings, and it rewards the player by collecting "supermonkeys". The total time for completing the three tasks per session is 20–25 min.

In Peijnenborgh et al. [71] review, most studies have participants that are at least 10 years old (7 studies, only 3 studies with children under 10). Similar moderate effect sizes for near transfer on measures of verbal working memory and visual spatial working memory were obtained. A small, though significant effect size for far transfer on decoding was obtained. Long term effects of working memory training were obtained for verbal (a moderate effect size) and visual working memory (small effect size), as well as for decoding (small).

In a meta-analytic study on cognitive training in ADHD, based on randomized controlled trials, [96], most of the cognitive trainings were unicomponential, such as 6 addressed working memory, and 4 addressed attention; two studies combined working memory training with attention, while other two studies combined inhibition with working memory. Only one study addressed in the content of the training working memory, inhibition, and cognitive flexibility. Results indicate a limited effect of these trainings to the components they address and limited to no effect on relieving clinical symptoms of ADHD. An interesting result, however prone to caution, is an indication of a superior effect of multi-component training versus uni-component trainings of executive functions. Only 4 studies, however, were addressing 2 or 3 components. It is not clear whether the result is in relation to the length of the training, as the authors emphasize.

In the most recent meta-analytic review of randomized controlled trials (RCTS) with blinded and objective outcomes, on cognitive training in the case of ADHD individuals [97] identified 36 eligible RCTS, of which 17 addressed working memory training, while 13 were multi-process, 5 addressed attention, and only 1 inhibition. Of the 31 studies addressing cognitive training in children, 16 had a training that was run at home. Of the 14 studies addressing working memory in children/adolescents, 11 use a CWMT, 2 WMT Minneslek, and 1 a WM n-back. 11 cognitive training studies in children and adolescents employed a multi component training paradigm. However, while the type of working memory training does not vary a lot, for the multi-component ones, it is the opposite. When analyzing the results, and distinguished between uni-component and multi-component training, there were no notable differences in effects. We analyzed the content of the multi-component trainings. Happy neuron [98] has a rich content on visual perception, visual attention and visual memory. Another program is Activate. It addresses sustained attention, response inhibition, cognitive flexibility, working memory, pattern recognition and categorization. Johnstone et al. [99] used In-house GNG, comprising two types of tasks: a go/no go task, and a visual spatial working meory task. Kollins et al. [100] used AKL-T01 to address attention and cognitive control (interference control). Medina et al. [101] used a cognitive training that addresses many more executive functions, such as inhibition, cognitive flexibility, planning, working memory, updating, decision making. Improvements in verbal working memory and visual working memory were obtained, though effect sizes were small to medium. However, there was no effect of computerized training on attention or inhibition, reading, arithmetic. On a long term, effect was visible within 6 months, in verbal working memory, reading comprehension, executive functions scores from rating measures.

McKay et al. [102] developed inhibitory control training on VR, called Alfi VR. The task is an anticipated response stop-signal task. It trains reactive, proactive, and selective inhibition. The difficulty increases. The task is embedded in a game scenario, in which the users play the role of a wizard that has the task of protecting a magic crystal from a dragon. The intervention is addressing ADHD adolescents. While motivating, engaging, it requires further research on its effectiveness.

Meyer et al. [103] addressed inhibition training through a program NeuroScout. It uses a randomized with active control. The program requires different movements performed on the screen, such as tapping, dragging, pressing. The experimental condition had an adaptive treatment. When compared to the active control group, receiving a similar training however, non-adaptive, a trend of improvement on symptoms of inattention based on parents were apparent. Both groups improved performance on the stop signal task. The results support the trainability of inhibition.

5 Conclusions

Overall, in terms of cognitive training paradigms, most studies use repeated practice on cognitive tasks, rather than a strategy-based or processual paradigm. Most studies addressing cognitive functions through computerized cognitive training do not use developmental models of executive functions. Therefore, some executive functions may have been addressed earlier, and this is especially the case for a delayed development. Other executive functions are less studied given the typical development. For instance, even though many computerized cognitive trainings are addressed to children older than 10, the content for higher order cognitive functions is scarce. This is the case for planning, organizing, interference control, problem-solving, metacognitive strategies. Robledo-Castro et al. [104] underline the need for cognitive training to be process-oriented. Digital technologies have a great potential to run a process approach. Still regarding content, there is accumulating evidence of a positive effect in terms of far transfer for using combined training of domain-general cognitive skills and domain-specific skills. Lately, more multi-componential programs have been developed and tested. However, objective data so far does not support the idea of a superior treatment to uni-component one at least in terms of transfer to academic skills and performance. There is need for research on this matter, for a thorough planning of a training schedule. By opening to different technologies, a processual approach based on solid learning theories can be embraced. As such, more active involvement in cognitive tasks could be implemented. In reference, inhibition training with VR seems to be promising. Also, training content needs to be better linked to functional tasks. This way, it rewards the child with skills that he/she can apply in daily life, to respond to their needs. Another issue is to conduct more research at younger ages in the case of neurodevelopmental disabilities.

Another important aspect that we should consider is the near and far transfer effects. Transfer effect may depend on the type of the task and how successfully one strategy is applied. Moreover, the transfer effects may be significantly higher for one specific EF compared to others, for example transfer effects on WM compared to IN or CF [105]. Also, the near transfer effect seems to be higher compared to far-transfer effect [106]. The generalizability of the skills is also linked with the context where the training takes place. Pasqualotto et al. [69] in their meta-analysis found that computerized or non-computerized trainings are more effective in training EF when implemented in an ecological environment. Therefore, the advantage of using computer-based training is that most of them are accessible directly from participant's homes or offered in a school setting.

There are also some possible mediators that can influence the effects of digital games on EF, for example the existence of a comorbidity with ADHD, which can influence their performance in the IH tasks, or the presence of an affective disorders which was highly associated with poor cognitive flexibility and shifting [107]. Another important variable that should be considered is the type of measurement, there are either other reported measurement or direct tasks which can be used to assess the effectiveness of the training. While direct task measurements can be more accurate, teacher or parent reported measurements may provide an more ecological view of the children's skills.

Acknowledgements The research leading to these results is in the frame of the "EMPOWER. Design and evaluation of technological support tools to empower stakeholders in digital education" project, which has received funding from the European Union's Horizon Europe programme under grant agreement No. 101060918. However, the views and opinions expressed are those of the authors(s) only and do not necessarily reflect those of the European Union. Neither the European Union nor the granting authority can be held responsible for them.

References

1. Leung RC, Vogan VM, Powell TL, Anagnostou E, Taylor MJ (2016) The role of executive functions in social impairment in Autism Spectrum Disorder. Child Neuropsychol 22(3):336–344. https://doi.org/10.1080/09297049.2015.1005066
2. Iversen RK, Lewis C (2021) Executive function skills are linked to restricted and repetitive behaviors: three correlational meta analyses. Autism Res 14(6):1163–1185. https://doi.org/10.1002/aur.2468
3. De Vries M, Geurts H (2015) Influence of autism traits and executive functioning on quality of life in children with an autism spectrum disorder. J Autism Dev Disord 45:2734–2743. https://doi.org/10.1007/s10803-015-2438-1
4. Nemeth DG, Chustz KM (2020) Executive functions defined. In: Evaluation and treatment of neuropsychologically compromised children, pp 107–120
5. Velikonja T, Fett AK, Velthorst E (2019) Patterns of nonsocial and social cognitive functioning in adults with autism spectrum disorder: a systematic review and meta-analysis. JAMA Psychiatr 76(2):135–151. https://doi.org/10.1001/jamapsychiatry.2018.3645
6. Demetriou EA, Lampit A, Quintana DS, Naismith SL, Song YJ, Pye JE et al (2018) Autism spectrum disorders: a meta-analysis of executive function. Mol Psychiatr 23(5):1198–1204. https://doi.org/10.1038/mp.2017.75
7. Kenworthy L, Anthony LG, Naiman DQ, Cannon L, Wills MC, Luong-Tran C, Werner MA, Alexander KC, Strang J, Bal E, Sokoloff JL, Wallace GL (2014) Randomized controlled effectiveness trial of executive function intervention for children on the autism spectrum. J Child Psychol Psychiatr 55(4):374–383. https://doi.org/10.1111/jcpp.12161
8. O'Neill B, Gillespie A (2014) Assistive technology for cognition. Psychology Press, Hove, UK

9. Puentedura RR (2006) Transformation, technology, and education. In: Paper presented at the Strengthening Your District through Technology workshops, coordinated by the Maine School Superintendents Association. http://hippasus.com/resources/tte/
10. Bouck EC, Savage M, Meyer NK, Taber-Doughty T, Hunley M (2014) High-tech or low-tech? Comparing self-monitoring systems to increase task independence for students with autism. Focus Autism Other Dev Disabil 29(3):156–167. https://doi.org/10.1177/1088357611 45287
11. Friedman NP, Miyake A (2017) Unity and diversity of executive functions: individual differences as a window on cognitive structure. Cortex 86:186–204. https://doi.org/10.1016/j.cortex.2016.04.023
12. Diamond A (2013) Executive functions. Annu Rev Psychol 64:135–168. https://doi.org/10.1146/annurev-psych-113011-143750
13. Kerns KA, Macoun S, MacSween J, Pei J, Hutchison M (2017) Attention and working memory training: a feasibility study in children with neurodevelopmental disorders. Appl Neuropsychol Child 6(2):120–137. https://doi.org/10.1080/21622965.2015.1109513
14. 15. Calub CA, Benyakorn S, Sun S, Iosif AM, Boyle LH, Solomon M et al (2022) Working memory training in youth with autism, fragile X, and intellectual disability: a pilot study. Am J Intellect Dev Disabil 127(5):369–389. https://doi.org/10.1352/1944-7558-127.5.369
15. Macoun SJ, Schneider I, Bedir B, Sheehan J, Sung A (2021) Pilot study of an attention and executive function cognitive intervention in children with autism spectrum disorders. J Autism Dev Disord 51:2600–2610. https://doi.org/10.1007/s10803-020-04723-w
16. Erickson LC, Thiessen ED, Godwin KE, Dickerson JP, Fisher AV (2015) Endogenously and exogenously driven selective sustained attention: contributions to learning in kindergarten children. J Exp Child Psychol 138:126–134. https://doi.org/10.1016/j.jecp.2015.04.011
17. May T, Rinehart NJ, Wilding J, Cornish K (2015) Attention and basic literacy and numeracy in children with autism spectrum disorder: a one-year follow-up study. Res Autism Spectrum Disord 9:193–201. https://doi.org/10.1016/j.rasd.2014.10.010
18. Murza KA, Schwartz JB, Hahs-Vaughn DL, Nye C (2016) Joint attention interventions for children with autism spectrum disorder: a systematic review and meta-analysis. Int J Lang Commun Disord 51(3):236–251. https://doi.org/10.1111/1460-6984.12212
19. Shalev L, Tsal Y, Mevorach C (2007) Computerized progressive attentional training (CPAT) program: effective direct intervention for children with ADHD. Child Neuropsychol 13(4):382–388. https://doi.org/10.1080/09297040600770787
20. Spaniol MM, Shalev L, Kossyvaki L, Mevorach C (2018) Attention training in autism as a potential approach to improving academic performance: a school-based pilot study. J Autism Dev Disord 48(2):592–610. https://doi.org/10.1007/s10803-017-3371-2
21. Spaniol MM, Mevorach C, Shalev L, Teixeira MCT, Lowenthal R, de Paula CS (2021) Attention training in children with autism spectrum disorder improves academic performance: a double-blind pilot application of the computerized progressive attentional training program. Autism Res 14(8):1769–1776. https://doi.org/10.1002/aur.2566
22. Cohen RA, Sparling-Cohen YA, O'Donnell BF (1993) Critical issues in neuropychology. In: The neuropsychology of attention. Plenum Press. https://doi.org/10.1007/978-1-4419-7463-1
23. Chen MT, Chang YP, Marraccini ME, Cho MC, Guo NW (2022) Comprehensive attention training system (CATS): a computerized executive-functioning training for school-aged children with autism spectrum disorder. Int J Dev Disabil 68(4):528–537. https://doi.org/10.1080/20473869.2020.1827673
24. Ionescu T (2012) Exploring the nature of cognitive flexibility. New Ideas Psychol 30:190–200. https://doi.org/10.1016/j.newideapsych.2011.11.001
25. Cristofori I, Cohen-Zimerman S, Grafman J (2019) Executive functions. In: Handbook of clinical neurology, vol 163, pp 197–219
26. D'Cruz AM, Ragozzino ME, Mosconi MW, Shrestha S, Cook EH, Sweeney JA (2013) Reduced behavioral flexibility in autism spectrum disorders. Neuropsychology 27(2):152–160. https://doi.org/10.1037/a0031721

27. Schmitt LM, Bojanek E, White SP, Ragozzino ME, Cook EH, Sweeney JA, Mosconi MW (2019) Familiality of behavioral flexibility and response inhibition deficits in autism spectrum disorder (ASD). Mol Autism 10:47
28. Shaffer RC, Schmitt LM, Reisinger DL, Coffman M, Hor P, Goodwin MS et al (2023) Regulating together: emotion dysregulation group treatment for ASD youth and their caregivers. J Autism Dev Disord 53(5):1942–1962. https://doi.org/10.1007/s10803-022-05461-x
29. Varanda CDA, Fernandes FDM (2017) Cognitive flexibility training intervention among children with autism: a longitudinal study. Psicol: Reflexão e Crítica, 30
30. Dandil Y, Baillie C, Tchanturia K (2020) Cognitive remediation therapy as a feasible treatment for a young person with anorexia nervosa and autism spectrum disorder comorbidity: a case study. Clin Case Stud 19(2):115–132
31. Nappo R, Crisci G, Ciaramella F, Boccia V, Carillo C, Giugliano M et al (2021) Assessment and training of executive functions in children through a game-based software: preliminary usability data from therapists' perspective. In: PSYCHOBIT
32. Mayer RE, Plass JL, Homer BD (2023) Executive functions training game. https://steinhardt.nyu.edu/create/research/executive-functions-training-games
33. Cao Y, Huang T, Huang J, Xie X, Wang Y (2020) Effects and moderators of computer-based training on children's executive functions: a systematic review and meta-analysis. Front Psychol 11:580329
34. Kray J, Eber J, Karbach J (2008) Verbal self-instructions in task switching: a compensatory tool for action-control deficits in childhood and old age? Dev Sci 11:223–236. https://doi.org/10.1111/j.1467-7687.2008.00673.x
35. Karbach J, Kray J (2009) How useful is executive control training? Age differences in near and far transfer of task-switching training. Dev Sci 12:978–990. https://doi.org/10.1111/j.1467-7687.2009.00846.x
36. Danielsson H, Henry L, Messer DJ, Rönnberg J (2012) Strengths and weaknesses in executive functioning in children with intellectual disability. Res Dev Disabil 33(2):600–607. https://doi.org/10.1016/j.ridd.2011.11.004
37. Spaniol M, Danielsson H (2022) A meta-analysis of the executive function components inhibition, shifting, and attention in intellectual disabilities. J Intellect Disabil Res 66(1–2):9–31. https://doi.org/10.1111/jir.12878
38. Tungate AS, Conners FA (2021) Executive function in down syndrome: a meta-analysis. Res Dev Disabil 108:103802. https://doi.org/10.1016/j.ridd.2020.103802
39. Kirk HE, Gray K, Rigby DM, Cornish KM (2015) Cognitive training as a resolution for early executive function difficulties in children with intellectual disabilities. Res Dev Disabil 38:145–160. https://doi.org/10.1016/j.ridd.2014.12.026
40. Bennett SJ, Holmes J, Buckley S (2013) Computerized memory training leads to sustained improvement in visuospatial short-term memory skills in children with down syndrome. Am J Intellect Dev 118(3):179–192. https://doi.org/10.1352/1944-7558-118.3.179
41. Van der Molen MJ, Van Luit JE, Van der Molen MW, Klugkist I, Jongmans MJ (2010) Effectiveness of a computerised working memory training in adolescents with mild to borderline intellectual disabilities. J Intellect Disabil Res 54(5):433–447. https://doi.org/10.1111/j.1365-2788.2010.01285.x
42. Söderqvist S, Nutley SB, Ottersen J, Grill KM, Klingberg T (2012) Computerized training of non-verbal reasoning and working memory in children with intellectual disability. Front Hum Neurosci 6:271. https://doi.org/10.3389/fnhum.2012.00271
43. Aksayli ND, Sala G, Gobet F (2019) The cognitive and academic benefits of Cogmed: a meta-analysis. Ed Res Rev 27:229–243. https://doi.org/10.1016/j.edurev.2019.04.003
44. Lanfranchi S, Pulina F, Carretti B, Mammarella IC (2017) Training spatial-simultaneous working memory in individuals with Down syndrome. Res Dev Disabil 64:118–129. https://doi.org/10.1016/j.ridd.2017.03.012
45. Mammarella IC, Toso C, Caviola S (2010) Memoria di Lavoro Visuo-spaziale. Erickson, Trento

46. Pulina F, Carretti B, Lanfranchi S, Mammarella IC (2015) Improving spatial-simultaneous working memory in down syndrome: effect of a training program led by parents instead of an expert. Front Psychol 6:1265. https://doi.org/10.3389/fpsyg.2015.01265
47. Danilesson H, Zottarel V, Palmqvist L, Lanfranchi S (2015) The effectiveness of working memory training with individuals with intellectual disabilities-a meta-analytic review. Front Psychol 6:1230. https://doi.org/10.3389/fpsyg.2015.01230
48. Kirk HE, Gray KM, Ellis K, Taffe J, Cornish KM (2016) Computerised attention training for children with intellectual and developmental disabilities: a randomised controlled trial. J Child Psychol Psychiatr 57(12):1380–1389. https://doi.org/10.1111/jcpp.12615
49. Corter HM, McKinney JD (1966) Cognitive training with retarded children. Research Report, U.S. Office of Education, Division of Handicapped Children and Youth: Washington, D.C.
50. Rostambeygi P, Ghaemi Z, Khakshour A, Yeganeh S, Abasi Z, Poorbarat S. The effect of cognitive flexibility training on reduction of cognitive problems in adolescents with intellectual disabilities. Int J Pediatr 9(8):14254–14265. https://doi.org/10.22038/ijp.2020.51136.4059
51. Orsolini M, Melogno S, Latini N, Penge R, Conforti S (2015) Treating verbal working memory in a boy with intellectual disability. Front Psychol 6:1091. https://doi.org/10.3389/fpsyg.2015.01091
52. Wu J, Peng J, Li Z, Deng H, Huang Z, He Y, Tu J, Cao L, Huang J (2023) Multi-domain computerized cognitive training for children with intellectual developmental disorder: a randomized controlled trial. Front Psychol 13:1059889. https://doi.org/10.3389/fpsyg.2022.1059889
53. Torra Moreno M, Canals Sans J, Colomina Fosch MT (2021) Behavioral and cognitive interventions with digital devices in subjects with intellectual disability: a systematic review. Front Psychiatr 12:647399. https://doi.org/10.3389/fpsyt.2021.647399
54. Bruttin CD (2011) Computerised assessment of an analogical reasoning test: effects of external memory strategies and their positive outcomes in young children and adolescents with intellectual disability. Educ Child Psychol 28(2):18–32. https://doi.org/10.53841/bpsecp.2011.28.2.18
55. Ko EJ, Sung IY, Yuk JS, Jang DH, Yun G (2020) A tablet computer-based cognitive training program for young children with cognitive impairment: a randomized controlled trial. Medicine (Baltimore) 99(12):e19549. https://doi.org/10.1097/MD.0000000000019549
56. Di Lieto MC, Castro E, Pecini C, Inguaggato E, Cecchi F, Dario P, Cioni G, Sgandurra G (2020) Improving executive functions at school in children with special needs by educational robotics. Front Psychol 10:2813. https://doi.org/10.3389/fpsyg.2019.02813
57. Beccaluva EA, Riccardi F, Gianotti M, Barbieri J, Garzotto F (2021) VIC—A tangible user interface to train memory skills in children with intellectual disability. Int J Child Comput Interact 32:100376. https://doi.org/10.1016/j.ijcci.2021.100376
58. Yoshimasu K, Barbaresi WJ, Colligan RC, Killian JM, Voigt RG, Weaver AL, Katusic SK (2011) Written-language disorder among children with and without ADHD in a population-based birth cohort. Pediatrics 128(3):e605–e612. https://doi.org/10.1542/peds.2010-2581
59. Pham AV, Riviere A (2015) Specific learning disorders and ADHD: current issues in diagnosis across clinical and educational settings. Curr Psychiatr Rep 17(6):38. https://doi.org/10.1007/s11920-015-0584-y
60. Barquero LA, Wilson LM., Benedict SL, Lindström ER, Harris HC, Cutting LE (2012) Executive functions in learning disorders. In: Hunter SJ, Sparrow EP (eds) Executive function and dysfunction: identification, assessment and treatment. Cambridge University Press, Cambridge, pp 131–140. https://doi.org/10.1017/CBO9780511977954.012
61. Menghini D, Finzi A, Benassi M, Bolzani R, Facoetti A, Giovagnoli S, Ruffino M, Vicari S (2010) Different underlying neurocognitive deficits in developmental dyslexia: a comparative study. Neuropsychologia 48(4):863–872. https://doi.org/10.1016/j.neuropsychologia.2009.11.003
62. Johnson ES, Humphrey M, Mellard DF, Woods K, Swanson HL (2010) Cognitive processing deficits and students with specific learning disabilities: a selective meta-analysis of the literature. Learn Disabil Q 33. https://doi.org/10.1177/073194871003300101

63. Hooper SR, Swartz CW, Wakely MB, de Kruif REL, Montgomery JW (2002) Executive functions in elementary school children with and without problems in written expression. J Learn Disabil 35(1):57–68. https://doi.org/10.1177/002221940203500105
64. Farah R, Ionta S, Horowitz-Kraus T (2021) Neuro-behavioral correlates of executive dysfunctions in dyslexia over development from childhood to adulthood. Front Psychol 12:708863. https://doi.org/10.3389/fpsyg.2021.708863
65. Maehler C, Schuchardt K (2016) Working memory in children with specific learning disorders and/or attention deficits. Learn Individ Differ 49:341–347. https://doi.org/10.1016/j.lindif.2016.05.007
66. Lonergan A, Doyle C, Cassidy C, MacSweeney Mahon S, Roche RA, Boran L, Bramham J (2019) A meta-analysis of executive functioning in dyslexia with consideration of the impact of comorbid ADHD. Cogn Psychol 31(7):725–749. https://doi.org/10.1080/20445911.2019.1669609
67. Agostini F, Zoccolotti P, Casagrande M (2022) Domain-general cognitive skills in children with mathematical difficulties and dyscalculia: a systematic review of the literature. Brain Sci 12:239. https://doi.org/10.3390/brainsci12020239
68. Bombonato C, Del Lucchese B, Ruffini C, Di Lieto MC, Brovedani P, Sgandurra G, Cioni G, Pecini C (2023) Far transfer effects of trainings on executive functions in neurodevelopmental disorders: a systematic review and metanalysis. Neuropsychol Rev 2023. https://doi.org/10.1007/s11065-022-09574-z
69. Pasqualotto A, Mazzoni N, Bentenuto A, Mule A, Benso F, Venuti P (2021) Effects of cognitive training programs on executive function in children and adolescents with autism spectrum disorder: a systematic review. Brain Sci 11(10):1280. https://doi.org/10.3390/brainsci11101280
70. Merzenich MM (2013) Soft-wired: how the new science of brain plasticity can change your life. Parnassus, San Francisco, CA
71. Peijnenborgh JC, Hurks PM, Aldenkamp AP, Vles JS, Hendriksen JG (2016) Efficacy of working memory training in children and adolescents with learning disabilities: a review study and meta-analysis. Neuropsychol Rehabil 26(5–6):645–672. https://doi.org/10.1080/09602011.2015.1026356
72. Nelwan M, Kroesbergen EH (2016) Limited near and far transfer effects of jungle memory working memory training on learning mathematics in children with attentional and mathematical difficulties. Front Psychol 7:1384. https://doi.org/10.3389/fpsyg.2016.01384
73. Chen X, Ye M, Chang L, Chen W, Zhou R (2018) Effect of working memory updating training on retrieving symptoms of children with learning disabilities. J Learn Disabil 51(5):507–519. https://doi.org/10.1177/0022219417712015
74. Capodieci A, Romano M, Castro E, Di Lieto MC, Bonetti S, Pecini C (2022) Executive functions and rapid automatized naming: a new tele-rehabilitation approach in children with language and learning disorders. Children (Basel, Switzerland) 9(6):822. https://doi.org/10.3390/children9060822
75. Nazari S, Hakiminejad F, Hassanzadeh S (2022) Effectiveness of a process-based executive function intervention on arithmetic knowledge of children with Developmental Dyscalculia. Res Dev Disabil 127:104260. https://doi.org/10.1016/j.ridd.2022.104260
76. Muñez D, Lee K, Bull R, Khng KH, Cheam F, Rahim RA (2022) Working memory and numeracy training for children with math learning difficulties: evidence from a large-scale implementation in the classroom. J Educ Psychol 114(8):1866–1880. https://doi.org/10.1037/edu0000732
77. Di Giusto V, Purpura G, Zorzi CF, Blonda R, Brazzoli E, Meriggi P, Reina T, Rezzonico S, Sala R, Olivieri I, Cavallini A (2023) Virtual reality rehabilitation program on executive functions of children with specific learning disorders: a pilot study. Front Psychol 14:1241860. https://doi.org/10.3389/fpsyg.2023.1241860
78. Bertoni S, Franceschini S, Puccio G et al (2021) Action video games enhance attentional control and phonological decoding in children with developmental dyslexia. Brain Sci 11:171. https://doi.org/10.3390/brainsci11020171

79. American Psychiatric Association, DSM-5 Task Force (2013) Diagnostic and statistical manual of mental disorders: DSM-5™, 5th edn. American Psychiatric Publishing, Inc.. https://doi.org/10.1176/appi.books.9780890425596
80. Thapar A, Cooper M (2016) Attention deficit hyperactivity disorder. Lancet 387(10024):1240–1250. https://doi.org/10.1016/S0140-6736(15)00238-X
81. Brocki KC, Eninger L, Thorell LB et al (2010) Interrelations between executive function and symptoms of hyperactivity/impulsivity and inattention in preschoolers: a two year longitudinal study. J Abnorm Child Psychol 38:163–171. https://doi.org/10.1007/s10802-009-9354-9
82. Sjöwall D, Bohlin G, Rydell A-M, Thorell LB (2017) Neuropsychological deficits in preschool as predictors of ADHD symptoms and academic achievement in late adolescence. Child Neuropsychol 23(1):111–128. https://doi.org/10.1080/09297049.2015.1063595
83. Fan L, Wang Y (2023) The relationship between executive functioning and attention deficit hyperactivity disorder in young children: a cross-lagged study. Curr Psychol 42(25):21375–21383. https://doi.org/10.1007/s12144-022-03233-5
84. Willcutt EG, Doyle AE, Nigg JT, Faraone SV, Pennington BF (2005) Validity of the executive function theory of attention-deficit/hyperactivity disorder: a meta-analytic review. Biol Psychiatr 57(11):133646. https://doi.org/10.1016/j.biopsych.2005.02.006
85. Barkley RA (1997) Behavioral inhibition, sustained attention, and executive functions: constructing a unifying theory of ADHD. Psychol Bull 12:65–94
86. Ramos-Galarza C, Pérez-Salas C (2021) Moderator role of monitoring in the inhibitory control of adolescents with ADHD. J Atten Disord 25(2):188–198. https://doi.org/10.1177/1087054718776478
87. Kofler MJ, Rapport MD, Bolden J, Sarver DE, Raiker JS (2010) ADHD and working memory: the impact of central executive deficits and exceeding storage/rehearsal capacity on observed inattentive behavior. J Abnorm Child Psychol 38(2):149–161. https://doi.org/10.1007/s10802-009-9357-6
88. Chang YK, Liu S, Yu HH, Lee YH (2012) Effect of acute exercise on executive function in children with attention deficit hyperactivity disorder. Arch Clin Neuropsychol 27(2):225–237. https://doi.org/10.1093/arclin/acr094
89. Tsuchiya E, Oki J, Yahara N, Fujieda K (2005) Computerized version of the Wisconsin card sorting test in children with high-functioning autistic disorder or attention-deficit/hyperactivity disorder. Brain Develop 27(3):233–236
90. Santos FE, Bastos AP, Andrade LC, Revoredo K, Mattos P (2011) Assessment of ADHD through a computer game: an experiment with a sample of students. In: 2011 third international conference on games and virtual worlds for serious applications, pp 104–111. IEEE
91. Lim CG, Poh XWW, Fung SSD, Guan C, Bautista D, Cheung YB et al (2019) A randomized controlled trial of a brain-computer interface based attention training program for ADHD. Plos One 14(50):e0216225. https://doi.org/10.1371/journal.pone.0216225
92. Dovis S, Van der Oord S, Wiers RW, Prins PJ. (2015) Improving executive functioning in children with ADHD: training multiple executive functions within the context of a computer game. A randomized double-blind placebo controlled trial. PloS One 10(4):e0121651. https://doi.org/10.1371/journal.pone.0121651
93. Marcelle ET, Ho EJ, Kaplan MS, Adler LA, Castellanos FX, Milham MP (2018) Cogmed working memory training presents unique implementation challenges in adults with ADHD. Front Psychiatr 9:388. https://doi.org/10.3389/fpsyt.2018.00388
94. Prins PJ, Brink ET, Dovis S, Ponsioen A, Geurts HM, de Vries M, van der Oord S (2013) "Braingame Brian": toward an executive function training program with game elements for children with ADHD and cognitive control problems. Games Health J 2(1):44–49. https://doi.org/10.1089/g4h.2013.0004
95. Memosyne Ltd (2011) Jungle Memory Retrieved from http://lb.junglememory.com
96. Cortese S, Ferrin M, Brandeis D, Buitelaar J, Daley D, Dittmann RW, Holtmann M, Santosh P, Stevenson J, Stringaris A, Zuddas A, Sonuga-Barke EJS, Guidelines EADHD (2015) Cognitive training for attention deficit/hyperactivity disorder: meta-analysis of clinical and

neuropsychological outcomes from randomized controlled trials. J Am Acad Child Adolesc Psychiatr 54(3):164–174. https://doi.org/10.1016/j.jaac.2014.12.010
97. Westwood SJ, Parlatini V, Rubia K et al (2023) Computerized cognitive training in attention-deficit/hyperactivity disorder (ADHD): a meta-analysis of randomized controlled trials with blinded and objective outcomes. Mol Psychiatr 28:1402–1414. https://doi.org/10.1038/s41380-023-02000-7
98. Bikic A, Østergaard Christensen T, Leckman JF, Bilenberg N, Dalsgaard S (2017) A double-blind randomized pilot trial comparing computerized cognitive exercises to Tetris in adolescents with attention-deficit/hyperactivity disorder. Nord J Psychiatr 71(6):455–464. https://doi.org/10.1080/08039488.2017.1328070
99. Johnstone SJ, Roodenrys S, Blackman R, Johnston E, Loveday K, Mantz S, Barratt MF (2012) Neurocognitive training for children with and without AD/HD. ADHD Atten Def Hyp Disord 4:11–23. https://doi.org/10.1007/s12402-011-0069-8
100. Kollins SH, DeLoss DJ, Cañadas E, Lutz J, Findling RL, Keefe RSE, Epstein JN, Cutler AJ, Faraone SV (2020) A novel digital intervention for actively reducing severity of paediatric ADHD (STARS-ADHD): a randomised controlled trial. Lancet Digit Health 2(4):e168–e178. https://doi.org/10.1016/S2589-7500(20)30017-0
101. Medina R, Bouhaben J, de Ramón I, Cuesta P, Antón-Toro L, Pacios J, Quintero J, Ramos-Quiroga JA, Maestú F (2021) Electrophysiological brain changes associated with cognitive improvement in a pediatric attention deficit hyperactivity disorder digital artificial intelligence-driven intervention: randomized controlled trial. J Med Internet Res 23(11):e25466. https://doi.org/10.2196/25466
102. McKay E, Kirk H, Coxon J, Courtney D, Bellgrove M, Arnatkeviciute A, Cornish K (2022) Training inhibitory control in adolescents with elevated attention deficit hyperactivity disorder traits: a randomised controlled trial of the Alfi virtual reality programme. Brit Med J 12:e061626. https://doi.org/10.1136/bmjopen-2022-061626
103. Meyer KN, Santillana R, Miller B, ClappW WM, Bridgman-Goines K, Sheridan MA (2020) Computer-based inhibitory control training in children with attention-deficit/hyperactivity disorder (ADHD): evidence for behavioral and neural impact. Plos One 15(11):e0241352. https://doi.org/10.1371/journal.pone.0241352
104. Robledo-Castro C, Castillo-Ossa LF, Corchado JM (2023) Artificial cognitive systems applied in executive function stimulation and rehabilitation programs: a systematic review. Arab J Sci Eng 48(2):2399–2427. https://doi.org/10.1007/s13369-022-07292-5
105. Cao Y, Huang T, Huang J, Xie X, Wang Y (2020) Effects and moderators of computer-based training on children's executive functions: a systematic review and meta-analysis. Front Psychol 26(11):580329. https://doi.org/10.3389/fpsyg.2020.580329
106. Kassai R, Futo J, Demetrovics Z, Takacs ZK (2019) A meta-analysis of the experimental evidence on the near- and far-transfer effects among children's executive function skills. Psychol Bull 145:165–188. https://doi.org/10.1037/bul0000180
107. Hollocks MJ, Jones CRG, Pickles A, Baird G, Happé F, Charman T, Simonoff E (2014) The association between social cognition and executive functioning and symptoms of anxiety and depression in adolescents with autism spectrum disorders. Autism Res 7:216–228

Best Practices to Improve Autonomy of People on the Spectrum Using Handheld Devices

Guadalupe Montero de Espinosa Espino
and Luis Perez de la Maza

Abstract

Technology use for people on the autism spectrum is progressively gaining broader scientific evidence to withhold its implementation. Handheld devices with specific or off-the-shelf developments, if appropriately implemented and responding to needs, can provide a relevant asset to improve autonomous functioning in some critical areas for people on the autism spectrum, like Communication, Social Interaction, Self-Regulation, Self-Management, and Independent Living. Along the text, we review and propose some options for these critical adaptative areas of development.

Keywords

Technology support • Autism spectrum disorder • Handheld devices • Independent living • Home automation • Smart home devices

1 Introduction

The use of mobile devices has grown exponentially in the last decade, becoming an integral part of daily life for many people. These devices include smartphones, tablets, and other integrated elements such as voice assistants, smartwatches, headsets, or home automation devices designed for general use. While these devices

G. Montero de Espinosa Espino (✉)
Inclusive Education Department, Smile and Learn, Madrid, Spain
e-mail: guadalupe.montero@smileandlearn.com

L. Perez de la Maza
Board, Fundación AUCAVI, Madrid, Spain
e-mail: lpmaza@fundacionaucavi.org

were not built to provide specific support for medical, accessibility, or other specialized needs, they have become an indispensable tool for many people.

As this digital ecosystem evolves, it brings about a continuous stream of enhancements and innovations that will lead to the emergence of novel applications for these devices, expanding their functionality to cover a broader range of activities in people's everyday lives.

For autistic people mobile devices offer a non-stigmatizing tool that provides access to digital resources, compensating for possible difficulties while facilitating social participation.

The integration of Artificial Intelligence (AI) developments in mobile devices is transforming the way people perform daily tasks. It's worth highlighting the significant role that this technology plays in this transformation, as its use is becoming increasingly widespread, and it's happening at a fast pace. AI-based developments promise many benefits for people on the autism spectrum, enabling personalized experiences that are accessible and adjusted to everyday life.

Data processing allows mobile devices to learn from user interactions and execute actions automatically, while voice assistants provide control over a development environment. These features are highly beneficial for independent living and can generate task automation based on common activities, situations, and user needs. This includes planning tasks, reminders and alarms, environmental control management through home automation devices, or sending alerts and communications to other people.

In addition, natural language processing technologies offer promising features to support people on the autism spectrum, including automated subtitling or translations, voice and text control, predictive text keyboards, gaze control, and descriptions of images and videos. These features increase accessibility and can facilitate understanding and interaction.

This chapter provides an overview of how mobile devices, using integrated or commonly used software, can offer support to enhance the autonomy of people on the autism spectrum in various areas of their development. By incorporating these elements naturally into daily life, mobile devices can provide new possibilities for people on the autism spectrum to lead more independent lives.

2   Framework

The rapidly developing and evolving landscape of handheld technologies often implies a lack of formal support for their implementation, especially when dealing with an extremely neurodiverse population such as those within the autism spectrum. We use a foundational framework to empower the use of these technologies, with the aim of achieving the highest planned outcomes. Two distinct approaches, originating from different sources and with different targets and developments, but nonetheless coherent and mutually reinforcing, are used to explain the framework that underpins this work.

The first component is the World Health Organization's International Classification of Functioning, Disability, and Health, commonly known as ICF [23, 24]. We specifically focus on the category of Activities and Participation, which includes Learning and Applying Knowledge, General Tasks and Demands, Communication, Mobility, Self-Care, Domestic Life, Interpersonal Interactions and Relationships, Major Areas of Life, and Community, Social, and Civic Life. Additionally, we consider the related qualifiers of Barriers and Facilitators as reference points to structure the developments cited further.

The second component is the assessment structure derived from the ABAS-3 [11], a multidimensional and standardized assessment tool employed to evaluate the functional skills required for daily living. The areas covered by this tool include Communication (speech-language and communication skills needed for interacting with others), Community Use (skills required for functioning in the community), Functional Academics (functional pre-academics and academics), School/Home Living (skills needed for basic care in a home or school/classroom setting), Health and Safety (skills needed to safeguard health and respond to illness and injury), Leisure (skills required for engaging in and planning leisure and recreational activities), Self-Care (skills needed for personal care), Self-Direction (skills required for independence, responsibility, and self-control), Social Skills (skills needed to interact socially and build relationships), Motor Skills (basic fine and gross motor skills needed for movement, environmental manipulation, and more complex activities), and Work Skills (skills needed for successful functioning and employment in a work setting).

With these two elements, we summarize the main content within the following areas: Communication, Self-Management, Self-Regulation, Social Interaction, and Independent Living. For each of these areas, we consider the challenges stemming from the autism condition as barriers, as well as the opportunities provided by current developments in handheld devices that, when appropriately implemented, can serve as significant facilitators, as we will explore in more detail.

3   Advantages of the Use of Technologies for Autistic People

Handheld devices and their connected elements are particularly useful for autistic people due to their alignment with the cognitive style of individuals with this condition. Handheld devices present information in a highly visual manner, allow a predictable use of programs and contexts and offer many stimulus control options. These characteristics make mobile devices an excellent tool for individuals on the autism spectrum.

Many technological devices rely on screens to display their interfaces, though there are also devices that use other sensory pathways, such as smart speakers or headphones. The use of screens often includes visual and intuitive designs, particularly in smartphones and tablets. This may be particularly beneficial for individuals on the autism spectrum who tend to process information visually [10].

Digital resources operate in a predictable and consistent manner, with well-defined and homogeneous processes based on achieving specific goals. This provides an advantage over some human responses in terms of consistency and facilitates structured learning.

It is important to note that technology offers various options to stimulate and control user interactions. These options include controlling parameters such as brightness and volume, as well as canceling notifications that may cause distractions. These choices allow for personal preferences to be considered and create more appropriate and pleasant interaction environments for users. Additionally, there are several accessibility options available that can be adjusted to meet the varying needs of autistic individuals. This enables to ensure a safe and satisfactory experience.

A significant number of individuals on the autism spectrum have expressed a preference for technological support over other forms of intervention. Studies have confirmed this preference, highlighting the benefits of using technology to support autistic individuals. These benefits include improved attention, increased motivation, and reduced anxiety [9]. Therefore, it's important to consider technology as a viable option when planning interventions for autistic individuals.

Technology can be used as a support resource to develop personal autonomy skills. Mobile devices are portable and have experienced the incorporation of new functionalities in recent years. Additionally, the variety and quality of applications available in the market make them very powerful tools to facilitate the daily lives of people on the autism spectrum. All these reasons support the use of technologies in this context.

4 Areas of Application

The following distribution of contents aims to be clarifying for the readers to engage in the provision of support for people on the autism spectrum. It's not a rigid classification as the overlapping of outcomes involved in the addressed developments or suggestions is clear. The intention is to organize content focusing primarily on some of the more outstanding features and their functionality towards that specific adaptative area.

4.1 Communication

4.1.1 Context

Effective communication is fundamental to navigating our surroundings and fostering relationships with those around us. This is frequently a challenge for those with autism, where communication remains a central area of difficulty. In the *Diagnostic and Statistical Manual of Mental Disorders* (DSM-5), communication is a critical component of diagnosing autism spectrum disorders. These criteria underscore the significance of evaluating and comprehending communication obstacles, encompassing verbal and nonverbal communication and social reciprocity, in those with ASD [1].

Communication is essential for autistic individuals, as it empowers them to engage more meaningfully with their surroundings and society. According to Kasari and Smith [13], communication is a critical factor in developing social skills and enabling people on the autism spectrum to adjust to the world around them. Effective communication empowers them to communicate their basic needs such as hunger or pain, as well as express their thoughts, interests, and desires, thereby significantly improving their relationship with the environment.

Effective communication plays a crucial role in the language and social skills development of autistic individuals. According to Lord et al. [14], communication at an early stage is a significant predictor of language development and social adaptation in autistic children. Through communication, they can learn to recognize and respond to social cues, which helps them form meaningful relationships and lead active life in society.

The DSM-5 has put a spotlight on the importance of communication in diagnosing autism spectrum disorders, highlighting its fundamental role in the lives of individuals on the autism spectrum. The cited research shows that communication is vital in the development and adjustment of people on the autism spectrum and reinforces the need for effective communication strategies and support to improve their quality of life.

This section aims to provide an overview of how mobile devices and next-gen technology can inclusively support autistic individuals through commonly used handheld devices and software, rather than delving into existing developments for AC implementation.

4.1.2 Challenges

Autistic individuals present complex and diverse communication needs that can range from a complete absence of communicative intention and the lack of means to communicate, to pragmatic difficulties in speech and social use of language. These wide needs require individualized analysis and assessment to provide the best support for each person, as the most common areas of concern involve functional communication, language development, nonverbal communication, social communication, and communication environments.

Functional communication support is crucial to enable autistic individuals to effectively express basic needs, desires, and emotions. Augmentative Communication Systems are sometimes necessary to facilitate communication with others and according to Odom et al. [18] the use of Speech Generating Devices (SGD) is considered an evidence based practice.

Language development is a multidimensional process that may develop at different levels in autistic individual, often generating disharmonic profiles due to these differences and requiring personalized intervention strategies that focus on personal strengths and compensate for difficulties based on centers of interest and using specific methodologies with evidence of success in autistic people.

Nonverbal communication, such as expression, movement, and intonation, adds up to speech and provides complexity to communication for autistic individuals who face the challenge of decoding these elements appropriately and applying them in their own communicative interactions. It is common to require support for interpreting these components to communicate with others in an effective manner that can ensure understanding.

Social communication involves participating in conversations, taking turns, and understanding communication rules in different social contexts. These are very complex issues that can lead to a lack of opportunities for functional participation and even social isolation without proper support.

Effective communication requires adapting to the partner's level of understanding, particularly with written text that cannot be further explained. Complex texts often need to be simplified through "Easy Read", a cognitive accessibility strategy that benefits autistic individuals and helps them better comprehend their surroundings. Moreno et al. [16] emphasize the importance of this strategy as well as other techniques that contribute to enhance the cognitive accessibility of texts.

Communication environments can also pose challenges for autistic individuals, as they may be complex and inaccessible. Adaptations or specific strategies may be necessary to promote participation, such as eliminating environmental stimuli, reducing the number of participants, or using visual supports to facilitate the consistency of the information exchanged and contribute to facilitating shared contextual references.

4.1.3 Opportunities

The use of technology has greatly aided in improving communication for autistic individuals, due to its potential to offer a very versatile and multimodal tool that can be made more accessible, allowing for easier use in everyday situations and providing valuable support for those with autism.

Augmentative Communication (AC) systems were initially developed to increase, improve or enhance communication possibilities using images, text or combinations of both. These systems offer a permanent visual aid and voice output, enabling communication with people without the need for a shared language. Over time, these communication systems also called Speech Generating Devices have advanced in design, functionality, and methodology. From traditional PECS to current communicators, a coherent and aligned approach can support good practices in AC for autistic individuals.

Some people may find it difficult to communicate in person. In such situations, messaging applications and emails can provide a less demanding setting to communicate with others. Additionally, these means allow for the use of visual aids which can be helpful in conveying information. Group communication can also be challenging, but applications that simplify the experience and facilitate conversation order and speaker identification can be useful. Employing cognitive accessibility strategies that use visual aids and simplify speech can enhance understanding.

There are numerous resources available to help people on the autism spectrum communicate more effectively in their daily lives, including mobile applications and different web-based developments. For example, social media and digital networking have provided new opportunities for communication and socialization among autistic individuals. Platforms such as Facebook, X (former Twitter), and Instagram have become valuable tools for connecting with others in a more structured and less intimidating environment. Recent studies, such as those reported in the systematic review published by Hassrick et al. [12], have found that social networks can be particularly beneficial for autistic adolescents and young adults.

By connecting with like-minded individuals, these platforms can facilitate communication and friendship building. Additionally, asynchronous communication on social networks allows for more time to process and respond to interactions, reducing the pressure of real-time communication.

When it comes to using social media for autistic individuals, it's important to keep in mind the need for guidance and supervision. This responsibility often falls on the parents, caregivers, and educators who should provide support and help navigate the safe and appropriate use of social media. It's also crucial to educate autistic individuals about online privacy and how to have secure interactions in virtual environments. Overall, social media and digital platforms can be excellent tools for enhancing communication and social interaction for those with autism. However, it's essential to balance the use of these tools with social skills training and appropriate supervision to ensure positive and safe experiences online.

Messaging applications, for instance, have proven to be extremely helpful in this regard. They make it easier for people on the autism spectrum to express themselves and connect with others, which can help them build stronger relationships and feel more confident in social situations. Whether it's through text messages, voice messages, or video calls, these apps are a valuable tool for anyone who wants to communicate more effectively with others.

Using messaging applications can be a great advantage for many people who struggle with face-to-face communication. These resources allow for delayed responses, giving time to process information and craft a message. They also reduce the need for non-verbal communication, replacing it with emojis that offer a precise indication of the message.

These apps can facilitate social participation and offer limited and understandable communicative contexts, making it easier to participate in groups. Additionally, these applications can be adjusted to different abilities or strengths, as they are developed in various channels such as writing, audio, or sending images.

Artificial Intelligence (AI), through Natural Language Processing (NLP) techniques, is contributing significantly to the development of products that will help people on the autism spectrum develop their communication skills in both expressive and receptive components.

Developments in technology are making language more accessible and user-friendly. Natural Language Processing techniques are being used to create tools that can identify complex words within a text and offer simpler alternatives or synonyms. One noteworthy example is Easier,[1] a project developed by researchers at Universidad Carlos III de Madrid. This innovative tool highlights complex words in a text and provides various resources to aid users in improving their reading and comprehension skills. These resources consist of synonyms, definitions, and pictograms that are customized to the context of each complex word. The Glossary feature offered by Easier is particularly valuable for individuals with cognitive challenges. As this technology evolves, it has the potential to enhance access to written language for all individuals with cognitive accessibility needs, including those with autism. By reinforcing communication skills and improving their understanding of language and the world around them, these tools can help individuals with cognitive disabilities better connect with their environment.

Finally, it's necessary to mention and recognize that the weight of video calls in our everyday existence is crucial, especially given the COVID-19 outbreak and the subsequent lockdowns in 2020 and 2021. These virtual meetings have emerged as indispensable means of communication that affect diverse facets of our routine, whether it's for socializing, unwinding, or supporting educational and professional endeavors. For autistic individuals, video calls can provide great support and have similarities to messaging apps in terms of reducing social demands during conversations. However, group video calls may still be stressful and challenging for some individuals.

To help improve cognitive accessibility, it is important to create products with simple and intuitive designs, visual aids, and other elements that aid in comprehension. Artificial Intelligence and Natural Language Processing can assist by providing tools that simplify texts and generate conversation summaries, allowing autistic individuals to access information visually and in a more understandable way.

The Access2Meet Project[2] of the Carlos III University of Madrid is currently developing a video conferencing tool with an adapted interface that shows interesting advances in terms of the features developed to offer specific answers to existing cognitive needs [15].

4.1.4 Best Practices

Effective communication and language skills are crucial for autistic individuals, and evidence-based practices play a key role in achieving this goal. These practices are grounded in scientific research and have been proven effective through numerous studies. They can be applied as part of a comprehensive treatment model (CTM) [17] like the Early Start Denver Model [5] in the early ages or used to target specific skills.

---

[1] http://easier.hulat.uc3m.es/.
[2] https://access2meet.uc3m.es/.

One of the most heavily researched approaches for improving communication skills in some autistic individuals is AC (Augmented Communication). These systems utilize symbols, pictures, communication boards, and electronic devices to help those with speech difficulties express their needs, wants, and thoughts. The Picture Exchange Communication System (PECS) is a particularly effective AC method, as demonstrated in a study conducted by Flippin, Reszka, and Watson [8]. This system allows autistic individuals to use pictures to communicate, which is especially helpful for those who struggle with verbal language.

It's worth noting that Augmented Communication Systems can and should be tailored to meet the unique needs of everyone, making it a versatile tool for promoting effective communication. By personalizing symbols and pictures, autistic individuals can express their preferences and needs in a more specific and meaningful way.

Developing effective social communication skills is crucial for autistic individuals, and social skills training is a proven approach to achieving this goal. By improving these abilities, autistic individuals can more confidently engage in social interactions and communicate more effectively.

Another important benefit of social skills training is that it takes place in real-life contexts, providing autistic individuals with valuable opportunities to practice their newly acquired skills. This hands-on experience allows them to apply what they have learned in meaningful situations, ultimately leading to a more fulfilling social life and a greater sense of belonging within their community.

All these evidence-based best practices can be reinforced with the use of technology-based tools such as those described above, which can amplify personal capabilities and support generalization processes in everyday life situations.

4.2 Self-management

4.2.1 Context

Personal autonomy is crucial for people on the autism spectrum to achieve self-realization, reduce dependence on others, and contribute to society. It is a fundamental aspect of achieving inclusion and making a meaningful impact in the world.

Despite these individual differences, that will determine the type and level of support they need, developing self-management skills is always a goal to pursue because of their significance and impact on daily life.

The term "personal autonomy" refers to a person's ability to make decisions and control their own life independently and autonomously. When it comes to autism, personal autonomy not only means the ability to take care of oneself and make daily decisions but also includes managing the specific challenges associated with the disorder. Self-management skills include planning, organization, and decision-making, among others.

Fostering personal autonomy and self-management skills in autistic individuals is crucial for various reasons. Firstly, it enhances their independence and quality of life, allowing them to make choices that positively impact their well-being and happiness. Additionally, the adquisition of these abilities decreases their reliance on caregivers and the constant need for assistance, which ultimately decreases the burden of caregiving on families and society.

Personal autonomy plays a vital role in promoting social inclusion. It empowers autistic individuals by enhancing their communication, interaction, and independence, which in turn enables them to take part in various areas of daily life, such as education, employment, and social relationships. As a result, it helps in creating a more inclusive and diverse society, where everyone, irrespective of their neurodiversity, can achieve their full potential.

4.2.2 Challenges

Many people on the autism spectrum need assistance in developing their self-management abilities to achieve a self-sufficient lifestyle. These abilities frequently involve executive functions, which are cognitive faculties such as memory retention, decision-making, problem-solving, and planning.

People on the autism spectrum may face difficulties in coping with daily life and adapting to unexpected situations due to deficits in their executive functions [19]. Therefore, the development of executive functions is crucial for autistic individuals to achieve greater independence in their daily lives. The common need for structure and rigidness present in many people on the autism spectrum derives from these difficulties with this complex cognitive feature: executive functioning.

Autistic individuals have specific needs in the areas of planning and organization. It is important to develop explicit strategies to support decision-making and strengthen working memory. This will enable them to remember what they have learned and apply it in various situations. Such support is crucial for autistic people to achieve their goals, be as independent as possible within their capabilities, and actively participate in society.

4.2.3 Opportunities

Mobile devices come equipped with a variety of applications designed to help individuals perform daily activities with applications that allow them to remember events, plan tasks, or take note of ideas. These tools, in their manipulative version, are particularly important for people on the autism spectrum, as they can facilitate greater independence and autonomy by helping to manage daily tasks in different contexts. By transferring these tools to a mobile device, autistic individuals can more easily use them in different settings, promoting the development of crucial life skills. Handheld devices increase the accessibility and functionality of all resources related to planning, organizing, and structuring.

It is necessary to consider the specific needs and cognitive style of autistic individuals when using these resources. Some native applications on devices may be complex, on such occasions, using specific, simple, and intuitive applications can provide complete visual information, including images if it is necessary.

It is also important to note that these resources shouldn't be used passively. Instead, individuals must be able to actively configure the contents to plan and achieve an appropriate level of self-sufficiency.

Collaborative features are often included in applications and programs that can be used across different devices linked to a single user account. One such feature is a shared calendar, which can provide support for autistic individuals by allowing a facilitator to remotely assist with time and activity management.

Developing self-management skills in daily life can be significantly aided by using technology. Technological supports can vary depending on the individual's needs, so the first step is to analyze those needs and determine the level of support necessary to perform various activities.

Once the individual's needs have been identified, appropriate resources can be selected. It is important to consider personal competencies to ensure that the chosen resources are easily understandable and usable.

Common technological resources used to support self-management include alarms, timers, and schedules. These resources can be used as both general-purpose applications or specific aids. Personal preferences should also be considered when selecting and using these resources to ensure maximum comfort and effectiveness.

4.2.4 Best Practices

Good practices for self-management skills are mainly based on the use of visual aids that contribute to improving the permanence of information to compensate for possible difficulties related to attention difficulties, executive functions, etc.

These visual aids should be adjusted to the cognitive and comprehension level of the person and can be used to improve the management of tasks, or temporal notions such as duration and order, and of the physical environment. All these aspects are easier to manage with the use of technological tools that allow the incorporation of variations and changes in a simple, effective, and high-quality way, and also offer many interaction options that improve the use with respect to conventional tools such as agendas in a physical/analogical format.

In addition, it is essential not only to have the appropriate tools to carry out activities and tasks autonomously but also to have a social environment that provides the necessary opportunities to develop them.

4.3 Self-regulation

4.3.1 Context

Self-regulation is a key process in human development that enables individuals to manage their emotions, behaviors, and cognitive responses based on environmental demands and personal goals. However, for autistic individuals, self-regulation becomes particularly essential and challenging. People on the autism spectrum often experience difficulties in social communication, exhibit rigid patterns of behavior and interaction, and have limitations in their ability to understand the perspectives of others, known as the Theory of Mind. As Baron-Cohen [3] emphasized, *"Theory of Mind, which involves the ability to attribute mental states to oneself and others, can be especially challenging in the context of autism."*

There is a direct correlation between self-regulation and quality of life for autistic individuals in society. Cognitive and behavioral inflexibility can lead to difficulties in adapting to changing situations, which can result in intense emotional responses or meltdowns. Inadequate self-regulation can increase stress and anxiety, exacerbating the tendencies toward inflexibility observed in autistic people. In addition, difficulty in communication and Theory of Mind also has an impact on self-regulation. Autistic individuals may have trouble expressing their needs and understanding their own and others' emotions, which can lead to frustration and increased anxiety.

This, in turn, affects their ability to self-regulate effectively. It is crucial to address self-regulation in autistic individuals to promote their well-being and their ability to lead an autonomous and satisfying life. This includes developing adaptive self-regulation strategies that enable them to manage their emotions and behaviors more effectively in a variety of situations. Teaching self-regulation skills can help autistic individuals to participate more successfully in daily activities and reduce the interference of autism symptoms on their global functioning.

4.3.2 Challenges

Autistic individuals have specific needs regarding the acquisition and development of self-regulation skills due to the unique characteristics of this disorder.

Autistic individuals often have difficulty identifying and managing their emotions, which may lead to emotional outbursts. Thus, they need specific strategies and support to regulate their emotions, such as learning to recognize emotional cues and using self-regulation techniques.

Problem-solving skills are essential for coping with stressful situations, and individuals within the autism spectrum can benefit from learning strategies to cope effectively with anxiety-provoking situations. Creating structured and predictable environments can help reduce anxiety in autistic individuals. They need clear routines and environments that minimize surprises and unpredictable situations.

Sensory sensitivity is common in autism, and it is crucial to consider individual sensory needs while providing sensory-appropriate activities and environments. Engaging in sensory-appropriate activities can be beneficial for autistic individuals to help them cope with anxiety and stress.

4.3.3 Opportunities

The utilization of native applications on mobile devices can be an effective means for individuals to engage in self-regulation. Such applications can assist with scheduling and reminders, as well as monitoring physical health using relaxation exercises, physical exercise tracking, and biometric measurement. Wearable technology can further enhance these capabilities, particularly concerning sensory aspects and the measurement of biometric parameters.

Smartwatches and physical activity bracelets, allow for continuous monitoring of parameters such as heart rate and can be configured to issue alerts when certain thresholds are exceeded. This functionality can facilitate the detection of moments of outburst [22], thereby improving self-awareness and enabling autistic individuals to better manage stress and anxiety.

These kind of devices are usually associated with health monitoring applications, which often offer a suite of features, that allow individuals to review their health history, establish new habits based on data, and track their progress toward meeting health goals. Such applications are also directly linked to physical exercise, which has been shown to be an effective means for improving self-regulation skills in those with autism.

The design of these resources, along with activity level measurements, provides a suitable foundation for establishing individualized exercise challenges. By enabling control over one's own body and actions, these resources can improve personal well-being and have numerous positive impacts, as outlined in the study by Dickinson and Place [6].

Modern health developments frequently incorporate mobile applications that offer tailored breathing exercises via smartphones and smartwatches. These exercises can effectively support autistic individuals in reducing anxiety levels by following customizable and visually guided breathing instructions. The intuitive design of these exercises provides an easily accessible tool for individuals struggling to focus on breathing techniques.

Other applications for handheld devices focus on mindfulness, meditation, and personal records. Both resources enable autistic people to observe their own emotional expressions more deeply to set personal challenges and develop strategies to improve their management.

Finally, it is worth emphasizing that smart headphones can also be very useful for people on the autism spectrum. The noise-cancellation feature of these devices can help create a comfortable and calm environment in noisy places which can be stressful for individuals with auditory hypersensitivity. This can help them participate in social settings more comfortably. Some models of smart headphones also have a feature that allows the modulation of different frequencies, which can help reduce sounds that are particularly bothersome to the user when using technology.

The ability to self-regulate is dependent on personal self-awareness, recognizing the elements that cause unease, anxiety, or discomfort, and understanding the physical and emotional signals that indicate one's mental state. This helps autistic individuals to employ prevention strategies that can avoid triggering an outburst or to utilize self-regulation strategies at the appropriate time to help them recover a normal arousal level more easily.

Self-regulation strategies vary from person to person, and it's important for everyone to determine which ones are most effective and comfortable for them in different contexts. Technological resources such as mood trackers and guided stress-reducing resources can be extremely helpful for monitoring and recording moods or significant body parameters.

By utilizing common and widely available devices, such as smartphones, smartwatches and smart headphones, autistic individuals can benefit from these supports without feeling stigmatized using specialized equipment.

4.3.4 Best Practices

Ensuring the well-being and development of autistic individuals requires effective management of anxiety, emotions, and stress. Given that autism is frequently associated with difficulties in communication, social interaction, and sensory sensitivities, regulating emotions poses a considerable obstacle. To overcome this challenge, a range of evidence-based practices and strategies are used to offer necessary support to people on the autism spectrum.

Cognitive-behavioral strategies have been proven to be effective therapeutic approaches for autistic individuals to cope with anxiety, emotions, and stress. These techniques aim to identify and modify negative thoughts and behaviors, allowing autistic individuals to recognize harmful patterns and replace them with more positive and adaptive responses. This results in better emotional regulation and more effective management of anxiety and stress [7].

In addition to cognitive-behavioral strategies, regular exercise is also a helpful tool in managing anxiety, emotions, and stress in both autistic adults and children. Physical activity leads to the release of endorphins, which can improve mood and reduce anxiety. Tailoring physical activities to the individual needs of the autistic person can also be an effective tool for emotional self-regulation, providing an opportunity to release tension and manage energy.

Developing self-regulation skills is crucial for autistic individuals to effectively manage anxiety, emotions, and stress. Through techniques such as deep breathing, utilizing calming cues, and identifying physical signs of anxiety, people on the autism spectrum can become more adept at understanding and controlling their emotional responses [21]. Fostering self-regulation is a vital step towards empowering autistic individuals to manage their emotions and navigate challenging situations.

These strategies can each play a significant role in mitigating anxiety, emotions, and stress for people on the autism spectrum. Depending on their unique needs and circumstances, a combination of these techniques may be necessary to achieve positive outcomes in emotional self-regulation.

4.4 Social Interaction

4.4.1 Context

Social interaction plays a fundamental role in personal autonomy and development of autistic individuals. However, it is also one of the defining characteristics of ASD according to the DSM-5. The diagnostic criterion establishes that persistent deficits in social communication and interaction are present, which means that many people on the autism spectrum face difficulties in stablishing meaningful relationships with others.

Although social interaction represents a significant challenge, it is essential for the well-being and growth of autistic individuals. In today's increasingly connected world, social interaction occurs not just in physical environments but also in digital ones. This digital space offers new opportunities to learn and to develop social skills, but it is important to understand the rules governing it and to know the tools that can facilitate social interaction.

This social interaction is very important as it promotes inclusion and acceptance in the environment, allowing interaction with other people, reducing isolation, and increasing opportunities for participation.

4.4.2 Challenges

One of the foremost needs is to establish meaningful relationships with others. However, due to challenges with social interactions, people on the autism spectrum often face exclusion and isolation [4]. Barriers such as lack of shared interests, limited participation in group activities, or difficulties in accessing social events can be encountered.

Autistic individuals may struggle to understand the rules implicit in social interactions or adopt a rigid and inflexible attitude when the rules are explained to them explicitly [2]. Understanding the codes of conduct that govern social interactions is a major challenge as it relates to a core characteristic of the disorder.

Finally, communication difficulties can be a significant obstacle to personal relationships. These difficulties can result in challenges in understanding the correct assignment of meanings, tones, and intentions, as well as expressive and conversational skills. Specific support is required to mediate these communicative exchanges and generate effective environments and situations of social communication.

4.4.3 Opportunities

Technology not only facilitates communication but also supports evidence-based interventions such as social skills training. These resources aid in participation and generalize learning to natural development contexts.

The digital world has provided an essential environment for social interaction in the past, with much less accessible devices and developments (with IRCs, MSN, etc. on PCs). Currently, this fact has only increased, enabling all this interaction in a limitless context regarding space and time with handheld devices. These tools must be incorporated into daily life since failure to use them will definitively lead to exclusion from reference groups by not participating in these "new" social forums.

The most frequently used media will differ according to the age, environment, and ability of each autistic person, but will generally include messaging applications, e-mail, video calls, and social networks, and eventually as it evolves surely the metaverse, and other virtual settings.

All these digital resources that involve communication and exchange with other people are governed by a set of rules called netiquette that provides recommendations for behavior in the use of these resources, with well-known examples such as writing in capital letters that are equivalent to shouting or the use of emojis to indicate non-verbal aspects of a text such as the expression of feelings associated with what has been commented.

Knowing this netiquette is a great advantage for people on the autism spectrum as they will be able to enrich their digital interactions in a more structured, visual, and understandable way than in face-to-face interactions, thus providing the opportunity to participate with a higher degree of complexity and having more time to decode and elaborate the different interactions, while reducing the stress of multichannel interactions that are very demanding sensory wise.

Also in this area, as in communication, it is necessary to highlight the important contributions being made by technologies based on the use of Artificial Intelligence. These developments offer a backup resource to ensure the social pulse interaction. Currently, it's widespread that communication doesn't necessarily co-occur, with an increasing number of studies involving youth social and communicative interaction reinforcing these appreciations. This scenario offers more ground for social interaction supported by technology for people on the spectrum as a normalized pattern. Also, the global connection existing through internet has broken down barriers to interacting and socializing among others with similar interests regardless of space and time making it fully functional.

The unstoppable development of AI is a very promising scenario. Currently many off-the-shelf tools frequently used for the generation of texts, translations, or digital content of any kind, incorporate or are adding AI features, for example, the cases of GrammarlyGo[3] or Canva.[4]

When reviewing a text with Grammarly you can choose different socio-emotional approaches to change the sense or perception of your message. These features enhance better social interaction with a very small effort, reducing stress, and increasing perception of control and success in social interaction. Some experimental developments such as KokoMind[5] provide a mixed ground of resources combining the power of AI from Chat GPT4,[6] social and interaction database from movies, and Theory of Mind based contents to build a massive database to work with.

4.4.4 Best Practices

Ensuring knowledge of the rules managing the social context is a critical outcome to facilitate meaningful participation of people on the autism spectrum in social settings both in the digital and physical world.

Handheld devices offer support to adjust the person's response in a specific setting almost in real-time. Wearables haven't developed as much as was expected to provide a life assistant that could interpret appropriately emotional responses of others, or at least they haven't evolved sufficiently to be effective, but eventually,

---

[3] https://www.grammarly.com/ai.
[4] https://www.canva.com/magic-design/.
[5] https://github.com/CHATS-lab/KokoMind.
[6] https://openai.com/gpt-4.

some of the current research might make a difference, and devices like Google glass might take a key role.

To ensure social success in interaction both ends need to be efficiently addressed: understanding a partner and adjusting to the context to respond appropriately. Wearables providing real time readings on biometrics related to anxiety, etc. provide explicit input that properly addressed will result in avoiding difficulties and managing distressful situations in advance of a possible meltdown or blackout.

Some apps aimed at monitoring noise can also provide a good insight to help monitor and regulate social interaction to keep the pattern of the interaction, lessening the effort in simultaneously keeping track of too many parameters apart from the content of the interaction.

4.5   Independent Living

4.5.1   Context

Independent living is a fundamental aspiration for all, but it holds particular significance for people on the autism spectrum. While the concept of autonomy is a common goal in adulthood, the unique challenges associated with autism often make achieving independent living a complex and demanding endeavor. The fact that services related to independent living frequently imply a lifelong span, is a key difference from other support services that have a defined time set. While educational systems, employment legislation, etc. provide a certain framework for different areas and the response of needs related to those contexts, in relation to independent living there is no framework to be found and the disparities in the concept, settings, resources, possibilities, etc. are so broad that makes it difficult to address as a unique reality.

Some figures from the Autism Society (USA), from the Autism Housing Network show that only 7% of autistic adults surveyed have access to support to live outside of their family home and over 75% of autistic adults report their top concern in securing housing is not being able to afford it. These numbers suggest a major need to provide support in this area.

All cognitive abilities implied in independent living are challenged or distorted with the vulnerabilities related to peculiar or altered communication and social interaction characteristics, like literal understanding, reading other's intentions, etc. all of which can lead to an extremely exposed consumer. The huge commercial pressure in advertising and sales policies can lead to increased feelings of insecurity, decreased self-esteem, lack of control, etc. Safety features are also critical content to address, both personal and community safety, as this can imply major difficulties in relation to domestic accidents, etc.

This area is also extremely sensitive as it involves major privacy features, that commonly are not shared among the community, regarding money use, habits, schedules, time distribution, and many other features that relate to your own personal way of living, that hugely varies between any individual.

For functional purposes, we'll be focusing on a scheme of supervised housing or supported independent living.

4.5.2 Challenges

Autistic individuals present complex and diverse needs in relation to independent living that can range from a sustained time extensive need of support to punctual specific training for taking the leap from a family setting to another living setting.

The management of a house is a massive task of executive functioning. In fact, it's an unbearable sequence of executive function features that simultaneously must be monitored, reset, etc. Health, safety, food, sleep, cleaning plus all the economic features involved. People on the spectrum frequently have difficulties in executive functioning, so the high demand for these skills implied in independent living can easily become overwhelming for many people who already must deal with very high levels of stress derived from social interactions.

The essence of independent living implies a major exposure to vulnerability related to autism features that are extremely conditioning for these settings. Core abilities involved in independent living involve social, cognitive, and communication skills.

4.5.3 Opportunities

Three key branches in this area can be identified: home automation [20]; voice assistants and smart home devices.

The amount of home automation devices available off the shelf is huge. Programing features of these devices offer the possibility of reinforcing adaptative routines that can benefit autistic people as the reduction of self-monitoring and the need of multitasking or at least to refocus attention continuously. This kind of setting in which blinds, lights, plugs, doors, TVs, or other major electronic appliances such as dishwashers, stoves, etc. can be programmed to comply with schedules and or existing rules, devices can be limited in their use time and therefore reduce anxiety and provide certainty and structure with the appearance of lack of direct supervision. This approach empowers self-esteem and increases independence for autistic people, providing easier and higher rates of environmental control as well as increasing security and certainty of many possible issues for the person and/or his support team.

The availability of all kinds of sensors, to track doors, windows, cabinets, etc. can play a relevant role in reminding situations, and responsibilities, being able to establish different sensory settings throughout the day can improve sleep patterns, manage temperatures not having to consistently monitor the weather, and specify comfortable temperature that relates to outside temperature automatically, reduce sensory overload, by having the vacuum work while the person leaves the house, and so many routines that can be combined: light intensity, TV volume, blinds position, etc.

The Internet of Things (IoT) opens a great world of possibilities depending on the appliances we refer to. Fridges are close to being able to remind of expiring dates on foods stored in, manage the availability of specific items, (like eggs or milk), and link the stock with a proposed shopping list. Cooking robots like Thermomix, are connected to the internet, and when choosing a recipe from a slightly visual menu it can send to your handheld device a shopping list with all the goods required for the recipe. TVs can be programmed on time frames to ensure not interfere with work or study time. Small kitchen devices such as kettles, air fryers, etc. can also be controlled manually or programmed as a marker for shifting attention between tasks in addition to their developed features.

Voice assistants are a clear asset in this approach. Among the main features they offer is accessibility, on a mono channel interaction, limiting sensory overload with a huge consistency in their response, in a very short time of interaction most people refer to as reinforcing and engaging. Voice assistants increase engagement, by simplifying access to information, providing a social interaction training partner, etc.

Several studies have proposed the use of automated solutions in homes to enhance the living conditions of people on the autism spectrum (i.e., Embodied Empowerment[7] or SENSHOME Project[8]). These studies offer guidance on the implementation of domotic elements to improve sensory adjustment based on individual needs. Additionally, they suggest incorporating visual and sound elements in the living environment to promote personal autonomy and a better understanding of activities and context.

It is important to establish clear goals for a home automation system designed for autistic individuals. This will simplify the process of selecting and arranging the appropriate resources, which may be both specific to the individual's needs and commonly used.

Service providers are increasingly adopting these technologies in homing settings. Entities like Autismo Avila,[9] APNABI,[10] or Autismo Sevilla[11] in Spain have developed different home automation in their home services all with very satisfying results, though very few formal studies.

Amazon Alexa, Google Assistant, and Siri (Apple) are voice assistants that may be available through a mobile device but also employ the support of a smart speaker. These types of devices rely on voice interaction, so their use may be inaccessible to minimally verbal individuals on the autism spectrum.

Other formats employed by these speakers include the use of screens, which confers greater accessibility for many people by including visual elements in the interaction.

4.5.4 Best Practices

Ethics are a major concern when providing support in home services. The number of available sensors and devices in the market can offer very accessible resources

---

[7] http://www.jellevandijk.org/embodiedempowerment/.
[8] https://senshome.projects.unibz.it/en/home-2/.
[9] https://www.autismoavila.org.
[10] https://www.apnabi.eus.
[11] https://www.autismosevilla.org.

to ensure privacy while increasing safety and control for the support team, without a physical presence.

The reduction of cameras within the scope of privacy, such as in dorms, toilets, etc. is a good practice to keep coherence with safety statements related to intimacy, self-protection, etc.

Ensuring a "menu" on paper on features like environments or settings established on the voice assistants can help ensure the knowledge and use of the devices by any person.

Having supervised accounts for shopping environments ensures error free use and prevents from abuse or rigidness. Having the users request their needs the order must be authorized by a third person that has the capability of readjusting if necessary.

Amazon's Alexa allows through *Blueprints* to develop personalized skills to respond to specific interests or needs.

5   Conclusion

The current amount of solid scientific evidence is little, to ensure a positive correlation between the use of handheld devices and an improvement in independence levels. Although we can conclude by firsthand testimonies, surveys, and recorded impressions from diverse support teams that there is a clear perception of a positive effect, and undoubtedly no harm or possible side effect that raises concerns. Any implementation should be the consequence of an assessment of the person, and his/her context trying to provide a response to the displayed needs. Advanced setup features are required to ensure the adjustment of device capabilities and the person's needs. The adoption of current technology by people on the spectrum is not only an opportunity but also a need in order not to sustain the digital divide.

References

1. American Psychiatric Association (2013) Diagnostic and statistical manual of mental disorders, 5th edn. https://doi.org/10.1176/appi.books.9780890425596
2. Attwood A (1997) Asperger's syndrome: a guide for parents and professionals. Jessica Kingsley Publishers
3. Baron-Cohen S (1985) Does the autistic child have a "theory of mind"? Cognition 21(1):37–46. https://doi.org/10.1016/0010-0277(85)90022-8
4. Bauminger N, Kasari C (2000) Loneliness and friendship in high-functioning children with autism. Child Dev 71(2). https://doi.org/10.1111/1467-8624.00156
5. Dawson G, Rogers S, Munson J, Smith M, Winter J, Greenson J, Varley J (2010) Randomized, controlled trial of an intervention for toddlers with autism: the early start denver model. Pediatrics 125(1):e17–e23. https://doi.org/10.1542/peds.2009-0958
6. Dickinson K, Place M (2014) A randomised control trial of the impact of a computer-based activity programme upon the fitness of children with autism. Autism Res Treat 2014:419653. https://doi.org/10.1155/2014/419653

7. Factor RS, Swain DM, Antezana L, Muskett A, Gatto AJ, Radtke SR, Scarpa A (2019) Teaching emotion regulation to children with autism spectrum disorder: outcomes of the stress and anger management program (STAMP). Bull Menninger Clin 83(3):235–258. https://doi.org/10.1521/bumc.2019.83.3.235
8. Flippin M, Reszka S, Watson LR (2010) Effectiveness of the picture exchange communication system (PECS) on communication and speech for children with autism spectrum disorders: a meta-analysis. Am J Speech Lang Pathol 19(2):178–195. https://doi.org/10.1044/1058-0360(2010/09-0022)
9. Goldsmith TR, LeBlanc LA (2004) Use of technology in interventions for children with autism. J Early Intensive Behav Interv 1(2):166–178. https://doi.org/10.1037/h0100287
10. Grandin T (2009) Thinking in pictures. Bloomsbury Publishing
11. Harrison PL, Oakland T (2015) Adaptive behavior assessment system, 3rd edn. Carlen Henington and Tony Wu
12. Hassrick EM, Holmes LG, Sosnowy C, Walton J, Carley K (2021) Benefits and risks: a systematic review of information and communication technology use by Autistic People. Autism Adulthood: Challeng Manag 3(1):72–84. https://doi.org/10.1089/aut.2020.0048
13. Kasari C, Smith T (2013) Interventions in schools for children with autism spectrum disorder: methods and recommendations. Autism: Int J Res Pract 17(3):254–267. https://doi.org/10.1177/1362361312470496
14. Lord C, Risi S, DiLavore PS, Shulman C, Thurm A, Pickles A (2006) Autism from 2 to 9 years of age. Arch Gen Psychiatr 63(6):694–701. https://doi.org/10.1001/archpsyc.63.6.694
15. Moreno L, Martínez P, Alarcon R (2022) Requirements and design patterns for an accessible video conferencing tool. In: Proceedings of the XXII international conference on human computer interaction, pp 1–9. https://doi.org/10.1145/3549865.3549894
16. Moreno L, Petrie H, Martínez P, Alarcon R (2023) Designing user interfaces for content simplification aimed at people with cognitive impairments. Univ Access Inf Soc 1–19. https://doi.org/10.1007/s10209-023-00986-z
17. Odom SL, Boyd BA, Hall LJ, Hume K (2010) Evaluation of comprehensive treatment models for autistic individuals spectrum disorders. J Autism Dev Disord 40:425–436. https://doi.org/10.1007/s10803-009-0825-1
18. Odom SL, Collet-Klingenberg L, Rogers SJ, Hatton DD (2010) Evidence-based practices in interventions for children and youth with autism spectrum disorders. Prev Sch Fail: Alternat Educ Children Youth 54(4):275–282. https://doi.org/10.1080/10459881003785506
19. Ozonoff S, Pennington BF, Rogers SJ (1991) Executive function deficits in high-functioning autistic individuals: relationship to theory of mind. J Child Psychol Psychiatr 32(7):1081–1105. https://doi.org/10.1111/j.1469-7610.1991.tb00351.x
20. Santo J, Kirilo CZ, Nogueira M, Santos N, Machado RJ, Lozano LCM, Carvalho J (2021) Home automation for people with autism spectrum disorder. In: International conference on computational science and its applications. Springer International Publishing, Cham, pp 119–141. https://doi.org/10.1007/978-3-030-86976-2_9
21. Torrado JC (2018) Tecnologías móviles y wearables para la autorregulación emocional de personas con Trastornos del Espectro Autista (Doctoral dissertation, Universidad Autónoma de Madrid)
22. Torrado JC, Gomez J, Montoro G (2017) Emotional self-regulation of autistic individuals spectrum disorders: smartwatches for monitoring and interaction. Sensors (Basel, Switzerland) 17(6):1359. https://doi.org/10.3390/s17061359
23. World Health Organization (2001) ICF: international classification of functioning, disability, and health. Switzerland, Geneva
24. World Health Organization (2013) How to use the ICF: a practical manual for using the international classification of functioning, disability and health (ICF). Exposure draft for comment. Geneva, Switzerland

Using *eCoaching* to Promote Independent and Effective Functioning of Neurodiverse Learners

Laura C. Chezan, Annemarie L. Horn, Jin Liu, and Whitney Idol

Abstract

One of the critical factors that contribute to the effectiveness of evidence-based practices (EBPs) to promote positive social-communication, behavioral, and academic outcomes for neurodiverse learners is implementation fidelity or the extent to which EBPs are implemented as planned. Learning to implement EBPs with fidelity requires explicit training and multiple practice opportunities. One approach to promote the adoption and implementation fidelity of EBPs with neurodiverse learners across settings consists of providing effective training to educators and parents to implement specific and complex interventions correctly. *e*Coaching is an evidence-based training that has been demonstrated to improve the implementation fidelity of EBPs in educators and parents. In this chapter, we will provide an overview of *e*Coaching and discuss its application to educators, neurodiverse learners, and parents. We will begin by defining the concept of *e*Coaching with bug-in-ear (BIE) technology. Next, we will provide a historical overview of the evolution of *e*Coaching with BIE technology and discuss the different terms used to refer to this training approach. Then, we

L. C. Chezan (✉)
Department of Human Movement Studies and Special Education, Old Dominion University, Norfolk, USA
e-mail: lchezan@odu.edu

A. L. Horn · W. Idol
School of Teacher Education and Leadership, Radford University, Radford, USA
e-mail: alhorn1@radford.edu

W. Idol
e-mail: widol@radford.edu

J. Liu
Department of Educational Leadership and Policy Studies, University of Texas at Arlington, Arlington, USA
e-mail: jin.liu@uta.edu

will discuss several considerations related to the successful and ethical implementation of *e*Coaching with BIE technology. We will continue by reviewing empirical studies that examined the effects of *e*Coaching with BIE technology on skill acquisition in educators, neurodiverse learners, and parents. Finally, we will end the chapter by presenting directions for future research and practice on *e*Coaching with BIE technology.

Keywords

*e*Coaching • Neurodiverse learners • Evidence-based practices • Educators • Families

1 Introduction

Federal mandates, such as the *Every Student Succeeds Act* (ESSA) [1] and the *Individuals with Disabilities Education Improvement Act* (IDEIA) [2] require educators to use practices grounded in scientific research when teaching neurodiverse learners. Furthermore, the IDEIA mandates that parents of learners with disabilities must be part of their children's educational decision-making process including the selection, development, and implementation of interventions. A large body of empirical evidence exists identifying evidence-based practices (EBPs) that have been demonstrated to promote positive social-communication, behavioral, and academic outcomes for neurodiverse learners and, consequently, enhance their quality of life [3–6]. EBPs are practices evaluated through rigorous research that (a) are supported by empirical evidence, (b) have been tested across diverse groups of learners, (c) promote positive learner outcomes, and (d) reduce the research-to-practice gap [7–9].

One critical factor that contributes to the effectiveness of EBPs is the implementation fidelity or the extent to which an intervention is implemented as planned [10]. Despite its significant importance to the successful use of EBPs with neurodiverse learners, the implementation fidelity of these interventions remains a challenge in education [11, 12]. Several reasons for the low level of implementation fidelity of EBPs are the insufficient training received by educators in their academic training programs and the lack of generalization to classroom settings [11, 13, 14], and the limited support received by parents to use EBPs with their children at home [15]. For example, educators reported both the limited training on EBPs and the low level of confidence in using these interventions as the main factors that hinder the adoption and use with fidelity of EBPs with learners with disabilities [16–18].

One approach to promote the adoption and implementation fidelity of EBPs with neurodiverse learners across settings consists of providing effective training to educators and parents to implement specific and complex interventions correctly. *e*Coaching is an evidence-based training that has been demonstrated to improve the implementation fidelity of EBPs in educators and parents [19, 20] and to promote positive outcomes when delivered directly to neurodiverse learners [21, 22]. Our purpose in this chapter is to provide an overview of *e*Coaching and to discuss its application to educators, neurodiverse learners, and parents. First, we will define the concept of *e*Coaching with bug-in-ear (BIE) technology. Second, we will provide a historical overview of the evolution of *e*Coaching with BIE technology and discuss the different terms used to refer to this training approach. Third, we will discuss several considerations related to the successful and ethical implementation of *e*Coaching with BIE technology. Fourth, we will review empirical studies that examined the effects of *e*Coaching with BIE technology on skill acquisition in educators, neurodiverse learners, and parents. Finally, we will end the chapter by presenting directions for future research and practice on *e*Coaching with BIE technology.

2 Defining *e*Coaching with Bug-In-Ear Technology

A lack of consensus exists in the literature on how *e*Coaching with BIE technology is defined. For example, Rock and colleagues [23] broadly define *e*Coaching as "a relationship in which one or more persons' effective teaching skills are intentionally and potentially enhanced through online interactions with another person" (p. 162). *e*Coaching has also been defined as a relationship mediated through email or other media [24] or as a relationship between a coach and a coachee mediated through technology with the goal of facilitating the coachee's learning [25]. Other definitions of *e*Coaching refer to a coach or consultant providing feedback to another person remotely through a videoconferencing platform [10, 26] or through a wireless earpiece (i.e., BIE communication device) from the same location at a distance [27]. In this book chapter, we will use the last two definitions of *e*Coaching because of their appropriateness and relevance to the field of education and neurodiverse learners.

*e*Coaching provided remotely through an online videoconferencing platform has been referred to in the literature as *e*Coaching with online BIE technology [23]. One of the main advantages of *e*Coaching with online BIE technology is that the coach can provide immediate feedback without being onsite while allowing the coachee to practice the target behavior multiple times within a session [11, 23, 28]. *e*Coaching provided through a wireless earpiece from the same location at a distance has been referred to as Covert Audio Coaching (CAC) [27–29]. One of the main benefits of CAC is that the coach can provide prompting and immediate feedback to the coachee in a natural and unintrusive way without being in their physical proximity, which reduces the likelihood of stigmatization, especially for neurodiverse learners [29, 30]. Furthermore, CAC allows the coach to provide immediate feedback privately without disrupting the ongoing activities taking place in schools and community settings [10]. Neurodiverse learners who have received CAC report the intervention to be useful in improving their social-communication skills [30, 31].

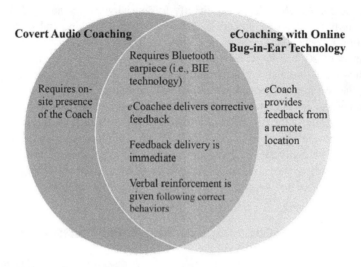

Fig. 1 Comparison of Covert Audio Coaching and eCoaching with online bug-in-ear technology

Figure 1 highlights the similarities and differences between *e*Coaching with online BIE technology and CAC. Although the *e*Coaching with online BIE technology extends the utility of coaching because of the remote nature in which feedback is delivered [11, 32], both *e*Coaching methods are valuable and effective in promoting skill acquisition and positive learner outcomes [20]. It is important to mention that the location of the coach should be determined based on the goal of the intervention, the target population receiving the intervention, and the contextual variables (e.g., resources, trained staff, leadership) that may influence the implementation of *e*Coaching. For example, when the goal of *e*Coaching is to teach neurodiverse learners socially significant behaviors that enhance their learning and independence, it may be preferable to use CAC which allows the coach to be onsite but at a distance. However, when the goal of *e*Coaching is to enhance the implementation fidelity of EBPs used by educators or parents, *e*Coaching with online BIE technology may be preferred over CAC because it allows the coach to provide immediate feedback remotely without traveling to a specific location [32].

3 The Evolution of eCoaching with Bug-In-Ear Technology

The concept of BIE technology received increased attention in the 1950s when researchers started to investigate the effectiveness of technology-enabled training on teaching learners without disabilities to engage in a variety of skills in different fields of study such as psychology, medicine, and education. In psychology, Korner and Brown [33] used for the first time the "mechanical third ear device" with students during clinical psychology field supervision. The researchers described the "mechanical third ear device" as a useful tool that allowed supervisors to prompt and provide private, immediate feedback to students conducting interviews with patients during supervision and concluded that the use of the device was a promising approach for training professionals in the field of clinical psychology [33]. Similarly, Baum and Lane [34] investigated the effectiveness of a BIE communication device for training graduate students to administer intelligence tests during their academic training in psychometry. In medicine, Hunt [35] used a BIE communication device to teach interview skills to medical students and to train dentists studying pedodontics.

The BIE communication device was first used in the field of education in 1971. Herold and colleagues [36] described the applicability and effectiveness of a portable radio communication system (i.e., BIE communication device) on providing feedback to teachers during classroom activities. The researchers reported that the use of the BIE communication device produced better results than the traditional approach to supervision which did not allow coaches to provide immediate corrective feedback [32]. Beginning with 1980s, additional studies in which researchers examined the effects of BIE communication devices have been published in the field of education [37–39].

For example, Giebelhaus [38] demonstrated the effectiveness of immediate feedback provided through a "mechanical third ear device" (i.e., BIE communication device) on preservice teachers' correct use of instructional behaviors such as stating the lesson objectives, emphasizing the importance of the topic discussed, or providing practice opportunities during classroom activities. In more recent studies, researchers have also shown positive effects of immediate corrective feedback provided through a "wireless FM listening system" (i.e., BIE technology) on preservice teachers' use of the three-term contingencies in their classrooms [27] or the delivery of instruction to learners with disabilities [40]. Other terms have also been used in the literature to refer to the BIE communication device, including "wireless earphone" or "electronic audio-cueing system" [32].

Over the last 40 years, numerous researchers have examined the effectiveness of BIE technology on teaching a variety of skills to learners without disabilities. Recently researchers have focused their attention to the applicability of BIE technology to learners with disabilities and demonstrated its effectiveness on promoting positive outcomes [28–30]. Bennett and colleagues [28] argued that terms such as "mechanical third ear" or "BIE communication device" refer to the tools used to provide feedback and do not accurately describe the training approach. Consequently, they proposed the term CAC as a training method that allows the delivery of prompts and immediate feedback through a two-way communication system and headsets from a distance [28].

The empirical evidence documenting the effectiveness of BIE technology on promoting skill acquisition in learners with and without disabilities and the advancements in the field of technology over the last 40 years provided a solid foundation for the development of online BIE technology. In recent years, procedural changes in the delivery of feedback through BIE technology have occurred because of technological innovations and, thus, a new terminology emerged.

Specifically, Geißler [41] introduced the term *e*Coaching to refer to coaching sessions in which feedback was provided via electronic media such as emails, telephone, or Internet. *e*Coaching defined by Geißler has also been referred to as virtual coaching, online coaching, remote coaching, or digital coaching [42].

In the field of special education, Rock and colleagues [32] introduced the term *e*Coaching with online BIE technology to refer to coaching sessions in which immediate feedback was provided to coachees through videoconferencing and a BIE communication device. Rock and colleagues examined the effects of *e*Coaching with online BIE technology on the teachers' use of research-based teaching strategies. Findings revealed that the training was effective in increasing teachers' use of praise statements and research-based teaching strategies. Furthermore, the teachers reported that *e*Coaching with online BIE technology was a useful and acceptable training approach. This study was the first empirical demonstration to show that the delivery of immediate feedback using BIE technology does not require the physical presence of a coach onsite if the BIE technology is paired with videoconferencing and, thus, made a noteworthy contribution to the field of special education.

After the publication of the study conducted by Rock and colleagues [32], numerous researchers have adopted *e*Coaching with online BIE technology to deliver training and support to educators [11, 43], neurodiverse learners [21, 44], and parents [19, 45]. Several factors have contributed to the adoption of *e*Coaching with online BIE technology in the field of special education, including multiple opportunities for application-based learning [46], its acceptability and usefulness in promoting acquisition, generalization, and maintenance of skills [23, 32, 47]. As new technologies are being developed, *e*Coaching with online BIE technology will continue to evolve over time and influence training practices and their implementation in education.

4   Considerations of *e*Coaching with BIE Technology

Several considerations are critical when implementing *e*Coaching with BIE technology. The first consideration when using *e*Coaching with BIE technology is the delivery of performance feedback (PF) during the sessions. PF has been defined as the written or verbal information about one's performance on one or multiple target behaviors that allows the individual to modify their behavior with the goal of improving learning [48, 49]. Three characteristics of PF should be considered to promote a successful implementation of *e*Coaching with BIE technology. First, the delivery of PF should be immediate. Immediate PF has been defined as feedback delivered within 3 s of the target behavior [23, 43, 50, 51]. Researchers have demonstrated that immediate PF is more effective in promoting learning compared to delayed PF in most situations [46, 52].

Second, PF delivered when a behavior is performed incorrectly should be corrective, behavior specific, and positive (i.e., corrective feedback) [51]. In other words, corrective PF should be objective and clearly state the behavior that was not implemented or implemented incorrectly during the *e*Coaching session. An example of corrective PF is "When you provide two choices of activities to the child, you have to wait for the child to request one of two activities before you allow them to engage with the activity." When the behavior is implemented correctly, PF should also be behavior specific and positive by acknowledging the correct performance of the target behavior (i.e., affirmative feedback). An example of affirmative feedback is "You used the token economy correctly when you gave Ann a token immediately after she raised her hand to ask a question during math class." To promote a change in behavior, it is critical that PF is delivered consistently across sessions. Immediacy, specificity, quality, and consistency are essential features of PF that allow a coachee to shape their behavior within the context of multiple practice opportunities [11, 51].

Third, goodness of fit in terms of the PF style (i.e., running commentary versus key words and phrases) [11] should be considered prior to implementing *e*Coaching with BIE technology. To promote the successful implementation of *e*Coaching with BIE technology and to maximize its effectiveness in facilitating learning, the PF style has to be individualized and aligned with the level of support needed by a coachee to acquire the target behaviors. For example, simple key words or phrases (e.g., "Be specific.") may be sufficient to shape an educator's behavior, whereas a neurodiverse learner may need more substantial support such as the coach modeling the correct response to learn the target behavior [21].

The second consideration when using *e*Coaching with BIE technology is the technology needed to successfully implement the sessions. When using *e*Coaching with online BIE technology, a fast and reliable wireless internet connectivity, and a videoconferencing platform such as Zoom, Skype, or WebEx are needed for livestreaming the sessions [50]. Coachees should have access to a computer, a wide-angle camera, a Bluetooth adapter, and a Bluetooth earpiece, whereas the coach should have access to a headset with microphone and a webcam with microphone unless they are built in the computer [23, 32]. Recently, researchers have recommended more sophisticated technologies such as a Swivel and a telepresence robot [53]. Swivel is a device that automatically follows a person wearing a transmitter, whereas a telepresence robot can physically move in a specific location while being controlled remotely by an observer [10]. Although the Swivel and the telepresence robot are very useful in providing opportunities for coaching across environments, they are more costly and may not be affordable to everyone.

When using CAC that requires the physical presence of the coach onsite but at a distance, the internet connectivity, the videoconferencing platform, the webcam, and the computer are not needed to provide immediate PF. In this case, the coach and coachee are usually connected through a phone and a Bluetooth device or other types of wired and wireless FM radio technologies. Regardless of the type of *e*Coaching with BIE technology and the devices used during the session, it is recommended to provide training to coachees on how to use the equipment prior to implementing *e*Coaching [26]. Furthermore, it is important to test the audio and video equipment and the internet connectivity prior to beginning the *e*Coaching session to avoid potential disruptions due to technology issues and to maximize the effectiveness of the *e*Coaching with BIE technology [10].

The third consideration when using *e*Coaching with BIE technology is its ethical implementation in research and practice. The videoconferencing platform used to connect synchronously during the *e*Coaching sessions, and the storage of the videorecorded files must be password protected and compliant with the Health Insurance Portability and Accountability Act (HIPAA) [54] and Family Educational Rights and Privacy Act (FERPA) [55] to minimize risks related to a breach in confidentiality. Furthermore, researchers and practitioners who use *e*Coaching with online BIE technology to conduct research or provide services to neurodiverse learners and their families must obtain informed consent prior to training implementation [10]. When *e*Coaching with online BIE technology is provided in a setting where other individuals not involved in training are present, researchers should also obtain informed consent from these individuals [56].

5   Applications of *e*Coaching with BIE Technology

5.1   *e*Coaching with BIE Technology for Educators

Providing immediate PF through *e*Coaching with BIE technology is an EBP for improving instruction [46]. Researchers have demonstrated that *e*Coaching with online BIE technology has been effective in increasing educators' implementation fidelity of EBPs to promote a variety of social-communication, behavioral, employment, and academic skills in neurodiverse learners [11, 43, 57–59].

5.2   Prompting

Prompting is an EBP consisting of the delivery of a supplemental cue in addition to an instruction to increase the likelihood that a learner will respond correctly [60]. For example, an educator may tell a learner "Show me the red circle" (i.e., instruction) while simultaneously pointing to a red circle placed on the table (i.e., prompting) to increase the likelihood that the learner will touch the red circle. Although prompting is one of the most frequently used EBPs, some educators reported that they have not received training on how to use prompting correctly with their learners [17]. Therefore, researchers have examined the effects of *e*Coaching with online BIE technology on increasing educators' implementation fidelity of prompting in applied settings.

Modeling is a type of prompt used to demonstrate the correct performance of a target behavior and it has been used with neurodiverse learners [61]. Nevertheless, researchers have reported that some educators struggle to generalize the use of modeling across a variety of novel routines in the classroom [62]. To expand the empirical evidence on generalization, Grygas Coogle and colleagues [63] examined the effects of *e*Coaching with online BIE technology on educators' use of modeling to promote functional communication in autistic children across child-led, teacher-lead, and mealtime routines. During the *e*Coaching sessions, the coach provided prompts at a rate of one per minute and immediate corrective or affirmative PF to educators on their use of modeling to promote communication in autistic children during the three types of classroom routines. The purpose of the corrective PF was to provide guidance on how to use a strategy correctly, whereas the purpose of affirmative PF was to acknowledge an educator's correct and independent use of modeling. Results revealed that educators increased their use of modeling to promote communication in autistic children and they reported the intervention as being socially valid. Furthermore, generalization data revealed that one educator used modeling within all routines, whereas another educator used modeling only in two of the three routines. The study conducted by Coogle and colleagues [63] highlights the need to program for generalization when training educators by providing PF across multiple activities.

Time delay is a unique prompting procedure consisting of the insertion of a brief interval of time or a pause between the delivery of an instruction and the provision of a prompt to allow the learner to emit an independent response [60]. Although time delay is an EBP for neurodiverse learners, the application of this procedure to teach new skills is very often limited to the classroom setting [43]. To extend its use in the natural environment, Horn and colleagues [43] evaluated the effects of a constant time delay (CTD) and *e*Coaching intervention package on the acquisition, generalization, and maintenance of job skills (i.e., sorting clothing by size on rack) in four transition-age autistic learners with co-occurring intellectual disability (ID) in a clothing store. Results indicated that *e*Coaching with online BIE technology increased the educator's implementation fidelity of CTD and all learners acquired the target job skill. Furthermore, results revealed that the learners generalized and maintained the newly acquired skills. The educator and learners reported that *e*Coaching with online BIE technology was a socially valid intervention that could be used to teach job-related skills to neurodiverse learners.

5.3 Behavior Specific Praise

Behavior specific praise (BSP) is an EBP consisting of a behavior-specific statement and positive reinforcement of a target behavior [64]. An example of BSP is an educator saying, "Nice job raising your hand" to a learner immediately after they raise their hand to ask a question. BSP has been effective in increasing learner engagement [65] and promoting a positive learning environment [66]. Considering the low complexity level of BSP and its potential benefits in promoting positive learner outcomes, researchers have used job-embedded *e*Coaching with BIE online technology to train educators to provide PF to paraeducators using BSP during instructional activities with neurodiverse learners [59, 67].

Scheeler and colleagues [59] examined the effects of *e*Coaching with BIE technology on paraeducators' acquisition of BSP. All sessions took place in a classroom setting during instructional activities that focused on academic and social behavior goals. Results indicated that eCoaching with BIE technology was effective in promoting paraeducators' use of contingent BSP with autistic learners and the participants rated the training as efficient and feasible. The ecological validity of this study was enhanced by the delivery of eCoaching by educators during typical instructional activities in the classroom which may promote sustainability of the intervention over time. Horn and colleagues [67] conducted a similar job-embedded training with paraeducators working with transition-age autistic learners. However, Horn and colleagues used eCoaching with online BIE technology to provide PF on paraeducators' use of BSP in a different context, namely 1:1 independent work with learners. Findings suggested that eCoaching with online BIE technology was not only effective in promoting the correct use of BSP but also rated as a socially valid intervention for paraeducators. Moreover, results showed improvements in learners' social-communicative behaviors such as eye contact, facial expression, and verbalization/vocalization contingent on the delivery of BSP by the paraeducator.

5.4 Naturalistic Communication Interventions

Incidental Teaching (IT) is an EBP consisting of an adult first modifying a child's natural environment and contriving opportunities for child-initiated interactions to request access to a preferred item, activity, or assistance and then using prompts and natural reinforcers to promote skill acquisition [58]. IT is considered a naturalistic communication intervention and has been most frequently used to teach language skills to neurodiverse learners who have communication and language delays. A large body of research has demonstrated the effectiveness of IT in teaching a multitude of skills to neurodiverse learners across different environments [68, 69].

Rosenberg and colleagues [58] evaluated the effects of eCoaching with online BIE technology on paraeducators' implementation of IT to teach self-advocacy statements to neurodiverse learners. All study sessions took place in a school setting during instructional activities targeting learners' self-advocacy statements. Results revealed a functional relation between eCoaching with online BIE technology and paraeducators' accurate use and rate of IT. Neurodiverse learners also increased their use of self-advocacy statements after paraeducators received eCoaching on the use of IT. Furthermore, both the paraeducators and the learners maintained the newly acquired skills after eCoaching ended. This study made a noteworthy contribution to the field of special education because it was the first experimental investigation of eCoaching with online BIE technology with paraeducators.

Embedded learning opportunities (ELO) is a type of naturalistic communication intervention in which an adult intentionally creates an opportunity for a child to communicate, prompts the child to emit a correct response, and provides access to the desired outcome contingent on the child's prompted or independent correct response [70]. For example, an educator who wants to increase a child's vocal responses may hold a bubble container in the child's sight but out of reach, prompt the child to vocalize, and then blow bubbles contingent on the child's vocalization. ELOs have been effective in teaching a variety of skills, including social-communication skills to neurodiverse learners and communication and language delays [71, 72].

Grygas Coogle and colleagues [70] compared the effects of eCoaching with online BIE technology and electronic PF on the correct use of ELOs by preservice special education preschool teachers working with autistic children. eCoaching with online BIE technology consisted of immediate corrective and affirmative PF delivered to teachers during typical activities with children in the classroom. Delayed PF consisted of corrective and affirmative PF provided to teachers within 1 h of completing the observation session. Findings revealed that although delayed PF increased teachers' correct use of ELOs compared to baseline, the addition of eCoaching with online BIE technology resulted in a more substantial improvement. Findings also indicated that teachers maintained the use of ELOs after the intervention ended, but only one of the three teachers generalized the strategy with novel routines not included in training. One of the limitations of the study was that the researchers did not conduct a component analysis to determine which of the two interventions was responsible for the increase in teachers' use of ELOs or whether the change in behavior was a combined effect of the two interventions. Despite this limitation, the study conducted by Google and colleagues adds empirical evidence to the limited body of research examining the effects of multiple types of PF on improving teachers' use of ELOs and generalization of skills.

5.5 Opportunities to Respond

Opportunities to respond (OTR) is an EBP consisting of an educator providing an instruction, waiting for a response, and providing a prompt to promote a student correct response [73]. Researchers have demonstrated that providing learners with multiple OTR increases their academic engagement during instruction, promotes appropriate behavior, and results in more correct responses [74, 75]. In addition, educators who use OTR in their classrooms are more likely to develop efficient behavior classroom management systems [73]. Although OTR is an easy-to-implement EBP that does not require intensive training and has benefits for educators and learners, many educators do not embed OTR in their daily instructional practices or provide limited OTR especially to learners with low levels of academic performance [74]. Thus, researchers have focused on training educators to use OTR with neurodiverse learners.

Randolph and colleagues [57] examined the effects of eCoaching with online BIE technology on educators' correct use of OTR with autistic learners in the classroom. All study sessions were conducted during typical activities in the classroom. eCoaching consisted of the researcher observing the activity and providing prompts and PF to educators on the use of OTR. Results indicated that educators' implementation fidelity and number of OTR increased after eCoaching and an improvement in learners' correct responses has also been documented. In addition, three of the four educators who participated in the study perceived *e*Coaching as being a helpful and feasible training approach in a classroom, whereas one educator reported that receiving prompts and PF during instructional activities was disruptive. The study conducted by Randolph and colleagues added empirical evidence to the literature on effective training approaches to promote the adoption and use of EBPs with fidelity in classroom settings.

In summary, developing and implementing effective training approaches to promote the adoption and use of EBPs with neurodiverse learners remains one of the critical aspects of educator preparation programs and professional development. Educators' use of EBPs with fidelity has been associated with improvements in learners' social-communication, behavioral, employment, and academic outcomes. The limited body of literature on *e*Coaching with BIE technology has shown that *e*Coaching can be used to teach and provide educators with the support needed to implement a wide variety of EBPs in their classrooms with neurodiverse learners [57, 58].

6 *e*Coaching with BIE Technology for Neurodiverse Learners

Researchers have examined the effects of *e*Coaching with BIE technology on the acquisition and generalization of various skills in neurodiverse learners [21, 28, 76, 77]. The research on the effectiveness of *e*Coaching with BIE technology on teaching employment, social-communication, and academic skills to neurodiverse learners is in its infancy. However, the limited empirical evidence on this topic suggests that *e*Coaching with BIE technology can enhance the behavioral repertoire of neurodiverse learners.

6.1 Employment Skills

Obtaining and maintaining employment has been associated with an improved quality of life for neurodiverse learners [78]. The United States Department of Labor Bureau of Labor Statistics [79] reported that only 19% of learners with disabilities were employed in 2021 compared to 64% of typical learners. The percentage of employment rates is even lower for neurodiverse learners: 39.4% for learners with multiple disabilities, 37.2% for autistic learners, and 33% for learners with ID [80, 81]. To better prepare neurodiverse learners for competitive employment, researchers have examined the effectiveness of *e*Coaching with online BIE technology and CAC on teaching job interview skills [21], clerical skills [29], and job task engagement [43, 82].

Horn and colleagues [21] investigated the effects of *e*Coaching with online BIE technology on the acquisition and maintenance of job interview skills in three transition-age autistic learners. All study sessions occurred via the Zoom videoconferencing platform. The intervention consisted of immediate PF delivered via online BIE technology during mock interview sessions in which the learners practiced responses to job interview questions. Results demonstrated a functional relation between *e*Coaching with online BIE technology and an increase in the level of performance on job interview skills for the learners included in the study. The acquired skills maintained up to 6 weeks postintervention. Furthermore, learners reported that they enjoyed receiving immediate PF from the coach during the mock job interview sessions. This study extends the limited literature on *e*Coaching with online BIE technology while demonstrating that this training approach is effective and acceptable for teaching soft skills, such as performance during job interviews to neurodiverse learners.

Bennett and colleagues [28] evaluated the effects of CAC on promoting employment skill fluency and maintenance in autistic learners. The intervention consisted of the coach providing immediate corrective and supportive statements on the steps of a task analysis for folding T-shirts using a two-radio communication system with headsets. All study sessions took place in the student lounge of the school and the coach implemented the intervention while onsite but at a distance. Results demonstrated that CAC was effective in producing fluency of folding T-shirts in the four learners who participated in the study. Moreover, findings revealed that the learners maintained the acquired skills for several weeks after the intervention ended and generalized the skills to their community-based worksite. One of the noteworthy contributions of this study is the focus on fluency of employment skills, an aspect that is very often overlooked in research and practice. Fluency has been defined as one's ability to complete a task both accurately and rapidly [83] and has been associated with generalization of skills [84]. Furthermore, fluency is a critical aspect of competitive employment and, thus, effective training programs should focus not only on acquisition but also on fluent behaviors in neurodiverse learners [28].

6.2 Social-Communication Skills

Social-communication skills are those skills that allow one to effectively communicate and interact socially with partners in the natural environment and include, but are not limited to, gaining a social partner's attention, engaging in culturally and contextually appropriate greetings, or initiating and maintaining conversations [85]. Many neurodiverse learners are characterized by deficits in social-communication skills and encounter challenges in communicating effectively during daily interactions [86, 87]. Although typically developing learners acquire social-communication skills through observation and imitation, neurodiverse learners require effective and systematic instruction to learn effective social-communication skills [85]. Several researchers have examined the effectiveness of CAC on teaching neurodiverse learners conversation skills in the workplace environment [22, 30, 44, 88], social interactions skills [82], and question asking [31].

Chezan and colleagues [30] examined the effects of CAC on the acquisition and maintenance of self-initiated conversations in three young autistic adults with co-occurring moderate ID. The study sessions were conducted in a recreational fitness facility where the young adults completed their employment training and had opportunities to engage in conversations with coworkers. The coach observed from a distance and prompted the learners through a BIE communication device to initiate a conversation with a coworker when an opportunity arose throughout the day. Findings showed that CAC was effective in promoting acquisition and maintenance of self-initiated conversations in neurodiverse learners and was perceived as acceptable both by the coach and by the learners. One of the most important contributions of this study is that the CAC took place in the natural environment where learners received employment training and their job coach implemented CAC during learners' engagement in conversations with coworkers which increased the social validity of the study.

Gregory and colleagues [88] conducted a study to investigate the effects of eCoaching with online BIE technology and online modules on promoting on-topic conversation skills in four autistic learners. Study sessions were conducted in a different location for each learner, including a dining hall on a university campus, the lobby of a business school building, and a local café. During the online instructional module phase, learners were required to watch one of two online modules targeting social-communication skills. During the eCoaching with online BIE technology, the coach and the learners were connected via a videoconferencing platform. The coach provided prompts and immediate PF through a BIE communication device during learners' conversations with peers. The researchers conducted a component analysis of the intervention package which revealed that eCoaching with online BIE technology was the most effective intervention in promoting acquisition of on-topic conversations for the learners included in this study. Furthermore, the learners reported that eCoaching with online BIE technology was helpful in improving their conversation skills and was preferred over in-person coaching that required the physical presence of the coach during conversations with peers.

In summary, the ability to initiate and maintain conversations with social partners and successfully obtain and maintain competitive employment are critical to the development of meaningful relationships, financial independence, and satisfaction with life. Engaging in conversations and completing job tasks are complex skills, and neurodiverse learners may require systematic and effective instruction to be successful and function effectively in their communities. eCoaching with online BIE technology and CAC are two effective and socially valid approaches supported by empirical evidence that have led to acquisition, fluency, and maintenance of employment related and social-communication skills in neurodiverse learners.

6.3 *eCoaching* with BIE Technology for Parents

One of the critical aspects of effective instructional programs for neurodiverse learners is family engagement. Family engagement refers to the inclusion of parents in the development, implementation, and evaluation of programs and activities designed to promote their children's development and well-being [89]. Researchers have demonstrated that family engagement has the potential to promote positive social and academic outcomes in neurodiverse learners [90, 91]. Furthermore, when parents use EBPs with their children in home and community settings and provide multiple opportunities for practice, children are more likely to generalize the newly acquired skills [92]. Thus, it is critical to use effective training to teach parents how to implement EBPs with their children [93]. The limited existing body of literature on the effectiveness of *e*Coaching with online BIE technology and CAC on training parents to implement interventions with their neurodiverse children shows promising results.

Oliver and Brady [94] conducted a study to examine the effects of CAC on mothers' interactions with their autistic children. All study sessions were conducted in the children's home during tasks and routines, such as making an art project, taking a bath, or getting dressed. During intervention sessions, the coach provided immediate PF to mothers via a BIE communication device on the use of prompts and praise with their children while observing from a distance. After the intervention ended, the researchers assessed mothers' generalization of the acquired skills to untrained tasks and routines. Results demonstrated that CAC was effective in increasing the level of mothers' interactions with their children and the skills generalized to tasks and routines not used in training. Furthermore, data revealed an increase in children's accurate completion of target tasks and routines after their mothers received CAC. This study represents the first empirical evaluation of the effects of CAC on training parents of neurodiverse children to implement effective interventions in home settings. One of the most important contributions of this study is the evaluation of skill generalization and the measurement of children's outcomes as a secondary variable.

Hamberger and colleagues [19] examined the effects of *e*Coaching with online BIE technology on increasing the use of natural communication opportunities by parents of young autistic children with language delays. Natural communication opportunities consisted of several strategies including providing choices, pausing during routines, using time delay, asking questions, and modeling specific behaviors. All sessions were implemented in the participants' homes during play activities. The coach provided prompts and immediate PF through a BIE communication device and videoconferencing. Findings demonstrated that *e*Coaching with online BIE technology was effective in increasing the use of natural communication opportunities in parents of young autistic children with language delays and the skills maintained after the intervention ended. Furthermore, parents rated the intervention to be acceptable and effective in improving their children's communication and reported that they would recommend it to other parents. An important aspect of this study was the use of *e*Coaching with online BIE technology as the only intervention to train parents how to implement EBPs rather than using an intervention package. Using only one intervention to teach parents how to use EBPs may reduce the time and costs associated with intervention packages while decreasing the complexity of training and increasing parents' adherence to training.

Drew and colleagues [45] examined the effects of an intervention package consisting of behavioral parent training and *e*Coaching with online BIE technology on promoting implementation fidelity of functional communication training in four parents of autistic children. All sessions were conducted in the participants' homes during typical routines including dinner, room cleaning, and toothbrushing. In the first phase, researchers used behavioral skills training consisting of didactic instruction, modeling, rehearsal, and feedback to teach parents to use functional communication training. In the second phase, researchers used *e*Coaching through online BIE technology to provide immediate PF to parents during the target family routines. Results indicated that the intervention package was effective in promoting high levels of implementation fidelity in parents' use of functional communication training and increased children's appropriate behavior while reducing challenging behavior. In addition, parents reported the intervention as being acceptable, feasible, and useful in promoting appropriate behavior in their children in the home setting. This study provides initial empirical evidence that *e*Coaching with online BIE technology can be used effectively to teach parents to use complex interventions and to promote children's positive outcomes.

In summary, parents' engagement is a critical aspect of successful implementation of effective educational programs for neurodiverse learners. Parents' use of EBPs with fidelity during typical routines in the home setting provides children with multiple learning and practice opportunities and leads to generalization and maintenance of new skills. Therefore, it is important to use effective training methods to teach parents to correctly implement EBPs with their children during typical family routines in the natural environment. The limited empirical evidence on *e*Coaching with online BIE technology and CAC demonstrate that these training methods are effective in training parents of neurodiverse learners to use EBPs that enhance learners' communication repertoire.

7   Directions for Future Research and Practice

Several aspects related to the use of *e*Coaching with BIE technology with educators, neurodiverse learners, and parents have conceptual and practical implications and warrant discussion. First, as we mentioned at the beginning of this chapter, a wide variability exists in how *e*Coaching with BIE technology has been defined and the terminology used to refer to this training approach in the literature. The multitude of definitions of *e*Coaching with BIE technology and inconsistencies in terminology pose challenges to the synthesis of findings across published studies on this topic and, thus, limits the interpretation of findings and the conclusions drawn. Researchers should focus their efforts on developing a clear and objective definition of *e*Coaching with BIE technology and use a consistent terminology to accurately describe the type of eCoaching used to train educators, parents, and neurodiverse learners.

Second, even though researchers have emphasized the importance of the immediacy, specificity, quality, and consistency of PF as essential dimensions of eCoaching with BIE technology, great variability exists in the literature regarding the delivery of PF. For example, some researchers provided PF on a timed schedule during the eCoaching sessions [56], whereas others provided PF aligned with the teacher's behavior [95]. Similarly, some researchers provided PF throughout the eCoaching sessions when an opportunity arose [59], whereas others provided PF at the end of the eCoaching session [96]. These variations in the delivery of PF pose challenges to accurately comparing findings across studies and drawing valid conclusions about the effectiveness of PF and eCoaching with BIE technology on promoting positive outcomes [46]. One potential solution to address this limitation is the development of guidelines for the use and evaluation of PF to promote consistent implementation of eCoaching with BIE technology across researchers and practitioners and, thus, minimize the potential influence on procedural changes on the effectiveness of the training.

Third, the main purpose of eCoaching with BIE technology in education is to train educators and parents to implement EBPs with fidelity and neurodiverse learners to function effectively and independently in the natural environment. However, as soon as the training goals have been achieved, the intervention should be gradually withdrawn to allow individuals to perform the acquired skills independently and to reduce dependence on the coach. Although researchers have highlighted the importance of fading eCoaching with BIE technology after the targeted intervention goals have been achieved [50, 59], this aspect is often overlooked in published studies. The question that arises is whether researchers are fading the eCoaching with BIE technology in their studies but do not describe these procedures or they do not fade the training. Researchers conducting future studies should also include fading procedures as a component of training procedures and examine the most effective and efficient approaches to fading the training.

Fourth, eCoaching with BIE technology has been perceived as an acceptable and useful training approach by most educators, neurodiverse learners, and parents. Although social validity of eCoaching with BIE technology has been reported in most of the published studies one aspect requires further investigation, namely the social validity of eCoaching with BIE technology reported by neurodiverse learners. Most learners perceived the training as acceptable; however, some learners reported that they did not like wearing the BIE communication device [30]. Therefore, it is important to not only examine learners' perception about this training approach at the end of the study, but also to involve learners in the selection of the most appropriate communication device or a different training in those cases when the BIE technology is not viewed as acceptable. Selecting interventions aligned with the learner's personal and cultural values and preferences is a critical requirement of any effective educational plan [97].

Finally, one aspect that has gained attention in recent years is the implementation of artificial intelligence (AI) in coaching. AI is broadly defined as the use of digital technologies to enhance, replace, or support human activity [24]. The research on AI in coaching is in its infancy. The limited existing evidence suggests that one reason for considering the use of AI in coaching is its ability to enhance one's performance [98], time efficiency in collection data, and a partnership between the coach and AI in which each partner leverages the strengths of the other [24]. Despite its potential benefits, the use of AI in coaching could also have negative effects or limitations that require further examination. One of such limitations is the inability of AI to shift from a predetermined algorithm (e.g., coachee-problem-solution) to a systemic perspective that requires consideration of contextual variables present in the coachees' environment and their influence on one's behavior [99]. As the adoption of AI in various domains of our lives including education is inevitable, it is imperative that researchers investigate and develop guidelines for promoting the effective and ethical use of AI in coaching with educators, neurodiverse learners, and parents.

References

1. Every Student Succeeds Act of 2015, 129 U. S. C. 1802 *et seq*. (2015). https://www.congress.gov/114/plaws/publ95/PLAW-114publ95/pdf
2. Individuals with Disabilities Education Improvement Act of 2004, 20 U.S.C. § 1400 *et seq*. (2004). https://sites.ed.gov/idea/statute-chapter-33
3. Alexander JL, Ayres KM, Smith KA (2015) Training teachers in evidence-based practice for autistic individuals spectrum disorder: a review of the literature. Teach Educ Spec Educ 38(1):13–27. https://doi.org/10.1177/0888406414544551
4. Council for Exceptional Children (2014) Council for exceptional children standards for evidence-based practices in special education. Teach Except Child 80(4):504–511. https://doi.org/10.1177/0040059914531389
5. Horner RH, Kratochwill TR (2012) Synthesizing single-case research to identify evidence-based practices: some brief reflections. J Behav Educ 21(3):266–272. https://doi.org/10.1007/s10864-012-9152-2
6. Steinbrenner JR, Hume K, Odom SL, Morin KL, Nowell SW, Tomaszewsk B, Szendrey S, McIntyre NS, Yücesoy-Őzkan S, Savage MN (2020) Evidence-based practices for children, youth, and young adults with autism. University of North Carolina at Chapel Hill, Frank Porter Graham Child Development Institute, National Clearinghouse on Autism Evidence and Practice Review Team
7. Singer GHS, Agran M, Spooner F (2017) Evidence-based and values-based practices for people with severe disabilities. Res Pract Persons Severe Disabil 43:62–72. https://doi.org/10.1177/1540796916684877
8. Slocum TA, Detrich R, Wilczynski SM, Spencer TD, Lewis T, Wolfe K (2014) The evidence-based practice of applied behavior analysis. Behav Anal 37(1):41–56. https://doi.org/10.1007/s40614-014-0005-2
9. Spencer TD, Detrich R, Slocum TAn(2012) Evidence-based practice: a framework for making effective decisions. Educ Treat Child 35(2):127–151. https://doi.org/10.1353/etc.2012.0013
10. Mason RA, Gregori E, Smith JE, Austin A, Crosley H (2022) Implementation of evidence-based practices. In: Chezan LC, Wolfe K, Drasgow E (eds) Evidence-based practices for supporting autistic individuals spectrum disorder. Rowman & Littlefield
11. Horn AL, Rock ML (2022) Practice with feedback makes permanent: *e*Coaching with bug-in-ear technology during clinical experiences. Invited article. J Spec Educ Prep 2(1):58–69. https://doi.org/10.33043/JOSEP.2.1.58-69

12. Simpson RL (2005) Evidence-based practices and students with autism spectrum disorders. Focus Autism Other Dev Disabil 20(3):140–149. https://doi.org/10.1177/10883576050200030201
13. Scheeler MC (2008) Generalizing effective teaching skills: the missing link in teacher preparation. J Behav Educ 17:145–159. https://doi.org/10.1007/s10864-007-9051-0
14. Vollmer TR, Sloman KN, St-Peter Pipkin C (2008) Practical implications of data reliability and treatment integrity monitoring. Behav Anal Pract 1:4–11. https://doi.org/10.1007/BF03391722
15. Pituch KA, Green VA, Didden R, Lang R, O'Reilly MF, Lancioni GE, Sigafoos J (2011) Parent reported treatment priorities for children with autism spectrum disorder. Res Autism Spectr Disord 5(1):135–143. https://doi.org/10.1016/j.rasd.2010.03.003
16. Brock ME, Huber HB, Carter EW, Juarez AP, Warren ZE (2014) Statewide assessment of professional development needs related to educating students with autism spectrum disorder. Focus Autism Other Dev Disabil 29(2):67–79. https://doi.org/10.1177/1088357614522290
17. Chezan LC, McCammon MN, Wolfe K, Drasgow E, Tabacu L (2023) Teachers' familiarity, confidence, training, and use of function-based interventions for learners with autism spectrum disorder in school settings. J Phys Dev Disabil 35:863–887. https://doi.org/10.1007/s10882-022-09885-2
18. Hsiao YJ, Sorensen Petersen S (2019) Evidence-based practices provided in teacher education and in-service training programs for special education teachers of students with autism spectrum disorder. Teach Educ Spec Educ 42(3):193–208. https://doi.org/10.1177/2F0888406418758464
19. Hamberger RJ, Evmenova AS, Coogle CG, Regan KS (2022) Parent coaching in natural communication opportunities through bug-in-ear technology. Top Early Childh Spec Educ 42(3):234–245. https://doi.org/10.1177/02711214221119031
20. Schaefer JM, Ottley JR (2018) Evaluating immediate feedback via bug-in-ear as an evidence-based practice for professional development. J Spec Educ Technol 33(4):247–258. https://doi.org/10.1177/0162643418766870
21. Horn AL, Chezan LC, Bobzien JL, Rock ML, Alturki A, Karadimou O (2023) You're hired! Effects of eCoaching transition-age students with autism during job interview preparation. Career Dev Transition Except Ind (Advance online publication). https://doi.org/10.1177/21651434231198492
22. Downey A, Kearney KB, Adams K, Brady MP, Berlingo L, Kenney S (2022) Effects of remote audio coaching during workplace conversations for college students with intellectual disabilities. J Vocat Rehabil 58:317–327. https://doi.org/10.3233/JVR-230020
23. Rock ML, Schumacker RE, Gregg M, Howard PW, Gable RA, Zigmond N (2014) How are they now? Longer term effects of eCoaching through online bug-in-ear technology. Teach Educ Spec Educ 27(2):161–181. https://doi.org/10.1177/0888406414525048
24. Clutterbuck D (2010) The future of AI in coaching. In: Clutterbuck D, Hussain Z (eds) Virtual coaching, virtual mentoring. Information Age
25. Boyce LA, Hernez-Broome (2010) E-coaching: consideration of leadership coaching in a virtual environment. In: Clutterbuck D, Hussain Z (eds) Virtual coaching, virtual mentoring. Information Age
26. Regan K, Weiss MP (2020) Bug-in-ear coaching for teacher candidates: what, why, and how to get started. Interv Sch Clin 55(3):178–184. https://doi.org/10.1177/1053451219842218
27. Scheeler MC, McAfee JK, Ruhl KL, Lee DL (2006) Effects of corrective feedback delivered via wireless technology on preservice teacher performance and student behavior. Teach Spec Educ 29:12–22. https://doi.org/10.1177/088840640602900103
28. Bennett KD, Ramasamy R, Honsberger T (2013) Further examination of covert audio coaching on improving employment skills among secondary students with autism. J Behav Educ 22:103–119. https://doi.org/10.1007/s10864-013-9168-2
29. Bennett KD, Ramasamy R, Honsberger T (2013) The effects of covert audio coaching on teaching clerical skills to adolescents with autism spectrum disorder. J Autism Dev Disord 43:585–593. https://doi.org/10.1007/s10803-012-1597-6

30. Chezan LC, Drasgow E, Grybos EM (2020) Conversation skills and self-initiated interactions in young adults with autism and intellectual disability. Res Autism Spectr Disord 75:1–12. https://doi.org/10.1016/j.rasd.2020.101554
31. Mason RA, Gregori E, Wills HP, Kamps D, Huffman J (2020) Covert audio coaching to increase question asking by female college students with autism: proof of concept. J Dev Phys Disabil 32:75–91. https://doi.org/10.1007/s10882-019-09684-2
32. Rock ML, Gregg M, Thead BK, Acker SE, Gable RA, Zigmond NP (2009) Can you hear me now? Evaluation of an online wireless technology to provide real-time feedback to special education teachers-in-training. Teach Educ Spec Educ 32(1):64–82. https://doi.org/10.1177/0888406408330872
33. Korner IN, Brown WH (1952) The mechanical third ear. J Consult Psychol 16:81–84
34. Baum D, Lane JR (1976) An application of the "bug-in-the ear" communication system for training psychometrists. Counselor Educ Supervis 15:309–310. https://psycnet.apa.org/doi/ https://doi.org/10.1002/j.1556-6978.1976.tb02010.x
35. Hunt DD (1980) "Bug-in-the-ear" technique for teaching interviewing skills. J Med Educ 55(11):964–966
36. Herold P, Ramirez M, Newkirk J (1971) A portable radio communication system for teacher education. Educ Technol 11(11):30–32. https://www.jstor.org/stable/44423318
37. Bowles EP, Nelson RO (1976) Training teachers as mediators: efficacy of a workshop versus the bug-in-ear technique. J Sch Psychol 14(1):15–25. https://doi.org/10.1016/0022-4405(76)90058-3
38. Giebelhaus CR (1994) The mechanical third ear device: a student teaching supervision alternative. J Teach Educ 45:365–373. https://doi.org/10.1177/0022487194045005009
39. van der Mars H (1988) The effects of audio-cueing on selected teaching behaviors of an experienced elementary physical education specialist. J Teach Phys Educ 8(1):64–72. https://doi.org/10.1123/jtpe.8.1.64
40. Goodman J, Brady MP, Duffy ML, Scott J, Pollard NE (2008) The effects of "bug-in-ear" supervision on special education teachers' delivery of learn units. Focus Autism Other Dev Disabil 23(4):207–216. https://doi.org/10.1177/1088357608324713
41. Geißler H (ed) (2008) E-coaching. Schneider Verlag Hohengehren
42. Geißler H (2010) E-coaching: an overview. In Clutterbuck D, Hussain, Z (eds) Virtual coaching, virtual mentoring. Information Age
43. Horn AL, Gable RA, Bobzien JL, Tonelson S, Rock M (2020) Teaching young adults job skills using a constant time delay and eCoaching intervention package. Career Dev Transit Except Individ 43(1):29–39. https://doi.org/10.1177/2165143419828983
44. Joseph B, Kearney KB, Brady MP, Downey A, Torres A (2021) Teaching small talk: on-topic conversational exchanges in college students with intellectual and developmental disabilities using remote audio coaching. Behav Modif 45(2):251–271. https://doi.org/10.1177/0145445520975174
45. Drew CM, Machaliceck W, Crowe B, Glugatch L, Wei Q, Ertuk B (2023) Parent-implemented behavioral interventions with telehealth for older children and adolescents. J Behav Educ 32:585–604. https://doi.org/10.1007/s10864-021-09464-z
46. Sinclair AC, Gesel SA, LeJeune LM, Lemons CJ (2020) A review of the evidence for real-time performance feedback to improve instructional practice. J Spec Educ 54(2):90–100. https://doi.org/10.1177/0022466919878470
47. Rock ML, Gregg M, Gable RA, Zigmond N, Blanks B, Howard P, Bullock L (2012) Time after time online: an extended study of virtual coaching during distant clinical practice. J Technol Teach Educ 20(3):277–304. https://www.learntechlib.org/primary/p/38623/
48. Daniels AC (2016) Bringing out the best in people: how to apply the astonishing power of positive reinforcement, 3rd edn. Aubrey Daniels International
49. Shute VJ (2008) Focus on formative feedback. Rev Educ Res 78(1):153–189. https://doi.org/10.3102/0034654307313795
50. Horn AL, Rock ML, Chezan LC, Bobzien JL, Karadimou O, Alturki A (2023) eCoaching during Mursion™ simulations to increase the occurrence, variety, and equity of behavior specific

praise. J Spec Educ Technol (Advance online publication). https://doi.org/10.1177/01626434231152893
51. Scheeler MC, Ruhl KL, McAfee JK (2004) Providing performance feedback to teachers: a review. Teach Educ Spec Educ 27(4):396–407. https://doi.org/10.1177/088840640402700407
52. Fallon LM, Collier-Meek MA, Maggin DM, Sanetti LMH, Johnson AH (2015) Is performance feedback for educators an evidence-based practice? A systematic review and evaluation based on single case research. Except Child 81(2):227–246. https://doi.org/10.1177/0014402914551738
53. Zoder-Martell KA, Markelz AM, Floress MT, Skriba HA, Sayyah LEN (2020) Technology to facilitate telehealth in applied behavior analysis. Behav Anal Pract 13:596–603. https://doi.org/10.1007/s40617-020-00449-4
54. Health Insurance Portability and Accountability Act. 45 C. F. R. § 160 & 164 (2002). https://www.hhs.gov/sites/default/files/privacysummary/pdf
55. Family Educational Rights and Privacy Act (FERPA). 34 C. F. R. § 99 (2001). https://www2.ed.gov/policy/gen/guid/fpco/ferpa/index.html
56. Grygas Coogle C, Ottley JR, Rahn NL, Storie S (2018) Bug-in-ear eCoaching: impacts on novice early childhood special education teachers. J Early Interv 40(1):87–103. https://doi.org/10.1177/1053815117748692
57. Randolph KM, Duffy ML, Brady MP, Wilson CL, Scheeler MC (2020) The impact of iCoaching on teacher-delivered opportunities to respond. J Spec Educ Technol 35(1):15–25. https://doi.org/10.1177/0162643419836414
58. Rosenberg NE, Artman-Meeker K, Kelly E, Yang X (2020) The effects of a bug-in-ear coaching package on implementation of incidental teaching by paraprofessionals in a K-12 school. J Behav Educ 29:409–432. https://doi.org/10.1007/s10864-020-09379-1
59. Scheeler MC, Morano S, Lee DL (2018) Effects of immediate feedback using bug-in-ear with paraeducators working with students with autism. Teach Educ Spec Educ 41(1):24–38. https://doi.org/10.1177/0888406416666645
60. Wilczynski SM, Magnusen A, Sundberg S, Seifert B (2022) Evidence-based practice: finding the right treatment that works. In: Chezan LC, Wolfe K, Drasgow E (eds) Evidence-based practices for supporting autistic individuals spectrum disorder. Rowman & Littlefield
61. Cooper JO, Heron TE, Heward WL (2020) Applied behavior analysis, 3rd edn. Pearson Education
62. Grygas Coogle C, Rahn NL, Ottley JR (2015) Pre-service teacher use of communication strategies upon receiving immediate feedback. Early Child Res Q 32:105–115. https://doi.org/10.1016/j.ecresq.2015.03.003
63. Grygas Coogle C, Rahn NL, Ottley JR, Storie S (2016) ECoaching across routines to enhance teachers' use of modeling. Teach Educ Spec Educ 39(4):227–245. https://doi.org/10.1177/0888406415621959
64. Royer DJ, Lane KL, Dunlap KD, Ennis RP (2019) A systematic review of teacher-delivered behavior-specific praise on K-12 student performance. Remedial Spec Educ 40(2):112–128. https://doi.org/10.1177/0741932517751054
65. Ennis RP, Royer DJ, Lane KL, Dunlap KD (2020) Behavior-specific praise in pre-K-12 settings: Mapping the 50 year knowledge base. Behav Disord 45(3):131–147. https://doi.org/10.1177/0198742919843075
66. McLeskey J, Barringer MD, Billingsley B, Brownell D, Kennedy M, Lewis T, Maheady L, Rodriguez J, Scheeler MC, Winn J, Ziegler D (2017) High-leverage practices in special education. Council for Exceptional Children & CEEDAR Center
67. Horn AL, Rock ML, Douglas K, Bean K, Layden SJ, Roitsch J (2022) The effects of teacher delivered bug in ear coaching on paraeducators and students. Educ Train Autism Dev Disabil 57(3):287–302
68. Charlop-Christy MH, Carpenter MH (2000) Modified incidental teaching sessions: a procedure for parents to increase spontaneous speech in their children with autism. J Posit Behav Interv 2(2):98–112. https://doi.org/10.1177/109830070000200203

69. Kroeger KA, Nelson WM (2006) A language programme to increase the verbal production of a child dually diagnosed with down syndrome and autism. J Intellect Disabil Res 50(2):101–108. https://doi.org/10.1111/j.1365-2788.2005.00734.x
70. Grygas Coogle C, Ottley JR, Storie S, Rahn NL, Kurowski-Burt A (2020) Performance-based feedback to enhance preservice teachers' practice and preschool children's expressive communication. J Teach Educ 71(2):188–202. https://doi.org/10.1177/0022487118803583
71. Snyder P, Hemmeter ML, McLean M, Sandall S, McLaughlin T, Algina J (2018) Effects of professional development on preschool teachers' use of embedded instruction practices. Except Child 84:213–232. https://doi.org/10.1177/0014402917735512
72. Wong C, Odom SL, Hume KA, Cox AW, Fettig A, Kucharczyk S, Brock ME, Plavnick JB, Fleury VP, Schultz TR (2015) Evidence based practices for children, youth, and young adults with autism spectrum disorder: a comprehensive review. J Autism Dev Disord 45:1951–1966. https://doi.org/10.1007/s10803-014-2351-z
73. Cavanaugh B (2013) Performance feedback and teachers' use of praise and opportunities to respond: a review of the literature. Educ Treat Child 36(1):111–136. https://doi.org/10.1353/etc.2013.0001
74. Haydon T, Conroy MA, Scott TM, Sindelar PT, Barber BR, Orlando AM (2010) A comparison of three types of opportunities to respond on student academic and social behaviors. J Emot Behav Disord 18(1):27–40. https://doi.org/10.1177/1063426609333448
75. Haydon T, Macsuga-Gage AS, Simonsen B, Hawkins R (2012) Opportunities to respond: a key component of effective instruction. Beyond Behav 22(1):23–31. https://doi.org/10.1177/107429561202200105
76. Allen KD, Burke RV, Howard MR, Wallace DP, Bowen SL (2012) Use of audio cuing to expand employment opportunities for adolescents with autism spectrum disorders and intellectual disabilities. J Autism Dev Disord 42:2410–2419. https://doi.org/10.1007/s10803-012-1519-7
77. Kearney KB, Torres A (2022) Teaching job search skills to college students with intellectual and developmental disabilities through screensharing and remote audio coaching. Educ Train Autism Dev Disabil 57(2):167–176
78. Shogren KA, Shaw LA, Little TD (2016) Measuring the early adult outcomes of young adults with disabilities: developing constructs using NLTS2 data. Exceptionality 24:45–61. https://doi.org/10.1080/09362835.2015.1064416
79. U.S. Bureau of Labor Statistics (2022) Persons with a disability: barriers to employment, types of assistance, and other labor-related issues summary. U.S. Bureau of Labor Statistics. https://www.bls.gov/news.release/dissup.nr0.htm
80. Newman L, Wagner M, Cameto R, Knokey AM, Shaver D (2010) Comparisons across time of the outcomes of youth with disabilities up to 4 years after high school: a report of findings from the National Longitudinal Transition Study (NLTS) and the National Longitudinal Transition Study-2 (NLTS2). NCSER 2010-3008. National Center for Special Education Research
81. Newman L, Wagner M, Knokey AM, Marder C, Nagle K, Shaver D, Wei X (2011) The post-high school outcomes of young adults with disabilities up to 8 years after high school: a report from the National Longitudinal Transition Study-2 (NLTS2). NCSER 2011-3005. National Center for Special Education Research
82. Gibson CB, Carter EW (2016) Promoting social interactions and job independence for college students with autism and intellectual disability: a pilot study. J Autism Dev Disord 46:3583–3596. https://doi.org/10.1007/s10803-016-2894-2
83. Binder C (1988) Precision teaching: measuring and attaining exemplary academic achievement. Youth Policy 10(7):12–15
84. Vargas JS (2009) Behavior analysis for effective teaching. Routledge
85. Sigafoos J, Carnett A, O'Reilly MF, Lancioni GE (2022) Evidence-based practices to enhance social competence. In: Chezan LC, Wolfe K, Drasgow E (eds) Evidence-based practices for supporting autistic individuals spectrum disorder. Rowman & Littlefield

86. Chesnut SR, Wei T, Barbard-Brak L, Richman DM (2017) A meta-analysis of social communication questionnaire: screening for autism spectrum disorder. Autism 21(8):920–928. https://doi.org/10.1177/1362361316660065
87. Loukusa S, Mäkinen L, Kuusikko-Gauffin S, Ebeling H, Leinonnen E (2018) Assessing social-pragmatic inferencing skills in children with autism spectrum disorder. J Commun Disord 73(1):91–105. https://doi.org/10.1016/j.jcomdis.2018.01.006
88. Gregori E, Mason R, Wang D, Griffin Z, Iriarte I (2022) Effects of telecoaching on conversation skills for high school and college students with autism spectrum disorder. J Spec Educ Technol 37(2):241–252. https://doi.org/10.1177/01626434211002151
89. Meadan H, Pearson JN (2022) Collaborative partnerships: Parents and families. In: Chezan LC, Wolfe, K, Drasgow E (eds) Evidence-based practices for supporting autistic individuals spectrum disorder. Rowman & Littlefield
90. Jeynes WH (2017) A meta-analysis: the relationship between parental involvement and Latino student outcomes. Educ Urban Soc 49(1):4–28. https://doi.org/10.1177/0013124516630596
91. Sheridan SM, Smith TE, Kim EM, Beretvas SN, Park S (2019) A meta-analysis of family-school interventions and children's social-emotional functioning: moderators and components of efficacy. Rev Educ Res 89(2):296–332. https://doi.org/10.3102/0034654318825437
92. Rosenbaum S., Simon P (eds) (2016) Speech and language disorders in children: implications for the social security administration's supplemental security income program. The National Academies Press. https://doi.org/10.17226/21872
93. Meadan H, Snodgrass MR, Meyer LE, Fisher KW, Chung MY, Halle JW (2016) Internet-based parent implemented intervention for young children with autism: a pilot study. J Early Interv 38(1):3–23. https://doi.org/10.1177/1053815116630327
94. Oliver P, Brady MP (2014) Effects of covert audio coaching on parents' interactions with young children with autism. Behav Anal Pract 7:112–116. https://doi.org/10.1007/s40617-014-0015-2
95. Grygas Coogle C, Ottley JR, Storie S, Rahn NL, Kurowski Burt A (2017) ECoaching to enhance special educator practice and child outcomes. Infants Young Child 30(1):58–75. https://doi.org/10.1097/IYC.0000000000000082
96. Gorton K, Allday RA, Lane JD, Ault MJ (2022) Effects of brief training plus electronic feedback on increasing quantity and intonation of behavior specific praise among preschool teachers. J Behav Educ 31:731–750. https://doi.org/10.1007/s10864-020-09427-w
97. Wilczynski SM (2017) A practical guide to finding treatments that work for people with autism. Elsevier Inc.
98. Terblanche N, Cilliers D (2020) Factors that influence users' adoption of being coached by an artificial intelligence coach. Philos Coach: Int J 5(1):61–70. https://doi.org/10.22316/poc/05.1.06
99. Cavanagh M, Lane D (2012) Coaching psychology coming of age: the challenges we face in the messy world of complexity. Int Coach Psychol Rev 7(1):75–90

Digital Interventions for Attention Deficit/Hyperactivity Disorder

11

Leonhard Marten, Anna Kaiser, and Alexander Häge

Abstract

In this chapter, we summarize available digital interventions utilized for assessment and therapy of ADHD. During the COVID-19 pandemic the use of digital tools in clinical psychology became prominent due to restrictions of in-person therapy. Since multiple interventions have been introduced over the last decade, we aim to provide an overview of different web- and PC-based (telemedicine, cognitive and behavioral interventions, neurofeedback) and mobile Health interventions as well as wearables/sensors and virtual reality-based tools. For each topic, we have focused on the therapeutic concept, its implementation and efficacy.

Keywords

Attention-deficit/hyperactivity disorder • Digital interventions • Mobile health • Telemedicine • Computerized interventions • Neurofeedback • Mobile games • Wearables • Virtual reality

---

L. Marten (✉) · A. Kaiser · A. Häge
Department of Child and Adolescent Psychiatry and Psychotherapy, Central Institute of Mental Health, Mannheim, Germany
e-mail: leonhard.marten@zi-mannheim.de

A. Kaiser
e-mail: anna.kaiser@zi-mannheim.de

A. Häge
e-mail: alexander.haege@zi-mannheim.de

© The Author(s), under exclusive license to Springer Nature Switzerland AG 2024
C. Costescu (ed.), *Digital Technologies for Learning and Psychological Interventions*,
Integrated Science 33, https://doi.org/10.1007/978-3-031-76414-1_11

1 Introduction

Attention-deficit/hyperactivity disorder (ADHD) is a neurodevelopmental disorder characterized by three core symptoms. Inattention, hyperactivity and impulsivity can all be prominent [1]. Epidemiological studies report prevalence rates of around 5% in children and 2.8% in adults. In child and adolescent psychiatry, ADHD is among the most frequent disorders [2].

National and international evidence-based treatment-guidelines recommend a multimodal, personalized (tailored to the individual characteristics and needs of a patient) intervention approach, depending on age, symptom severity, and probable comorbidities. To improve psychiatric health care innovatively is a permanent challenge in clinical research, and recently, boosted by the inevitable restrictions during the Covid-19 pandemic, digital alternatives to common treatment interventions became more and more relevant. Besides the telemedical approach (digitalizing face to face interventions via videoconferencing), a lot of different concepts like computer programs, mobile applications, wearable sensors and the use of virtual or augmented reality tools were introduced in the past decade. When introducing these relatively new interventions, it is important to highlight treatment concepts they are based on, as well as (if available) validation data, as a lot of interesting digital intervention approaches, that are partially already available (like mobile applications claiming therapeutic effects [3]) are still under development and do not find clinical application yet.

2 Digital Interventions for ADHD

2.1 Clustering Digital Interventions for ADHD

Digital interventions, also referred to as 'digital health interventions' (DHI) or 'digital therapeutics' (DTx) are generally defined as 'interventions that provide information, support and therapy (emotional, decisional, behavioral and neurocognitive) for physical and/or mental health problems via a technological or digital platform' [4], following psychoeducational and/or mainly behaviorally-focused psychotherapeutic intervention strategies. There are many different types of digital interventions targeting diverse treatment areas like cognitive functioning, behavioral management and organization, treatment adherence, self-regulation and social skills. Besides treatment, digital tools are also used for diagnosis/assessment to monitor behavior and emotions. They can be tailored for children, adolescents or their caregivers (mostly parents), and used in different settings (e.g. at home or in school). To provide an organized overview, we have subdivided interventions by the technological medium on which they are delivered, and elaborated on the application settings. We also discussed different users and therapeutic target areas within the specific tools.

2.1.1 Web- and PC-Based Interventions
Telemental Health
Telemedicine refers to remotely performing or supporting medical services (diagnosis, treatment) to patients through telecommunications technology [5]. Applied in ADHD therapy, it describes the use of video-teleconferencing tools to provide pharmaco- and psychotherapeutic interventions to affected children, adolescents and their parents, and is referred to as 'telemental health'. Access to in-person clinical care can be limited due to many different reasons, as resources can be limited both for clinicians and recipients. Telemental health interventions, consequently, try to compensate these limitations, and can either be delivered in real-time or asynchronous by sharing recordings on patient portals, websites or social media [6]. Especially during the COVID-19 pandemic, the use of telemedical services rapidly increased [7].

Clinicians can deliver psychotherapeutic interventions, e.g. psychoeducational content, to children and adolescents via web-cam and video-conferencing tools. Pharmacological treatment can be supported by discussing effectiveness, side effects, and adherence with the patient and their caregivers online while they stay in their home-setting. Other psychosocial interventions, like behavioral parent trainings (mostly a mix of psychoeducation and training of behavioral skills and techniques), either individually or in a group setting have also been implemented remotely. The online-setting lowers the participation threshold, as it enables simplified appointment planning, and lowers the organizational effort such as transportation or child care. Positive results regarding acceptance and feasibility of telemental health interventions have been reported from patients as well as clinicians [8], and within the last couple of years increasing research comparing the effectiveness of face-to-face interventions with those carried out via online-videoconferencing has been conducted. For example, online parent trainings have shown comparable effects to trainings carried out in a face-to-face setting on parental knowledge, treatment adherence and child behavior [8, 9]. The COVID-19-induced shift from in-person to online therapies lends hope for an increase of studies comparing their effectiveness in the near future [10].

Computerized Cognitive Training
Many digital interventions for ADHD focus on improving cognitive functioning. Multiple studies have shown that individuals with ADHD perform worse in tests of various cognitive skills which are important for functioning both in academic surroundings like performing in school or at work, but also in daily life [11]. Besides the ability to maintain attention and stay focused on a specific stimulus or task over a certain period of time, other higher-order cognitive, executive functions like response inhibition, working memory, action planning, attention shifting, or reward management can also be impacted.

The principle underlying cognitive training is to improve these cognitive skills by repetitive exposure and practice of tasks that require one or several of the above-mentioned neurocognitive functions. Often, different exercises targeting multiple cognitive domains are combined and addressed via structured computerized cognitive training (CCT) programs. Users have the possibility to access the training content on different levels, as the difficulty can be adapted to every (possibly evolving) subjective skill level over time. This is intended to boost neuronal connectivity and result in a transfer of abilities to situations which depend on the same neural networks [12, 13]. This is thought to also transfer into daily-life functioning by improving performance in a variety of situations across different settings. Performing training sessions on a PC-interface (monitor) makes it possible to access the interventions in different settings (clinical setting, at home or even at school), automatically tracks progress, and offers direct feedback of the performance result. The training content derives from the specific domain that is targeted and ranges from tasks that require to inhibit responses to certain cues, maintain and direct the attentional focus, organizational tasks like planning or goal setting, to tasks demanding to memorize information over a certain time period.

With increasing technological options, more complex interfaces for CCT can be and have been designed. Today, a wide variety of web- and PC-based cognitive training softwares which comprise content for multiple target areas is available [13, 14]. A very popular approach that developers consider is the method of gamification of their CCT-program with the idea to bring game elements into cognitive training to increase user-motivation, usability/intuitiveness for the target age group and long-term engagement [15]. Also, embedding a therapeutic training intervention into a computerized game can make it attractive and enjoyable, especially for younger children. So called "serious games" try to combine educational and playful elements. Elements that are used to gamify an intervention can be *achievement and progression-oriented*, like implementing a Box [Definition] starts **Serious Games** Serious games are (video-) games that include entertaining and motivating dynamics while providing some kind of training or education towards a certain skill. Being easy to access, attractive and enjoyable they are especially used in child and adolescent psychiatry to train certain cognitive or behavioral skills. Box [Definition] ends reward system (e.g. points, medals), feedback loops (positive, to reinforce an action/behavior or negative, to reduce an action/behavior), challenges (adding a time limit or a limited error-range represented by lives) or features to map progress (e.g. a progress-bar, achievable levels). *Social-oriented* game elements focus on social interaction with competitive elements, *immersion-oriented* game elements on wrapping the training procedure into a storyline, or visual and auditory representation like creating an avatar or using sound effects [16]. Gamified versions of cognitive training content have been shown to be more challenging, as well as more motivating compared to non-gamified training tasks [16].

Many research data support the effectiveness of CCT on cognitive functioning in ADHD-patients. In latest findings, significant, moderate short-term improvements on working memory and executive functioning (test-) performance are consistently demonstrated. Symptom-related measures like attention-scores are also positively affected [13, 17]. Yet, these effects are rather specific, i.e. limited to the setting of the trained task. Consequently, further research is required to investigate possible effects of CCT on ADHD-symptomatology or the application of the improved cognitive skills in other settings. CCT at this time can therefore not be recommended as first-line or standalone options for ADHD treatment [12, 13, 18].

CCT-tasks are also very frequently used to assess neurocognitive deficits in children and adolescents. Examples for established tasks to measure these deficits are the stop signal task (measuring response inhibition), continuous performance tasks (measuring response inhibition as well as sustained attention) or sequencing/recognition tests (measuring working memory). Stimuli are presented on monitors and performed using mouse and keyboard input. There is an effort to utilize results of such tests to create a neurocognitive skill profile or as diagnostic (information that contributes to accurately predict the occurrence of ADHD) or prognostic (information that contributes to accurately predict the efficacy of different treatment-options like pharmaco- and psychotherapeutic interventions) markers with so far mixed findings [19–21].

Computerized Behavioral Interventions

The development of social as well as emotion regulation skills plays an important role in building and maintaining interpersonal relationships [22]. ADHD symptoms like inattention or impulsivity can be impairing factors in this process as they can limit children and adolescents in behaving according to social norms. For example, not interrupting someone speaking, reading social cues or regulating emotions, especially in stressful or frustrating situations, can be very challenging. The concept behind behavioral interventions promoting social and emotional skills is to practice prosocial behavior and regulatory processes, e.g. by interacting in social situations via role play.

In computerized behavioral interventions, this approach is digitalized. Using web- and computer based serious games children can train their time management-, planning- and social skills by mastering different challenges. One example for interacting in a social environment is playing a commanding character that is required to act prosocial, planning explorations and solving labyrinths on time ([23], for children between 8 and 12 years old). In another example which was created based on the flanker effect, the stroop task, the stop signal task (SST) and the continuous performance test (CPT), players require self-control, planning skills, the skill to delay impulsive responses (to instant rewards), emotional self-regulation, and to endure increasing waiting times to successfully manage different levels [24]. These tools have, like many in this relatively new field, only recently been developed, and therefore their efficacy lacks confirmed clinical evidence. In a meta-analysis following Cochrane standards [25] including in-person as well as digitally supported social skill interventions, no significant effects on social or emotional competences could be shown while ADHD core symptoms were improved (although with only small effect size).

In school settings, the idea of using a monitor interface to implement a behavioral classroom intervention was introduced, in which the contribution of each child to a shared group goal in combination with feedback (e.g. rewarding images) is displayed via diagram on a screen [26]. Furthermore, first studies have investigated the use of robots mimicking human interaction with children [27]. Overall, the implementation of computerized behavioral interventions resembles, at least to some degree, a shift or even replacement of human interaction (e.g. between practitioner and patient). Considering the rapid increase of technological possibilities, the development of further behavioral intervention approaches in the future should be critically examined and evaluated.

Neurofeedback

Neurofeedback (NF) implements the approach of training self-regulation of neurophysiological activity which is associated with the core symptoms and altered in patients with ADHD, [2]. Thereby, neuronal activity is measured e.g. via electroencephalography (EEG) by one or more electrodes placed on the scalp. This activity is then transformed into a visual or acoustic signal and fed back online to the patient/participant via a computer, for example, by an avatar moving up and down. The task of the participants is to move the avatar up or down by focusing on the screen and trying to regulate his/her EEG activity in the desired direction. The final aim is a "normalization" with regard to the altered EEG activity and, ideally, a consequent improvement of ADHD symptoms.

Several different EEG-NF training protocols have been implemented in ADHD so far. Those which have received the best evaluation are the NF training of the frequency bands and the training of slow cortical potentials [28]. For frequency-band trainings the general goal is to decrease slower θ and/or increase faster β band frequencies (reduce the θ/β ratio [29], or increase the faster sensorimotor rhythm in SMR training). The training of slow cortical potentials aims at learning to intentionally increase and decrease cortical excitability over short periods of time.

However, as indicated by extensive research, no reliable characteristic neurophysiological ADHD pattern (biomarker) seems to exist [30, 31]. Nevertheless, gaining control over one's brain activity and related attentional states continues to be a valid treatment goal as improvements have been shown on a neurophysiological level, cognitive level and in some studies, even on a phenotypical/clinical level. The estimation of effectiveness of NF depends strongly on which type of evidence is considered [32, 33]. Efficacy is low for specific effects on core symptoms in RCTs using blinded ratings and stringent, semi-active controls, but medium to high if additional evidence is considered. With regard to clinical symptoms in ADHD children, medium effects on symptoms of inattention were found that increase to large at follow-up (FU) assessments [34, 35]. For adolescents and adults, effects were also identified for symptoms of hyperactivity/impulsivity (besides significant effects on symptoms of inattention), with a medium effect size at post-assessment and FU [36]. Significant symptom improvement is generally found in unblind/most proximal ratings (raters that are unblind/know about the patients/participants treatment with NF). For possibly blinded/distal raters (e.g. teachers, that do not know about treatment allocation), significant effects for standard training protocols have consistently been shown [37]. Further, higher improvement for more intense treatment (but not for treatment duration) and the use of a high-quality EEG equipment was found [38, 39].

NF is more effective than non-active control groups, but not better active controls for symptoms of inattention (at pre-post [40]); NF is superior to waiting list and physical activity, but not better compared to methylphenidate (MPH [41, 42]). Generally, MPH is significantly more efficacious than NF on overt behavioral ADHD core-symptoms; however, some studies indicate lower dropouts for NF compared to MPH in children, but this needs to be confirmed in future research. For adolescents and adults, no dropout differences were found for a follow-up (FU) assessment. Further, an additive effect of NF combined with medication at 12-week FU (for parents rating with regards to global ADHD and inattention symptoms) was revealed, but effects failed to sustain 6 months after treatment [43]. No benefits on domains of executive functioning were found in most studies [44].

To summarize, although some effects of NF on symptoms of ADHD were revealed, so far, there is no convincing evidence that these effects are specific and related to/due to an improved learned control over the targeted brain activity despite recent studies also including personalization and training in different relevant settings (clinic, school, home). Instead, nonspecific treatment effects (e.g. improved self-efficacy, positive reinforcement, and learning to sit still and attend) might be relevant and contribute in large part to the positive clinical outcomes identified in earlier research [45].

More technically sophisticated NF approaches, such as tablet-based NF [46, 47], tomographic NF, fMRI-NF or near-infrared spectroscopy feedback (feedback of hemoglobin oxygenation) are currently explored [48]. These new techniques might represent promising new strategies for treating symptoms of ADHD.

2.1.2 Mobile Health

In the last decades, the integration of mobile devices like phones or tablets in our day to day life significantly increased. With steady development of their capability, the focus of digital interventions has shifted from web- and pc-based interventions to those that can be accessed through mobile devices. These mobile interventions offer increased flexibility, allowing not only the delivery of interventions, but also the organization of treatments, and serving as sensors to track behaviors or physical data in combination with sensoring devices (see Sect. 2.1.3). Digital interventions delivered on mobile devices like phones or tablets are summarized under the term 'mobile Health' (m-Health, [27]).

Intervention Applications/Mobile Games

The most common approach in interventional mobile applications for treating ADHD in children and adolescents, involves the use of mobile games that incorporate therapeutic content, thus categorizing them as 'serious games' (see Sect. 2.1.1.2). Similar to the games described above serious mobile games can address various treatment areas. Numerous ADHD-themed mobile Apps are available online or through app stores, many of which qualify as mobile games. These interventions cover a wide spectrum ranging from cognitive training and psychoeducation to hypnosis or music therapy [3]. However, clinical evidence to prove their

Fig. 1 In-app interface of a game-based attention training application played on a phone—EndeavorRx by Akili

effectiveness is limited. In a recent meta-analysis aiming to comprehensively identify clinically evaluated video games for ADHD, twelve mobile games focusing on ADHD treatment with available quantitative data were identified. These games focused on attention, memory and behavioral characteristics, asking players to respond to specific cues and carry out particular actions such as avoiding obstacles or selecting objects with specific attributes in a distracting environment. Memory-related tasks like remembering the order of a sequence of items that appear again later in the game, or association tasks like matching differently presented items, are also included [49].

Games seeking to improve attention are often based on the Go-/No Go test paradigm, that requires participants to react to so called Go-stimuli, whereas reaction to No-Go-stimuli should be inhibited. An often used example for such a game is the first prescribable mobile game for ADHD treatment that was authorized by the American Food and Drug Administration (FDA). Specifically designed for children aged 8–12 years, this game involves guiding an avatar through a dynamic game interface, collecting targets and avoiding obstacles (Fig. 1). These game features, together with training content, were shown to moderate training effects of mobile applications seeking to enhance cognitive functioning [17]. Results regarding the effectiveness of game-based m-Health interventions are mixed. The interventions were shown to significantly improve attention when measured task-specific (with a digital attention test, [50]). Parent reported attention-scores have consistently shown significant improvements, while ratings provided by teachers and participants on well validated clinical attention-rating scales have not [50, 51]. A similar concern, as mentioned in the chapter on computerized cognitive training, arises when evaluating reports of improved attention: can these results be transferred into real world context? Some authors argue that these cognitive improvements are domain specific and cannot be generalized to other contexts. In contrast, others stress methodological issues, such as the validity of instruments like the Test of Variables of Attention (TOVA; [52]) and try to include subjective ratings along with assessments of impairment.

Still, very few therapeutic mobile games have undergone stringent clinical evaluation [49]. Therefore, more well-designed clinical trials are needed to provide precise insights into their effectiveness. It is important not to disregard the potential positive influence of m-Health interventions in form of mobile games on attention. Furthermore, highlighting the high compliance rates, little adverse effects (a critical comment can be found in Chap. 3), and the ability to personalize the treatment intensity to a level that is optimally challenging for each individual by adjusting the task difficulty is important. However, it is worth noting that the efficacy of m-Health interventions compared to the state of the art treatments, such as (combined) pharmacotherapy and behavioral interventions (especially in severe cases), falls short. Some authors suggest recommending them as supplementary treatments, in cases with low to moderate symptom severity, alongside other non-pharmacological interventions.

Applications for Assessment, Monitoring and Treatment Planning
M-Health applications are not limited to ADHD treatment, they are also valuable for assessment, monitoring and treatment planning. Many available applications serve as assessment instruments for tracking emotions or behavior. The underlying concept is to collect data to support diagnosis and monitor treatment effects, while encouraging self-reflection and emotional awareness. This procedure follows the ecological momentary assessment (EMA; [53]) concept, which intends to repeatedly sample emotions and behavior in real time and in the situational, natural environment. For example, some apps are used as emotion or mood trackers: mobile phone notifications act as reminders indicating a momentary assessment of the current emotional state, and users provide their rating in whatever setting (social interaction, school, at home etc.) they might be in. Mobile-delivered assessment can also be externally directed to parents or teachers of children and adolescents.

Within the complex landscape of ADHD symptoms, problems related to organizing, scheduling, being on time or remembering appointments are common issues for ADHD-patients. M-health interventions aim to provide support in these areas, offering assistance and solutions. They can play a crucial role in improving medication adherence, ensuring patients take their medication in the correct dosage and at the right time. Mobile applications for tracking and monitoring pharmacotherapy have features like reminding notifications or journaling surfaces. These apps can also be useful for clinicians, as they can monitor important data like adherence or side effects. Some applications even combine supporting behavioral treatment planning with delivering interventions. Children, adolescents or caregivers can access psychoeducational content, exercises, monitor emotions and behavior, review their progress and receive reminders to use the app according to the treatment plan that was elaborated with a clinician [54] (Fig. 2).

2.1.3   Wearables/Sensors

This category includes wearable devices and sensors, which are somehow affixed to the human body and mostly used to assess symptom-related data to support

Fig. 2 In-app interface of a smartphone-based parent training intervention that is currently in the validation process. It combines interventional with organizational characteristics. Imagery content provided by medigital®

ADHD diagnosis. They are sometimes classified as mobile-health interventions [4, 49], as they are often used in combination with mobile phones/smartphones. Here, we aim to briefly introduce some available tools that do not fall into this category, as they are applicable without using mobile-phone or tablet interfaces.

Wearables and sensors are capable of providing activity data, often focusing on measuring movement. With regard to ADHD, these devices primarily concentrate on assessing hyperactivity symptoms by tracking movement patterns. For instance, in a study investigating movement patterns of children and adolescents between 6 and 16 years of age, Muñoz-Organero and colleagues [55] trained a recurrent neural network to characterize patterns in the movement of normally developing children, and used the network model to identify differences in the movement patterns of ADHD participants. They assessed movement by attaching so called tri-axial accelerometers on ankles and wrists of the children. Those accelerometers are small sensors that are able to measure an objects (or in this regard, a persons) acceleration in space and therefore precisely depict the motion properties happening in a certain time span. After monitoring the movement for a continuous 24 h, the movement patterns of the ADHD subgroup could be differentiated, surprisingly in the range of medium and low intensity movements.

Further, also wearable tools for supporting behavioral intervention are being developed. For example, a 'kinesiofeedback' tool (promoting feedback regarding the amount or intensity of movement) seeking to support self-behavioral inhibition was introduced [56]. Here, a technical device that collects accelerometer-delivered information on children's movement in class, is attached to the children, sending them feedback (via vibration) whenever a certain movement threshold was exceeded, reminding them to follow their therapeutic goals regarding certain thresholds of physical activity in a learning environment. Others developed the idea for the development of self-regulation tools based on the use of smartwatches [57]. Smartwatches would allow for a combined approach, as they are able to track behavior, physical data (e.g. sleep quality), but also communicate interventional content (like behavioral feedback via prompts). Their natural design as a typically used device could also prevent stigmatization of users in social settings like school.

It is important to mention, that research regarding these tools is still in an early, rather exploratory state [27], and needs to be tested in randomized clinical trials, that can also be important for empirically investigating the validity of diagnostic measures [58] before they can be implemented in daily clinical practice.

2.1.4 Virtual/Augmented Reality

Within the last very recent years, (research) interest in the development of virtual/augmented reality (VR-)based options for ADHD diagnosis and interventions has substantially grown resulting in more and more publications in the field [59, 60]. VR offers immersive, interactive and highly experiential virtual scenarios, thereby generating enormous therapeutic opportunities such as the possibility to simulate ecologically valid realities where symptoms are relevant for diagnostic or treatment purpose [61–65]. Therefore, VR might not only be a promising tool for therapeutic but also for diagnostic purpose within a broader, more holistic mental-health assessment approach [66]. VR could be considered as an "embodied technology" with the following aspects providing a definition: 1) the use of external tools that provide sensory information (mainly visual, auditory, and haptic) to interact with the virtual environment; (2) internal tools, which allow the collection of information on the user's movement and position regarding their interaction with the system (for example, through gloves, trackers, exoskeletons, or a mouse); (3) systems for reproducing graphic images created by the virtual environment; and (4) software and databases that shape objects in the virtual world, using their shape, texture, or movement [59]. Especially with regard to therapeutic purpose, VR environments are supposed to enhance the quality of experience, motivation, and learning, consequently probably enhancing treatment effects [67].

Early studies on VR and ADHD mainly focused on adult patient populations using VR for exploring (improvements with regard to) motor skills and driving performance after (psychopharmacological) treatment thereby simulating driving situations in the VR-setting. More recent research rather focuses on the augmentation of the diagnostic accuracy of standardized tests by implementing them in a VR-environment and on the therapeutic options of VR for improving symptoms as well as cognitive functioning skills.

With regard to VR as a tool for clinical assessment enabling real-time assessment within real-like environments, a systematic review by Geraets and colleagues [68] found one study on ADHD participants comparing young, mostly adult, males with and without ADHD. Similar to research in children, this study concerned a VR-assisted neuropsychological test (Nesplora Aquarium test) that continues the wave of 2D computerized continuous performance tasks (CPTs) for assessment of attention, working memory, and processing speed [69–71]. In their meta-analysis, Parsons and colleagues [69] compared 2D CPTs to VR-based CPTs in ADHD children, exploring the probably enhanced ecological validity of the 3D-version. The authors were able to show that VR-based CPT-versions also reliably differentiate attention performance in ADHD children but only subtle differences between the two versions (2D versus 3D) were found.

A meta-analysis by Romero-Ayuso and colleagues [59] quantitatively summarized the relevant literature on the effectiveness of VR-based interventions on cognitive deficits for ADHD children and adolescents and found improvements with regard to attentional vigilance and (sustained) attention measures with an increase in the number of correct responses and a decrease in the number of omission errors (typically linked to symptoms of inattention). No effects were observed for impulsivity. A more recent meta-analysis by Corrigan and colleagues [72], found strong effects with large effect sizes in favor of VR-based interventions on outcomes of global cognition, attention, and memory. More specifically, Bioulac and colleagues [73] tested a new virtual classroom cognitive remediation program compared to methylphenidate (MPH) or a psychotherapy group in a randomized clinical trial including 51 ADHD children aged 7–11 years. They found that the cognitive remediation program delivered in a virtual classroom reduces distractibility in ADHD children (with significantly higher numbers of correct hits on the virtual classroom and CPT) and that these improvements were equivalent to those for MPH treatment.

To summarize, some promising findings exist with regards to the use of VR in ADHD diagnosis and therapy. However, further studies including larger numbers of participants are needed for more valid conclusions and for solid clinical recommendations.

3 Digital Interventions in ADHD: Balancing Opportunities and Risks

Various digital interventions provide opportunities for improved treatment and earlier detection of ADHD. Additionally, they promise support of ADHD therapy in multiple ways. Specifically, services delivered via the internet, apps, and even social media have the advantage of reaching a wider range of patients and families as well as potentially reducing the barriers to seeking help. Furthermore, the availability of outpatient services and psychotherapies, whether individual or group-based, is limited in many regions. Therefore, approaches that do not require face-to-face contact could prove highly beneficial in such contexts.

Children and adolescents spend significant portions of their time with and in the internet, social media, and corresponding mobile applications. This provides a valuable channel for connecting with them. Despite the obvious opportunities and advantages that digital approaches offer, it is essential to note that there can also be negative aspects associated with them, requiring careful consideration and caution [74]. We know that ADHD children and ADHD adolescents often engage in dysfunctional and excessive use of the internet, online gaming and social media [75]. There is a clear association between increased internet and social media use and ADHD [75]. The newly defined gaming disorder in DSM-V and ICD-11 also shows a significant link with ADHD, as does a worrisome use of online games and social media, although not yet classified as pathological [76–78]. Such behaviors can lead to developmental problems and family conflicts, escalating already existing issues.

The use of social media and online gaming itself does not necessarily have negative effects for children and adolescents, especially if kept within reasonable time limits. However, it can indirectly jeopardize the development of children and adolescents [79] as they spend many hours online or on their mobile phones, neglecting other crucial aspects essential for their development, such as face-to-face interactions with peers, direct engagement, forming personal relationships, and activities such as sports and spending time outdoors.

Shifting therapeutic action into the digital realm raises concerns that the aforementioned worrying trends may increase further. Careful consideration and future research of such new digital approaches are needed in order to avoid adverse outcomes for children, adolescents, and families.

It has been noted with criticism by many therapists that video-based therapies weaken the personal relationship between therapist and patient. The nature and intricacies of face-to-face encounters significantly differ from those in online/video-based therapy settings without direct, face-to-face contact [80]. Online, perception is limited significantly, e.g. by minimal yet relevant delays and loss of tactile, olfactory and other sensory qualities. Additionally, group therapies, particularly crucial for children and adolescents dealing with behavioral problems, may be limited in their effectiveness within an online setting.

Content on platforms like YouTube, TikTok, and podcasts can help educate about various disorders, disseminate valuable information, and reach many children, adolescents, and parents. This outreach can potentially dispel prejudices and counteract stigmatization. However, misinformation and misrepresentation of disorders such as ADHD may also be spread publically with usually minimal to low moderation (and if necessary, even correction) of content. This has even led to an increase in functional disorders. This phenomenon has been observed and studied particularly in adolescents exhibiting tic-like symptoms as a result of consuming content related to tics, Tourette syndrome, or similar conditions [81, 82].

Similarly, some young individuals openly share experiences of anorexic behavior, self-harm, or suicidal thoughts on social media platforms, triggering the same behaviors in others and reinforcing dysfunctional thoughts and behaviors, especially among at-risk youth [83–85]. The automatic algorithmic recommendation of comparable content to children and adolescents on certain platforms after they have engaged with dysfunctional content is deeply concerning as harmful patterns are reinforced.

Overall, there is substantial evidence suggesting that digital interventions can serve as valuable supplements in the diagnostic process and treatment of ADHD patients. However, it is crucial not to overlook indications of associated risks and potential negative effects. These factors should be considered in the urgent need for further research in this field.

References

1. Faraone SV, Banaschewski T, Coghill D, Zheng Y, Biederman J, Bellgrove MA et al (2021) The World Federation of ADHD international consensus statement: 208 evidence-based conclusions about the disorder. Neurosci Biobehav Rev 128:789–818. https://doi.org/10.1016/j.neubiorev.2021.01.022
2. Drechsler R, Brem S, Brandeis D, Grünblatt E, Berger G, Walitza S (2020) ADHD: current concepts and treatments in children and adolescents. Neuropediatrics 51(5):315–335. https://doi.org/10.1055/s-0040-1701658
3. Păsărelu CR, Andersson G, Dobrean A (2020) Attention-deficit/hyperactivity disorder mobile apps: a systematic review. Int J Med Inform. 138:104133. https://doi.org/10.1016/j.ijmedinf.2020.104133
4. Hollis C, Falconer CJ, Martin JL, Whittington C, Stockton S, Glazebrook C, Davies EB (2017) Annual research review: digital health interventions for children and young people with mental health problems—A systematic and meta-review. J Child Psychol Psychiatr 58(4):474–503. https://doi.org/10.1111/jcpp.12663
5. Field M (1996) Telemedicine: a guide to assessing telecommunications in health care. National Academies Press (US), , Washington (DC)
6. Myers K, Vander Stoep A, Zhou C, McCarty CA, Katon W (2015) Effectiveness of a telehealth service delivery model for treating attention-deficit/hyperactivity disorder: a community-based randomized controlled trial. J Am Acad Child Adolesc Psychiatr 54(4):263–274. https://doi.org/10.1016/j.jaac.2015.01.009
7. Patel PD, Cobb J, Wright D, Turer RW, Jordan T, Humphrey A et al (2020) Rapid development of telehealth capabilities within pediatric patient portal infrastructure for COVID-19 care: barriers, solutions, results. J Am Med Inform Assoc 27(7):1116–1120. https://doi.org/10.1093/jamia/ocaa065
8. Fogler JM, Normand S, O'Dea N, Mautone JA, Featherston M, Power TJ, Nissley-Tsiopinis J (2020) Implementing group parent training in telepsychology: lessons learned during the COVID-19 pandemic. J Pediatr Psychol 45(9):983–989. https://doi.org/10.1093/jpepsy/jsa a085
9. DuPaul G, Kern L, Belk G, Custer B, Daffner M, Hatfield A, Peek D (2018) Face-to-face versus online behavioral parent training for young children at risk for ADHD: treatment engagement and outcomes. J Clin Child Adolesc Psychol 47:369–383. https://doi.org/10.1080/15374416.2017.1342544

10. Lakes KD, Cibrian FL, Schuck SEB, Nelson M, Hayes GR (2022) Digital health interventions for youth with ADHD: a mapping review. Comput Hum Behav Rep 6. https://doi.org/10.1016/j.chbr.2022.100174
11. de Oliveira Rosa V, Moreira-Maia CR, Wagner F, Simioni A, de Fraga Bassotto C, Moritz GR et al (2021) Computerized cognitive training for ADHD as an add-on treatment to stimulants: a randomized clinical trial. J Atten Disord 25(2):275–285. https://doi.org/10.1177/1087054718816818
12. Rapport MD, Orban SA, Kofler MJ, Friedman LM (2013) Do programs designed to train working memory, other executive functions, and attention benefit children with ADHD? A meta-analytic review of cognitive, academic, and behavioral outcomes. Clin Psychol Rev 33(8):1237–1252. https://doi.org/10.1016/j.cpr.2013.08.005
13. Westwood SJ, Parlatini V, Rubia K, Cortese S, Sonuga-Barke EJS, Banaschewski T et al (2023) Computerized cognitive training in attention-deficit/hyperactivity disorder (ADHD): a meta-analysis of randomized controlled trials with blinded and objective outcomes. Mol Psychiatr 28(4):1402–1414. https://doi.org/10.1038/s41380-023-02000-7
14. Rosa VO, Schmitz M, Moreira-Maia CR, Wagner F, Londero I, Bassotto CF et al (2017) Computerized cognitive training in children and adolescents with attention deficit/hyperactivity disorder as add-on treatment to stimulants: feasibility study and protocol description. Trends Psychiatr Psychother 39(2):65–76. https://doi.org/10.1590/2237-6089-2016-0039
15. Lumsden J, Edwards EA, Lawrence NS, Coyle D, Munafo MR (2016) Gamification of cognitive assessment and cognitive training: a systematic review of applications and efficacy. JMIR Serious Games 4(2):e11. https://doi.org/10.2196/games.5888
16. Vermeir JF, White MJ, Johnson D, Crombez G, Van Ryckeghem DML (2020) The effects of gamification on computerized cognitive training: systematic review and meta-analysis. JMIR Serious Games 8(3):e18644. https://doi.org/10.2196/18644
17. Ren X, Wu Q, Cui N, Zhao J, Bi HY (2023) Effectiveness of digital game-based trainings in children with neurodevelopmental disorders: a meta-analysis. Res Dev Disabil 133:104418. https://doi.org/10.1016/j.ridd.2022.104418
18. Cortese S, Ferrin M, Brandeis D, Buitelaar J, Daley D, Dittmann RW et al (2015) Cognitive training for attention-deficit/hyperactivity disorder: meta-analysis of clinical and neuropsychological outcomes from randomized controlled trials. J Am Acad Child Adolesc Psychiatr 54(3):164–174. https://doi.org/10.1016/j.jaac.2014.12.010
19. Molitor S, Langberg J (2017) Using task performance to inform treatment planning for youth with ADHD: a systematic review. Clin Psychol Rev 58:157–173
20. Fosco WD, Sarver DE, Kofler MJPAA (2018) Parent and child neurocognitive functioning predict response to behavioral parent training for youth with ADHD. Atten Deficit Hyperact Disord 10(4):285–295
21. Buitelaar J, Bölte S, Brandeis D, Caye A, Christmann N, Cortese S et al (2022) Toward precision medicine in ADHD. Front Behav Neurosci 16. https://doi.org/10.3389/fnbeh.2022.900981
22. Halle TG, Darling-Churchill KE (2016) Review of measures of social and emotional development. J Appl Dev Psychol 45:8–18. https://doi.org/10.1016/j.appdev.2016.02.003
23. Bul KCM, Franken IHA, Van Der Oord S, Kato PM, Danckaerts MV et al (2015) Development and user satisfaction of plan-it commander, a serious game for children with ADHD. Games Health J 4:502–512. https://doi.org/10.1089/g4h.2015.0021
24. Crepaldi M, Colombo V, Mottura S, Baldassini D, Sacco M, Cancer AAntonietti A (2020) Antonyms: a computer game to improve inhibitory control of impulsivity in children with attention deficit/hyperactivity disorder (ADHD). Information 11(4). https://doi.org/10.3390/info11040230
25. Storebo OJ, Elmose Andersen M, Skoog M, Joost Hansen S, Simonsen E, Pedersen N et al (2019) Social skills training for attention deficit hyperactivity disorder (ADHD) in children aged 5–18 years. Cochrane Database Syst Rev 6(6):CD008223. https://doi.org/10.1002/14651858.CD008223.pub3

26. Matic A, Hayes GR, Tentori M, Abdullah M, Schuck S (2014) Collective use of a situated display to encourage positive behaviors in children with behavioral challenges. In: 2014 ACM international joint conference on pervasive ubiquitous computing, pp 885–895. https://doi.org/10.1007/978-3-319-03647-28
27. Cibrian FL, Lakes KD, Schuck SEB, Hayes GR (2022) The potential for emerging technologies to support self-regulation in children with ADHD: a literature review. Int J Child-Comput Interact 31. https://doi.org/10.1016/j.ijcci.2021.100421
28. Aggensteiner PM, Brandeis D, Millenet S, Hohmann S, Ruckes C, Beuth S et al (2019) Slow cortical potentials neurofeedback in children with ADHD: comorbidity, self-regulation and clinical outcomes 6 months after treatment in a multicenter randomized controlled trial. Eur Child Adolesc Psychiatr 28(8):1087–1095. https://doi.org/10.1007/s00787-018-01271-8
29. Lee CSC, Chen TT, Gao QW, Hua CZ, Song R, Huang XP (2022) The effects of theta/beta-based neurofeedback training on attention in children with attention deficit hyperactivity disorder: a systematic review and meta-analysis. Child Psychiatr Hum Dev. https://doi.org/10.1007/s10578-022-01361-4
30. Kaiser A, Aggensteiner PM, Baumeister S, Holz NE, Banaschewski T, Brandeis D (2020) Earlier versus later cognitive event-related potentials (ERPs) in attention-deficit/hyperactivity disorder (ADHD): a meta-analysis. Neurosci Biobehav Rev 112:117–134. https://doi.org/10.1016/j.neubiorev.2020.01.019
31. Loo SK, McGough JJ, McCracken JT, Smalley SL (2018) Parsing heterogeneity in attention-deficit hyperactivity disorder using EEG-based subgroups. J Child Psychol Psychiatry 59(3):223–231. https://doi.org/10.1111/jcpp.12814
32. Brandeis D (2017) EEG neurofeedback in ADHD: new meta-analyses and multicentre trials. Eur Neuropsychopharmacol 27:S562–S563. https://doi.org/10.1016/s0924-977x(17)31082-9
33. Sonuga-Barke EJ, Brandeis D, Cortese S, Daley D, Ferrin M, Holtmann M et al (2013) Nonpharmacological interventions for ADHD: systematic review and meta-analyses of randomized controlled trials of dietary and psychological treatments. Am J Psychiatr 170(3):275–289. https://doi.org/10.1176/appi.ajp.2012.12070991
34. Rahmani E, Mahvelati A, Alizadeh A, Mokhayeri Y, Rahmani M, Zarabi H, Hassanvandi S (2022) Is neurofeedback effective in children with ADHD? A systematic review and meta-analysis. Neurocase 28(1):84–95. https://doi.org/10.1080/13554794.2022.2027456
35. Riesco-Matias P, Yela-Bernabe JR, Crego A, Sanchez-Zaballos E (2021) What do meta-analyses have to say about the efficacy of neurofeedback applied to children with ADHD? Review of previous meta-analyses and a new meta-analysis. J Atten Disord 25(4):473–485. https://doi.org/10.1177/1087054718821731
36. Fan HY, Sun CK, Cheng YS, Chung WL, Tzang RF, Chiu HJ et al (2022) A pilot meta-analysis on self-reported efficacy of neurofeedback for adolescents and adults with ADHD. Sci Rep 12(1). https://doi.org/10.1038/s41598-022-14220-y
37. Strehl U, Aggensteiner P, Wachtlin D, Brandeis D, Albrecht B, Arana M et al (2017) Neurofeedback of slow cortical potentials in children with attention-deficit/hyperactivity disorder: a multicenter randomized trial controlling for unspecific effects. Front Hum Neurosci 11:135. https://doi.org/10.3389/fnhum.2017.00135
38. Bussalb A, Congedo M, Barthélemy Q, Ojeda D, Acquaviva E, Delorme R, Mayaud L (2019) Clinical and experimental factors influencing the efficacy of neurofeedback in ADHD: a meta-analysis. Front Psychiatr 10:35. https://doi.org/10.3389/fpsyt.2019.00035
39. Van Doren J, Arns M, Heinrich H, Vollebregt MA, Strehl USKL (2019) Sustained effects of neurofeedback in ADHD: a systematic review and meta-analysis. Eur Child Adolesc Psychiatr 28(3):293–305. https://doi.org/10.1007/s00787-018-1121-4
40. Yan L, Wang S, Yuan Y, Zhang J (2019) Effects of neurofeedback versus methylphenidate for the treatment of ADHD: systematic review and meta-analysis of head-to-head trials. Evid Based Ment Health 22(3):111–117. https://doi.org/10.1136/ebmental-2019-300088
41. Meisel V, Servera M, Garcia-Banda G, Cardo E, Moreno I (2013) Neurofeedback and standard pharmacological intervention in ADHD: a randomized controlled trial with six-month follow-up. Biol Psychol 94(1):12–21. https://doi.org/10.1016/j.biopsycho.2013.04.015

42. Sudnawa KK, Chirdkiatgumchai V, Ruangdaraganon N, Khongkhatithum C, Udomsubpayakul U, Jirayucharoensak S, Israsena P (2018) Effectiveness of neurofeedback versus medication for attention-deficit/hyperactivity disorder. Pediatr Int 60(9):828–834. https://doi.org/10.1111/ped.13641
43. Lin FL, Sun CK, Cheng YS, Wang MY, Chung WL, Tzang RF et al (2022) Additive effects of EEG neurofeedback on medications for ADHD: a systematic review and meta-analysis. Sci Rep 12(1). https://doi.org/10.1038/s41598-022-23015-0
44. Louthrenoo O, Boonchooduang N, Likhitweerawong N, Charoenkwan K, Srisurapanont M (2022) The effects of neurofeedback on executive functioning in children with ADHD: a meta-analysis. J Attent Disord 26(7):976–984. https://doi.org/10.1177/10870547211045738
45. Aggensteiner PM (2021) Editorial: the complexity of neurofeedback and control of placebo effects. J Am Acad Child Adolesc Psychiatr 60(7):811–812. https://doi.org/10.1016/j.jaac.2021.05.008
46. Purper-Ouakil D, Blasco-Fontecilla H, Ros T, Acquaviva E, Banaschewski T, Baumeister S et al (2022) Personalized at-home neurofeedback compared to long-acting methylphenidate in children with ADHD: NEWROFEED, a European randomized noninferiority trial. J Child Psychol Psychiatr 63(2):187–198. https://doi.org/10.1111/jcpp.13462
47. Shin MS, Jeon H, Kim M, Hwang T, Oh SJ, Hwangbo M, Kim KJ (2016) Effects of smart-tablet-based neurofeedback training on cognitive function in children with attention problems. J Child Neurol 31(6):750–760. https://doi.org/10.1177/0883073815620677
48. Rubia K, Westwood S, Aggensteiner PM, Brandeis D (2021) Neurotherapeutics for attention deficit/hyperactivity disorder (ADHD): a review. Cells 10(8). https://doi.org/10.3390/cells10082156
49. Jiang H, Natarajan R, Shuy YK, Rong L, Zhang MW, Vallabhajosyula R (2022) The use of mobile games in the management of patients with attention deficit hyperactive disorder: a scoping review. Front Psychiatr 13. https://doi.org/10.3389/fpsyt.2022.792402
50. Kollins SH, DeLoss DJ, Cañadas E, Lutz J, Findling RL, Keefe RSE et al (2020) A novel digital intervention for actively reducing severity of paediatric ADHD (STARS-ADHD): a randomised controlled trial. Lancet Digit Health 2(4):e168–e178. https://doi.org/10.1016/s2589-7500(20)30017-0
51. Oh S, Choi J, Han DH, Kim E (2023) Effects of game-based digital therapeutics on attention deficit hyperactivity disorder in children and adolescents as assessed by parents or teachers: a systematic review and meta-analysis. Eur Child Adolesc Psychiatr. https://doi.org/10.1007/s00787-023-02174-z
52. Forbes G (1998) Clinical utility of the test of variables of attention (TOVA) in the diagnosis of attention-deficit/hyperactivity disorder. J Clin Psychol 54:461–476
53. Shiffman S, Stone AAMRH (2008) Ecological momentary assessment. Annu Rev Clin Psychol 4:1–32. https://doi.org/10.1146/annurev.clinpsy.3.022806.091415
54. Görtz-Dorten A, Frank M, Fessel A, Hofmann LMD (2022) Effects of a smartphone app-augmented treatment for children with oppositional defiant disorder/conduct disorder and peer-related aggressive behavior—A pilot study. Trials 23(1). https://doi.org/10.1186/s13063-022-06325-6
55. Munoz-Organero M, Powell L, Heller B, Harpin VParker J (2019) Using recurrent neural networks to compare movement patterns in ADHD and normally developing children based on acceleration signals from the wrist and ankle. Sensors (Basel) 19(13). https://doi.org/10.3390/s19132935
56. Garcia JJ, De Bruyckere H, Keyson DV, Romero N (2013) Designing personal informatics for self-reflection and self-awareness: the case of children with attention deficit hyperactivity disorder. In: Ambient intelligence. Springer, Cham. https://doi.org/10.1007/978-3-319-03647-2_8
57. Cibrian FL, Lakes KD, Tavakoulnia A, Guzman K, Schuck SHayes GR (2020) Supporting self-regulation of children with ADHD using wearables. In: Proceedings of the 2020 CHI conference on human factors in computing systems, pp 1–13. https://doi.org/10.1145/3313831.3376837

58. Janatzek S (2011) The benefit of diagnostic tests—From surrogate endpoints to patient-relevant endpoints. Z Evid Fortbild Qual Gesundhwes 105(7):504–509. https://doi.org/10.1016/j.zefq.2011.07.027
59. Romero-Ayuso D, Toledano-González A, Rodríguez-Martínez MDC, Arroyo-Castillo P, Triviño-Juárez JM, González P et al (2021) Effectiveness of virtual reality-based interventions for children and adolescents with ADHD: a systematic review and meta-analysis. Children (Basel) 8(2). https://doi.org/10.3390/children8020070
60. Valentine AZ, Brown BJ, Groom MJ, Young E, Hollis CHall CL (2020) A systematic review evaluating the implementation of technologies to assess, monitor and treat neurodevelopmental disorders: a map of the current evidence. Clin Psychol Rev 80:101870. https://doi.org/10.1016/j.cpr.2020.101870
61. Alqithami S, Alzahrani M, Alzahrani A, Mustafa A (2019) AR-therapist: design and simulation of an AR-game environment as a CBT for patients with ADHD. Healthcare (Basel) 7(4). https://doi.org/10.3390/healthcare7040146
62. Areces D, Dockrell J, Garcia T, Gonzalez-Castro P, Rodriguez C (2018) Analysis of cognitive and attentional profiles in children with and without ADHD using an innovative virtual reality tool. Plos One 13(8):e0201039. https://doi.org/10.1371/journal.pone.0201039
63. Cho BH, Kim S, Shin DI, Lee JH, Lee SM, Kim IY, Kim SI (2004) Neurofeedback training with virtual reality for inattention and impulsiveness. Cyberpsychol Behav 7(5):519–526. https://doi.org/10.1089/cpb.2004.7.519
64. Keshav NU, Vogt-Lowell K, Vahabzadeh A, Sahin NT (2019) Digital attention-related augmented-reality game: significant correlation between student game performance and validated clinical measures of attention-deficit/hyperactivity disorder (ADHD). Children (Basel) 6(6). https://doi.org/10.3390/children6060072
65. Kokol P, Vosner HB, Zavrsnik J, Vermeulen J, Shohieb S, Peinemann F (2020) Serious game-based intervention for children with developmental disabilities. Curr Pediatr Rev 16(1):26–32. https://doi.org/10.2174/1573396315666190808115238
66. Wiebe A, Kannen K, Selaskowski B, Mehren A, Thöne AK, Pramme L et al (2022) Virtual reality in the diagnostic and therapy for mental disorders: a systematic review. Clin Psychol Rev 98:102213. https://doi.org/10.1016/j.cpr.2022.102213
67. Cho BH, Ku J, Jang DP, Kim S, Lee YH, Kim IY et al (2002) The effect of virtual reality cognitive training for attention enhancement. Cyberpsychol Behav 5(2):129–137. https://doi.org/10.1089/109493102753770516
68. Geraets CNW, Wallinius M, Sygel K (2022) Use of virtual reality in psychiatric diagnostic assessments: a systematic review. Front Psychiatr 13:828410. https://doi.org/10.3389/fpsyt.2022.828410
69. Parsons TD, Bowerly T, Buckwalter JG, Rizzo AA (2007) A controlled clinical comparison of attention performance in children with ADHD in a virtual reality classroom compared to standard neuropsychological methods. Child Neuropsychol 13(4):363–381. https://doi.org/10.1080/13825580600943473
70. Coleman B, Marion S, Rizzo A, Turnbull J, Nolty A (2019) Virtual reality assessment of classroom—Related attention: an ecologically relevant approach to evaluating the effectiveness of working memory training. Front Psychol 10:1851. https://doi.org/10.3389/fpsyg.2019.01851
71. Pollak Y, Weiss PL, Rizzo AA, Weizer M, Shriki L, Shalev RS, Gross-Tsur V (2009) The utility of a continuous performance test embedded in virtual reality in measuring ADHD-related deficits. J Dev Behav Pediatr 30(1):2–6. https://doi.org/10.1097/DBP.0b013e3181969b22
72. Corrigan N, Păsărelu CR, Voinescu A (2023) Immersive virtual reality for improving cognitive deficits in children with ADHD: a systematic review and meta-analysis. Virtual Real 1–20. https://doi.org/10.1007/s10055-023-00768-1
73. Bioulac S, Micoulaud-Franchi JA, Maire J, Bouvard MP, Rizzo AA, Sagaspe P, Philip P (2020) Virtual remediation versus methylphenidate to improve distractibility in children with ADHD: a controlled randomized clinical trial study. J Atten Disord 24(2):326–335. https://doi.org/10.1177/1087054718759751

74. Abi-Jaoude E, Naylor KT, Pignatiello A (2020) Smartphones, social media use and youth mental health. CMAJ 192(6):E136–E141. https://doi.org/10.1503/cmaj.190434
75. Ra CK, Cho J, Stone MD, De La Cerda J, Goldenson NI, Moroney E et al (2018) Association of digital media use with subsequent symptoms of attention-deficit/hyperactivity disorder among adolescents. JAMA 320(3):255–263. https://doi.org/10.1001/jama.2018.8931
76. Hong JS, Bae S, Starcervic V, Han DH (2023) Correlation between attention deficit hyperactivity disorder. Internet Gaming Disord Gaming Disord J Atten Disord 27(11):1252–1262. https://doi.org/10.1177/10870547231176861
77. Dullur P, Krishnan V, Diaz AM (2021) A systematic review on the intersection of attention-deficit hyperactivity disorder and gaming disorder. J Psychiatr Res 133:212–222. https://doi.org/10.1016/j.jpsychires.2020.12.026
78. Gonzalez-Bueso V, Santamaria JJ, Fernandez D, Merino L, Montero E, Ribas J (2018) Association between internet gaming disorder or pathological video-game use and comorbid psychopathology: a comprehensive review. Int J Environ Res Public Health 15(4). https://doi.org/10.3390/ijerph15040668
79. Ulvi O, Karamehic-Muratovic A, Baghbanzadeh M, Bashir A, Smith J, Haque U (2022) Social media use and mental health: a global analysis. Epidemiologia (Basel) 3(1):11–25. https://doi.org/10.3390/epidemiologia3010002
80. Schuster R, Topooco N, Keller A, Radvogin E, Laireiter AR (2020) Advantages and disadvantages of online and blended therapy: replication and extension of findings on psychotherapists' appraisals. Internet Interv 21:100326. https://doi.org/10.1016/j.invent.2020.100326
81. Paulus T, Baumer T, Verrel J, Weissbach A, Roessner V, Beste C, Munchau A (2021) Pandemic tic-like behaviors following social media consumption. Mov Disord 36(12):2932–2935. https://doi.org/10.1002/mds.28800
82. Muller-Vahl KR, Pisarenko A, Jakubovski E, Fremer C (2022) Stop that! It's not Tourette's but a new type of mass sociogenic illness. Brain. 145(2):476–480. https://doi.org/10.1093/brain/awab316
83. Mento C, Silvestri MC, Muscatello MRA, Rizzo A, Celebre L, Pratico M et al (2021) Psychological impact of pro-anorexia and pro-eating disorder websites on adolescent females: a systematic review. Int J Environ Res Public Health 18(4). https://doi.org/10.3390/ijerph18042186
84. Wilksch SM, O'Shea A, Ho P, Byrne S, Wade TD (2020) The relationship between social media use and disordered eating in young adolescents. Int J Eat Disord 53(1):96–106. https://doi.org/10.1002/eat.23198
85. Susi K, Glover-Ford F, Stewart A, Knowles Bevis R, Hawton K (2023) Research review: viewing self-harm images on the internet and social media platforms: systematic review of the impact and associated psychological mechanisms. J Child Psychol Psychiatr 64(8):1115–1139. https://doi.org/10.1111/jcpp.13754

Moral Disengagement in Cyberbullying Through Serious Games in Neurodiverse Children

12

Paula Costa Ferreira, Ana Margarida Veiga Simão, Diana Stilwell, Sara L. Lopes, Fátima Trindade, Nádia Pereira, and Sofia Francisco

Abstract

Little attention has been given toward understanding how neurodiverse children develop their morality and engage in moral (dis)engagement mechanisms as they encounter cyberbullying situations. Furthermore, there is a lack of exploration into how their regulation of emotions can influence their moral behavior. In this chapter we discuss moral development and (dis)engagement, the risks of using the Internet, such as cyberbullying, as well as how serious games can serve as a promising resource to understand these processes and behaviors in neurodiverse children. We believe that this constitutes a new line of research which provides an important contribution to the well-being of these children,

---

P. Costa Ferreira (✉) · A. M. Veiga Simão · D. Stilwell · N. Pereira · S. Francisco
CICPSI, Faculdade de Psicologia, Universidade de Lisboa, Lisbon, Portugal
e-mail: paula.ferreira@edu.ulisboa.pt

A. M. Veiga Simão
e-mail: amsimao@psicologia.ulisboa.pt

D. Stilwell
e-mail: dianateixeira@edu.ulisboa.pt

N. Pereira
e-mail: nadia@edu.ulisboa.pt

S. Francisco
e-mail: sofia.francisco@campus.ul.pt

S. L. Lopes
Business School, Iscte-IUL, Lisbon, Portugal
e-mail: sara_lampreia_lopes@iscte-iul.pt

F. Trindade
PADS, Portuguese Association of Down Syndrome, Lisbon, Portugal
e-mail: fatimaptrindade2018@gmail.com

© The Author(s), under exclusive license to Springer Nature Switzerland AG 2024
C. Costescu (ed.), *Digital Technologies for Learning and Psychological Interventions*,
Integrated Science 33, https://doi.org/10.1007/978-3-031-76414-1_12

and opens avenues for future studies examining individual, behavioral, and contextual factors that determine how neurodiverse children interpret, react to, and cope using different strategies.

Keywords

Neurodevelopmental disorders • Moral development • Moral (dis)engagement • Cyberbullying • Serious games

1 Introduction

Technology has enabled innovative breakthroughs in how essential skills may be developed in children with neurodevelopment disorders, whether it be through the use of social networks while interacting with others or through digital games to train cognitive competencies and foster motivation in learning. As the use of technologies, such as social networks [11] and digital games rises, the risk of cyberbullying increases. This risk extends to those with neurodevelopmental disorders, including those with learning disabilities, autism spectrum disorder and attention deficit hyperactivity disorder (ADHD), making them potential victims, cyberbullies, or victim-cyberbullies [22, 37].

Therefore, it is critical for research to focus on how these children react to such phenomena and morally engage or disengage. This exploration is essential for understanding how these children's morality develops and guides their behavior, especially in situations like cyberbullying, where their ability to regulate their emotions is crucial.

Cyberbullying has been defined as relational intentional repeated harmful behavior with digital technologies where there is an imbalance of power between the cyberbully and the victim [42, 109]. As far as we know, little attention has been given to how neurodiverse children develop their morality and are able to engage in moral (dis)engagement mechanisms as they encounter cyberbullying situations, as well as to how their regulation of emotions can determine their moral behavior. We believe that this constitutes a new line of research offering a meaningful contribution to improving the well-being of these children.

Neurodevelopmental disorders have been considered a group of disorders characterized by developmental delays in cognitive and motor function, and include communication disorders, ADHD, autism spectrum disorder, motor disorders and specific learning disorders [4]. Specifically, the DSM-5 [4] has proposed that neurodevelopmental disorders comprise Intellectual Developmental Disorder, Communication Disorders (including Language Disorder, Speech Sound Disorder, Childhood-onset and fluency Disorder), Social Communication Disorder (impaired social verbal and nonverbal communication), Autism Spectrum Disorder, ADHD, Specific Learning Disorder, Motor Disorders (encompassing Developmental Coordination Disorder, Stereotypic Movement Disorder, and tic disorders including

Tourette Syndrome). Moreover, neurodevelopmental disorders have been considered as specific conditions in which the brain's development and growth are affected. Specifically, these disorders can affect children's emotions, self-control, behavior, memory, emotions, language, learning, and behavior. The disorders can also co-exist in certain individuals. Neurodiverse children can show delays and deficits in development early on and the latter can continue to occur throughout their lifespan. Some disorders may affect speech, behavior, and learning, whereas others may have an impact on intelligence, communication, and social skills, meaning that they may have difficulty with certain social interactions, such as cyberbullying. Furthermore, there is a lack of research concerning the involvement of neurodiverse students in cyberbullying situations [11] and how specific sociomoral behavior may be impaired in these situations [62].

In the sections below, we discuss moral development and (dis)engagement, the risks of using the Internet, such as cyberbullying, as well as how serious games can serve as a promising resource to understand these processes and behaviors in neurodiverse children.

2   Moral Development in Neurodiverse Children

Moral development is impacted by individual factors, such as cognitive changes, emotions, and even neurodevelopment, as well as contextual factors, including family, peers, and culture [8]. In terms of contextual factors, children's development of moral understanding and behavior can be influenced by their interactions with family, teachers, and peers. Morality can be considered a code of values and customs that guide social behavior and has been described as both descriptive and normative [39]. Descriptive morality encompasses rules of moral behavior according to a specific society or group, whereas normative morality constitutes a universal code of moral conduct which is followed by all rational individuals, regardless of their society or group's descriptive morality, as it mainly emphasizes fairness and no harm for all [39, 111]. Morality can help direct behavior and enable positive interpersonal relationships.

Some of the literature in this domain has focused on the influence of interpersonal relationships on children's moral development from a social domain theory perspective [89, 100], as well as from a socialization/internalization approach [51, 52]. Research from the social domain theory perspective has focused on how children distinguish moral from standard behavior based on the responses of those around them [88]. The literature on the socialization/internalization approach is based on how adults model behavior to children through different techniques and whether children internalize those values or not [38, 51]. According to this perspective, moral development entails children's compliance with and internalization of social norms and standard behavior. Moreover, within this approach, evidence has shown that parents' behavior may encourage children's internalization of specific values but that this process involves children's attributes [38]. In a related study, Kochanska [50] showed that children who experience gentle parenting discipline tend to have greater conscientious development. Such parenting practices have been shown to facilitate children's experience of moral emotions, such as guilt and empathy, as well as their self-identification as moral individuals [52]

In children's moral development, the family stands as one of the biggest determining interpersonal influences, since there is direct and indirect teaching of values, perceived justice (of right and wrong behavior, which has consequences to guide decision-making), perceived fairness (i.e., set boundaries on the distribution of resources and corresponding thoughts about sharing, respect, reciprocity, own rights and entitlement), personal balance (between own needs and wants, and the interests of the greater social environment), social roles (in providing and receiving social support to satisfy emotional needs, and develop kindness, generosity, and empathy), morality, and culture (culturally specific and universal general values across groups), as well as pro-social helping [87, 103, 106]. In opposition to pro-social helping, but still within the interpersonal domain, a review investigating social exclusion identified cultural similarities in assessing exclusion across diverse societies and cultures [43]. Hence, non-pro-social behavior can also be transferred from one generation to the next universally.

Regarding intrapersonal influences, moral issues tend to trigger strong affective responses. Hence, emotions seem to play a crucial role in moral development. Nonetheless, there is little consensus among researchers on how emotions could determine moral development. Specifically, the literature on pro-social behavior has proposed that emotions can lead individuals to engage in moral and altruistic behavior, thus suggesting that moral emotion can affect moral judgment in the context of moral dilemmas and therefore, contribute to moral development [29]. Moral judgments involve the ability to judge one's own and others' behavior as either right or wrong, and are associated with the theory of mind, as it is essential to understand others' beliefs, desires, and intentions to form adaptive moral judgments [47]. By middle childhood, typically developing children are more attentive to others' intentions behind their behavior than to the behavior itself when they assess the moral legitimacy of the behavior. This capacity to comprehend others' intentions is dependent on theory of mind [113].

Moral emotions can include empathy, sympathy, guilt, and shame. Empathy (i.e., *affective*: being able to feel what others feel; and *cognitive*: being able to take the others' perspective) and sympathy (i.e., understanding and apprehending others' emotional states by expressing concern and sorrow) are moral emotions oriented towards others, whereas guilt (i.e., an unpleasant feeling of regret with regards to an aversive event) and shame (i.e., similar to guilt, but involving a more passive response of disappointment with regards to deviant behavior) are oriented towards the self [29]. When empathy is fostered in children, for example, they are more likely to engage in pro-social behavior [29]. Furthermore, the literature has shown that young children can show concern and empathy towards others [30]. In fact, emotions offer feedback to children so that they may interpret different consequences of diverse behavior, such as pro-social or aggressive [102] and accidental vs intentional harm [23], even though individual differences have been found to influence children's emotional reactions [60].

From a neurodevelopmental perspective, affective and cognitive processes are necessary for moral development, which occurs through interpersonal engagement and social experience [23]. In fact, the dynamic relationship between these processes is essential for normative and adaptive socioemotional functioning, because it can prevent individual networks and interconnections that cause impairments in moral behavior. Moreover, emotions have a profound effect on the development of moral capacities, especially considering children who tend to exert greater empathic reactions and neural network responses [23]. Consequently, moral judgment begins to take shape early on through integrated knowledge about others' emotions and consequences, as well as one's own theory of mind.

Theory of mind has been proposed in the literature as individuals' cognitive capacity to understand others' minds [72]. It is the ability to consider others' thoughts, feelings, and beliefs [62]. Although emotions are key for moral development, moral decision-making entails reasoning as a fundamental pillar [101]. Moreover, moral reasoning is supported by different neural networks, such as the amygdala, the right posterior superior temporal sulcus, and the ventromedial prefrontal cortex [2, 114]. These networks enable an exchange of information between affective states, cognitions, and motivational processes which are involved in moral judgment.

Some of the literature has indicated that there seems to be some differences in moral judgment between neurodiverse children (such as autism spectrum disorder) and neurotypical developing children [39, 63]. A recent study found that although autistic and neurotypical children tended to make similar judgments regarding moral transgressions across diverse moral foundations (i.e., authority/respect, care/harm, fairness/reciprocity, in-group/loyalty, and purity/sanctity [40], the first were more likely to suggest punishment for harmless norm violations than the latter. What determined this suggestion was children's perceived severity of moral transgressions. Another study found that both children on the autism spectrum and typically developing children made correct moral judgments, even though the first tended to have more rigid criteria for what they considered to be morally transgressive behavior [58]. Moreover, typically developing children seemed to have greater cooperation with children who demonstrated morally sound behavior, as opposed to those on the autism spectrum, who did not differ regarding their peers' morality.

Neurodevelopmental disorders are conditions that affect brain functions. Some disorders are mild impairments, enabling those affected to function daily, whereas others are more severe disorders and require constant care. Neurodiverse children can experience difficulties with language and speech, motor skills, behavior, memory, learning, or other neurological functions [104]. In fact, there is cerebellar dysfunction in various developmental disorders, such as autism, ADHD, and developmental dyslexia, and damage to the cerebellum in childhood can have a lasting impact on movement, cognition, and emotion regulation [91]. Damage to the subgenual prefrontal cortex in early childhood for instance, has been linked to abnormal autonomic reactions to emotional experiences and reduced understanding of the grave consequences of injurious social behavior [10]. Consequently, younger children may experience more suffering than adults. Moreover, lesions of the human amygdala in early childhood have been linked to a loss of retrieval of emotionally arousing experiences and deficiencies in theory of mind [86]. Furthermore, damage to the ventromedial pre-frontal cortex has been associated with impairments in early childhood, leading to greater difficulties in moral reasoning [3].

3 Moral Disengagement in Neurodiverse Children

There are many brain disorders that can impair sociomoral behavior, such as autism spectrum disorders. In fact, when children display behavior that is morally disengaged from previous behavioral patterns, possible causative developmental disorders must be considered to help children cope with situations and other environmental factors, as well as their own ability to regulate behavior [62]. Moreover, without the control mechanisms of moral emotions and the consideration of others' perspectives, children with developmental disorders may not be able to behave according to their moral standards, even when they know what is morally right and wrong, as well as the consequences associated with their behavior.

From a social cognitive perspective [8], moral agency pertains to individuals' capacity to make moral judgments considering what they deem to be right or wrong and is fundamental for self-directedness that influences one's own intentional functioning in different situations. Intrinsically, moral reasoning is transformed into action through self-regulatory processes, and through the moral judgment of behavior, which is based on personal standards and contextual factors. Thus, moral actions are a product of a dynamic interplay of cognitive, affective, and social stimuli, and individuals are considered as moral agents within their immediate social context which influences them [8].

Moral agency may be inhibitive, where individuals can abstain from behaving in cruel manners, and proactive, where they refrain from engaging in inhumane behavior by engaging in prosocial behavior. Moral agency is determined by social influences [7] and the digital era has created a physical distance between those who are victimized, those who bully, and those who observe. Understanding how neurodiverse children function as moral agents is fundamental, since moral judgments of aggressive behavior, based on personal moral beliefs, may affect their own behavior. Furthermore, those with the same moral values can, in fact, behave differently in the same circumstance because they may be different regarding how they morally disengage from it [8, 105]. Hence, this perspective can help shed light on how and why children behave in specific ways during social interaction through social media, especially in aggressive situations.

In developing a moral self, children assume standards to guide their behavior. In this activated self-regulatory process, children engage in cognitive functions by monitoring their conduct and circumstances surrounding it, judging their behavior regarding their moral standards and regulating it considering potential consequences in pursuit of self-satisfaction and self-worth, and withdrawal from self-censure. Accordingly, children may engage in moral disengagement, which is when individuals engage in harmful behavior with the belief that moral standards do not apply to them in that particular context [8]. Furthermore, according to the social cognitive theory of moral agency, there are four loci of moral disengagement where moral self-censure is selectively disengaged during moral control. These include (1) the locus of behavior, (2) the agent of the behavior, (3) the outcomes that derive from the behavior, and (4) the receiver of the behavior [5]. There are different disengagement mechanisms which operate at each locus: (1) moral justification (virtuous ends to explain harmful means), euphemistic language (harmful behavior is considered benevolent), and exonerative comparison (harmful behavior will prevent more pain than it causes); (2) displacement of responsibility (own behavior stems from others' demands) and diffusion of responsibility (division of behavior, group decision-making, and collective behavior) to conceal personal accountability; (3) minimizing/disregarding the injurious consequences of one's own behavior; and (4) dehumanization (allocating unhuman qualities) and attributing blame to the recipient [6, 16, 26].

Selective moral disengagement can operate at an individual and social level, causing extensive harm [6]. For instance, evidence has shown how moral disengagement may predict children's aggressive behavior in cyberbullying [71]. Other studies, however, have shown no association between moral disengagement and cyberbullying [69]. Cyberbullying constitutes intentional repeated harmful acts by sending prejudicial material or being involved in other forms of social aggression through digital technologies [109]. Since cyberbullying is considered a major challenge in contemporary society [79], the decision-making processes, and the ability to understand one's own and others' perspectives, must be considered [70]. Children's understanding of their cognitive activities [72] may affect how they interact in their social environment and make assumptions regarding the conduct of others, and how they develop cognitively and emotionally [46, 56]. While some literature indicates that moral disengagement declines in adolescence, specifically between the ages of 14 and 16 [66], it is in this period that there is a greater prevalence of cyberbullying behavior [68].

Technology, such as digital games and social media, can contribute to the escalation of moral disengagement since face-to-face interaction is null, and sometimes anonymity is used to hide one's personal identity, which therefore, disables personal and social sanctions for socially condemnable behavior [105]. Moreover, individuals disconnect from moral judgment and, hence, withdraw from socially moral behavior without feeling personally responsible for it. To date, little to no research has investigated the impact of technology on the moral (dis)engagement of neurodiverse children when confronted with negative online situations, such as cyberbullying. In fact, as far as we know, little research has investigated the impact cyberbullying has on these children, what role they play, and how they react to the phenomenon.

4 Cyberbullying in Neurodiverse Children

The role of technology and the internet in promoting mental health is crucial for those with developmental disorders who face cerebral, learning, and relational challenges on a daily basis. These children tend to be more isolated and marginalized in face-to-face contexts and may experience positive interpersonal relationships through online communication [37]. Some literature has focused on the challenges neurodiverse children have in using social networks to interact with others and on how their social skills can be developed [82]. Accordingly, social media can improve the quality of the relationships neurodiverse children have with others through social media, their friendship quality, and their anxiety levels. In fact, social media use has been associated with good friendship quality in adolescents on the autism spectrum, which can moderate anxiety levels. Hence, social media may be a useful resource to foster friendships among autistic adolescents, which in turn, could foster better social skills. In fact, evidence has shown that neurodiverse children are more likely to self-disclose online than face-to-face, which can lead to improvements in resilience, a more positive self-image, and a greater sense of accomplishment [74].

Nonetheless, as neurodiverse children participate in online experiences, whether through digital games or social networks, the probability of having them exposed to inappropriate information and interactions can increase. While social networks can constitute an effective resource for neurodiverse children to interact with family and friends [11] the risks associated with cyberbullying and other inappropriate conduct and content, as well as their anticipation that their children may shift more towards online life, as opposed to offline, with parents tending to be careful about their children's social network use [115]. This parental cautiousness is expected, since neurodiverse children may be more prone to being involved in cyberbullying situations when compared to typically developing students [11].

Research informing about the prevalence of cyberbullying among neurodiverse youth is scarce [25, 41, 53, 54], whereas research on bullying among these children has been more amplified. These studies have shown that those with neurodevelopmental disorders tend to be more bullying victims, perpetrators, and bully/victims than those who are typically developing children [15, 90, 93]. Specifically, even though research has been limited, neurodiverse children are at a greater risk of being bullying and cyberbullying victims than those who do not have these conditions [1, 9, 11]namely those on the autism spectrum and with ADHD [25], and especially those who are included in non-inclusive education settings as they do not have as many opportunities to develop social and academic skills [17, 65], and experience greater acceptance and increased participation [79]. Specifically, those with ADHD have shown a greater tendency to be more involved in cyberbullying than those who did not have a diagnosis [25, 41]. Aditionaly, those with learning disabilities tend to experience higher incidences of being cybervictims [18], cyberbullies, and cyberbully-victims [9, 49], compared to typically developing children [41].

Neurodiverse children seem to be more vulnerable to this phenomenon in segregated educational contexts, as opposed to inclusive ones [41]. Neurodiverse children, such as ADHD for instance, tend to show an increased and problematic use of social media [24], which may lead to their involvement in cyberbullying situations. In fact, the danger of a maladaptive use of social media may be determined by the link between limited cognitive control and underdeveloped brain regions concerning gratification in social contexts. Furthermore, online and offline interactions among adolescents overlap often, creating a greater strain for them when perceiving and experiencing these situations. Moreover, experiencing cyberbullying victimization has a grave impact on the psychosocial wellness of neurodiverse children [19]. These children may experience low self-esteem and difficulties in interacting with others. Besides, ADHD children who have been cybervictims have been known to report more severe depression and suicidality, than those who were not victimized [112]. Those on the autism spectrum and more severe oppositional defiant disorder have also been found to be more engaged in cyberbullying victimization and perpetration, but the tendency is for them to be the targets of this type of behavior [44].

Research has shown that ADHD children for example, tend to experience more in-person victimization [28, 34, 84], cybervictimization or both [73, 81, 108] than those who have a typical development. In fact, evidence has shown that in-person victimization and cybervictimization are related to lower self-esteem and differentially associated with internalizing symptoms among ADHD children. Both types of victimization were linked to higher internalizing symptoms and lower self-esteem [33]. Due to a lack of social competencies and an adaptive use of social skills, children with developmental disorders have difficulty in dealing with obstacles in developmental transitions and tend to show secondary psychiatric symptoms, namely, anxiety and depression, which can further negatively impact their development and quality of life [12, 110]. For instance, ADHD children, dyslexic children and autistic children have reported greater social withdrawal, sadness, and difficulty in using executive functions [48, 78], because of difficulties in thinking critically, foreseeing future outcomes, and delaying responses. Moreover, in early adolescence, evidence has shown that those with neurodevelopmental disorders may have more difficulty engaging in self-directed behavior autonomously [27, 59]. Hence, interacting with others online becomes more challenging, specifically because parental supervision is not always available.

Some of the literature has shown that there is a greater prevalence rate of cyberbullying involvement in ADHD children, as opposed to those who do not suffer from a developmental disorder [41, 76, 112]. For instance, Tural and colleagues [99] found that ADHD adolescents who were not treated for their condition tended to suffer greatly from cyberbullying, isolation, physical aggression, sexual victimization, and the destruction of their personal belongings. On the other hand, these adolescents tended to engage in cyberbullying behavior more, as well as to destroy others' belongings more frequently, than those who were treated for their condition. A recent meta-analysis [45] found that online interaction may be more appealing to individuals within the autism spectrum, than interacting with others face-to-face. This may be so because they do not experience certain pressures, such as the need for eye-contact, quick response, and non-verbal behavior, which is usually a requisite for face-to-face interaction, but not online interaction. Nonetheless, the literature mentions the risks and vulnerabilities related to social media use. For instance [92], found that those on the autism spectrum tended to show signs of loneliness, and isolation, as well as cyberbullying involvement. Furthermore, those with neurodevelopmental disorders tend to use less social network sites but seem to experience as much cyberbullying as those who do not have these disorders [96]. In addition, not only has social media use been associated with cyberbullying experiences in those with developmental disorders [96], but these children feel profound unpleasant emotions regarding these situations [36].

Cyberbullying victimization and perpetration are common occurring phenomena among autistic children. Those who have been victimized tended to report greater depression, anxiety, and suicidality than those who were not victims [44]. Research has shown that those with and without neurodevelopmental disorders tend to display high prevalence rates of cyberbullying victimization, but that the latter show a significantly greater frequency of cybervictimization [55]. Moreover, a meta-analysis found that 44% of autistic individuals have experienced victimization (e.g., mostly cyber/bullying, child abuse, and crime victimization), although they did not consider the different types of victimization separately [97]. Accordingly, contexts with greater social support tended to have lower prevalence rates of victimization. Hence, it is critical for researchers and practitioners to focus on neurodiverse children and adolescents who may be more at risk of experiencing cyberbullying, whether they play the role of the victim, the cyberbully, or the bystander, so that they may be able to interpret these situations more accurately and develop strategies to deal with interpersonal relationships that are involved in this type of phenomena.

5 Serious Games to Assess Cyberbullying and Moral Disengagement

Digital games can include a great variety of digital applications, and some similar features, such as the gaming context, player participation, interaction, and multimedia [61]. These resources may be used as entertainment, but serious digital games can effectively train and help develop new competencies in those with neurodevelopmental disorders [20, 64, 67, 85, 94, 98]. A recent review has shown the positive effects of serious games on those with neurodevelopmental disorders, such as ADHD, because they offered opportunities for greater awareness, control of attention, and positive social interactions [57, 107]. Furthermore, serious games have been known to help those with disorders control impulsive and aggressive behavior and develop self-regulated behavior [107].

Moreover, serious games have been known to foster pleasant emotions and increased motivation to learn during gameplay [57, 77, 83, 107]. Evidence has shown that experiencing embodiment in serious virtual reality games seems to be an effective strategy for ADHD children because they are highly engaged, motivated, and able to develop self-regulation strategies [107].

Serious games have been known to foster prosociality in neurodiverse players including considerable behavioral change [77]. These games have also provided evidence that they can help those with neurodevelopmental disorder develop executive functions, self-control [83], and self-regulated thinking [21]. In fact, serious games based on virtual reality, for instance, have been known to improve self-consciousness, awareness of others, decision-making, adaptive behavior, and the regulation of emotions, thoughts and behavior [64]. This, in turn, tended to lead towards improved social interactions, empathetic decisions, and an improved sense of belonging. Furthermore, those with neurodevelopmental disorders revealed positive emotions and were more independent, self-confident, self-motivated, and even perceived training as a gratification. In Mitsea and colleagues study [64], it was emphasized that their serious game should offer opportunities for players to be observant, communicative, cooperative, expressive, and understanding of others. Nonetheless, it is crucial for professionals to acquire training, even when using resources, such as serious games, to be able to guide and monitor children's involvement during gameplay, as well as provide adequate feedback [64].

A recent study found positive prolonged training effects of digital game-based interventions in neurodiverse children, such as ADHD children or dyslexics suggesting that these types of resources are beneficial to develop social-cognitive skills in diverse remote or face-to-face educational settings [75]. For instance, game features are key aspects which may determine the effects of serious games in neurodiverse children. It is important to include training objectives while designing game features to develop children's cognitive abilities more efficiently. In fact, game features can contribute to children's interest, motivation [80], and learning process [95]. Neurodiverse children can also improve their attention [14] and academic skills with digital serious games, such as math abilities and reading fluency through training in visuospatial attention [13, 75].

Even though these resources benefit neurodiverse children in terms of executive functions and affective/motivational processes, to date, we have not yet found studies examining how these resources could be used to focus on these children's involvement in cyberbullying incidents and their moral (dis)engagement from these situations. Serious games constitute a resource that provides players with direct immersive experiences of different phenomena, such as bullying and cyberbullying, while raising awareness and empathy regarding the victims involved and teaching problem-solving strategies for different situations. There have been studies which proposed digital serious-game based interventions to examine the reactions of children and adolescents with typical development while promoting prosociality, fostering empathy, and investigating moral disengagement in cyberbullying situations.

As an example, Com@Viver is a game which was developed to foster prosociality, empathy, and moral engagement in cyberbullying situations [31, 32, 35]. This game contextualized cyberbullying situations within a fictional social network site for students and used social agents through scripted interaction. The results from this game were promising, since it did in fact, enable children and adolescents to improve their reactions to cyberbullying events. Specifically, those who experienced the game demonstrated more prosocial assertive behavior after the intervention in comparison with those who did not [32]. Moreover, over time, those who played the game tended to consider the cyberbullying situations more seriously and did not avoid assuming responsibility for intervening prosocially in the situation as much as the children who did not play the game. Furthermore, children who played the game revealed a lower tendency over time to invest aggressively against the cybervictim. The game also enabled children and adolescents to reveal greater cognitive empathy, empathic concern regarding the situation, and affective empathy than those who did not play the game. Additionally, those who played Com@Viver reported appraisals and factual cognitions against cyberbullying, and empathy towards the victim [32]. Lastly, this game was also used to examine specific moral disengagement mechanisms in cyberbullying situations through gamified tasks which were embedded into the game [35]. In fact, the most used moral disengagement mechanisms during gameplay by children and adolescents were blaming the victim and euphemistic labeling regarding the severity of the situation. We argue that if digital serious games can have beneficial effects on neurodiverse children in terms of cognitive and socio-emotional skills, then, it is likely that they can also enhance these children's prosociality and interpersonal relationships online and offline.

6   Conclusion

According to the literature we have mentioned in this chapter, little research has investigated the impact cyberbullying has on neurodiverse children, what role they play, and how they react to the phenomenon. Furthermore, how they morally engage or disengage from this type of phenomenon requires examination, considering the relevancy of emotions, as well as the different diagnoses. It would be interesting to combine a neurodevelopmental perspective with social cognitive theory to understand how moral development occurs in neurodiverse children and how moral emotions may or may not condition their behavior, whether through impulse or behavior. Furthermore, we propose that this line of research could use state-of-the-art technology, such as serious games incorporating artificial intelligence and social agents to inform parents and professionals how these processes occur in neurodiverse children. Longitudinal objective data retrieved from logfiles during gameplay could inform researchers and education professionals about these children's reactions to the phenomenon. This would provide detailed information that could help tailor develop training programs which are adapted to children's needs.

Acknowledgements This work received national funding from the Foundation for Science and Technology (FCT), I.P. (2022 02218.CEECIND), project *Te@ch4SocialGood: Promoting prosociality in schools to prevent cyberbullying* (PTDC/PSI-GER/1918/2020), and the Research Center for Psychological Science (CICPSI) (UIDB/04527/2020; UIDP/04527/2020).

References

1. Alhaboby ZA, Barnes J, Evans H, Short E (2019) Cyber-victimization of people with chronic conditions and disabilities: a systematic review of scope and impact. Trauma Violence Abuse 20:398–415
2. Allison T, Puce A, McCarthy G (2000) Social perception from visual cues: role of the STS region. Trends Cogn Sci 4:267–278. https://doi.org/10.1016/S1364-6613(00)01501-1
3. Anderson SW, Bechara A, Damasio H, Tranel D, Damasio AR (1999) Impairment of social and moral behavior related to early damage in human prefrontal cortex
4. APA (2013) Diagnostic and statistical manual of mental disorders: DSM-5^{TM}, 5th edn. American Psychiatric Publishing Inc., Arlington, VA, US
5. Bandura A (2002) Selective moral disengagement in the exercise of moral agency. J Moral Educ 31:101–119. https://doi.org/10.1080/0305724022014322
6. Bandura A (2003) The role of selective moral disengagement in terrorism and counterterrorism. In: Mogahaddam FM, Marsella AJ (eds) Understanding terrorism: psychosocial roots, consequences, and interventions. American Psychological Association, Washington, pp 121–150
7. Bandura A (2008) Toward an agentic theory of the self. In: Marsh HW, Craven RG, McInerey DM (eds) Advances in self research: self-processes, learning, and enabling human potential, vol 3. Information Age Publishing, Charlotte, NC, pp 15–49
8. Bandura A (2016) Moral disengagement: how people do harm and live with themselves. Macmillan, New York
9. Barringer-Brown C (2015) Cyber bullying among students with serious emotional and specific learning disabilities. J Educ Hum Dev 4. https://doi.org/10.15640/jehd.v4n2_1a4
10. Bechara A, Tranel D, Damasio H, Damasio AR (1996) Failure to respond autonomically to anticipated future outcomes following damage to prefrontal cortex
11. Beckman L, Hellström L, von Kobyletzki L (2020) Cyber bullying among children with neurodevelopmental disorders: a systematic review. Scand J Psychol 61:54–67
12. Bellini S (2004) Social skill deficits and anxiety in high-functioning adolescents with autism spectrum disorders. Focus Autism Other Dev Disabl 19:78–86. https://doi.org/10.1177/10883576040190020201
13. Benavides-Varela S, Zandonella Callegher C, Fagiolini B, Leo I, Altoè G, Lucangeli D (2020) Effectiveness of digital-based interventions for children with mathematical learning difficulties: a meta-analysis. Comput Educ 157. https://doi.org/10.1016/j.compedu.2020.103953
14. Bertoni S, Franceschini S, Ronconi L, Gori S, Facoetti A (2019) Is excessive visual crowding causally linked to developmental dyslexia? Neuropsychologia 130:107–117. https://doi.org/10.1016/j.neuropsychologia.2019.04.018
15. Blake JJ, Lund EM, Zhou Q, Kwok O-M, Benz MR (2012) National prevalence rates of bully victimization among students with disabilities in the United States
16. Bolinger D (1980) Language—The loaded weapon: the use and abuse of language today. Longman Publishing Group, New York, NY
17. Brown L, Long E, Udvari-Solner A, Schwarz P, Vandeventer P, Ahlgren C, Johnson F, Gruenewald L, Jorgensen J (1989) Should students with severe intellectual disabilities be based in regular or in special education classrooms in home schools? The Special and Regular Edcuation Classroom: Options in the Home School Divisions for Educational Services and Personnel Preparation

18. Campbell M, Hwang YS, Whiteford C, Dillon-Wallace J, Ashburner J, Saggers B, Carrington S (2017) Bullying prevalence in students with autism spectrum disorder. Aust J Spec Educ 41:101–122. https://doi.org/10.1017/jse.2017.5
19. Cavallo ND, Maggi G, Ferraiuolo F, Sorrentino A, Perrotta S, Carotenuto M, Santangelo G, Santoro C (2023) Neuropsychiatric manifestations, reduced self-esteem and poor quality of life in children and adolescents with neurofibromatosis type 1 (NF1): the impact of symptom visibility and bullying behavior. Children 10. https://doi.org/10.3390/children10020330
20. Cheah I, Shimul AS, Phau I (2022) Motivations of playing digital games: a review and research agenda. Psychol Mark 39:937–950. https://doi.org/10.1002/mar.21631
21. Cunha F, Campos S, Simões-Silva V, Brugada-Ramentol V, Sá-Moura B, Jalali H, Bozorgzadeh A, Trigueiro MJ (2023) The effect of a virtual reality based intervention on processing speed and working memory in individuals with ADHD—A pilot-study. Front Virtual Real 4. https://doi.org/10.3389/frvir.2023.1108060
22. Davis K, Iosif AM, Nordahl CW, Solomon M, Krug MK (2023) Video game use, aggression, and social impairment in adolescents with autism spectrum disorder. J Autism Dev Disord 53:3567–3580. https://doi.org/10.1007/s10803-022-05649-1
23. Decety J, Howard LH (2013) The role of affect in the neurodevelopment of morality. Child Dev Perspect 7:49–54. https://doi.org/10.1111/cdep.12020
24. Dekkers TJ, van Hoorn J (2022) Understanding problematic social media use in adolescents with attention-deficit/hyperactivity disorder (ADHD): a narrative review and clinical recommendations. Brain Sci 12
25. Didden R, Scholte RHJ, Korzilius H, De Moor JMH, Vermeulen A, O'Reilly M, Lang R, Lancioni GE (2009) Cyberbullying among students with intellectual and developmental disability in special education settings. Dev Neurorehabil 12:146–151. https://doi.org/10.1080/17518420902971356
26. Diener E (2006) Deindividuation: causes and consequences. Soc Behav Personal Int J 5:143–155. https://doi.org/10.2224/sbp.1977.5.1.143
27. Eaves LC, Ho HH (2008) Young adult outcome of autism spectrum disorders. J Autism Dev Disord 38:739–747. https://doi.org/10.1007/s10803-007-0441-x
28. Efron D, Wijaya M, Hazell P, Sciberras E (2021) Peer victimization in children with ADHD: a community-based longitudinal study. J Atten Disord 25:291–299. https://doi.org/10.1177/1087054718796287
29. Eisenberg N (2000) Emotion, regulation, and moral development. Annu Rev Psychol 51:665–697. https://doi.org/10.1146/annurev.psych.51.1.665
30. Eisenberg N, Spinrad TL, Sadovsky A (2006) Empathy-related responding in children. In: Killen M, Smetana JG (eds) Handbook of moral development. Lawrence Erlbaum Associates Publishers, pp 517–549
31. Ferreira PC, Simão AMV, Paiva A, Martinho C, Prada R, Rocha J (2022) Serious game-based psychosocial intervention to foster prosociality in cyberbullying bystanders. Psychosoc Interv 31:83–96. https://doi.org/10.5093/pi2022a5
32. Ferreira PC, Veiga Simão AM, Paiva A, Martinho C, Prada R, Ferreira A, Santos F (2021) Exploring empathy in cyberbullying with serious games. Comput Educ 166. https://doi.org/10.1016/j.compedu.2021.104155
33. Fogleman ND, McQuade JD, Mehari KR, Becker SP (2021) In-person victimization, cyber victimization, and polyvictimization in relation to internalizing symptoms and self-esteem in adolescents with attention-deficit/hyperactivity disorder. Child Care Health Dev 47:805–815. https://doi.org/10.1111/cch.12888
34. Fogleman ND, Slaughter KE, Rosen PJ, Leaberry KD, Walerius DM (2019) Emotion regulation accounts for the relation between ADHD and peer victimization. J Child Fam Stud 28:2429–2442. https://doi.org/10.1007/s10826-018-1297-8
35. Francisco SM, Ferreira PC, Veiga Simão AM (2022) Behind the scenes of cyberbullying: personal and normative beliefs across profiles and moral disengagement mechanisms. Int J Adolesc Youth 27:337–361. https://doi.org/10.1080/02673843.2022.2095215

36. Gillespie-Smith K, Hendry G, Anduuru N, Laird T, Ballantyne C (2021) Using social media to be 'social': perceptions of social media benefits and risk by autistic young people, and parents. Res Dev Disabil 118. https://doi.org/10.1016/j.ridd.2021.104081
37. Good B, Fang L (2015) Promoting smart and safe internet use among neurodiverse children and their parents. Clin Soc Work J 43:179–188. https://doi.org/10.1007/s10615-015-0519-4
38. Grusec JE, Goodnow JJ (1994) Impact of parental discipline methods on the child's internalization of values: a reconceptualization of current points of view
39. Haidt J (2001) The emotional dog and its rational tail: a social intuitionist approach to moral judgment. Psychol Rev 108:814–834. https://doi.org/10.1037/0033-295X
40. Haidt J, Joseph C (2008) The moral mind: how five sets of innate intuitions guide the development of many culture-specific virtues, and perhaps even modules. In: The innate mind. Oxford University Press
41. Heiman T, Olenik-Shemesh D, Eden S (2015) Cyberbullying involvement among students with ADHD: relation to loneliness, self-efficacy and social support. Eur J Spec Needs Educ 30:15–29. https://doi.org/10.1080/08856257.2014.943562
42. Hinduja S, Patchin JW (2010) Bullying, cyberbullying, and suicide. Arch Suicide Res 14:206–221. https://doi.org/10.1080/13811118.2010.494133
43. Hitti A, Mulvey KL, Killen M (2011) Social exclusion and culture: the role of group norms, group identity and fairness
44. Hu HF, Liu TL, Hsiao RC, Ni HC, Liang SHY, Lin CF, Chan HL, Hsieh YH, Wang LJ, Lee MJ, Chou WJ, Yen CF (2019) Cyberbullying victimization and perpetration in adolescents with high-functioning autism spectrum disorder: correlations with depression, anxiety, and suicidality. J Autism Dev Disord 49:4170–4180. https://doi.org/10.1007/s10803-019-04060-7
45. Hudson NA, Linnane JM, Rayner-Smith K (2023) Autism and social media: a systematic review of the user experience. Adv Autism 9:201–216. https://doi.org/10.1108/AIA-01-2023-0001
46. Hughes C (2004) What are the links between theory of mind and social relations? Review, reflections and new directions for studies of typical and atypical development. Soc Dev 13:590–619
47. Kahn PH (2004) Mind and morality. New Dir Child Adolesc Dev 107:73–83
48. Kegel NE (2010) Executive functioning in Asperger's disorder and nonverbal learning disabilities: a comparison of developmental and behavioral characteristics. Duquesne University
49. Kloosterman PH, Kelley EA, Craig WM, Parker JDA, Javier C (2013) Types and experiences of bullying in adolescents with an autism spectrum disorder. Res Autism Spectr Disord 7:824–832. https://doi.org/10.1016/j.rasd.2013.02.013
50. Kochanska G (1997) Multiple pathways to conscience for children with different temperaments: from toddlerhood to age 5
51. Kochanska G, Barry RA, Jimenez NB, Hollatz AL, Woodard J (2009) Guilt and effortful control: two mechanisms that prevent disruptive developmental trajectories. J Pers Soc Psychol 97:322–333. https://doi.org/10.1037/a0015471
52. Kochanska G, Koenig JL, Barry RA, Kim S, Yoon JE (2010) Children's conscience during toddler and preschool years, moral self, and a competent, adaptive developmental trajectory. Dev Psychol 46:1320–1332. https://doi.org/10.1037/a0020381
53. Kowalski RM, Fedina C (2011) Cyber bullying in ADHD and Asperger syndrome populations. Res Autism Spectr Disord 5:1201–1208. https://doi.org/10.1016/j.rasd.2011.01.007
54. Kowalski RM, Limber SP, Agatston PW (2012) Cyberbullying: bullying in the digital age. Wiley-Blackwell, Hoboken
55. Kowalski RM, Toth A (2018) Cyberbullying among youth with and without disabilities. J Child Adolesc Trauma 11:7–15. https://doi.org/10.1007/s40653-017-0139-y
56. Lalonde CE, Chandler MJ (1995) False belief understanding goes to school: on the social-emotional consequences of coming early or late to a first theory of mind. Cogn Emot 9:167–185. https://doi.org/10.1080/02699939508409007

57. Lan KY, Shih M-F (2018) Effective learning design of game-based 3D virtual language learning environments for special education students
58. Li J, Zhu L, Gummerum M (2014) The relationship between moral judgment and cooperation in children with high-functioning autism. Sci Rep 4. https://doi.org/10.1038/srep04314
59. Litner B (2003) Teens with ADHD: the challenge of high school. Child Youth Care Forum 32:137–158
60. Malti T, Gummerum M, Keller M, Buchmann M (2009) Children's moral motivation, sympathy, and prosocial behavior. Child Dev 80:442–460
61. Manesis D (2020) Digital games in primary education
62. Mendez MF (2009) The neurobiology of moral behavior: review and neuropsychiatric implications. CNS Spectr 14:608–620
63. Mercier H, Sperber D (2011) Why do humans reason? Arguments for an argumentative theory. Behav Brain Sci 34:57–74. https://doi.org/10.1017/S0140525X10000968
64. Mitsea E, Drigas A, Skianis C (2023) VR gaming for meta-skills training in special education: the role of metacognition, motivations, and emotional intelligence. Educ Sci (Basel) 13:639. https://doi.org/10.3390/educsci13070639
65. Morrison GM, Furlong MJ, Smith G (1994) Factors associated with the experience of school violence among general education, leadership class, opportunity class, and special day class pupils. Educ Treat Child 17:359–369
66. Paciello M, Fida R, Tramontano C, Lupinetti C, Caprara GV (2008) Stability and change of moral disengagement and its impact on aggression and violence in late adolescence. Child Dev 79:1288–1309. https://doi.org/10.1111/j.1467-8624.2008.01189.x
67. Papanastasiou G, Drigas A, Skianis C (2022) Serious games: how do they impact special education needs children. Tech Educ Human 2:41–58
68. Pereira F, Spitzberg BH, Matos M (2016) Cyber-harassment victimization in Portugal: prevalence, fear and help-seeking among adolescents. Comput Human Behav 62:136–146. https://doi.org/10.1016/j.chb.2016.03.039
69. Perren S, Gutzwiller-Helfenfinger E (2012) Cyberbullying and traditional bullying in adolescence: differential roles of moral disengagement, moral emotions, and moral values. Euro J Dev Psychol 9:195–209. https://doi.org/10.1080/17405629.2011.643168
70. Pfeifer JH, Blakemore SJ (2012) Adolescent social cognitive and affective neuroscience: past, present, and future. Soc Cogn Affect Neurosci 7:1–10. https://doi.org/10.1093/scan/nsr099
71. Pornari CD, Wood J (2010) Peer and cyber aggression in secondary school students: the role of moral disengagement, hostile attribution bias, and outcome expectancies. Aggress Behav 36:81–94. https://doi.org/10.1002/ab.20336
72. Premack D, Woodruff G (1978) Does the chimpanzee have a theory of mind? Behav Brain Sci 1:515–526. https://doi.org/10.1017/S0140525X00076512
73. Przybylski AK, Bowes L (2017) Cyberbullying and adolescent well-being in England: a population-based cross-sectional study. Lancet Child Adolesc Health 1:19–26. https://doi.org/10.1016/S2352-4642(17)30011-1
74. Raskind MH, Margalit M, Higgins EL (2014) Hammill Institute on Disabilities
75. Ren X, Wu Q, Cui N, Zhao J, Bi H-Y (2023) Effectiveness of digital game-based trainings in children with neurodevelopmental disorders: a meta-analysis. Res Dev Disabil 133:104418. https://doi.org/10.1016/j.ridd.2022.104418
76. Del Rey R, Casas JA, Ortega-Ruiz R, Schultze-Krumbholz A, Scheithauer H, Smith P, Thompson F, Barkoukis V, Tsorbatzoudis H, Brighi A, Guarini A, Pyzalski J, Plichta P (2015) Structural validation and cross-cultural robustness of the European Cyberbullying Intervention Project Questionnaire. Comput Human Behav 50:141–147. https://doi.org/10.1016/j.chb.2015.03.065
77. Rodrigo-Yanguas M, Martin-Moratinos M, Blasco-Fontecilla H, Menendez-Garcia A, Carlos Gonzalez-Tardon B, Royuela A (2021) A virtual reality game (The Secret Trail of Moon) for treating attention-deficit/hyperactivity disorder: development and usability study. JMIR Serious Games. https://doi.org/10.2196/preprints.26824

78. Rommelse NNJ, Geurts HM, Franke B, Buitelaar JK, Hartman CA (2011) A review on cognitive and brain endophenotypes that may be common in autism spectrum disorder and attention-deficit/hyperactivity disorder and facilitate the search for pleiotropic genes. Neurosci Biobehav Rev 35:1363–1396
79. Sabella RA, Patchin JW, Hinduja S (2013) Cyberbullying myths and realities. Comput Human Behav 29:2703–2711
80. Sailer M, Hense JU, Mayr SK, Mandl H (2017) How gamification motivates: an experimental study of the effects of specific game design elements on psychological need satisfaction. Comput Human Behav 69:371–380. https://doi.org/10.1016/j.chb.2016.12.033
81. Salmivalli C, Sainio M, Hodges EVE (2013) Electronic victimization: correlates, antecedents, and consequences among elementary and middle school students. J Clin Child Adolesc Psychol 42:442–453. https://doi.org/10.1080/15374416.2012.759228
82. van Schalkwyk GI, Marin CE, Ortiz M, Rolison M, Qayyum Z, McPartland JC, Lebowitz ER, Volkmar FR, Silverman WK (2017) Social media use, friendship quality, and the moderating role of anxiety in adolescents with autism spectrum disorder. J Autism Dev Disord 47:2805–2813. https://doi.org/10.1007/s10803-017-3201-6
83. Schena A, Garotti R, D'Alise D, Giugliano S, Polizzi M, Trabucco V, Riccio MP, Bravaccio C (2023) IAmHero: preliminary findings of an experimental study to evaluate the statistical significance of an intervention for ADHD conducted through the use of serious games in virtual reality. Int J Environ Res Public Health 20. https://doi.org/10.3390/ijerph20043414
84. Sciberras E, Ohan J, Anderson V (2012) Bullying and peer victimisation in adolescent girls with attention-deficit/hyperactivity disorder. Child Psychiatr Hum Dev 43:254–270. https://doi.org/10.1007/s10578-011-0264-z
85. Shahmoradi L, Mohammadian F, Rahmani Katigari M (2022) A systematic review on serious games in attention rehabilitation and their effects. Behav Neurol 2022
86. Shaw P, Lawrence EJ, Radbourne C, Bramham J, Polkey CE, David AS (2004) The impact of early and late damage to the human amygdala on "theory of mind" reasoning. Brain 127:1535–1548. https://doi.org/10.1093/brain/awh168
87. Shweder R, Mahapatra M, Kagan J, Lamb S, Miller J (1987) The emergence of morality in young children
88. Smetana JG (1999) The role of parents in moral development: a social domain analysis. J Moral Educ 28:311–321. https://doi.org/10.1080/030572499103106
89. Smetana JG (2006) Social-cognitive domain theory: Consistencies and variations in children's moral and social judgments. In: Handbook of moral development, pp 119–153
90. Sterzing PR, Shattuck PT, Narendorf SC, Wagner M, Cooper BP (2012) Bullying involvement and autism spectrum disorders: prevalence and correlates of bullying involvement among adolescents with an autism spectrum disorder. Arch Pediatr Adolesc Med 166:1058–1064. https://doi.org/10.1001/archpediatrics.2012.790
91. Stoodley CJ (2016) The cerebellum and neurodevelopmental disorders. Cerebellum 15:34–37
92. Suzuki K, Oi Y, Inagaki M (2021) The relationships among autism spectrum disorder traits, loneliness, and social networking service use in college students. J Autism Dev Disord 51:2047–2056. https://doi.org/10.1007/s10803-020-04701-2
93. Swearer SM, Wang C, Maag JW, Siebecker AB, Frerichs LJ (2012) Understanding the bullying dynamic among students in special and general education. J Sch Psychol 50:503–520. https://doi.org/10.1016/j.jsp.2012.04.001
94. Terras MM, Boyle EA, Ramsay J, Jarrett D (2018) The opportunities and challenges of serious games for people with an intellectual disability. Br J Edu Technol 49:690–700. https://doi.org/10.1111/bjet.12638
95. Tokan MK, Imakulata MM (2019) The effect of motivation and learning behaviour on student achievement. S Afr J Educ 39. https://doi.org/10.15700/saje.v39n1a1510
96. Triantafyllopoulou P, Clark-Hughes C, Langdon PE (2022) Social media and cyber-bullying in autistic adults. J Autism Dev Disord 52:4966–4974. https://doi.org/10.1007/s10803-021-05361-6

97. Trundle G, Jones KA, Ropar D, Egan V (2023) Prevalence of victimisation in autistic individuals: a systematic review and meta-analysis. Trauma Violence Abuse 24:2282–2296
98. Tsikinas S, Xinogalos S (2019) Studying the effects of computer serious games on people with intellectual disabilities or autism spectrum disorder: a systematic literature review. J Comput Assist Learn 35:61–73. https://doi.org/10.1111/jcal.12311
99. Tural Hesapcıoglu S, Kandemir G (2020) Association of methylphenidate use and traditional and cyberbullying in adolescents with ADHD. Pediatr Int 62:725–735. https://doi.org/10.1111/ped.14185
100. Turiel E (1983) The development of social knowledge: morality and convention. Cambridge University Press, New York, NY
101. Turiel E (2010) The relevance of moral epistemology and psychology for neuroscience. In: Zelazo PD, Chandler M, Crone E (eds) Developmental social cognitive neuroscience. Psychology Press, New York, pp 313–331
102. Turiel E, Killen M (2010) Taking emotions seriously: the role of emotions in moral development. Emotions, aggression, and morality in children: bridging development and psychopathology. American Psychological Association, Washington, pp 33–52
103. Turiel E, Perkins SA (2004) Flexibilities of mind: conflict and culture. Hum Dev 47:158–178
104. U.S. Environmental Protection Agency (2013) America's children and the environment, 3rd edn., Washington, D.C.
105. da Veiga Simão AMV, Ferreira P, Francisco SM, Paulino P, de Souza SB (2018) Cyberbullying: shaping the use of verbal aggression through normative moral beliefs and self-efficacy. New Media Soc 20:4787–4806. https://doi.org/10.1177/1461444818784870
106. Wainryb C (2006) Moral development in culture: diversity, tolerance, and justice. In: Killen M, Smetana JG (eds) Handbook of moral development. Lawrence Erlbaum Associates Publishers, pp 211–240
107. Weerdmeester J, Cima M, Granic I, Hashemian Y, Gotsis M (2016) A feasibility study on the effectiveness of a full-body videogame intervention for decreasing attention deficit hyperactivity disorder symptoms. Games Health J 5:258–269. https://doi.org/10.1089/g4h.2015.0103
108. Wigderson S, Lynch M (2013) Cyber-and traditional peer victimization: unique relationships with adolescent well-being. Psychol Violence 3:297–309. https://doi.org/10.1037/a0033657
109. Willard N (2005) Educators guide to cyberbullying and cyberthreats
110. Wilson AM, Deri Armstrong C, Furrie A, Walcot E (2009) The mental health of canadians with self-reported learning disabilities. J Learn Disabil 42:24–40. https://doi.org/10.1177/0022219408326216
111. Wilson JQ (1993) The moral sense
112. Yen CF, Chou WJ, Liu TL, Ko CH, Yang P, Hu HF (2014) Cyberbullying among male adolescents with attention-deficit/hyperactivity disorder: prevalence, correlates, and association with poor mental health status. Res Dev Disabil 35:3543–3553. https://doi.org/10.1016/j.ridd.2014.08.035
113. Young L, Cushman F, Hauser M, Saxe R (2007) The neural basis of the interaction between theory of mind and moral judgment
114. Young L, Dungan J (2012) Where in the brain is morality? Everywhere and maybe nowhere. Soc Neurosci 7:1–10
115. Zhu R, Hardy D, Myers T (2022) Community led co-design of a social networking platform with adolescents with autism spectrum disorder. J Autism Dev Disord 52:38–51. https://doi.org/10.1007/s10803-021-04918-9

Computer-Supported Collaborative Learning and the Regulation of Learning in Neurodiverse Children

Paula Costa Ferreira, Ana Margarida Veiga Simão, Diana Stilwell, Sara L. Lopes, Diogo Domingues, Fátima Trindade, and Nádia Pereira

Abstract

This chapter presents how the regulation of learning, individually and collectively, in a computer-supported learning environment, can benefit neurodiverse children. We review the literature on self-regulation, co-regulation, and shared regulation of learning throughout the learning process within a technology context. Additionally, we investigate the type of regulation that neurodiverse students can engage in while employing specific self-regulation, co-regulation, and shared regulation strategies to reach objectives. This chapter aims to present current literature and empirical evidence on this subject and provide recommendations for best practices so that researchers and education professionals can help children reflect metacognitively on their learning processes and attribute

---

P. Costa Ferreira (✉) · A. M. Veiga Simão · D. Stilwell · N. Pereira
CICPSI, Faculdade de Psicologia, Universidade de Lisboa, Lisbon, Portugal
e-mail: paula.ferreira@edu.ulisboa.pt

A. M. Veiga Simão
e-mail: amsimao@psicologia.ulisboa.pt

D. Stilwell
e-mail: dianateixeira@edu.ulisboa.pt

N. Pereira
e-mail: nadia@edu.ulisboa.pt

S. L. Lopes
Business School, Iscte-IUL, Lisbon, Portugal
e-mail: sara_lampreia_lopes@iscte-iul.pt

F. Trindade
PADS, Portuguese Association of Down Syndrome, Lisbon, Portugal
e-mail: fatimaptrindade2018@gmail.com

D. Domingues
Facukdade de Psicologia, Universidade de Lisboa, Lisbon, Portugal
e-mail: diogohfd@gmail.com

value to their learning experiences and decision-making processes with the help of digital interactive tools, which can be used and adapted to meet their needs and can be made available in classrooms.

1 Introduction

Learners are influenced by the reciprocity of intrapersonal, behavioral, and environmental factors when managing their actions to accomplish tasks. This enhancement of learners' self-regulatory skills enables them to autonomously make choices and trace learning paths in order to achieve goals [1, 2]. Additionally, the regulation of learning is inherently social as it can be shaped by contextual factors, developed through social participation, and embedded within social activity systems [3]. Understanding how learners can engage in individual and collective learning tasks in order to improve their performance becomes increasingly important for educational practices. This becomes more challenging when these learners are neurodiverse children. Neurodevelopmental disorders have been considered as intellectual disabilities, including communication disorders, attention-deficit/hyperactivity disorder, autism spectrum disorder, motor disorders, and specific learning disorders [4].

Computer-supported collaborative learning (CSCL) provides opportunities for learners to agentically engage in and share the regulation of learning and the co-construction of knowledge with digital media [5] and is a promising approach to enable neurodiverse students to develop higher-order skills. CSCL implies a synchronized, reciprocal effort to build shared knowledge [6] and to regulate learning [6, 7]. Since learners may have difficulty in participating regularly and with quality in collaborative learning environments, the literature [5, 6, 8] has suggested that research needs to focus on how CSCL is used in specific domains and what its resultant effects are, since much of the research in this area is domain neutral. Furthermore, Roschelle [6] mentioned how research should also focus on understanding how specific technological resources available in schools can be used to foster CSCL. Kirschner and Erkens [5] pointed out how it is also important to examine how the social space of a classroom fosters collaboration and how the sociability provided by the characteristics of the technology used may determine the social presence of learners during collaborative activities. Lastly, Hadwin and colleagues [9] posited that research should study and develop ways of analyzing shared regulation in a social space and use different study designs and analytical methods that reveal how regulation of learning may shift from individual to shared.

2   The Regulation of Learning in Neurodiverse Children

Self-regulation may be considered as a process through which students convert cognitive ability into task-related competencies and is a product of a continuous interaction between individuals, the task at hand, and the environment [1, 2, 10]. This process is cyclical and involves feelings, self-generated thoughts, and actions which are anticipated, planned, and adjusted to reach specific goals, depending on previous feedback. It has also been defined as the adaptive and effective use of metacognitive and cognitive strategies to reach specific task goals [11]. Self-regulation can be accomplished through self-observation, self-judgment, and self-reaction, and may be influenced by self-efficacy, which is an individual's assessment of their ability to effectively perform a task in a given situation [1]. Furthermore, self-regulation involves the interaction between affect/motivation, cognition/metacognition, competencies, and the context in which it develops [12].

Self-regulation is differentiated from metacognition since the latter has been defined as the regulation and monitoring of cognition. That is, it refers to what individuals know about their cognitive activity and how this is used to manage cognitive action during efforts to learn, whereas self-regulation involves monitoring and controlling emotional, motivational, and social dimensions of mental functioning [13]. Some authors have proposed several dimensions of metacognition, such as metacognitive knowledge, metacognitive processes, and metacognitive experiences [14, 15]. The first has been described as learners' awareness and understanding of cognitive processes and products, whereas the second is considered as individuals' capacity to monitor and self-regulate cognitive activities during efforts to learn. The third has been proposed as the experiences in which learners are engaged consciously and affectively to reach goals. Other authors have referred to metacognitive knowledge as the beliefs, declarative knowledge, theories about goals, strategies, and cognitive functions of an individual; to metacognitive skills as procedural knowledge and strategies, involving planning, self-monitoring and evaluating; and to metacognitive experiences as overt processes of cognitive monitoring during efforts to learn [16].

Research on self-regulation has provided evidence that neurodiverse children tend to have less metacognitive and task knowledge and are less likely to use this type of information to properly self-regulate their efforts to learn and perform tasks [17]. Moreover, neurodiverse children tend to have difficulties with emotion and motivation regulation, which leads them to self-doubt, low task engagement, and maladaptive beliefs about the learning process [18]. In fact, a lack of effective self-regulation skills may determine whether or not neurodiverse children have more difficulties with academic performance [19]. Other studies have highlighted that neurodiverse children may demonstrate difficulties in self-regulating their behavior, emotions, motivation, and learning [20]. Therefore, considering self-regulation, and consequently, self-regulated learning explicitly, as critical factors in the learning process of neurodiverse children, is crucial. For instance, the literature has suggested that autistic adolescents are able to self-regulate their learning [21]. Accordingly, being aware of the learning process has been found to be determining for memory and learning [22, 23]. The literature has suggested that having an awareness of memory performance predicts academic performance in children [24].

Children who can monitor their memory effectively and are able to engage in self-directed speech tend to be more accurate in their responses when questioned about situations [25–27]. A systematic review focused on the differential development and use of self-directed speech, has highlighted that it is an important self-regulatory tool, in neurodiverse children [28]. Specifically, children with developmental language disorder (DLD), autism spectrum disorder (ASD), and attention deficit hyperactivity disorder (ADHD) tend to show a maturational delay in terms of self-directed speech. In fact, autistic children tend to not use inner speech to regulate thinking. Nonetheless, this may be determined by cognitive aspects and specificities of tasks. Furthermore, the development of self-directed speech may be hinged by their social and learning contexts, involving those who surround the child on a daily basis, such as parents and teachers, and the quality of their interaction.

Self-regulated learning has been defined as an intrinsic motivational oriented process in the transfer of knowledge and skills to novel contexts [11]. It has also been considered as the degree to which students participate actively in their own learning process through planning, monitoring, and self-evaluation, which from a social cognitive perspective, involves metacognitive, motivational, and behavioral aspects of learning [29, 30]. Self-regulated learning includes three cyclical phases proposed by Zimmerman [30], namely, forethought (i.e. self-motivational beliefs and task analysis), performance (self-observation and self-control), and self-reflection (self-reaction and self-judgment), along with the associated learning strategies that may be used during the regulation of learning [31]. In ADHD children for instance, the motivational and goal directed features of self-regulated learning are compromised [32]. Nonetheless, cognitive and metacognitive strategies are essential in self-regulated learning associated with positive learning outcomes [33, 34].

Self-regulated learning competencies involve awareness of how learners think during efforts to learn to manage their learning behavior and regulate their motivation to reach goals. Dignath and colleagues [35] suggested that both metacognition and motivation are essential elements of self-regulated learning across diverse domain areas. Large effects on learners' overall academic achievement have been found when they experienced self-regulated learning interventions focusing on both metacognitive strategies and motivational regulation. Moreover, learners tend to use different strategies, depending on individual differences and the domain area task, indicating that each domain area is different in the strategic and motivational way with which they approach it. In fact, learners tend to approach the different domain areas differently [35].

Self-regulated learning competencies may be used by neurodiverse children as a way of avoiding engaging in dysfunctional behavior [36, 37]. Not being able to self-regulate emotions adaptively, for instance, may constitute a risk factor for developing covert and overt processes and behavior in neurodiverse children, such as depression and misconduct [38, 39]. Empirical evidence has shown that in these cases, maladaptive emotion regulation may be associated with impairments in working memory, inhibition, and attention shifting and explain covert and overt processes and behavior [40]. In fact, maladapted emotional regulation strategies and deficits in executive functioning seem to be interconnected in neurodiverse children, especially since inhibitory control, reasoning, planning, and problem solving are required for adaptive emotional regulation [41, 42]. Moreover, maladaptive emotion regulation strategies used by neurodiverse children, such as rumination, avoiding information, and repetitive behavior, have been associated with high levels of anxiety, which is prejudicial to their psychological and physical health [43].

Some of the literature has posited that education professionals should focus on effective learning environments, where learners are given the opportunity to generate their own learning goals, allowing them to experience meaningful activities within their learning context. In addition, how students self-regulate their learning should be considered also with regard to their socio-emotional goals. That is, if they are encouraged to solve problems in collaborative learning contexts, they are most likely to develop important learning strategies because firstly they must attribute value to the task at hand by following their own goal structure, and secondly, they must attribute meaning to the learning context, which implies interpersonal behavior, social support and demands [44].

Some of the literature has focused on meta-skills, which involve higher-order skills encompassing metacognitive, social-emotional, and motivational processes [45, 46]. Meta-skills allow learners to develop adaptive self-motivation and self-regulation in different contexts using strategies to overcome possible obstacles [45–48]. These skills enable learners to acknowledge and consciously regulate learning to reach personal goals through reflection [49]. Affective meta-skills involve emotional awareness, emotional regulation, and empathy [45]. whereas social meta-skills involve social interaction, collaboration, and conflict resolution [50], and motivation processes, involve internal motivation as opposed to external gratification [51]. All these meta-skills are crucial for neurodiverse children to develop in CSCL environments.

Järvelä and Hadwin [3]. have proposed that it is important to understand the regulation process of learning of oneself, as well as others', including feelings, beliefs, motivations behavior, and actions, in addition to understanding how knowledge of tasks, goals, and strategies are regulated during collaborative work. The authors suggest that whether learners succeed in collaborative learning depends on several factors pertaining to the regulation of learning.

The regulation of learning is more than the regulation of processes and outcomes related to domain task execution. It includes learning and collaboration processes, where learners monitor and evaluate progress, adopting strategies that may assist a group in working more effectively and efficiently together. Furthermore, when regulation is collective, meta-emotional, meta-motivational, and metacognitive knowledge is developed regarding collaborative learning processes (i.e., negotiating and managing task requirements/goals).

Moreover, Järvelä and Hadwin [3] and Hadwin and colleagues [9] suggested three types of regulation of learning. Specifically, they differentiate between the self-regulation of learning, where learners may bring personal self-regulatory skills and strategies to a group; the co-regulation of learning, where learners provide support to each other to help self-regulatory competence progress within a group; and the shared regulation of learning, where learners are metacognitively aware, share motivational regulation and manage strategies to achieve a common goal. We consider these different types of regulation to be important for neurodiverse children during learning, namely self-regulation as individual learning, and co- and shared regulation as collaborative learning. Recently, Alonso-Campuzano and colleagues [52] investigated how collaborative storytelling could constitute a useful resource to promote cognitive and social skills in neurodiverse children. They found a positive effect of collaboration on learners' performance in telling stories, as opposed to individual work. Students had access to different tools, including paper-based or digital resources.

Figure 1 shows an outline of a CSCL environment, which we discuss more in the next section. Specifically, in these environments, the child self-regulates through different phases, as proposed by Zimmerman [30], and brings to the collaborative learning space what they have learned and developed through this process [3]. The child is in control and manages their own learning through individual agency and its various components, such as intentionality (i.e., the child forms intentions to engage in specific behavior), forethought (i.e., the child anticipates possible outcomes and obstacles), self-reactiveness (i.e., the child monitors their own behavior and learning process through self-regulation), and self-reflectiveness (i.e., the child reflects about the entire learning process and forms further intentions and anticipates strategy use) [1]. Colleagues can engage in co-regulation, as well as the teacher, to guide the child to reach personal goals. Classmates can co-regulated and help the child (and vice versa) reach their personal goals through proxy agency [1]. During this process, children can enhance their communication skills progressively through prosocial assertiveness. Moreover, classmates can engage in shared regulation with the child through collective agency [1]. where children work together to obtain a common desired goal. Through this mode of agency, children may improve their communication skills via prosocial negotiation. Moreover, the teachers serve as guides in this student collective agency and monitor children's use of technology during efforts to learn.

Figure 1 also shows the technology component of CSCL in neurodiverse children, where different digital resources can sustain the regulation of learning, whether individual, co-regulated, or shared. These resources can include diverse features to support the different modes of human agency and forms of regulating learning and be used systematically in classroom settings by learners with the guidance of their teacher. Lastly, CSCL environments involve the use of metacognitive, social-emotional, and motivational strategies by learners. These strategies can be developed and trained through teacher guidance, as well as diverse technological resources.

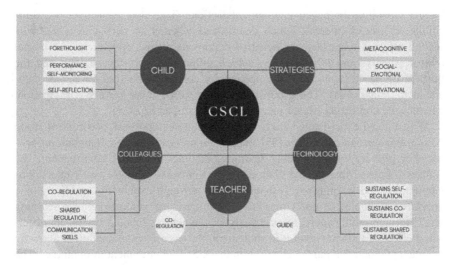

Fig. 1 A CSCL environment model for neurodiverse children

3   Neurodiverse Children and CSCL Environments

In this section, we discuss further details regarding CSCL environments, including examples of technological resources and collaborative efforts which foster effective interaction that can benefit neurodiverse children. Effective interaction has been defined in the literature as group engagement where all members of the group actively participate to collaborate in problem-solving by communicating, negotiating, and evaluating group performance with minimal distractions [53, 54]. Fischer and colleagues [7] for instance, studied how participant-generated procedural knowledge (i.e., internal scripts) could often be inaccurate and how externally generated scripts could assist students in learning collaboratively because they complement internal scripts. External scripts did not determine but guided students' collaborative activities by specifying instructions, sequencing information, representing strategies, determining roles, and distributing activities through varying representations (e.g., textual or graphical) presented by external resources (e.g., a teacher or a Learning Management System—LMS). The authors referred that sound external collaboration scripts could foster student interaction. In participating in this type of activity, students developed more complex and collaborative procedural knowledge, which enabled them to improve their performance in a CSCL environment.

Määttä and colleagues [53] studied the efficacious interaction of two groups of fourth-grade students' task involvement in authentic science learning situations. The authors found three types of triggers that changed students' activity while working in groups. These included the individual progress trigger, the group progress trigger, and the contextual trigger. While the first pertained to each learner's positive or negative comments/actions (i.e., clear objectives vs. difficulties or loss of interest) which determined whether to persist in a task; the second referred to positive or negative comments/actions/evaluations (i.e. social reinforcement) from other learners which influenced task engagement; and the third involved elements from the pedagogical organization (i.e. teacher or camera in the classroom). The group progress triggered more learner participation, whereas the contextual trigger caused less student participation.

With a quasi-experimental study including a pretest, posttest, and control group design, Prinsen and colleagues [55] studied the impact of guided elaboration (feedback) on primary school students' learning outcomes in a CSCL environment. The authors proposed that guided elaboration is a process through which efficacious interactions and learning are fostered namely through explaining, justifying, and providing examples of one's reasoning, opinions, and perceptions of a learning task. Through multilevel regression analysis, the authors found a significant differential effect of the intervention in students in the experimental condition, allowing them to conclude that guided elaboration in a CSCL environment through feedback and reflection had the potential to positively influence how students interacted, and thus progress in collaborative learning experiences. The authors suggested that interventions should focus on developing student interactions (i.e., with colleagues, the teacher, and technological resources) that can enhance learning in CSCL environments.

Recent studies have highlighted the importance of providing teachers with training using Moodle [56] and using this tool to personalize learning [57]. In fact, some studies have provided evidence that using Moodle helped primary school neurodiverse children increase their cognitive abilities [58]. Moreover, this study suggested that Learning Management Moodle Systems could be an effective solution to solve learning problems for neurodiverse children. Angeli and Tsaggari [59] found how collaborative learning with a computer system that aided students in problem-solving (i.e., Athena and Odysseus in Egypt multimedia software) enhanced third-grade learners' performance in history class. However, the authors mentioned how the intervention only took a total of three hours and how future research should involve interventions with longer duration periods.

We found Määttä and colleague's conclusions [53] to be important for our chapter since they were able to confirm that the comments, actions, and evaluations from other learners influenced task engagement. Hence, we highlight how children can engage in collaborative regulation of learning, but within a CSCL environment, as suggested by Prinsen and colleagues [55]. Moreover, Ni [60] suggested the importance of using Moodle, for example, as a platform for human–computer interaction and speaking skills, which is what we also consider a useful tool for classroom use, specifically with neurodiverse children. Furthermore, Angeli and Tsaggari's [59] findings were important for this chapter to understand how a CSCL environment could provide opportunities for children to interact amongst each other. Design aspects of CSCL environments can support shared goals, discussions regarding goals, interactions between collaborators, and achievement outcomes, which impact motivational/emotional factors and enable teachers to provide more personalized feedback [61–63]. The success of learners in CSCL environments depends on which self-regulated learning competencies and strategies they bring to their group (self-regulated learning), as well as on the reciprocal support they provide each other to foster self-regulated learning competence within their group (co-regulated learning) [3]. Accordingly, learners can experience successful learning in CSCL environments if they engage in collective regulation of learning (shared regulated learning), by sharing the regulation of motivation and adequate coordination of strategies.

In collaborative learning, being able to interact with others is fundamental, even though some neurodiverse children may have difficulty interacting with others. Voss and colleagues [64]. Investigated whether an intervention designed to foster facial engagement and emotion recognition could enhance socialization in autistic children with wearable artificial intelligence. They performed a randomized clinical trial to examine the efficacy of the intervention and concluded that this technology reinforced facial engagement and emotion recognition and led these children towards improved social behavior. Zhang and colleagues [65]. Used an intelligent agent that could verbally communicate with autistic children and play collaborative puzzle games with them to measure their task performance and verbal communication behavior throughout gameplay. The children found the intelligent agent engaging and the collaborative gameplay enjoyable. Another recent study has also proposed that teachers can plan and execute collaborative storytelling exercises in a classroom setting, in view of the executive and social skills of neurodiverse children, as well as group dynamics, paper and digital resources, storytelling features, while supporting collaborative processes which emphasize social interaction and task demands [52].

In a systematic review, Marinelli and colleagues [66] found that there were very few serious games developed for neurodiverse children with evidence of efficacy. Those that have been developed focused on some elements of literacy but did not include spelling and text comprehension, for instance. Nonetheless, this study found that serious games constitute an effective resource to improve reading and meta-phonological skills, as well as to provide good opportunities for learner engagement and enjoyment. Since this systematic review revealed that there was low progress in terms of essential skills, the authors highlighted the need for further research in using serious games to improve essential competencies for learning in neurodiverse children.

Concurrently, a recent systematic review investigated the efficacy of virtual reality games as an intervention resource to train meta-skills (i.e., higher-order skills involving metacognitive, social-emotional, and motivational processes) in neurodiverse learners [67]. This review proposed that these games have the potential to support these learners in raising motivation and developing metacognitive and emotional intelligence skills. Moreover, a recent meta-analysis [68] has also revealed that digital game-based training can foster the cognitive abilities of neurodiverse children. Furthermore, task content and game features have a significant impact on these children's cognition over time, even when used remotely.

4 Future Directions for Research and Practice

Interventions based on self-regulation have been known to help neurodiverse children improve their academic performance [18, 69, 70] such as reading [71] and math [72, 73]. Intervention programs available for ADHD learners instance, can combine reparative metacognitive strategies, namely goal setting and plan execution [74]. Takacs and Kassai [75] for example, found that neurodiverse children benefit mostly from programs that foster the acquisition of self-regulation strategies which are embedded in their daily tasks. Specifically, they found a big effect-size (0.84) in a recent meta-analysis concerning the efficacy of self-regulation-based interventions that provide neurodiverse children new strategies, such as explicit strategy teaching programs, biofeedback-enhanced relaxation, and mindfulness [75]. Tsampouris and colleagues [72] proposed that intervention programs to enhance self-regulated learning in ADHD learners should be designed considering metacognition and cognitive flexibility. These programs could be curriculum-based while aiming to teach metacognitive questioning, self-monitoring, and self-evaluating as effective processes.

Programs based on explicitly teaching self-regulation strategies seem to be very effective for neurodiverse children [75]. For instance, these children can learn how to apply self-regulation skills, such as planning [76] and self-instruction [77] during efforts to learn. Zelazo and Lyons [78] have proposed that mindfulness meditation is appropriate to foster reflective development in terms of cognitive and emotional aspects in children, considering the latter get opportunities to regulate their attention, train executive skills, and reduce their levels of stress and anxiety.

Specifically with regards to technology use included in these training programs, Ren and colleagues [68] suggested that further research is necessary to examine retention effects of digital game-based training programs with neurodiverse children. That is, longitudinal training which could be extended over a consistent period of time, as opposed to one-session or short-time training. This could be a first step in understanding how neurodiverse children can experience the regulation of learning with digital media. Furthermore, by having teachers specifically trained in using CSCL environments, these children could be guided in using specific learning strategies when they engage in learning with these tools. These resources could enhance how they reflect on their learning experiences in a CSCL environment.

The implications for practice suggest that integrating technology into collaborative learning with neurodiverse children is a beneficial resource. It enables them to make intentional, responsible, and appropriate choices as they monitor their work and in receiving feedback from the technology used. This, in turn, creates new opportunities for their guided autonomy. This has implications concerning these learners' gratification because they could be empowered to improve performance at their own learning rhythm. Furthermore, psychologists and special education teachers could use these tools to aid them in guiding their students in regulating their learning more efficiently, individually, and collectively. To do so efficiently,

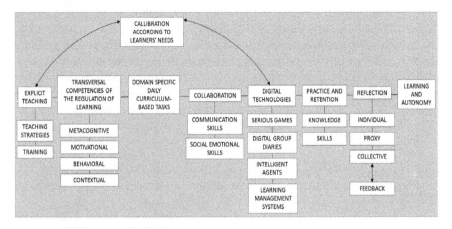

Fig. 2 Learning efforts in CSCL environments

it would be required to provide teachers with initial teacher training and in-service training on the use of such tools to promote self-regulated learning and enhance students' performance and engagement in class. Moreover, educational psychologists could help teachers with this type of training by exploring the potential and features of these tools in schools. Teachers and psychologists could focus on the design of instructional settings, by integrating technology in education to fit the needs of the learning process of neurodiverse children, which may aid them in regulating their learning.

It would be interesting to study in the future why children make the choices they do by having them interact with an interactive agent after their learning experience. Supplementing this approach with collaborative diary data would be valuable, as these data sources could help address the obstacles identified in the literature regarding collaborative work [8, 79]. Students could reflect collaboratively over a digital group diary and identify strengths, weaknesses, and obstacles to overcome using digital media to engage in the regulation of learning. This approach could also complement recent research and aid students in increasing their awareness of their interpersonal skills and how these may have an impact on their performance as a group [80]. Figure 2 shows how efforts to learn by neurodiverse children in CSCL environments can be fostered.

5 Conclusions

This chapter serves its purpose of discussing how neurodiverse children can benefit from the regulation of learning in CSCL environments, but more research and intervention are needed in this specific area. Furthermore, it holds practical value considering it presents a summary of studies which focus on empirically assessing ways and finding opportunities for neurodiverse learners to collaborate and share the regulation of learning, and how this collaboration and regulation may be supported by CSCL environments. Additionally, this chapter provides insights into how teachers may adapt technology that is available to them towards their students' needs in terms of promoting interaction through the regulation of learning when engaging in academic tasks. Investigating how technological tools inside the classroom could foster collaboration and the regulation of learning could ultimately enhance the pedagogical management of existing tools and provide innovative proposals for the design of contemporary learning environments for neurodiverse children.

Acknowledgements This work received national funding from the Foundation for Science and Technology (FCT), I.P. (2022 02218.CEECIND), and the Research Center for Psychological Science (CICPSI) (UIDB/04527/2020; UIDP/04527/2020).

References

1. Bandura A (2006) Toward a psychology of human agency. Perspect Psychol Sci 1(2):164–180
2. Zimmerman BJ (2000) Attaining self-regulation: a social cognitive perspective. In: Boekaerts M, Pintrich P, Zeidner M (eds) Handbook of self-regulation. Elsevier, San Diego, pp 13–39
3. Järvelä S, Hadwin A (2013) New Frontiers: Regulating Learning in CSCL. Educ Psychol 48(1):25–39
4. APA (2013) Diagnostic and statistical manual of mental disorders: DSM-5^{TM}, 5th edn. American Psychiatric Publishing Inc., Arlington, VA, US
5. Kirschner P, Erkens G (2013) Toward a framework for CSCL research. Educ Psychol 48(1):1–8
6. Roschelle J (2013) Special issue on CSCL: discussion. Educ Psychol 48(1):67–70
7. Fischer F, Kollar I, Stegmann K, Wecker C (2013) Toward a script theory of guidance in computer-supported collaborative learning. Educ Psychol 48(1):56–66
8. Le H, Janssen L, Wubbels T (2018) Collaborative learning practices: teacher and student perceived obstacles to effective student collaboration. Camb J Educ 48(1):103–122
9. Hadwin A, Oshige M, Gress C, Winne PH (2010) Innovative ways for using gStudy to orchestrate and research social aspects of self-regulated learning. Comput Hum Behav 26(5):794–805
10. Schunk DH (2001) Social-cognitive theory and self-regulated learning. In: Zimmerman BJ, Schunk DH (eds) Self-regulated learning and academic achievement: theoretical perspectives. Routledge, Mahwah, pp 125–151
11. Pintrich PR (2000) The role of goal orientation in self-regulated learning. In: Boekaerts M, Pintrich PR, Zeidner M (eds) Handbook of self-regulation. Elsevier, London, pp 451–502
12. Butler DL (2002) Qualitative approaches to investigating self regulated learning: contributions and challenges. Educ Psychol 37(1):59–63
13. Whitebread D, Pino Pasternak D (2010) Metacognition, self-regulation, and meta-knowing. In: Littleton K, Wood C, Kleine-Staarman J (eds) Elsevier handbook of education: new perspectives on learning and teaching. Elsevier, London, pp 673–711
14. Flavell JH (2002) Development of children's knowledge about the mental world. In: Hartup WW, Silbereisen RK (eds) Growing points in developmental science: an introduction. Psychology Press, Hove, pp 102–122
15. Vanderswalmen R, Vrijder J, Desoete A (2010) Metacognition and spelling performance in college students. In: Efklides A, Misailidi P (eds) Trends and prospects in metacognition research. Springer, New York, pp 367–394

16. Efklides A (2011) Interactions of metacognition with motivation and affect in self-regulated learning: the MASRL model. Educ Psychol 46(1):6–25
17. Jokić CAS, Whitebread D (2014) Examining change in metacognitive knowledge and metacognitive control during motor learning: what can be learned by combining methodological approaches? Psychol Top 23(1):53–76
18. Graham S, Harris KR (2003) Students with learning disabilities and the process of writing: a meta-analysis of SRSD studies. In: Swanson HL, Harris KR, Graham S (eds) Handbook of learning disabilities. Guilford, New York, pp 323–344
19. Sugden DA (1989) Skill generalization and children with learning difficulties. In: Sugden D (ed) Cognitive approaches in special education. Psychology Press, London, pp 82–99
20. Romero-Ayuso D, Alcántara-Vázquez P, Almenara-García A, Nuñez-Camarero I, Triviño-Juárez JM, Ariza-Vega P, Molina JP, González P (2020) Self-regulation in neurodiverse children "SR-MRehab: un colegio emocionante": a protocol study. Int J Environ Res Public Health 17(12):4198
21. Bowler DM, Gardiner JM, Grice S, Saavalainen P (2000) Memory illusions: false recall and recognition in adults with Asperger's syndrome. J Abnorm Psychol 109(4):663
22. Flavell JH (1979) Metacognition and cognitive monitoring: a new area of cognitive—Developmental inquiry. Am Psychol 34(10):906
23. Schneider W (1999) The development of metamemory in children. In: Gopher D, Koriat A (eds) Attention and performance XVII: cognitive regulation of performance: interaction of theory and application. MIT Press, Cambridge, pp 487–513
24. Pierce SH, Lange G (2000) Relationships among metamemory, motivation and memory performance in young school-age children. Br J Dev Psychol 18(1):121–135
25. Roebers CM, Fernandez O (2002) The effects of accuracy motivation on children's and adults' event recall, suggestibility, and their answers to unanswerable questions. J Cogn Dev 3(4):415–443
26. Waterman AH, Blades M (2011) Helping children correctly say "I don't know" to unanswerable questions. J Exp Psychol Appl 17(4):396
27. Waterman AH, Blades M, Spencer C (2004) Indicating when you do not know the answer: The effect of question format and interviewer knowledge on children's 'don't know' responses. Br J Dev Psychol 22(3):335–348
28. Mulvihill A, Carroll A, Dux PE, Matthews N (2020) Self-directed speech and self-regulation in childhood neurodevelopmental disorders: current findings and future directions. Dev Psychopathol 32(1):205–217
29. Zimmerman BJ (1989) A social cognitive view of self-regulated academic learning. J Educ Psychol 81(3):329–339
30. Zimmerman BJ (2013) From cognitive modeling to self-regulation: a social cognitive career path. Educ Psychol 48(3):135–147
31. Zimmerman BJ, Martinez Pons M (1986) Development of a structured interview for assessing student use of self-regulated learning strategies. Am Educ Res J 23(4):614–628
32. Sibley MH, Graziano PA, Ortiz M, Rodriguez L, Coxe S (2019) Academic impairment among high school students with ADHD: the role of motivation and goal-directed executive functions. J Sch Psychol 77:67–76
33. McWhaw K, Abrami PC (2001) Student goal orientation and interest: effects on students' use of self-regulated learning strategies. Contemp Educ Psychol 26(3):311–329
34. Karabenick SA, Dembo MH (2011) Understanding and facilitating self-regulated help seeking. New Direct Teach Learn 2011(126):33–43
35. Dignath C, Buettner G, Langfeldt H (2008) How can elementary school students learn self-regulated learning strategies most effectively? A meta-analysis on self-regulation trainning programmes. Educ Res Rev 3(2):101–129
36. Petersen LE (2014) Self-compassion and self-protection strategies: the impact of self-compassion on the use of self-handicapping and sandbagging. Personal Individ Differ 56:133–138

37. Thomas CR, Gadbois SA (2007) Academic self-handicapping: the role of self-concept clarity and students' learning strategies. Br J Educ Psychol 77(1):101–119
38. Kranzler A, Young JF, Hankin BL, Abela JR, Elias MJ, Selby EA (2016) Emotional awareness: a transdiagnostic risk factor for internalizing symptoms in children and adolescents? J Clin Child Adolesc Psychol 45(3):262–269
39. Mazefsky CA, White SW (2014) Emotion regulation: concepts & practice in autism spectrum disorder. Child and Adolesc Psychiatr Clin 23(1):15–24
40. Tajik-Parvinchi D, Farmus L, Tablon Modica P, Cribbie RA, Weiss JA (2021) The role of cognitive control and emotion regulation in predicting mental health problems in children with neurodevelopmental disorders. Child: Care Health Dev 47(5):608–617
41. Predescu E, Sipos R, Costescu CA, Ciocan A, Rus DI (2020) Executive functions and emotion regulation in attention-deficit/hyperactivity disorder and borderline intellectual disability. J Clin Med 9(4):986
42. Diamond A (2013) Executive functions. Annu Rev Psychol 64:135–168
43. Samson AC, Sokhn N, Van Herwegen J, Dukes D (2022) An exploratory study on emotion regulation strategy use in individuals with Williams syndrome, autism spectrum disorder and intellectual disability. Front Psych 13:940872
44. Boekaerts M (2002) Bringing about change in the classroom: strengths and weaknesses of the self-regulated learning approach—EARLI Presidential Address, 2001. Learn Instr 12(6):589–604
45. Prasittichok P, Klaykaew KK (2022) Meta-skills development needs assessment among undergraduate students. Heliyon 8(1)
46. Mitsea E, Drigas A, Mantas P (2021) Soft skills & metacognition as inclusion amplifiers in the 21st century. Int J Online Biomed Eng 17(4)
47. Drigas A, Mitsea E, Skianis C (2023) Meta-learning: a nine-layer model based on metacognition and smart technologies. Sustainability 15(2):1668
48. D'Amico A, Geraci A (2023) Beyond emotional intelligence: the new construct of meta-emotional intelligence. Front Psychol 14:1096663
49. Drigas A, Mitsea E (2021) 8 Pillars X 8 Layers model of metacognition: educational strategies, exercises & trainings. Int J Online Biomed Eng 17(8)
50. Senova M (2020) Meta-skills are the key to human potential. J Behav Econ Soc Syst 2(1):133–137
51. Ryan RM, Deci EL (2000) Intrinsic and extrinsic motivations: classic definitions and new directions. Contemp Educ Psychol 25(1):54–67
52. Alonso-Campuzano C, Iandolo G, Filosofi F, Tardivo A, Sosa-González N, Pasqualotto A, Venuti P (2023) Tangible digital collaborative storytelling in adolescents with intellectual disability and neurodevelopmental disorders. J Appl Res Intellect Disabil
53. Määttä E, Järvenoja H, Järvelä S (2012) Triggers of students' efficacious interaction in collaborative learning situations. Small Group Res 43(4):497–522
54. Soller A (2001) Supporting social interaction in an intelligent collaborative learning system. Int J Artif Intell Educ 12(1):40–62
55. Prinsen F, Terwel J, Zijlstra B, Volman MM (2013) The effects of guided elaboration in a CSCL programme on the learning outcomes of primary school students from Dutch and immigrant families. Educ Res Eval 19(1):39–57
56. Ulfatin N, Prestiadi D, Adha MA, Ariyanti NS, Saputra BR, Sjaifullah FW (2021) Mentoring teachers in the utilization of Moodle e-learning application to optimize learning success. In: Paper presented at the 2021 7th international conference on education and technology (ICET), Universitas Negeri Malang, East Java, Indonesia
57. Papanikolaou K, Boubouka M (2020) Personalised learning design in moodle. In: Paper presented at the 2020 IEEE 20th international conference on advanced learning technologies (ICALT), Tartu, Estonia
58. Swastika R, Prasodjo I, Daeroby D (2020) Development of electronic learning systems for special needs children (autism) at elementary school level in efforts to increase cognitive intelligence. J TAM (Technol Accept Model) 11(2):73–79

59. Angeli C, Tsaggari A (2016) Examining the effects of learning in dyads with computer-based multimedia on third-grade students' performance in history. Comput Educ 92:171–180
60. Ni C (2021) The human-computer interaction online oral English teaching mode based on Moodle platform. In: Paper presented at the 2021 IEEE Asia-pacific conference on image processing, electronics and computers (IPEC), Dalian, China
61. Coll C, Rochera M, Gispert I (2014) Supporting online collaborative learning in small groups: teacher feedback on learning content, academic task and social participation. Comput Educ 75:53–64
62. Druin A, Revelle G, Bederson BB, Hourcade JP, Farber A, Lee J, Campbell D (2003) A collaborative digital library for children: a descriptive study of children's collaborative behaviors and dialogue. J Comput-Assisted Learn 19(2):239–248
63. Mayer R, Estrella G (2014) Benefits of emotional design in multimedia instruction. Learn Instr 33:12–18
64. Voss C, Schwartz J, Daniels J, Kline A, Haber N, Washington P, Tariq Q, Robinson TN, Desai M, Phillips JM, Feinstein C (2019) Effect of wearable digital intervention for improving socialization in children with autism spectrum disorder: a randomized clinical trial. JAMA Pediatr 173(5):446–454
65. Zhang L, Amat AZ, Zhao H, Swanson A, Weitlauf A, Warren Z, Sarkar N (2020) Design of an intelligent agent to measure collaboration and verbal-communication skills of children with autism spectrum disorder in collaborative puzzle games. IEEE Trans Learn Technol 14(3):338–352
66. Marinelli CV, Nardacchione G, Trotta E, Di Fuccio R, Palladino P, Traetta L, Limone P (2023) The effectiveness of serious games for enhancing literacy skills in children with learning disabilities or difficulties: a systematic review. Appl Sci 13(7):4512
67. Mitsea E, Drigas A, Skianis C (2023) VR gaming for meta-skills training in special education: the role of metacognition, motivations, and emotional intelligence. Educ Sci 13(7):639
68. Ren X, Wu Q, Cui N, Zhao J, Bi H-Y (2023) Effectiveness of digital game-based trainings in children with neurodevelopmental disorders: a meta-analysis. Res Dev Disabil 133:104418
69. Fuchs LS, Fuchs D, Prentice K, Burch M, Hamlett CL, Owen R, Schroeter K (2003) Enhancing third grade student's mathematical problem-solving with self-regulated learning strategies. J Educ Psychol 95(2):306–315
70. Maccini P, Hughes CA (2000) Effects of problem-solving strategy on the introductory algebra performance of secondary students with learning disabilities. Learn Disabil Res Pract 15:10–21
71. Pressley M, Gaskin I (2006) Metacognitively competent reading comprehension is constructively responsive reading: how can such reading be developed in students? Metacogn Learn 1:99–113
72. Tsampouris G, Sampedro Requena BE (2022) Metacognitive strategies related with logical–mathematical thinking for adolescents with ADHD. Mathematics 10(11):1810
73. Schoenfeld AH (1992) Learning to think mathematically: problem-solving, metacognition and sense making in mathematics. In: Grouws DA (ed) Handbook of research on mathematics teaching and learning. MacMillan, New York, pp 334–370
74. Gawrilow C, Morgenroth K, Schultz R et al (2013) Mental contrasting with implementation intentions enhances self-regulation of goal pursuit in schoolchildren at risk for ADHD. Motiv Emot 37:134–145
75. Takacs ZK, Kassai R (2019) The efficacy of different interventions to foster children's executive function skills: a series of meta-analyses. Psychol Bull 145(7):653
76. Hannesdottir DK, Ingvarsdottir E, Bjornsson A (2017) The OutSMARTers program for children with ADHD: A pilot study on the effects of social skills, self-regulation, and executive function training. J Atten Disord 21(4):353–364
77. Meichenbaum DH, Goodman J (1971) Training impulsive children to talk to themselves: a means of developing self-control. J Abnorm Psychol 77(2):115–126
78. Zelazo PD, Lyons KE (2012) The potential benefits of mindfulness training in early childhood: a developmental social cognitive neuroscience perspective. Child Dev Perspect 6(2):154–160

79. Schmitz P, Perels F (2011) Self-monitoring of self-regulation during math homework behaviour using standardized diaries. Metacogn Learn 6:255–273
80. Slof B, Nijdam D, Janssen J (2016) Do interpersonal skills and interpersonal perceptions predict student in CSCL-environments? Comput Educ 97:49–60

Conclusion

Developing digital technologies for learning and psychological interventions involves careful consideration of various factors to ensure effectiveness, accessibility, and ethical use. Among the factors that were mentioned, discussed or considered in the chapters of this books we mention user-centered design, collaboration with end-user and interdisciplinary approach, evidence-based practices, customization and personalization, integration with existing systems, training and support, as well as ethical considerations.

To develop effective and accessible digital tools one's should consider understanding the needs, preferences, and capabilities of the target audience, in our case the particularities of neurodiverse children and adults. To better understand their needs, the recommendations are to involve stakeholders, neurodiverse individuals, caregivers, teachers in the design process to ensure the technology is user-friendly. To ensure that the design aligns with their needs one possibility is to develop prototypes and gather feedback through testing it with the end-users. The customization process involves incorporating adaptive learning features and design of the technological tool in a way that allows for accommodation to individual differences and evolving needs. Moreover, considerations for NDDs-specific design may include clear, predictable, easy to navigate interfaces and structured and consistent interactions with the platforms. For example, when developing digital tools for autistic people one's should consider the sensory sensitivities and design features that are mindful of sensory preferences, such as providing options for visual and auditory stimuli.

Another important conclusion that emerged from this book is related to evidence-based practices in the context of digital technologies. Evidence based practices are crucial for ensuring that the digital technologies designed for a specific population (i.e. ADHD children) are not only innovative but also have a positive impact on their development, learning and overall well-being. Firstly, the studies that test the effectiveness of digital tools should employ standardized measurement tools to measure the outcomes, then pre-and post-intervention assessment should be conducted to quantitatively measure the changes in the targeted skills.

The contents of the applications and their complexity should be customized to the children's abilities, preferences, and developmental level. Moreover, training and support for the multidisciplinary teams should be provided to maximize the benefits of the digital technology. The digital technology should integrate the input from educators, teachers, psychologists and parents to provide a well-rounded support system.

There are several conclusions that can be drawn from the chapters of this book. In regard to the first section that deals with the more general aspects of the development and use of digital technologies important conclusions emerged in regard to participatory design, machine learning use, digital biomarkers and the role of social robots in learning and psychological intervention. Therefore, after stating very clearly which are the advantages of using digital technologies for neurodiverse population (i.e. predictability, control of the learning situation, reduces speed at which information is presented, intrinsic reinforcement) the risks associated with the use of technology are presented (i.e. the high screen time to which children are exposed leading to compulsive internet use) each of the themes mentioned above is described in detail. The analysis described in the first chapter shows that the most used forms of personalization are: the possibility to add extra resources (e.g. image or sound), functionality (e.g. the contents and the functions may vary according to the users' needs), interface (e.g. fonts size, colors, background) and user-related data (e.g. different types of measurements, activity monitorization). Consequently, generalization and customization opportunities were discussed within the chapters to maximize the use of digital technologies for autistic individuals. Another possibility to increase the use and effectiveness of digital technologies is to use participatory design and use experimental designs that facilitate the representation of neurodiverse population. This book proposes some quality of research indicators that can be used both for single case designs and for clinical studies to assess the level of evidence available about a given practice. The description of participants, operationalizing the dependent variables, independent variables, base lines, control of internal validity and external validity are just some of the indicators described in the book as quality indicators for testing the effectiveness of digital technologies. Among the technology design, gamification is described to be a powerful resource for increasing engagement and improving the learning process. The use of narrative, challenges, progression, competition, feedback, avatars and different levels, are key elements in the app designs, as well as the accessibility of the contents for neurodiverse people.

The second major theme in the first section of this books is the use of digital biomarkers. Digital biomarkers are defined within this book as objectively measurable traits that serve as indicators either for signaling the presence of a general condition (i.e. diagnosis) or that can be used as a prognostic or risk related aspects of a neurodevelopmental disorder. Each biomarker has two major components, the input layer (components as measurement) and output layer (clinical outcome). Therefore, the role of the biomarkers in the assessment process and in treatment monitoring are described. The use of Magnetic Resonance Imaging, Electroencephalography and genetic predispositions are discussed for both attention and hyperactivity disorder and autism spectrum disorder. More recently, digital biomarkers derived from wearable devices, eye trackers, pupillometry or vocal biomarkers are the most investigated. While there are high promises in this domain, such as the ability to measure a greater variety of biomarkers faster, cheaper, and more accurately or the opportunity for bridging the access gap to healthcare, within this book we outline also the potential perils (e.g. accuracy and authenticity; autonomy and agency; access and availability) of the use of this new generation of biomarkers. Because of the heterogeneous nature of NDDs, no biomarker currently meets the standard of 80% sensitivity and 80% specificity. The complexity of the disorders, differences in imaging techniques, and confounding factors like comorbidities all contribute to the difficulty in identifying a definitive biomarker.

The third important theme from the first section of the book is use of social robots for assessment and interventions for children. Within this topic several important subjects are being discussed starting with the three main components the child, the robot and the intervention context. While different types of robots are described within the chapter the authors emphasize the importance of the role that the robot has considering the context in which is used, for example the role of a companion or mediator that offers support for interventions, or in educational setups the robots can the take the role of a tutor or peer. Whereas children may be different, and they may have different needs, the intervention context plays a pivotal role in shaping the whole interaction with the robot. The chapter explores how the robots design is tailored to the specific interventions that they are used for. Robot mediated therapy, mental well-being and education are the three samples described within the book and some case studies with robots as story tellers or therapy adjuvants are presented. Moreover, there is one special extra chapter where the authors discuss about the use of machine learning and artificial intelligence to support neurodiverse children through novel technologies. Technological tools like social robots or applications that can help parents, teachers and therapists or even that directly support the neurodiverse population require the development of machine learning algorithms for assessing the appropriate course of actions, for collecting and analyzing statistical data or to provide information about the child's engagement. Within this chapter two major roles of machine learning are described: one role concerns the gathering and analysis of the data and the other one concerns the interpretation of the data to serve a specific gool in assessment or in therapy.

The second section of this book deals with specific ways of using technologies for neurodiverse children for different purposes. One of the major themes that emergers from the second section is the use of digital tools for autistic population. Within the first chapter from the second section relevant studies that test the effectiveness of different digital technologies for autistic children are presented. Virtual reality is the first presented, and there are several studies showing the effectiveness of this technology for improving cognitive skills, social and communication skills, emotion regulation and recognition and daily living skills with great promising on short term but inconclusive results on the long term. Social robots and wearables are technologies that gained more interest lately and there are studies showing great improvements when used, especially in the social area of development. Whereas in the robot-based interventions there are rigorous studies showing positive outcomes, when using wearables, studies are still needed to confirm the effectiveness of that kind of digital technologies. When using computer-based interventions or mobile devices there are several studies showing the real benefit of such devices, even if they are used for improving executive functions or for increasing their autonomy or social interactions. All these digital technologies can help autistic individuals to live an independent life and there is solid scientific evidence that shows a positive association between the use of digital technologies and improvements in the independence levels of autistic individuals. One of the chapters describes techniques that can help not only autistic individuals, but also their teachers in the process of using digital technologies. The use of eCoaching with Bug-In-Ear Technology is described in details and the advantages of this method are discussed in relation with the use of prompting, behavior praise, opportunities to respond in behavioral intervention and in naturalistic communication interventions. Moreover, the effects of coaching using digital devices are discussed in relations to improvements in social and communication skills and employment skills for autistic individuals. While the positive outcomes are clearly outlined when using eCoaching with Bug-In-Ear Technology for different areas of development, the use of AI in coaching has limited existing evidence and cautions should be considered when using it for neurodiverse individuals.

The second major theme of this section of the book is the use of digital technologies for ADHD individuals. This theme has a dedicated chapter and is partly covered when discussing the use of digital technologies for improving executive functions in a distinct chapter. The most used digital technologies are computerized cognitive training, and the underlying mechanism for improving individuals' cognitive skills is repetitive exposure and practice of tasks that require one of several executive functions. Many publications support the effectiveness of serious games or computerized tasks in improving memory, attention, inhibition or cognitive flexibility, even if the transfer into daily-life functioning is not always as expected. One of the main characteristics of the games developed for computer or mobile use is that they are based on standardized tasks (e.g. Go-/No Go, Stroop Task) which helps in increasing the validity of the developed digital applications. Another type of technology widely used is neurofeedback and the studies in this domain mainly target clinical symptoms of ADHD. While some effects of neurofeedback on ADHD symptoms have been observed, there is still no convincing evidence that these effects are specifically due to improved control over targeted brain activity. This remains true even in recent studies that incorporate personalized approaches and training in various settings such as clinics, schools, and homes. Regarding wearables and sensors, as in the case of ASD, the use of these tools is still in an exploratory state and needs more studies to test their effectiveness. The use of virtual/augmented reality has been proven to be effective in reducing executive deficits, but it is still difficult to differentiate between the use of 2D and 3D versions. The most important risks and opportunities in the domain of digital technologies for ADHD are discussed in the end of the chapter emphasizing the importance of technology use in the diagnosis and treatment process of ADHD individuals.

Finally, cyberbullying, moral engagement and self-regulation strategies of neurodiverse children are discussed in the last chapters. Within these last chapters moral development and (dis) engagement and self-regulatory process are being discussed in the context of technology use. Cyberbullying, defined as intentional repeated harmful acts by sending prejudicial material or being involved in other forms of social aggression through digital technologies, is highly related to moral disengagement and is a great challenge nowadays. Neurodiverse children seem to be more vulnerable to this phenomenon due to their cognitive and social development and more tools are needed to help them identify such situations and deal with them. Even if the research in this domain is scarce, there are some studies that show the effectiveness of improving prosociality, empathy and moral engagement in improving children' reactions in cyberbullying situations. An overview about the studies in self-regulated learning is presented in the last chapter, whereas self-regulated learning has been defined as an intrinsic motivational oriented process in the transfer of knowledge and skills to novel contexts, for neurodiverse children self-regulated learning competencies may be used also as a way of avoiding engaging in dysfunctional behavior. Interventions based on self-regulation that use digital technologies for neurodiverse children that usually combine metacognitive strategies and motivational strategies proved to be effective and help children to take make intentional, responsible, and appropriate choices while encountering difficult situation especially online.

In conclusion, the development of digital technologies for neurodiverse populations must be guided by a deep understanding of user needs, rigorous evidence-based practices, and ethical considerations. By focusing on these areas, digital tools can be designed to effectively support learning and psychological interventions, ultimately improving the lives of neurodiverse individuals. Future studies should investigate the long-term efficacy of the digital technologies, as well as the generalization of digital interventions. Namely, more long-term studies are needed to assess the sustained impact of digital interventions on neurodiverse populations and there is a need to measure the transferability of this skills and to understand the factors that influence the successful use of learned skills in non-digital environments. In terms of machine learning and AI, there is a need for future research to develop and refine algorithms that can dynamically adapt content to the evolving needs of neurodiverse individuals. The algorithms should be capable of personalizing interventions based on real-time data, learning patterns and user preferences.

In regard to innovative technologies and emerging trends, research should continue to explore the potential of wearable technologies or digital biomarkers for monitoring and supporting neurodiverse individuals in real-time. This includes studying the efficacy of different devices in tracking behavioral and physiological markers. While investigating the effectiveness of emergent technologies, research should focus on making digital interventions accessible to neurodiverse populations across different cultural and socioeconomic background. This includes exploring how cultural differences impact the design and effectiveness of digital tools and developing low-cost scalable solutions that can be widely implemented.

Index

A
Accessibility in web-based learning for autism, 36
Assistive technology for independent living in autism, 205, 206

B
Biomarker-based diagnostics, 62
Biomarkers in neurodevelopmental disorders, 83–85, 87

C
Co-design in technology development for autism, 33, 151
Cognitive training in neurodevelopmental disorders, 138, 170, 172–174, 176, 177, 180, 181, 237, 238, 241, 292
Computer-aided diagnosis in neurodevelopmental disorders, 53
Computer-assisted learning for autism, 155
Computerized executive function training, 155, 165
Cyberbullying and digital safety, 262

D
Descriptive vs. interpretative algorithms, 109, 111
Designing interactive experiences with robots, 139, 141
Digital biomarkers for neurodevelopmental conditions, 83, 87
Digital coaching and educators, 216
Digital health, 96, 236
Digital interventions for executive functions, 237

Digital learning environments, 274, 277
Self-regulated learning, 293

E
Ecoaching and neurodevelopmental disorders, 211, 213, 221
Educational interventions for autistic children, 134–136, 151
Ethical AI in healthcare trials, 100
Evidence-based practices through eCoaching, 212

F
Framework for child-robot interaction, 125, 126

G
Game-based learning, 265, 281, 282
Gamified learning tools for autism, 238, 266

H
Handheld devices for autism interventions, 173, 201

I
Innovative technologies in autism support, 293

M
Mobile-based interventions, 153

N
Neurobiological traits in NDDs, 43, 44

P
Participatory design in autism interventions, 33, 290

R
Robot-assisted therapy for children, 110

S
Self-regulated learning, 275, 276, 281–283, 293
Signal processing: overt vs. covert indicators, 85
Social and moral development, 255, 257–259, 266
Stakeholder support in AI implementation, 100

Supporting parents and learners with neurodevelopmental disorders, 111

T
Technological tools in autism therapy, 291
Technology-based health interventions, 236, 237, 243, 244
Technology design for neurodiverse populations, 33, 290
Technology-enhanced learning, 213, 220
Technology support for Autism Spectrum Disorder (ASD), 43, 47, 51, 84, 151, 276

V
Visual supports for autism, 8, 194

W
Wearable technology in healthcare, 88, 200

www.ingramcontent.com/pod-product-compliance
Lightning Source LLC
Chambersburg PA
CBHW070048060125
19957CB00003B/71